AF207897

CARAVAGGIO

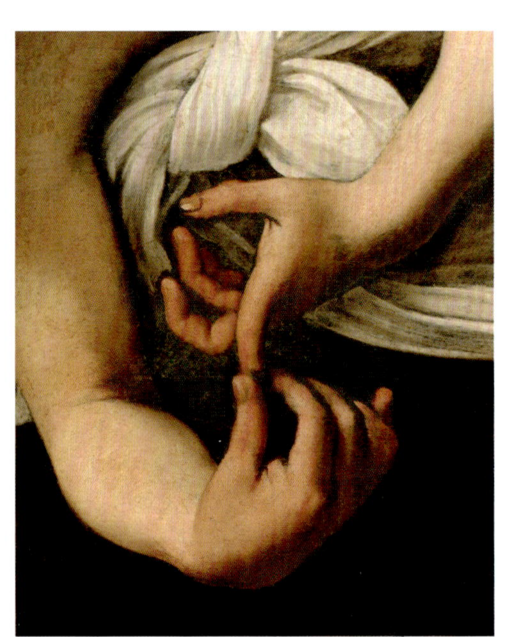

CARAVAGGIO

RUTH DANGELMAIER

p. 2

Saint Matthew and the Angel (second version, detail)

Saint Matthieu et l'Ange (deuxième version, détail)

Der hl. Matthäus und der Engel (zweite Fassung, Detail)

San Mateo y el ángel (segunda versión, detalle)

San Matteo e l'angelo (seconda versione, particolare)

De heilige Matteüs en de engel (tweede versie, detail)

1602, Oil on canvas/Huile sur toile, 292 × 186 cm, Chiesa di San Luigi dei Francesi, Roma

KÖNEMANN
© 2017 koenemann.com GmbH
www.koenemann.com

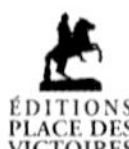
ÉDITIONS
PLACE DES
VICTOIRES

© Éditions Place des Victoires
6, rue du Mail – 75002 Paris
www.victoires.com
ISBN: 978-2-8099-1527-3
Dépôt légal: 3e trimestre 2017

Concept, Project Management: koenemann.com GmbH
Text: Ruth Dangelmaier
Editing: Kristina Scherer

Translation into French: Denis-Armand Canal
Translation into English, Spanish, Italian and Dutch: **TEXTCASE** Translation Agency

Layout: Nora Hein, Holy Design
Picture credits: akg-images gmbh; Bridgeman Images (p. 175)

ISBN: 978-3-95588-615-8 (international)

Printed in China by Shenzhen Hua Xin Colour-printing & Platemaking Co., Ltd

Contents   Sommaire   Inhalt   Índice   Indice   Inhoud

À propos

Caravaggio pushed the limits in both his art and his life. Stories are told about the brilliant painter and highly sensitive person drawn to the down and out such as prostitutes, players, and thugs while hanging out with Roman aristocracy all the while seeking to become Rome's new Michelangelo. He got into trouble with the law more than once, but he became famous for breaking the laws of late Renaissance painting and launching the backlash movements of Mannerism and the Baroque. The realism and emotional intensity of Caravaggio's work both

En art comme dans la vie, Caravage fut un transgresseur. Que d'histoires autour de ce peintre génial, empathique et hypersensible, si souvent attiré par la déchéance et la révolte ! Lui qui fréquentait à la fois les courtisanes, les joueurs et les spadassins – mais aussi l'aristocratie romaine – et qui voulait devenir le « nouveau Michel-Ange » de Rome. Il eut plus d'une fois maille à partir avec la justice ; surtout, il s'affranchit des conventions picturales de la Renaissance tardive et fut à l'origine des puissants mouvements du maniérisme

Caravaggio war im Leben wie in der Kunst ein Grenzgänger. Es ranken sich Geschichten um den genialen Maler und hochsensiblen Empathen, der einen inneren Drang zum Niederen und Abtrünnigen hatte, gleichzeitig mit Dirnen, Spielern und Schlägern sowie mit der römischen Aristokratie verkehrte und der neue Michelangelo Roms werden wollte. Er geriet mehr als einmal mit der Justiz in Konflikt, doch vor allem brach er die Gesetze der Malerei der Spätrenaissance und stand am Anfang der heftigen Gegenbewegung

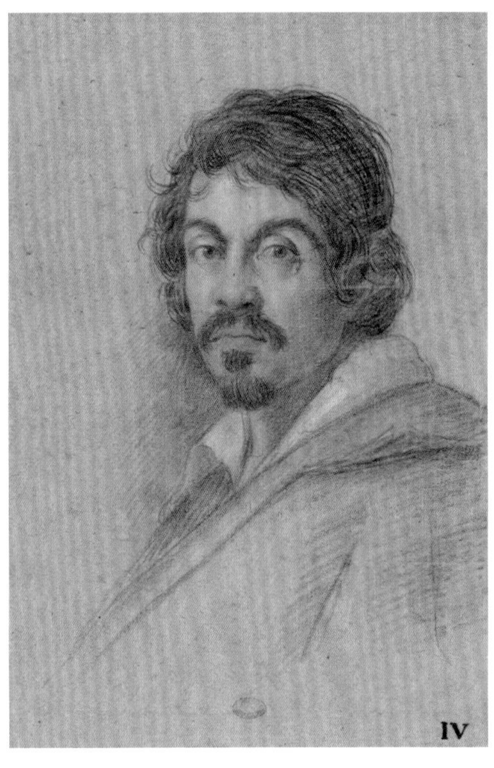

Ottavio Leoni (1578–1630)

Caravaggio

Caravage

c. 1621, Black and red chalk/Craie rouge et noire, rehauts blancs sur papier bleu,
23,4 × 16,3 cm, Biblioteca Marucelliana, Firenze

Caravaggio fue, tanto en la vida como en el arte, una figura de transición. Circulan multitud de historias sobre el genial pintor de empatía extrema, con su tendencia a la bajeza y la blasfemia, que frecuentaba la compañía de prostitutas, jugadores y matones por un lado y la aristocracia romana por otro, y que estaba destinado a convertirse en el nuevo Miguel Ángel de Roma. Si bien tuvo más de un problema con la justicia, infringió sobre todo las leyes de la pintura del Renacimiento tardío, ocupando su lugar al inicio de las intensas contracorrientes

Caravaggio sfidò sempre i confini, sia nella vita sia nell'arte. Sono molte le storie circa questo genio artistico, questo pittore empatico ed estremamente sensibile che era attratto interiormente verso gli umili e i rinnegati, che, contemporaneamente all'aristocrazia romana, frequentava prostitute, giocatori d'azzardo e delinquenti, e che desiderava convertirsi nel nuovo Michelangelo di Roma. Ebbe più di una volta problemi con la legge ma, soprattutto, ruppe le leggi della pittura del tardo Rinascimento e partecipò all'impetuosa rivoluzione

Zowel in zijn leven als in zijn kunst zocht Caravaggio grenzen op. De verhalen rond deze geniale, emotionele en scherpzinnige schilder verraden een innerlijke drang naar zelfdestructie, maar naast zijn omgang met prostituees, gokkers en criminelen bewoog hij zich in kringen van de Romeinse adel en streefde ernaar de nieuwe Michelangelo van Rome te worden. Hij kwam meermalen in aanraking met de wet, maar het waren vooral de wetten van de schilderkunst van de late Renaissance die hij overtrad, waarmee

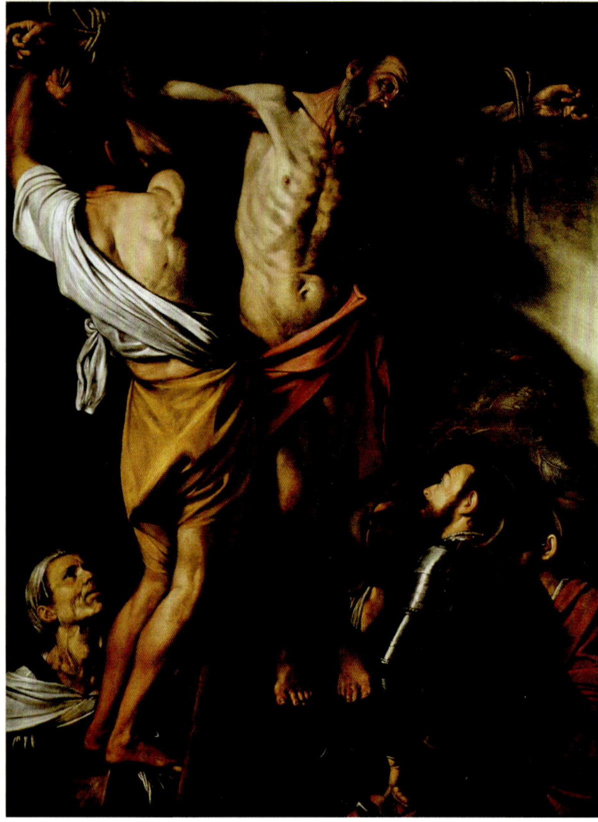

c. 1607, Oil on canvas/Huile sur toile, 202,5 × 152,7 cm, Cleveland Museum of Art, Cleveland

mesmerize and polarize its viewers, triggering reactions of fascination and rejection at the same time. As a master of chiaroscuro, this exceptional artist created what in the end are stunning images full of drama with a style that would influence generations of artists to come.

et du baroque. Le réalisme et l'intensité affective des œuvres de Caravage attirent le spectateur, suscitant la fascination en même temps que le rejet. Maître du clair-obscur, cet artiste exceptionnel a créé de fabuleux tableaux chargés de dramatisme, dont le style allait marquer les générations d'artistes suivantes.

des Manierismus sowie des Barock. Der Realismus und die emotionale Intensität der Werke Caravaggios ziehen den Betrachter in ihren Bann, polarisieren, lösen Faszination und zugleich Ablehnung aus. Als Meister des Chiaroscuro schließlich schuf der Ausnahmekünstler, dessen Stil nachfolgende Künstlergenerationen prägen sollte, eindrucksvolle Bilder voller Dramatik.

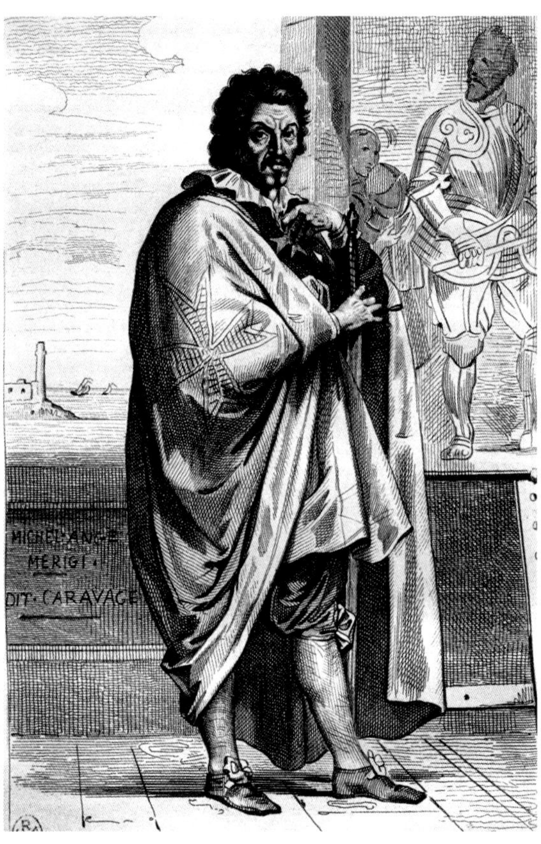

del Manierismo y el Barroco. El realismo
y la intensidad emocional de las obras
de Caravaggio atrapan al espectador de
forma controvertida, generando tanto
fascinación como rechazo. Como maestro
del chiaroscuro, este excepcional artista
creó imágenes impresionantes llenas
de dramatismo cuyo estilo habría de
ejercer su influencia en las siguientes
generaciones de artistas.

del Manierismo e del Barocco nei suoi
inizi. Il realismo e l'intensità emotiva
delle opere di Caravaggio attirano lo
spettatore, ne polarizzano l'attenzione
e suscitano al contempo fascinazione
e rifiuto. Maestro del chiaroscuro,
questo eccezionale pittore creò quadri
straordinari pieni di drammaticità, il cui
stile influenzò le seguenti generazioni
di artisti.

hij aan het begin stond van de intense
tegenbeweging van maniërisme en
barok. Het realisme en de emotionaliteit
van Caravaggio's werk betoveren de
beschouwer, polariseren en roepen
fascinatie en afwijzing op. Als meester
van het chiaroscuro schiep hij imposante
en dramatische werken, in een stijl
die enorme invloed op navolgende
generaties zou hebben.

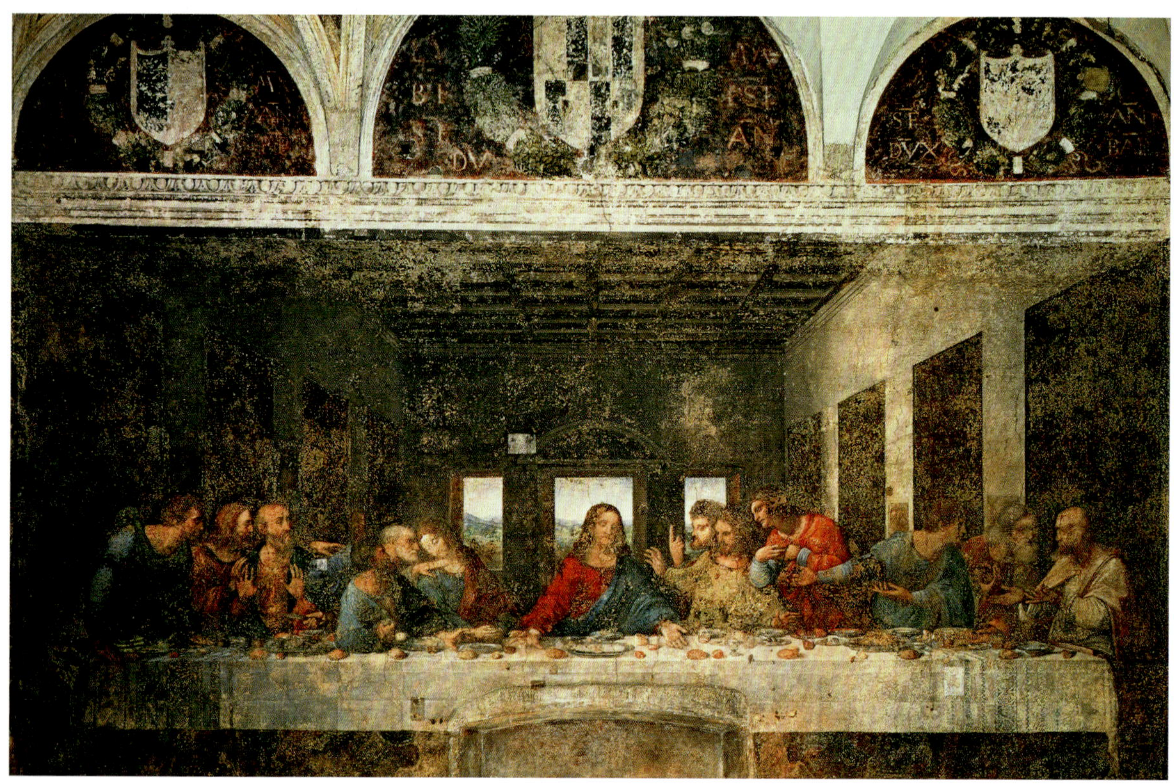

Youth and training in Milan

Michelangelo Merisi was born on
29 September 1571, probably in Milan. He
later took on the name Caravaggio based
on his parents' hometown in Lombardy.
Little his know about his early years
in Milan. At the age of 13, Caravaggio
began a four-year apprenticeship in
the studio of renowned painter Simone
Peterzano (c. 1540–1596). Caravaggio
had the opportunity to study Titian's
(1488/1490–1576) *Crown of Thorns* and
Leonardo da Vinci's (1452–1519) *Last*

Jeunesse et apprentissage à Milan

Michelangelo Merisi est né le
29 septembre 1571, probablement à
Milan. Il prit le nom de « Caravaggio »,
d'après celui de la petite ville lombarde
d'où ses parents étaient venus. On
sait peu de choses sur ses premières
années de jeunesse à Milan. À l'âge
de 13 ans, Caravage entra pour quatre
ans en apprentissage dans l'atelier
d'un peintre renommé, Simone
Peterzano (v. 1540–1596). Dans les églises
de Milan, il eut la possibilité d'étudier

Jugend und Lehre in Mailand

Michelangelo Merisi wurde am
29. September 1571 vermutlich in Mailand
geboren. Nach dem lombardischen
Herkunftsort seiner Eltern nannte er
sich Caravaggio. Über seine frühen
Jugendjahre in Mailand ist wenig
bekannt. Im Alter von 13 Jahren trat
Caravaggio eine vierjährige Lehrzeit im
Atelier des renommierten Malers Simone
Peterzano (ca. 1540–1596) an. In Santa
Maria delle Grazie hatte Caravaggio die
Gelegenheit, Tizians (1488/1490–1576)

Leonardo da Vinci (1452–1519)

The Last Supper

La Cène

Das Abendmahl

La cena

Ultima cena

Het Laatste Avondmaal

*c. 1495–97, Fresco/Fresque,
460 × 880 cm, Santa Maria delle
Grazie, Milano*

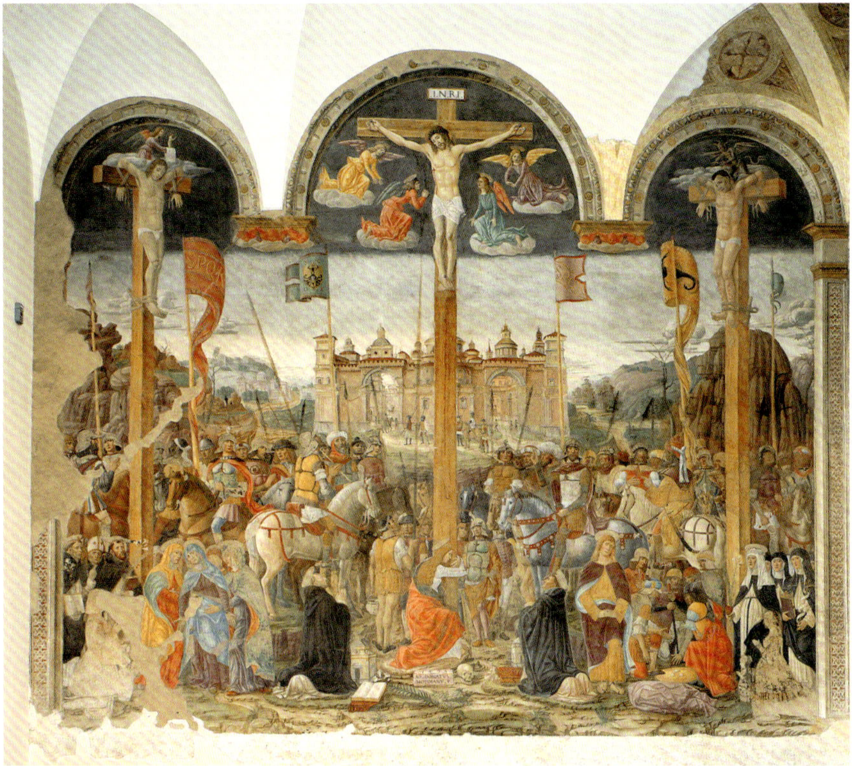

Giovanni Donato da Montorfano
(c. 1460–c. 1503)

Crucifixion

Crucifixion

Kreuzigung

Crucifixión

Crecefissione

Kruisiging

*c. 1495, Fresco/Fresque, Santa Maria
delle Grazie, Milano*

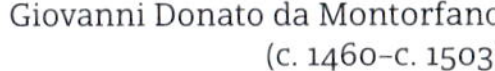

Juventud y aprendizaje en Milán

Michelangelo Merisi nació,
probablemente en Milán, el 29 de
septiembre de 1571. Se hacía llamar
Caravaggio, por la región de Lombardía
de la que procedían sus padres. Se
conoce más bien poco de sus primeros
años de juventud en Milán. A los 13 años
Caravaggio comienza un período de
aprendizaje de cuatro años en el taller
del famoso pintor Simone Peterzano
(ca. 1540–1596). Caravaggio tuvo la
oportunidad de estudiar, en Santa Maria

Giovinezza e formazione a Milano

Michelangelo Merisi nacque il
29 settembre 1571, probabilmente a
Milano. Prese il nome di Caravaggio dal
paese bergamasco di origine dei suoi
genitori. Sono poche le informazioni
disponibili circa gli anni della sua
giovinezza nel capoluogo lombardo.
All'età di 13 anni Caravaggio iniziò il
suo apprendistato di quattro anni nella
bottega del famoso pittore Simone
Peterzano (c. 1540–1596), ed ebbe la
possibilità di studiare nel Santa Maria

Jeugd en opleiding in Milaan

Michelangelo Merisi werd op
29 september 1571 vermoedelijk in
Milaan geboren. Hij noemde zich
naar het Lombardijnse geboortedorp
van zijn ouders: Caravaggio. Over
zijn vroege jeugd in Milaan is weinig
bekend. Op 13-jarige leeftijd werd
Caravaggio voor vier jaar aangenomen
als leerling in het atelier van de
gerenommeerde schilder Simone
Peterzano (ca. 1540–1596). In Santa Maria
delle Grazie van Milaan had Caravaggio

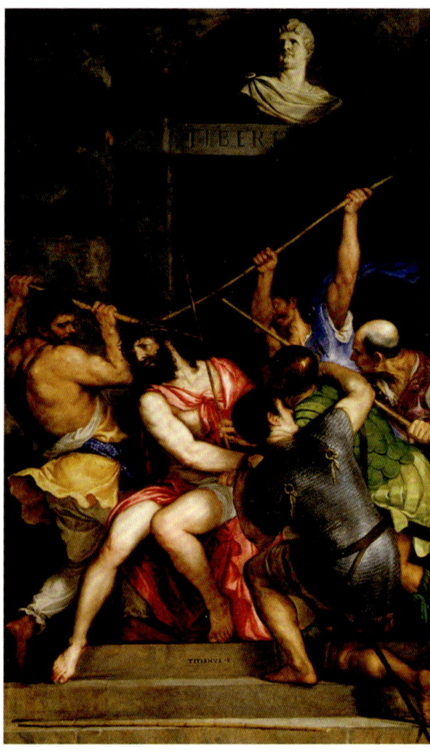

Tiziano (c. 1488/90–1576)

The Crown of Thorns

Le Couronnement d'épines

Die Dornenkrönung

La coronación de espinas

Incoronazione di spine

De Doornenkroning van Christus

c. 1542/43, Oil on panel/Huile sur bois,
303 × 181 cm, Musée du Louvre, Paris

Simone Peterzano (c. 1540–1596)

Venus and Cupid

Vénus et Cupidon

Venus und Cupido

Venus y Cupido

Venere e Cupido

Venus en Cupido

c. 1570–73, Oil on canvas/Huile sur toile,
135,2 × 206,9 cm, Pinacoteca di Brera, Milano

Supper in Santa Maria delle Grazie. The naturalistic representation of human moods and the simpler visual language of the Lombard school stood in contrast to the Mannerist overload of compositional and iconographic elements with a supremely colorful style reflected in his teacher Peterzano's works. After completing his apprenticeship with Peterzano, Caravaggio went to Rome.

Le Couronnement d'épines de Titien (1488/1490–1576) et *La Cène* de Léonard de Vinci (1452–1519). La représentation naturaliste des émotions humaines et le langage figuratif plus sobre de l'école lombarde étaient à l'opposé du style iconographique surchargé et violemment coloré du maniérisme à la mode, dont l'influence se faisait sentir dans les œuvres de Peterzano. À la fin de son apprentissage chez ce dernier, Caravage partit pour Rome.

Dornenkrönung und Leonardo da Vincis (1452–1519) *Abendmahl* zu studieren. Die naturalistische Darstellung menschlicher Gemütszustände und die schlichtere Bildsprache der lombardischen Schule standen im Gegensatz zum kompositorisch und ikonografisch überfrachteten, farbgewaltigen Stil des in Mode gekommenen Manierismus, dessen Einfluss sich in Peterzanos Werken niederschlug. Nach der Beendigung seiner Lehrzeit bei Peterzano ging Caravaggio nach Rom.

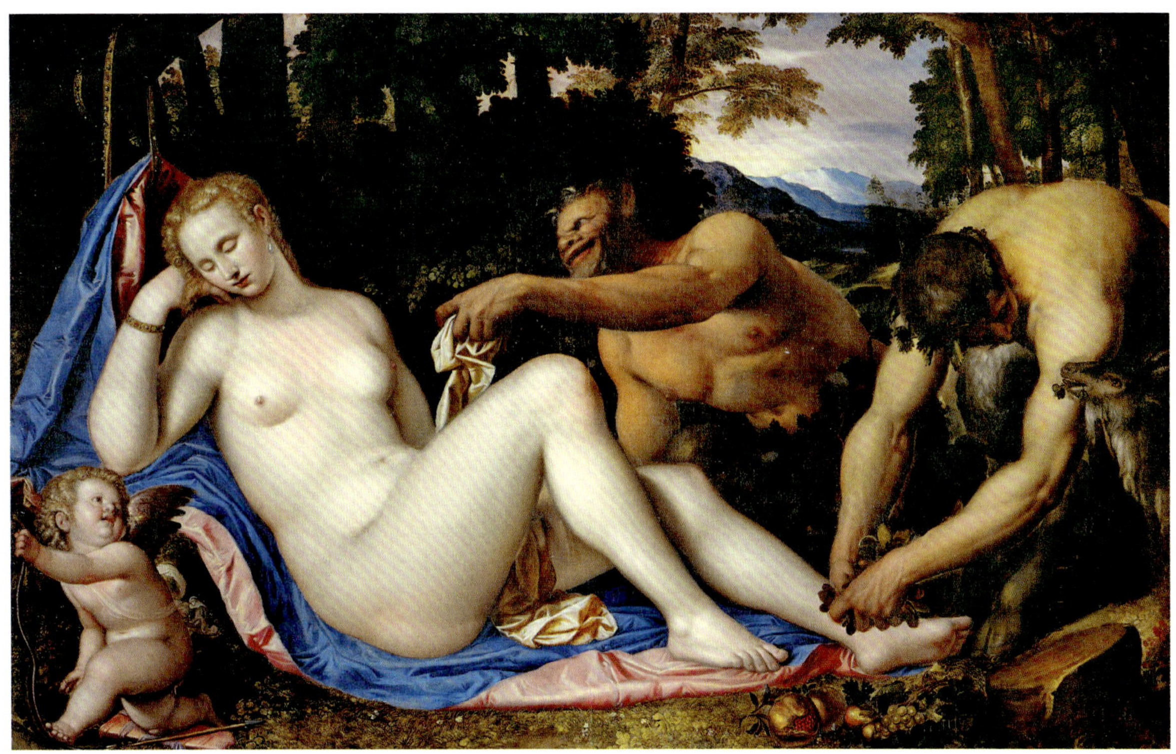

delle Grazie, *La coronación de espinas* de Tiziano (1488/1490–1576) y *La última cena* de Leonardo da Vinci (1452–1519). La representación naturalista de estados emocionales y el lenguaje pictórico más bien sobrio de la escuela lombarda se oponían al estilo excesivo, tanto en la composición como la iconografía, y de coloridos brillantes del Manierismo entonces en boga, y cuya influencia era patente en las obras de Peterzano. Tras terminar su aprendizaje con Peterzano Caravaggio se mudó a Roma.

delle Grazie l'*Incoronazione di spine* di Tiziano (1488/1490–1576) e l'*Ultima cena* di Leonardo da Vinci (1452–1519). La rappresentazione naturalistica degli stati d'animo umani e la semplicità del linguaggio plastico della scuola lombarda erano in contrasto con lo stile compositivo e iconografico sovraccarico e potentemente cromatico del Manierismo, una corrente che iniziava ad essere di moda e la cui influenza è riconoscibile nelle opere di Peterzano. Dopo la fine del suo apprendistato con Peterzano Caravaggio si trasferì a Roma.

de gelegenheid *De Doornenkroning van Christus* van Titiaan (1488/1490–1576) en *Het Laatste Avondmaal* van Leonardo da Vinci (1452–1519) te bestuderen. De naturalistische uitbeelding van gemoedstoestanden en de eenvoudiger beeldtaal van de Lombardijnse school druisten in tegen de iconografisch en compositorisch zo overvolle werken van het opkomende maniërisme, dat ook het werk van Peterzano beïnvloedde. Na voltooiing van zijn leertijd bij Peterzano trok Caravaggio naar Rome.

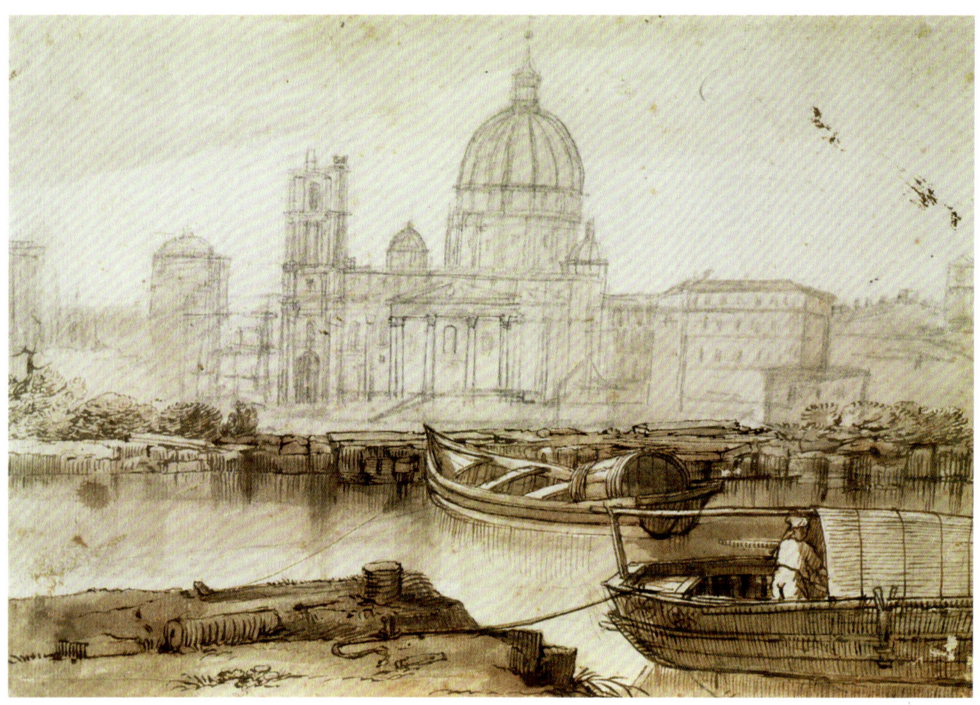

Becoming the painter to the Roman aristocracy

Shortly before the end of the 16th century, Rome had undisputedly once again become the center of Italian culture. The popes' urban renewal projects had turned the Eternal City into a colossal construction site with legions of builders and painters flocking to the city. The competition among the arts and artists was in full swing. Caravaggio likely arrive in Rome in 1592. He was introduced to Guiseppe Cesari (1568–1640), one of the most successful artists in the city. Caravaggio trained on classic models, learned metaphors and allegories, and

Promotion comme peintre de l'aristocratie romaine

Peu avant la fin du XVIe siècle, Rome était la capitale incontestée de l'Italie. La *renovatio Urbis* réalisée par les papes faisait alors de la Ville éternelle un immense chantier : des armées d'ouvriers en bâtiment et de peintres y constituaient de véritables colonies ; la concurrence des arts et des artistes battait son plein. Caravage arriva probablement à Rome en 1592, introduit par Giuseppe Cesari dit le Cavalier d'Arpin (1568–1640), un des artistes les plus demandés de la cité. Caravage se forma aux modèles classiques, apprit métaphores et

Aufstieg zum Maler der römischen Aristokratie

Rom war kurz vor dem Ende des 16. Jahrhunderts die unangefochtene Metropole Italiens. Die *renovatio urbis* der Päpste machte aus der ewigen Stadt eine Baustelle kolossalen Ausmaßes: Heerscharen von Bauleuten und Malern bildeten regelrechte Wohnkolonien – der Wettbewerb der Künste und Künstler war im vollen Gange. Vermutlich traf Caravaggio 1592 in Rom ein. Er wurde bei Guiseppe Cesari (1568–1640) eingeführt, einem der erfolgreichsten Künstler der Stadt. Hier schulte Caravaggio sich an klassischen Vorbildern, erlernte

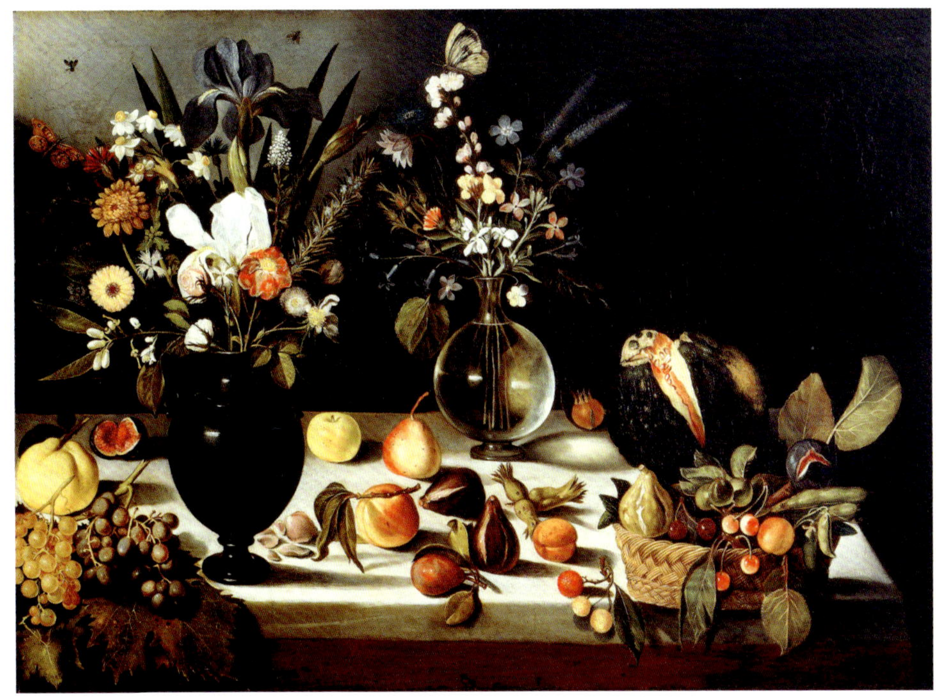

Ascenso del pintor a la aristocracia romana

A finales del XVI, Roma era la indiscutible metrópolis de Italia. La *renovatio urbis* de los Papas había convertido a la ciudad eterna en un espacio de obras de medidas colosales: huestes de constructores y pintores formaban verdaderas colonias residenciales, la competencia entre las artes y los artistas era intensa. Caravaggio llegó a Roma probablemente en 1592. Guiseppe Cesari (1568–1640), uno de los artistas más exitosos de la ciudad, le presentó en sociedad en la misma. Aquí Caravaggio estudió los clásicos, aprendiendo el lenguaje metafórico y

Ascesa a pittore dell'aristocrazia romana

Poco prima della fine del XVI secolo Roma era la metropoli indiscussa dell'Italia. La *renovatio urbis* dei papi convertì la città eterna in un cantiere di proporzioni colossali: legioni di costruttori e pittori vi fondarono vere e proprie colonie; la competizione delle arti e degli artisti era in pieno corso. Caravaggio giunse a Roma probabilmente nel 1592. Qui fu introdotto a Giuseppe Cesari (1568–1640), uno degli artisti di maggior successo della città, e studiò i modelli classici, ne imparò le metafore e le allegorie, e cominciò a dipingere fiori e frutta. Forse il giovane

Opkomst als schilder van de Romeinse aristocratie

Tegen het einde van de zestiende eeuw was Rome het onbetwiste centrum van Italië. De *renovatio urbis* die de pausen doorvoerden, maakte de Eeuwige Stad tot een bouwplaats van kolossale omvang: legers van bouwarbeiders en schilders vormden regelrechte woonwijken – in de kunsten heerste een bedrijvige concurrentie. Caravaggio moet in 1592 in Rome zijn gearriveerd, waar hij in de leer ging bij Giuseppe Cesari (1568–1640), een van de meest succesvolle schilders van de stad. Hier schoolde hij zich naar het voorbeeld

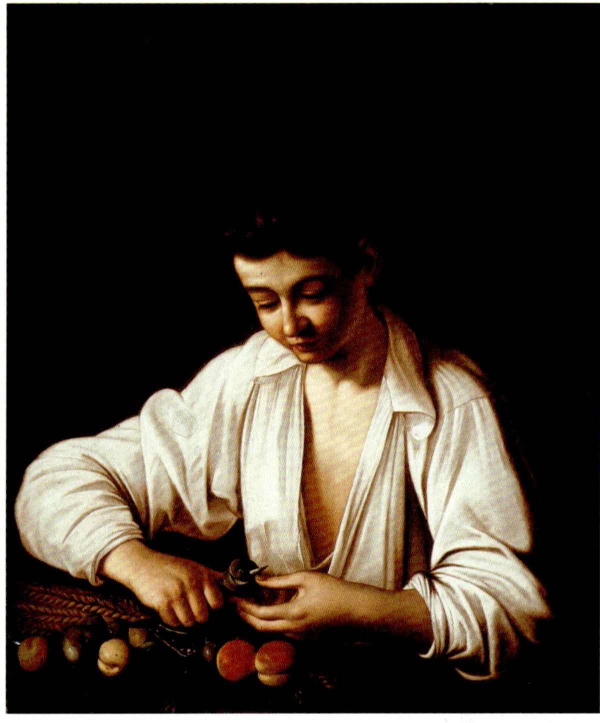

c. 1592, Oil on canvas/Huile sur toile, 75,5 × 64,4 cm, Private collection

began to paint flowers and fruit. He probably tried to set up his own studio with his friend, painter Mario Minniti (1577–1640), but it failed miserably. Before it led to any permanent damage to Caravaggio's reputation, Cardinal Francesco Maria del Monte (1549–1627) had taken him under his protection. This introduced Caravaggio to a world populated with the educated bourgeoisie, bankers, lawyers, and nobility, but his hot-headed temperament often got him into trouble with the law.

allégories, et commença de peindre des fleurs et des fruits. Le jeune artiste tenta peut-être de prendre son indépendance avec son ami peintre Mario Minniti (1577–1640) : ce fut un échec. Sur le point de tomber dans la déchéance sociale, Caravage fut sauvé par la protection du cardinal Francesco Maria del Monte (1549–1627). Fréquentant alors, outre ses collègues artistes, des bourgeois, des banquiers, des juristes et des nobles cultivés, il ne cessa pourtant d'avoir des ennuis avec la justice en raison de son caractère irascible.

Metaphern und Allegorien und begann Blumen und Früchte zu malen. Vermutlich versuchte der junge Künstler, sich mit seinem Malerfreund Mario Minniti (1577–1640) selbstständig zu machen, was jedoch kläglich scheiterte. Bevor es zum sozialen Abstieg kam, nahm der Kardinal Francesco Maria del Monte (1549–1627) Caravaggio unter seinen Schutz. Er verkehrte fortan außer mit Künstlerkollegen mit gebildeten Bürgern, Bankiers, Juristen und Adligen, geriet aufgrund seines hitzköpfigen Temperaments jedoch immer wieder mit dem Gesetz in Konflikt.

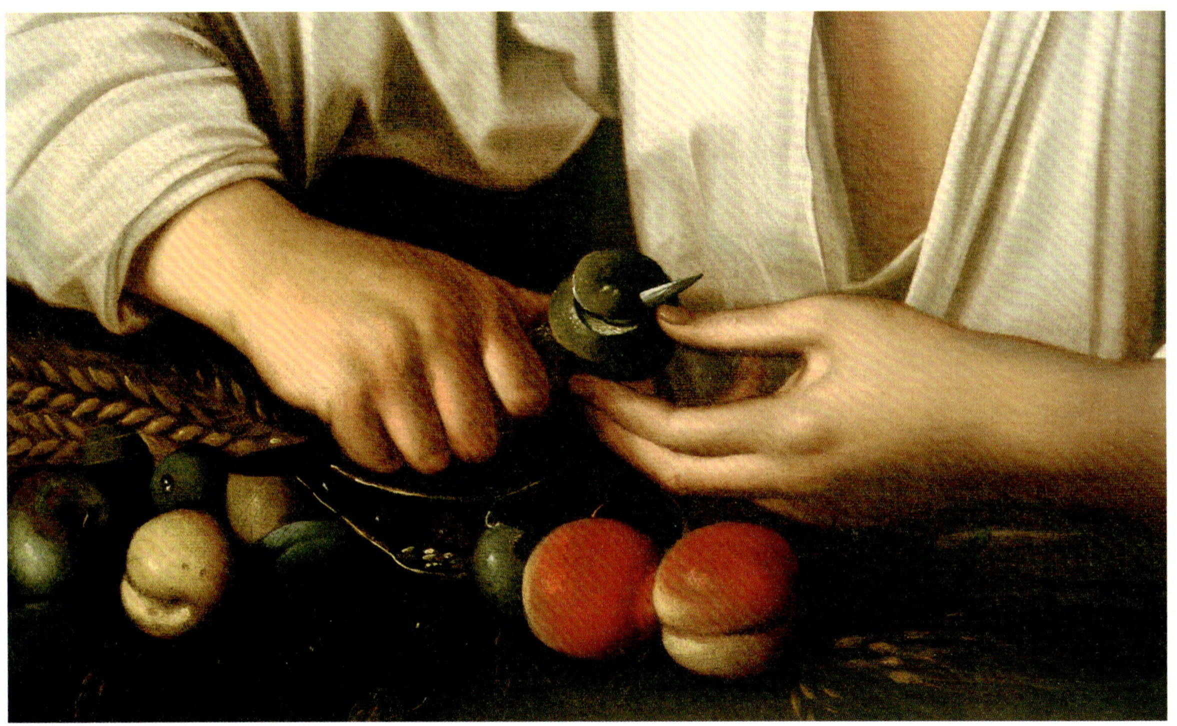

alegórico, y comenzó a pintar flores y frutas. Parece ser que el joven artista intentó hacerse independiente junto a su amigo pintor Mario Minniti (1577–1640), pero esta empresa falló estrepitosamente. Antes de que cayera en la miseria social, el Cardenal Francesco Maria del Monte (1549–1627) acogió a Caravaggio bajó su protección. A partir de ese momento el artista frecuentaría la compañía no solo de colegas artistas, sino también de ciudadanos ilustrados, banqueros, juristas y nobles, y sin embargo su impetuoso temperamento le llevaría a tener constantes problemas con la ley.

artista cercò di mettersi in proprio con il suo amico pittore Mario Minniti (1577–1640), ma l'intento fallì miseramente. Prima che cadesse nel declino sociale, il cardinal Francesco Maria del Monte (1549–1627) prese Caravaggio sotto la sua protezione. Da quel momento in poi, oltre ad altri artisti, il pittore frequentò cittadini istruiti, banchieri, avvocati e nobili, tuttavia continuò ad avere ripetutamente problemi con la giustizia a causa del suo temperamento da testa calda.

van de klassieken, verdiepte zich in metaforen en allegorieën en begon bloemen en vruchten te schilderen. De jonge kunstenaar moet hebben geprobeerd zich met zijn schildersvriend Mario Minniti (1577–1640) als zelfstandige te vestigen, maar dat mislukte jammerlijk. Voordat hij aan lager wal raakte, werd Caravaggio door kardinaal Francesco Maria del Monte (1549–1627) in dienst genomen, waardoor hij voortaan verkeerde met gecultiveerde burgers, bankiers, juristen en edellieden. Maar door zijn opvliegendheid kwam hij telkens weer in de problemen.

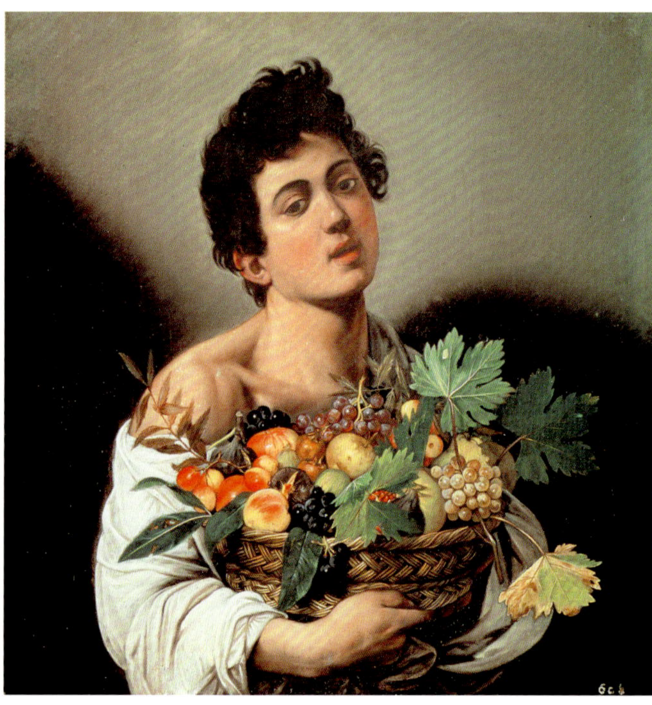

Early secular paintings

In his first years as a painter, Caravaggio mostly painted genre scenes intended for aristocratic clients. *Boy Peeling Fruit* and *Boy with Fruit Basket* are some of his earliest works to survive. With the half-length depictions, Caravaggio was following the rules of genre scenes with moralizing messages as had developed in the Netherlands, Venice, and northern Italy such as Giorgione's (1478–1510) depiction of Vanitas as *The Old Hag*. Aids to the interpretation of Caravaggio's pictures of boys with fruit, however, are rather limited. If the modeling of the boy in *Boy Peeling Fruit* has not quite

Premiers tableaux profanes

Dans ses premières années de peintre à Rome, Caravage créa surtout des scènes de genre, destinées à une clientèle noble. Le *Garçon pelant un fruit* et le *Jeune Garçon portant une corbeille de fruits* sont parmi ses toutes premières œuvres. Avec ces représentations en demi-figure, Caravage suit le type des scènes de genre à tendance moralisante, développé dans les Pays-Bas, à Venise et en Italie du Nord – à l'instar de *La Vieille* de Giorgione (1478–1510). Les éléments aidant à interpréter les représentations de jeunes garçons sont très limités pour Caravage. Si le modelé

Frühe profane Gemälde

In seinen ersten Jahren als Maler schuf Caravaggio hauptsächlich Genreszenen, die für adlige Auftraggeber bestimmt waren. Der *Knabe, eine Frucht schälend* und der *Junge mit dem Früchtekorb* gehören zu den frühesten Werken. Mit den halbfigurigen Darstellungen folgt Caravaggio dem in den Niederlanden, Venedig und Oberitalien entwickelten Bildtypus der Genreszene mit moralisierenden Hinweisen, der z.B. in der Vanitasdarstellung *Die alte Vettel* von Giorgione (1478–1510) zu finden ist. Von interpretatorischen Hilfsmitteln wie verdeutlichenden Symbolen kann

Giorgione (1478–1510)

The Old Hag* or *Time

La Vieille* ou *La Vecchia

Die alte Vettel* oder *Die Zeit

La anciana* o *El tiempo

La vecchia* o *Col tempo

De oude vrouw* of *De Tijd

c. 1506/07, Oil on canvas/Huile sur toile, 68 × 59 cm, Gallerie dell'Accademia, Venezia

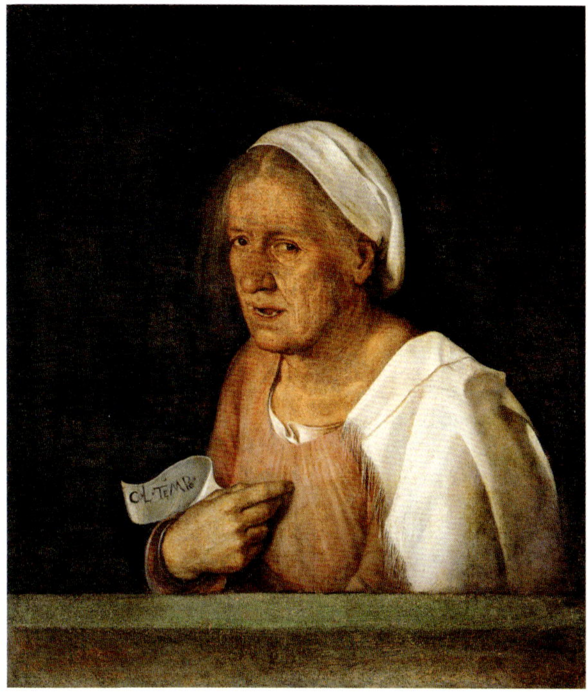

Pinturas profanas de juventud

En sus primeros años como pintor Caravaggio pintó sobre todo escenas costumbristas, destinadas para sus clientes nobles. El *Muchacho pelando fruta* y el *Muchacho con cesto de fruta* son dos de sus obras más tempranas. Sus representaciones de medio cuerpo siguen el modelo pictórico de los Países Bajos, Venecia y el norte de Italia para las escenas costumbristas con carácter moralista, como en la representación de la vanidad *La anciana* de Giorgione (1478–1510). En las imágenes de jóvenes de Caravaggio sin embargo solo puede hablarse parcialmente de instrumentos

La pittura profana degli inizi

Nei suoi primi anni da pittore Caravaggio dipinse per lo più scene di genere destinate a committenti aristocratici. A queste opere iniziali appartengono ad esempio i quadri *Ragazzo che monda un frutto* e *Fanciullo con canestro di frutta*. In queste rappresentazioni di mezze figure Caravaggio seguì il modello delle scene di genere con avvertenze moraleggianti sviluppato nei Paesi Bassi, a Venezia e nel nord Italia, al quale appartiene, tra gli altri, la rappresentazione della vanitas *La vecchia* di Giorgione (1478–1510). Tuttavia, le raffigurazioni di ragazzi di Caravaggio possono solo in parte essere

Vroege profane werken

In zijn eerste jaren als schilder creëerde Caravaggio vooral genrestukken voor adellijke opdrachtgevers. *Jongen die een vrucht schilt* en *Jongen met fruitmand* behoren tot deze vroegste werken. Met zijn halffiguren sloot Caravaggio aan op een genretype dat in de Nederlanden, Venetië en Noord-Italië was ontwikkeld en steevast een morele boodschap uitdroeg, zoals het vanitaswerk *De oude vrouw* van Giorgione (1478–1510). Caravaggio's knapenvoorstellingen lieten echter weinig ruimte voor morele interpretaties. Terwijl de modellering van de knaap in *Jongen die een vrucht*

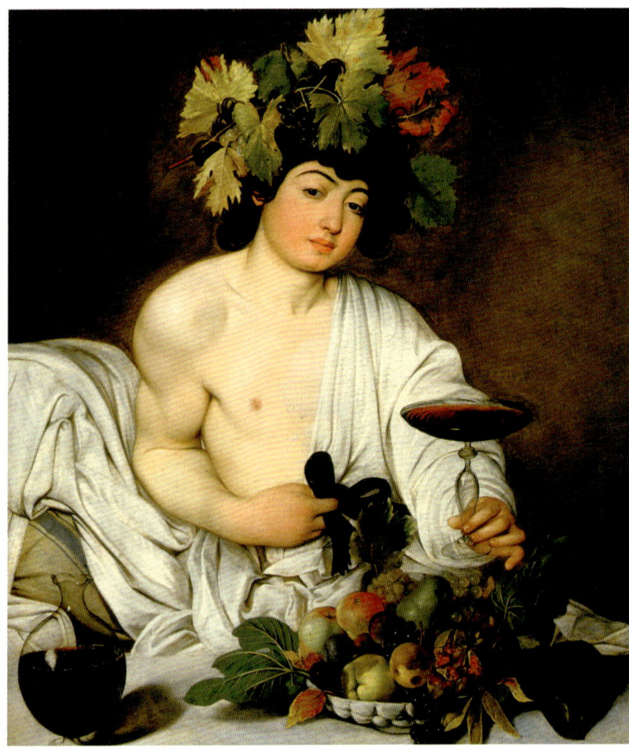

reached the standard of Caravaggio's later craft, *Boy with Fruit Basket* already shows the young artist's mastery, especially as a still-life painter, an art he fully mastered as seen in the later *Basket of Fruit*, the only still-life without figures by Caravaggio to survive.

Caravaggio's extraordinary feeling for depicting natural Details can be seen in his two portrayals of Bacchus: *Sickly Bacchus*, which also contains a self-portrait of the artist, and *Bacchus*. He also had a talent for displaying subliminal eroticism paired with a new aesthetic

du *Garçon pelant un fruit* ne révèle pas encore l'habileté qui sera plus tard si remarquable, le *Jeune Garçon portant une corbeille de fruits* montre déjà la maîtrise atteinte, surtout comme peintre de nature morte, qui connaîtra son apogée avec la *Corbeille de fruits* (seule nature morte autonome du peintre).

Le flair extraordinaire de Caravage pour la représentation des détails naturels ressort aussi de ses deux représentations de Bacchus : le *Jeune Bacchus malade* (où l'on voit un autoportrait du peintre) et le *Bacchus*.

in Caravaggios Knabendarstellungen aber nur bedingt die Rede sein. Erreicht die Modellierung des Jungen in *Knabe, eine Frucht schälend* noch nicht die von Caravaggio gewohnte Kunstfertigkeit, so zeigt sich in *Junge mit dem Früchtekorb* bereits die Meisterschaft des jungen Mannes, vor allem als Stilllebenmaler, die im später entstandenen *Obstkorb*, dem einzigen selbstständigen Stillleben Caravaggios, vollendet wird.

Caravaggios außerordentliches Gespür für die Abbildung von Natur Details tritt auch in den beiden Bacchusdarstellungen

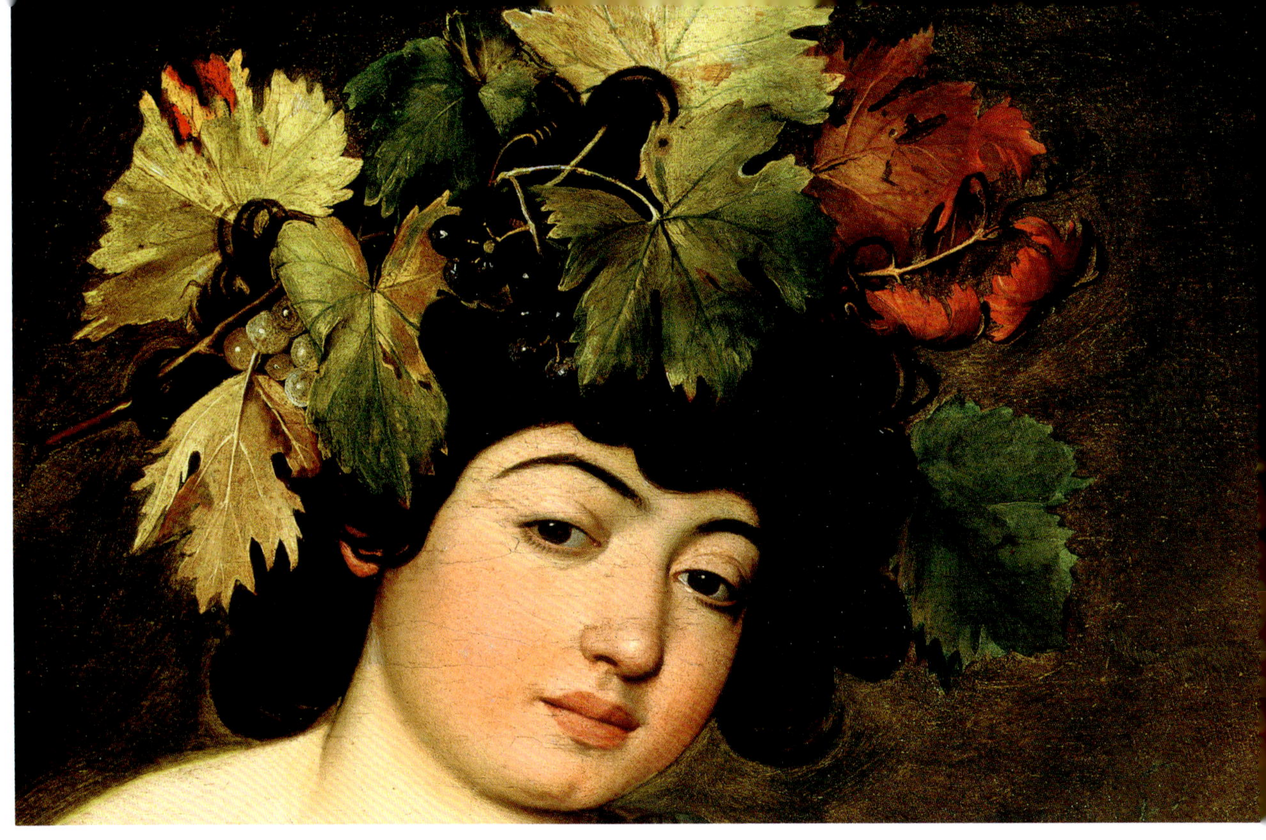

indicativos para la interpretación. Si
bien el modelado del joven en *Muchacho
pelando fruta* todavía no ha alcanzado la
artesanía característica de Caravaggio,
en el *Muchacho con cesto de fruta* ya se
muestra la maestría del joven, sobre
todo como pintor de bodegones, que
culminará con el posterior *Cesto de
fruta*, el único bodegón autónomo
de Caravaggio.

El extraordinario instinto de Caravaggio
para la representación de Detalles
naturalistas también es patente en sus
dos imágenes de Baco, *Baco enfermo*, en

considerate degli ausili interpretativi.
Se nella modellazione del fanciullo nel
dipinto *Ragazzo che monda un frutto* il
giovane Caravaggio non aveva ancora
raggiunto la sua consueta abilità artistica,
nel *Fanciullo con canestro di frutta* è già
evidente tutta la maestria, soprattutto
come pittore di nature morte, che
l'artista svilupperà poi appieno nell'opera
Canestra di frutta, la sua unica natura
morta indipendente.

Lo straordinario talento di Caravaggio
nel riprodurre i dettagli della natura si
palesa anche nelle due rappresentazioni

schilt nog niet het meesterschap van
de latere Caravaggio vertoont, verraadt
Jongen met fruitmand al de genialiteit van
de jonge kunstenaar, vooral als schilder
van stillevenachtige partijen, zoals hij
die in zijn latere *Fruitmand* – het enige
zelfstandige stilleven van Caravaggio –
zou perfectioneren.

Caravaggio's enorme gevoel voor
natuurlijke Details bleek ook uit zijn beide
Bacchus-schilderijen: *De zieke Bacchus*,
dat als zelfportret van de kunstenaar
word beschouwd, en *Bacchus*. Daarnaast
bezat hij een gave voor het uitbeelden

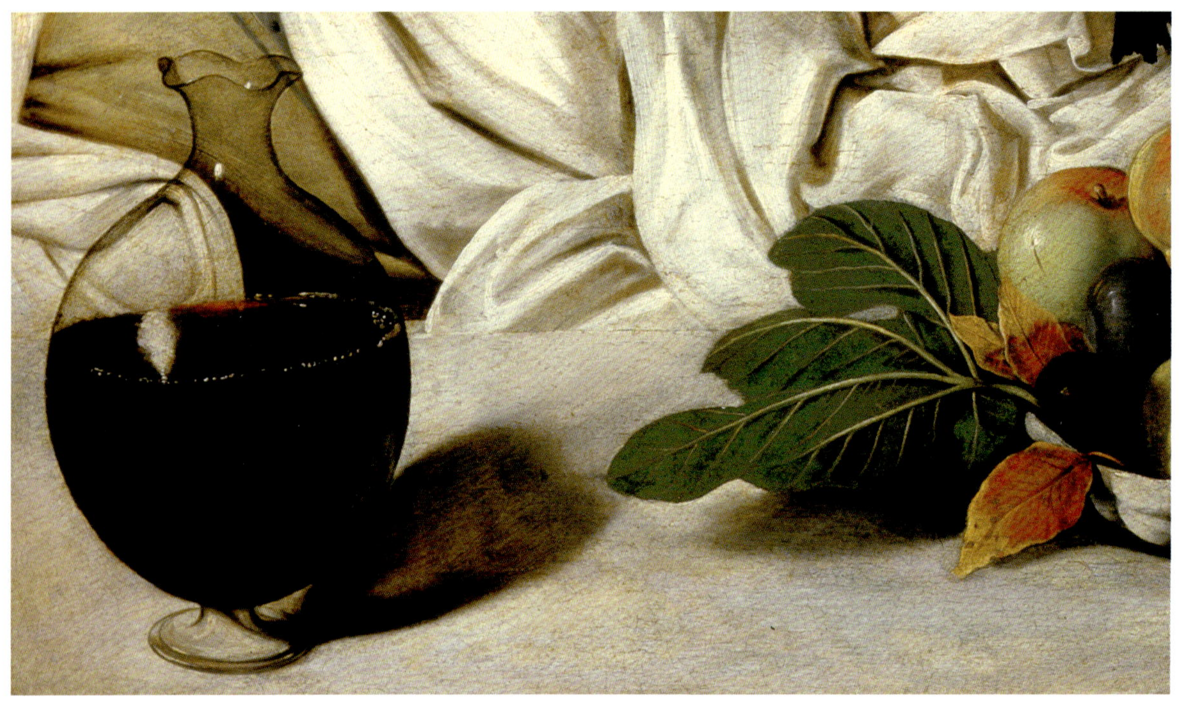

that moved beyond the artificially bent bodies and metallic colors of Mannerism. Paintings of *lutenists* had become quite popular in the period. Caravaggio painted more sensually than any of his contemporaries, with earthy colors and skillful play of light and dark. He found his models on the streets of Rome. Crowd scenes like the *Cheaters* and the *Fortuneteller* were previously unknown in Rome and structured in such a way that drew the viewer into the action. Details worked out with precision give information about the nature of the scene such as the ace hidden behind one player's back and the wily countenance

Il possède en outre un talent pour la suggestion d'un érotisme subliminal, joint à une esthétique nouvelle qui ne se soucie pas des corps artistement ployés et des couleurs métalliques de la peinture maniériste. Le sujet du *Joueur de luth* est alors en vogue. Caravage peint avec une sensualité qu'on ne relève chez aucun de ses concurrents ; ses couleurs sont terreuses, le jeu du clair-obscur atteste son savoir-faire. Il va chercher ses modèles dans les rues de Rome. Des scènes populaires comme celle des *Tricheurs* ou de *La Diseuse de bonne aventure* sont alors nouvelles dans le contexte artistique romain, et conçues

Der kranke Bacchus – in dem ein Selbstporträt des Künstlers gesehen wird – und *Bacchus* hervor. Darüber hinaus besaß er ein Talent für die Darstellung unterschwelliger Erotik gepaart mit einer neuen Ästhetik, die sich nicht kümmert um die künstlich verbogenen Körper und metallischen Farben der manieristischen Malerei. Auch das Thema des *Lautenspieler* erfreute sich großer Beliebtheit. Caravaggio malte so sinnlich wie keiner seiner Konkurrenten; seine Farben sind erdig, das Spiel von Hell und Dunkel ist gekonnt. Seine Modelle holte er sich von den Straßen Roms. Volksszenen wie

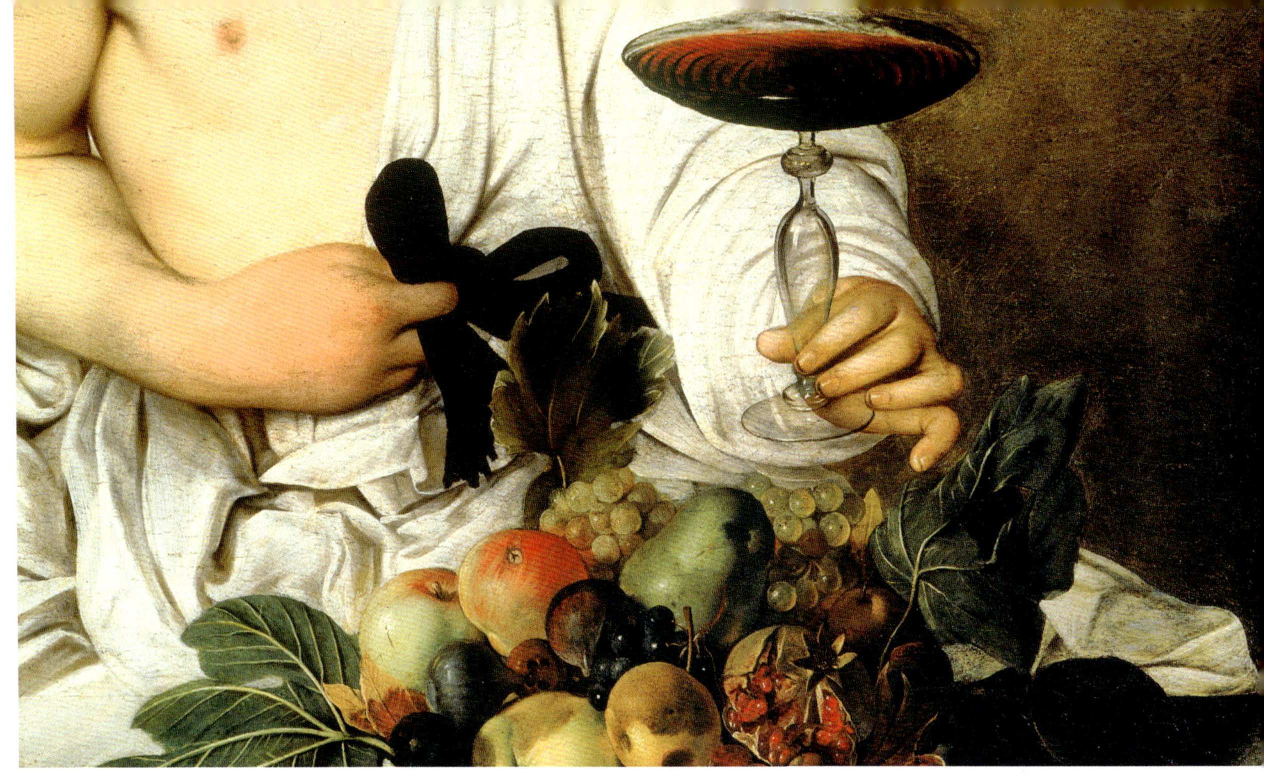

la que se ve un autorretrato del artista, y *Baco*. Además poseía un talento para la representación de un erotismo latente, unido a una nueva estética que no se centraba en los cuerpos artificialmente cubiertos y los colores metálicos de la pintura manierista. El motivo del *Tañedor de laúd* gozaba de gran aceptación. Caravaggio pintaba con una sensualidad sin parangón entre sus competidores, sus colores profundos, el juego entre luz y sombra de gran destreza. Encontraba sus modelos en las calles de Roma. Escenas populares como *Los jugadores de cartas* y *La buenaventura* eran novedosas para el contexto romano, y parecían empujar

di Bacco: *Bacchino malato*, che secondo alcuni studiosi sarebbe un autoritratto dell'artista, e *Bacco*. Caravaggio aveva però un grande talento anche per la rappresentazione erotica subliminale in combinazione con una nuova estetica che, a differenza della pittura manieristica, non si curava della torsione artistica dei corpi o dei colori metallici. Il motivo del *Suonatore di liuto* ha goduto sempre di grande popolarità. Le rappresentazioni di Caravaggio sono sensuali come nessun'altra; i suoi colori sono terrosi, e i suoi giochi di luce e ombra sono eseguiti magistralmente. Caravaggio traeva i suoi modelli dalle

van onderliggende erotiek, die hij paarde aan een nieuwe esthetiek waarin hij de kunstmatig verwrongen lichamen en metaalkleurige tinten van het maniërisme achter zich liet. Het motief van *de Luitspeler* was enorm populair en Caravaggio schilderde het beter dan zijn concurrenten; zijn kleuren zijn aards, het spel van licht en donker is subtiel. Zijn modellen vond hij in de straten van Rome. Volkse taferelen als *De valsspelers* en *De waarzegster* waren voor Romeinse begrippen nieuw en toonden een compositie waarin de beschouwer bij het uitgebeelde werd betrokken. Zorgvuldig uitgewerkte Details verwezen naar het

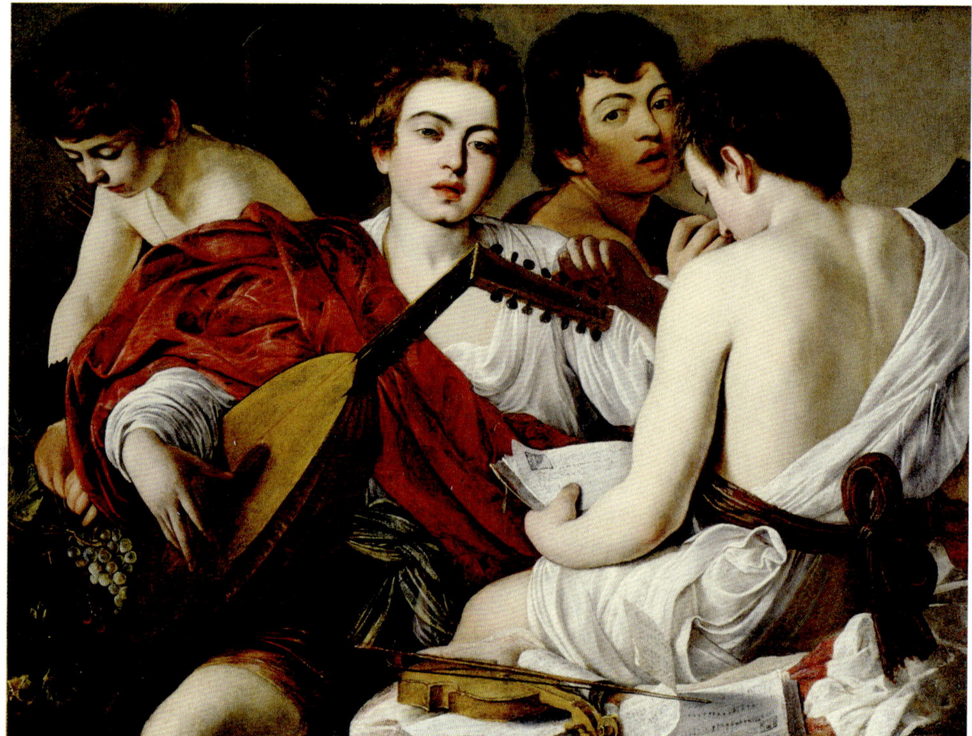

of the fortuneteller stealthily taking the ring off the young man's finger. Such negation of tradition and convention did not always receive a positive response, especially in Caravaggio's religious works.

de telle façon que le spectateur soit impliqué dans l'événement. Des détails précisément travaillés donnent des indications sur le caractère de la scène : l'as caché dans le dos du joueur, l'air roublard de la diseuse de bonne aventure qui tire doucement l'anneau que le jeune homme porte au doigt. Son non-respect de la tradition et de la convention n'est pas toujours bien accueilli, surtout dans ses œuvres sacrées.

die *Falschspieler* und die *Wahrsagerin* waren für römische Verhältnisse neu und derart aufgebaut, dass der Betrachter in das Geschehen hineingezogen wird. Genau herausgearbeitete Details geben Hinweise auf den Charakter der Szene: das Ass hinter dem Rücken des Spielers, der verschlagene Gesichtsausdruck der Wahrsagerin, die dem Jüngling den Ring vom Finger streift. Das Negieren von Tradition und Konvention wurde dabei nicht immer positiv aufgenommen – vor allen bei seinen sakralen Bildwerken.

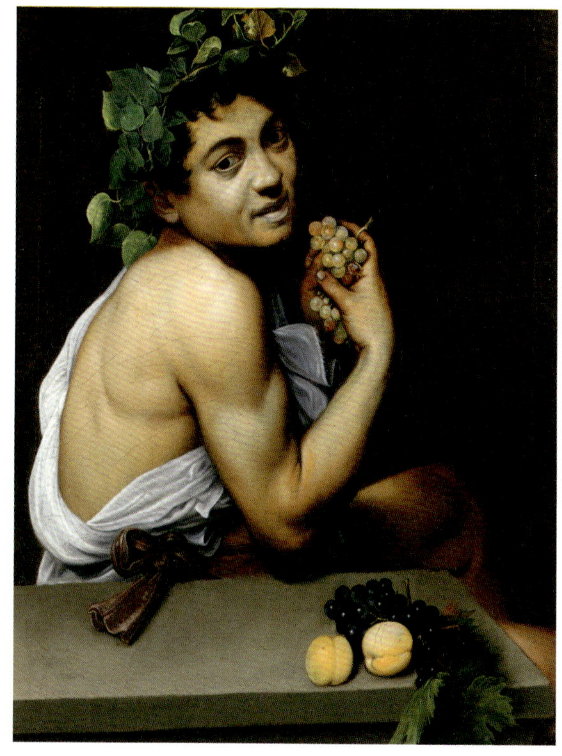

c. 1593, Oil on canvas/Huile sur toile, 67 × 53 cm, Galleria Borghese, Roma

al espectador al interior de la escena. Los Detalles profusamente trabajados aportan indicaciones sobre el carácter de la escena: el as a la espalda de uno de los jugadores, la expresión astuta de la gitana que extrae el anillo del dedo del joven. Su rechazo a la tradición y convención no fue siempre bien recibido, sobre todo en sus obras sacras.

strade di Roma. Scene di massa come *I bari* e *Buona ventura* costituivano una novità per i romani e furono dipinte in modo tale da rendere l'osservatore partecipe dell'azione. Dettagli riprodotti minuziosamente, quali l'asso dietro la schiena del giocatore e il volto scaltro della zingara che sfila l'anello dal dito del giovane, forniscono informazioni sulla natura della scena. Il rinnegamento della tradizione e delle convenzioni da parte di Caravaggio non fu però sempre ben accolto, soprattutto nelle sue opere di carattere sacro.

karakter van de scène: de ezel achter de rug van de spelers, de listige uitdrukking op het gezicht van de waarzegster die de ring van de vinger van de jongeling steelt. Caravaggio's minachting voor tradities en conventies werd hem niet door iedereen in dank afgenomen, vooral niet bij zijn sacrale schilderijen.

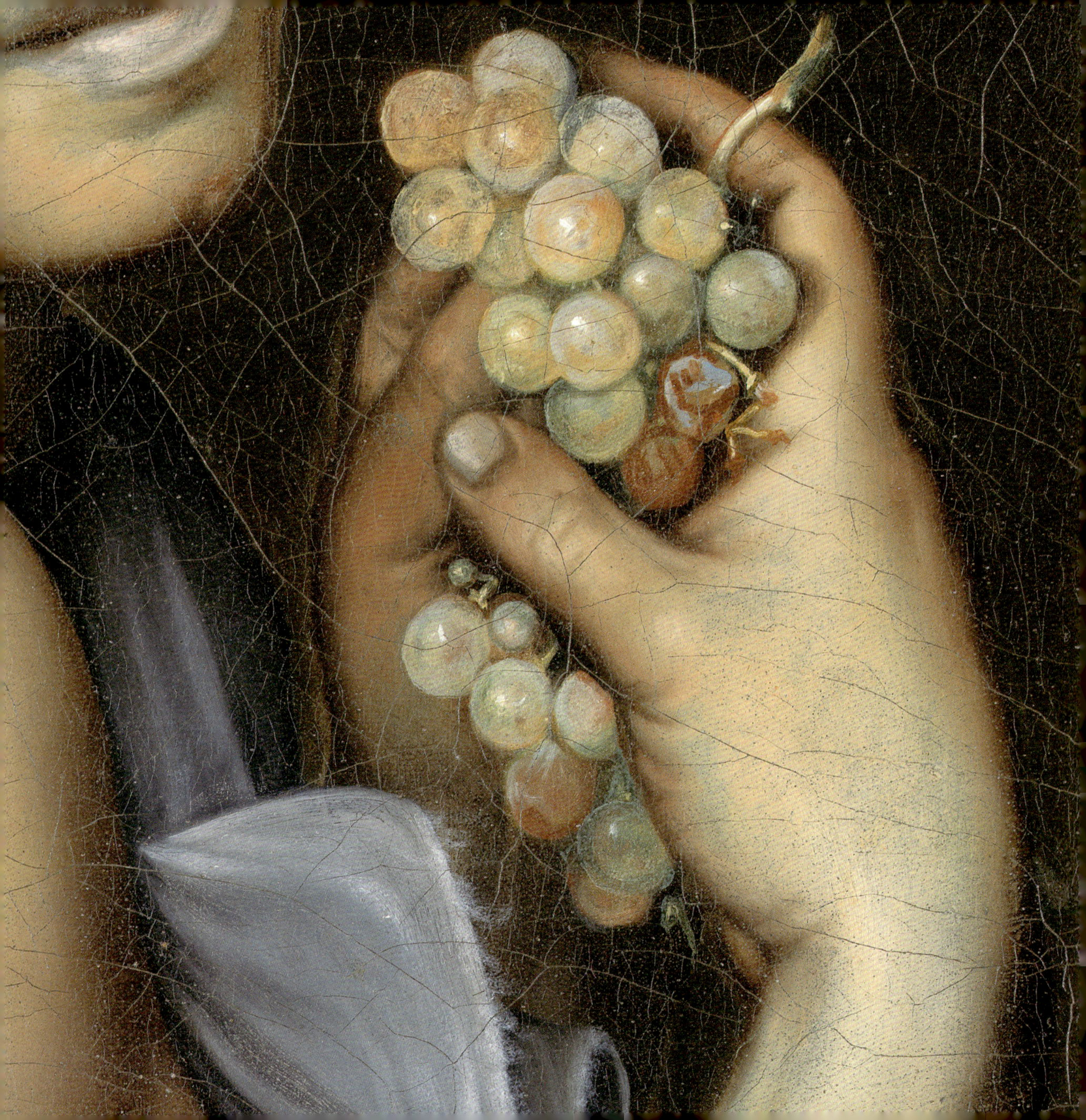

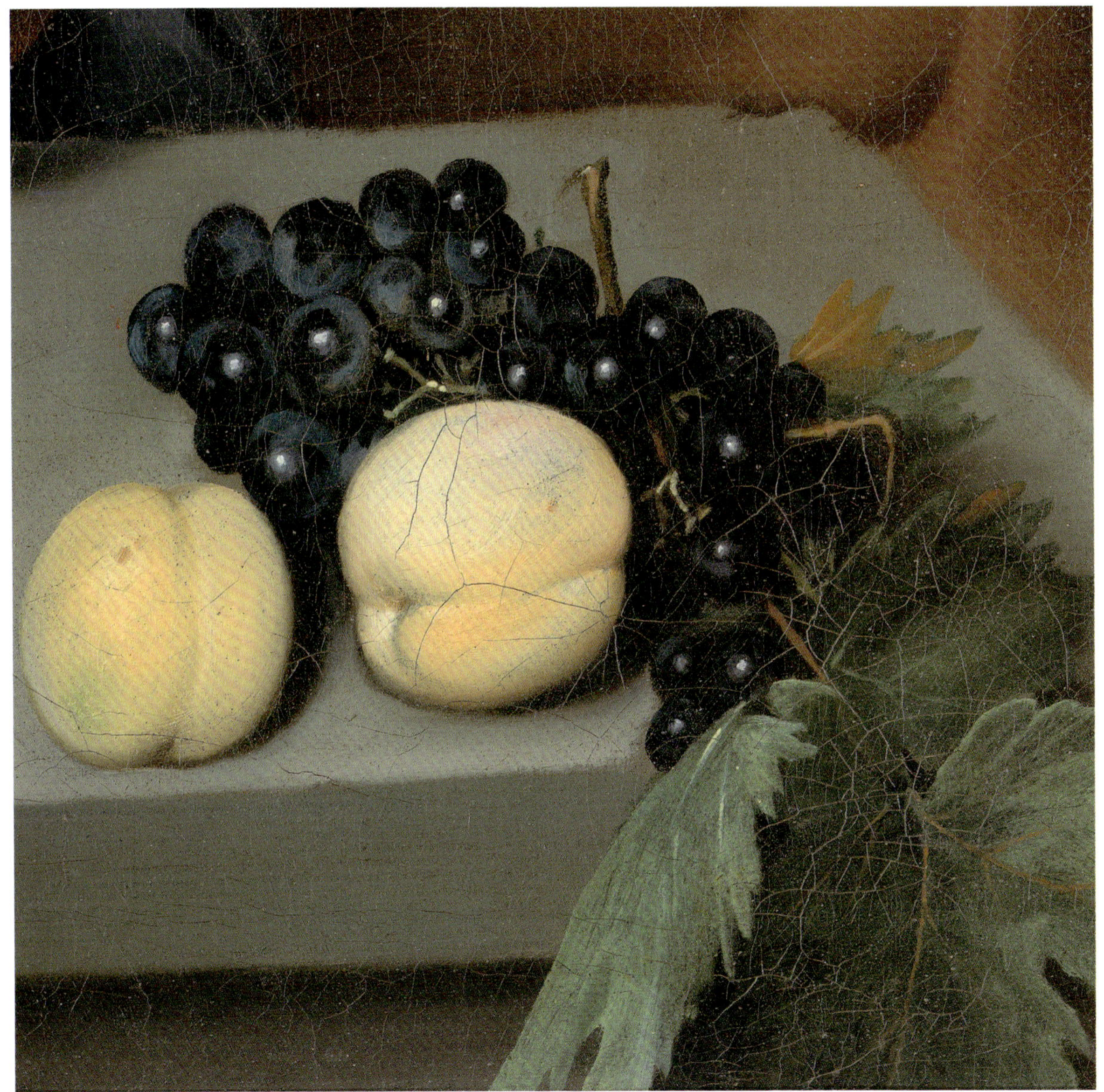

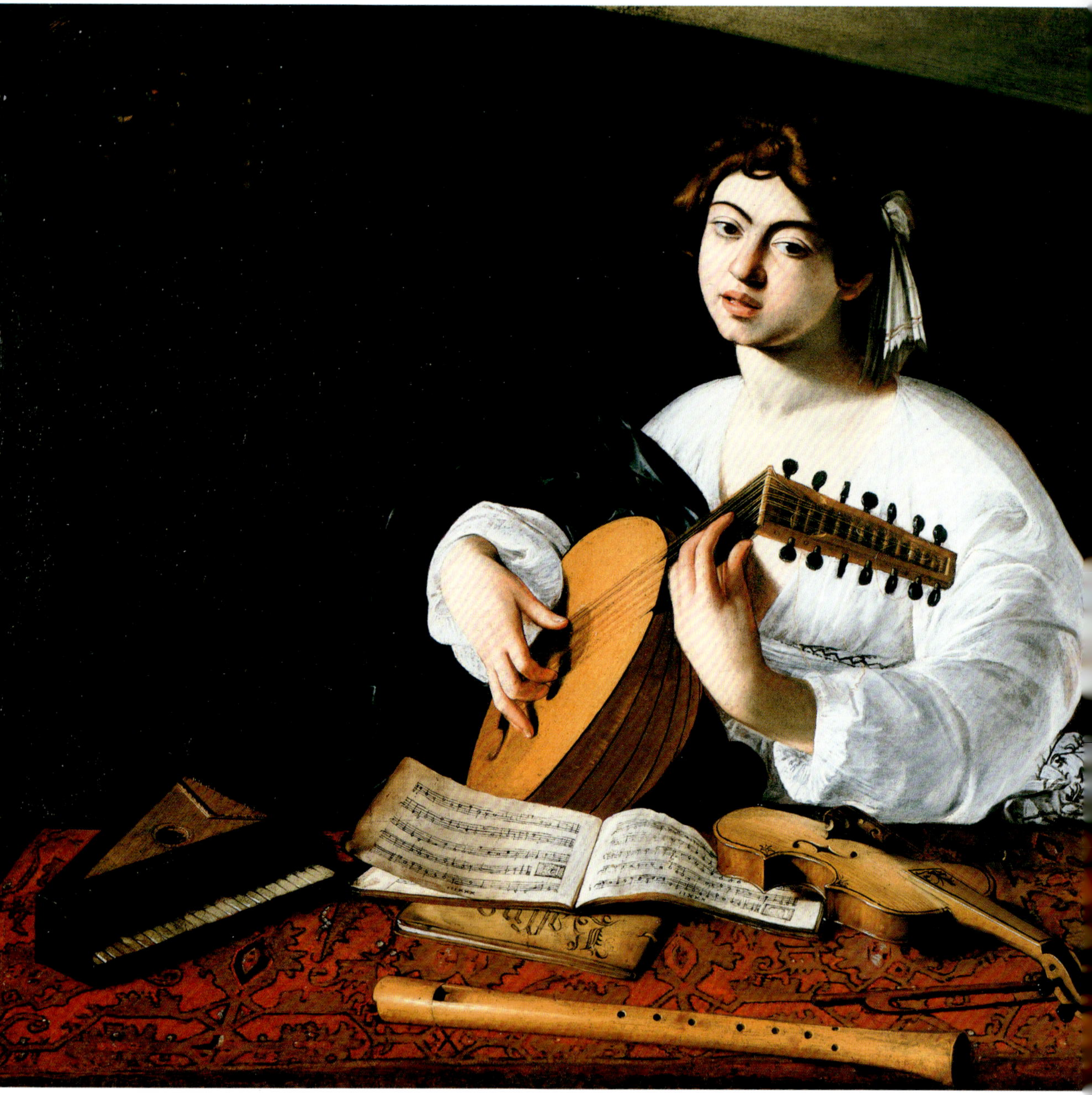

The Lutenist
Le Joueur de luth
Der Lautenspieler
El tañedor de laúd
Suonatore di liuto
De luitspeler

1595, Oil on canvas/Huile sur toile, 100 × 126,5 cm, Private collection

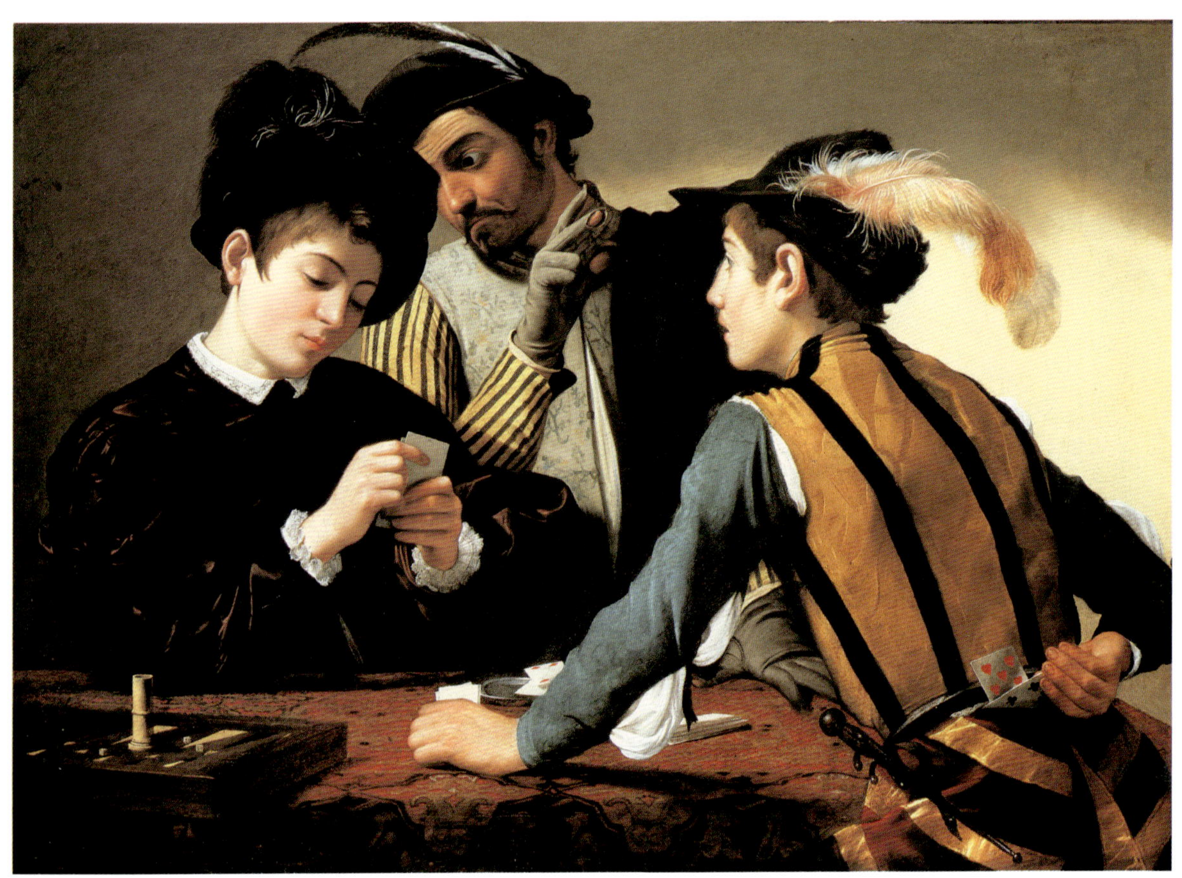

Cheaters

Les Tricheurs

Die Falschspieler

Los jugadores de cartas

I bari

De valsspelers

1594/95, Oil on canvas/Huile sur toile, 94,2 × 130,9 cm, Kimbell Art Museum, Fort Worth

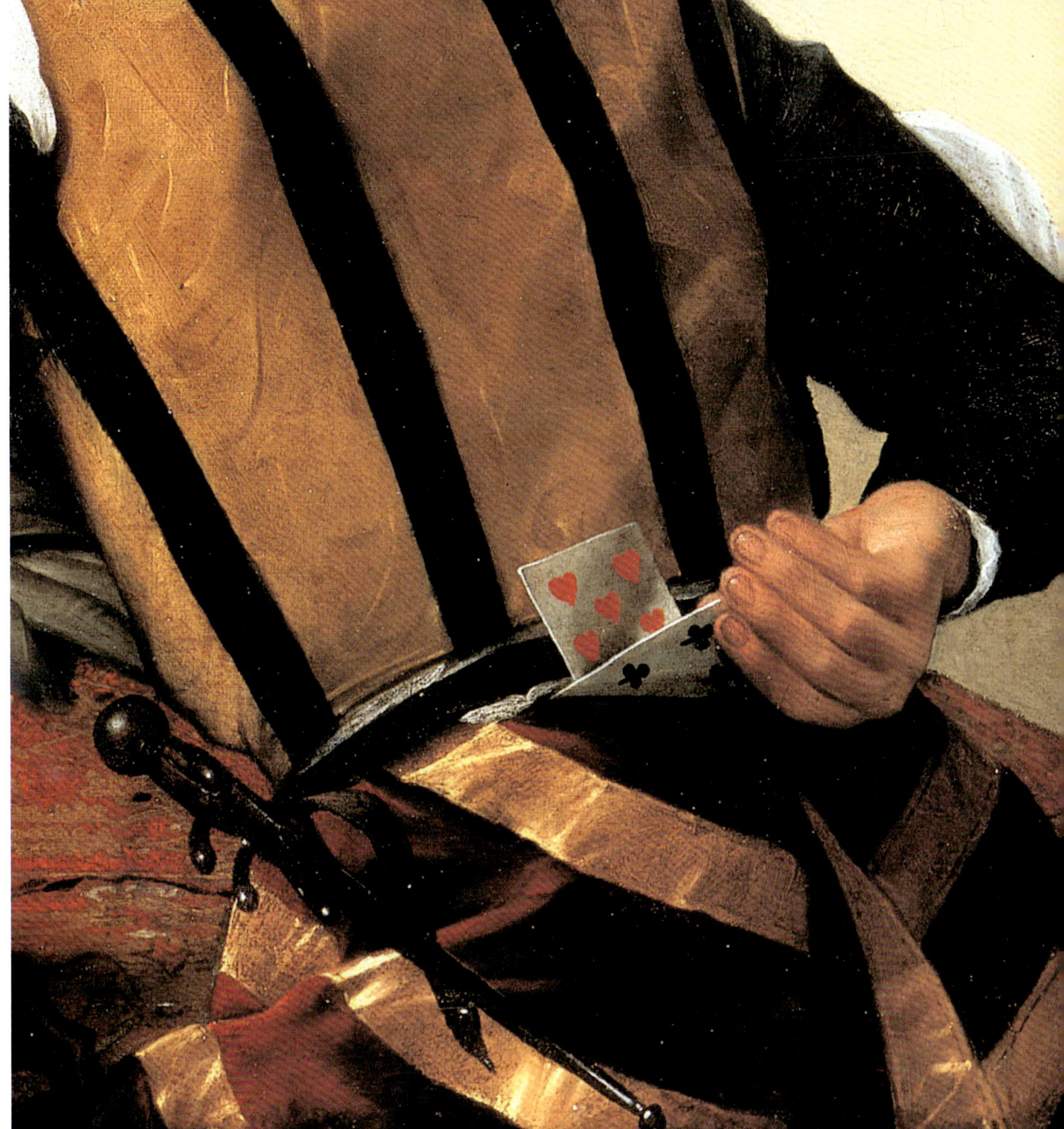

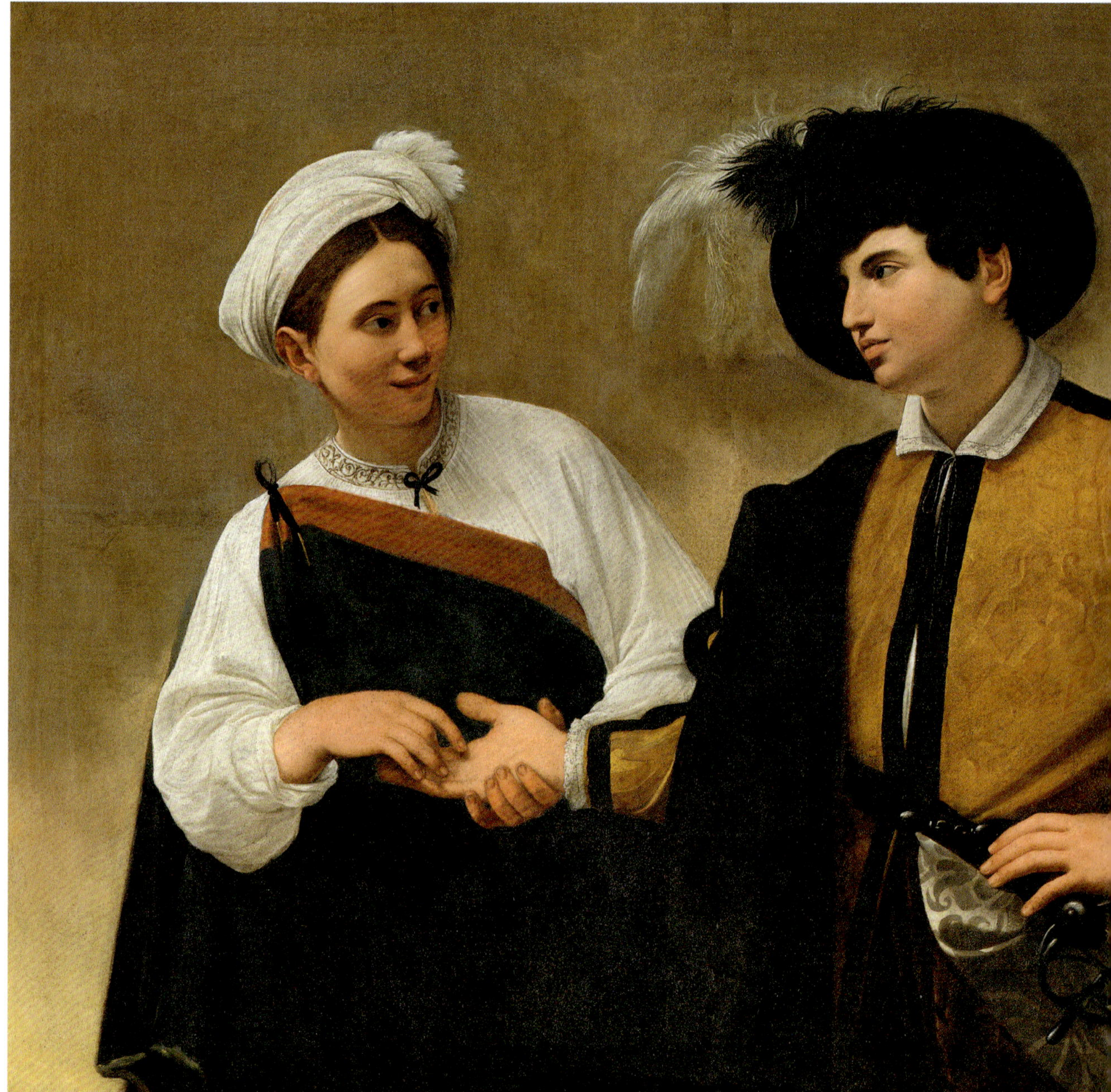

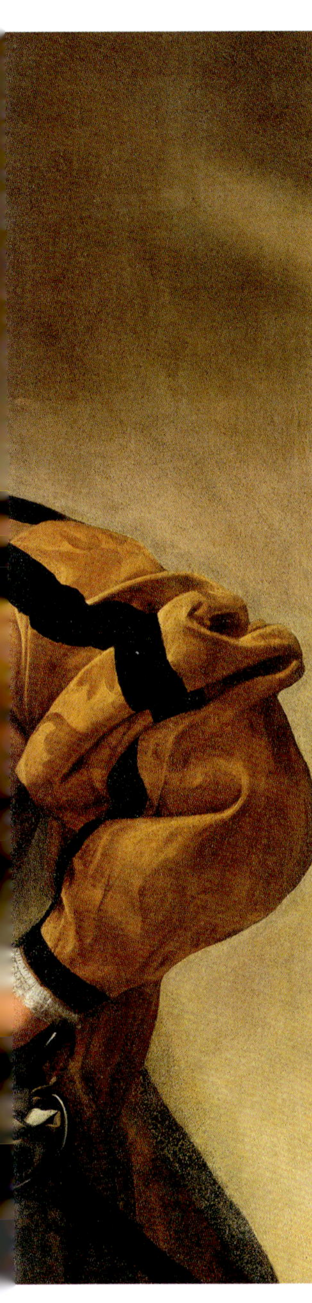

The Fortuneteller
La Diseuse de bonne aventure
Die Wahrsagerin
La buenaventura
La buona ventura
De waarzegster

1595, Oil on canvas/Huile sur toile, 115 × 150 cm, Pinacoteca Capitolina, Roma

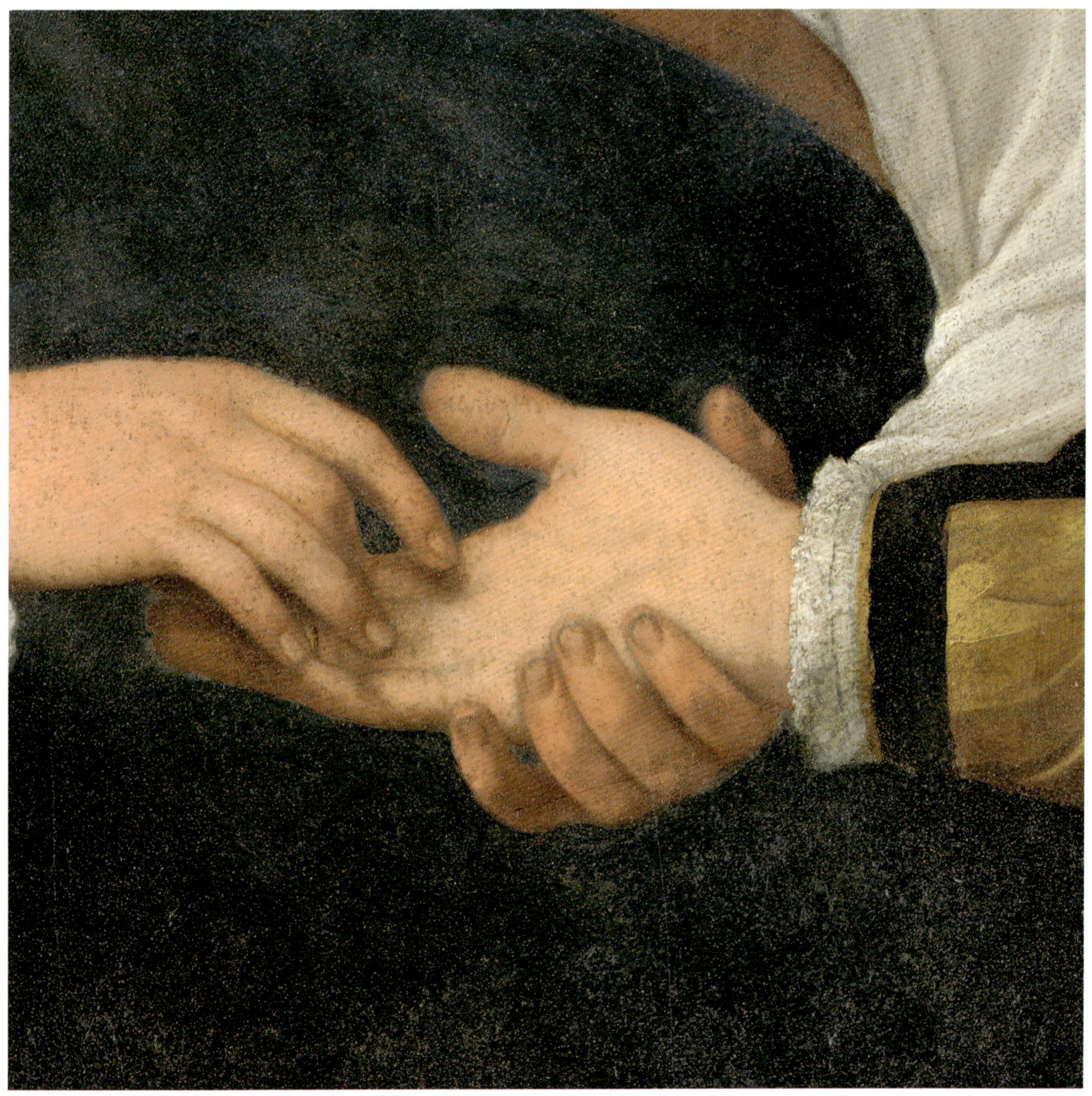

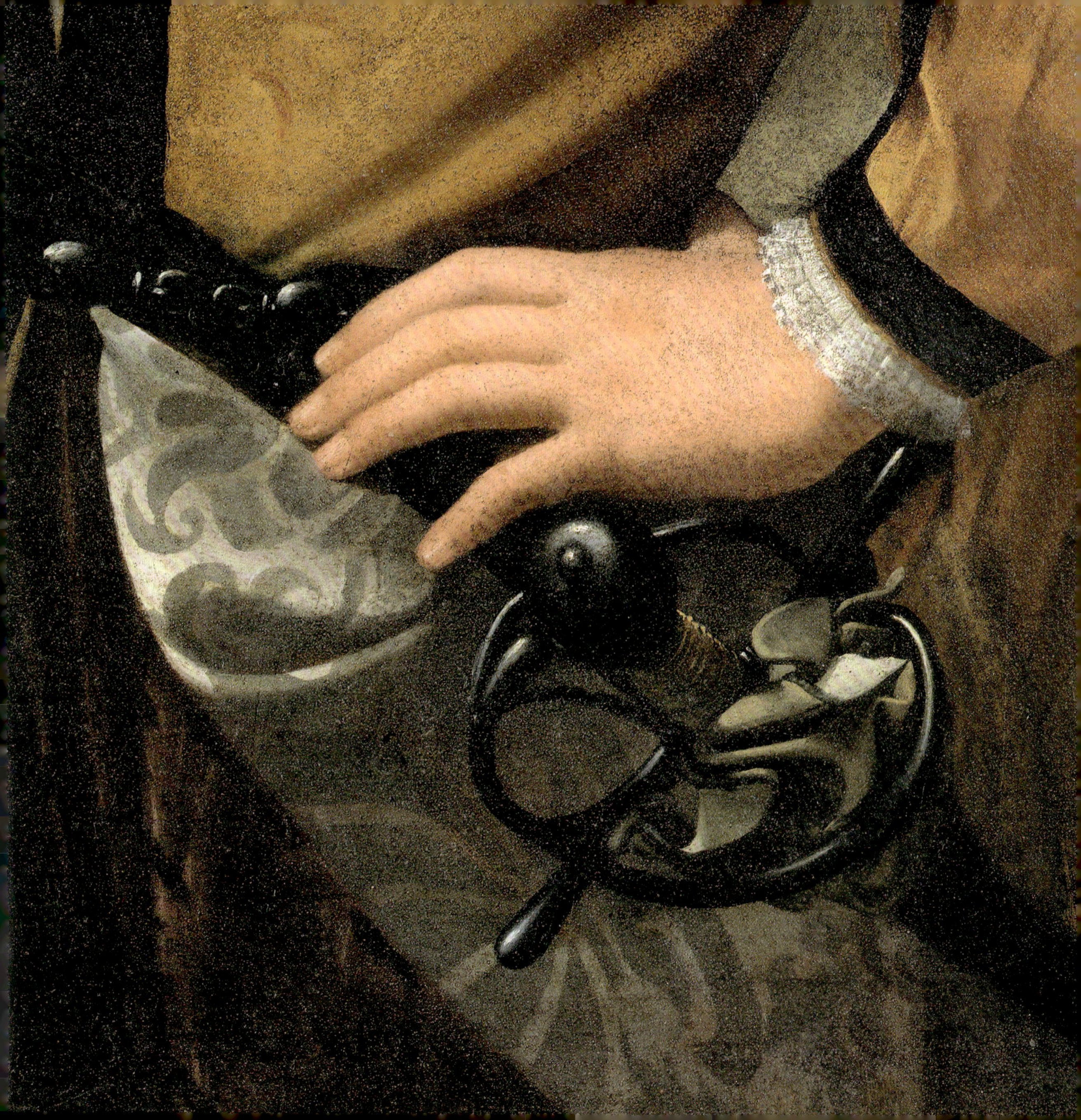

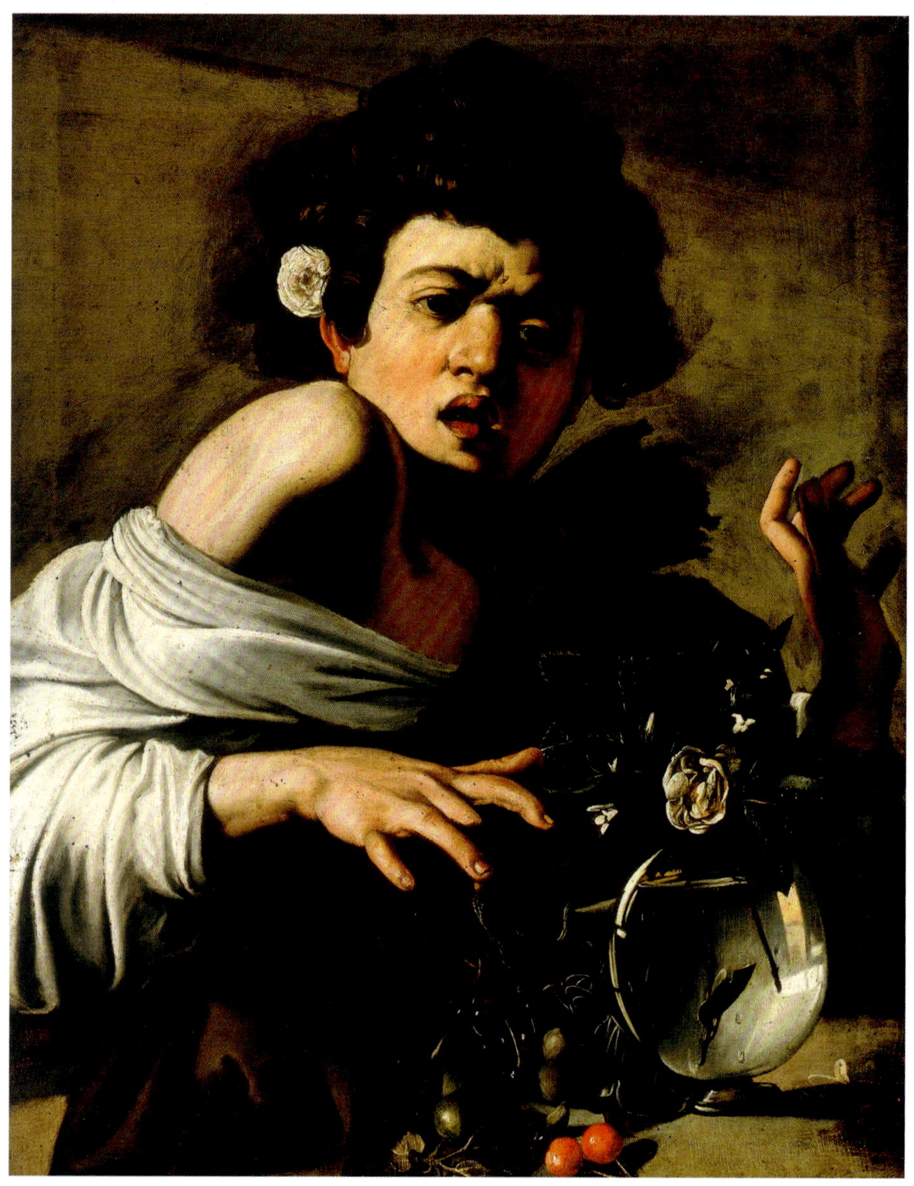

Boy Being Bitten by a Lizard (first version)

Garçon mordu par un lézard (première version)

Knabe, der von einer Eidechse gebissen wird (erste Fassung)

Chico mordido por una lagartija (primera versión)

Ragazzo morso da un ramarro (prima versione)

Jongen die door een hagedis wordt gebeten (eerste versie)

c. 1594/95, Oil on canvas/ Huile sur toile, 65,8 × 52,3 cm, Private collection

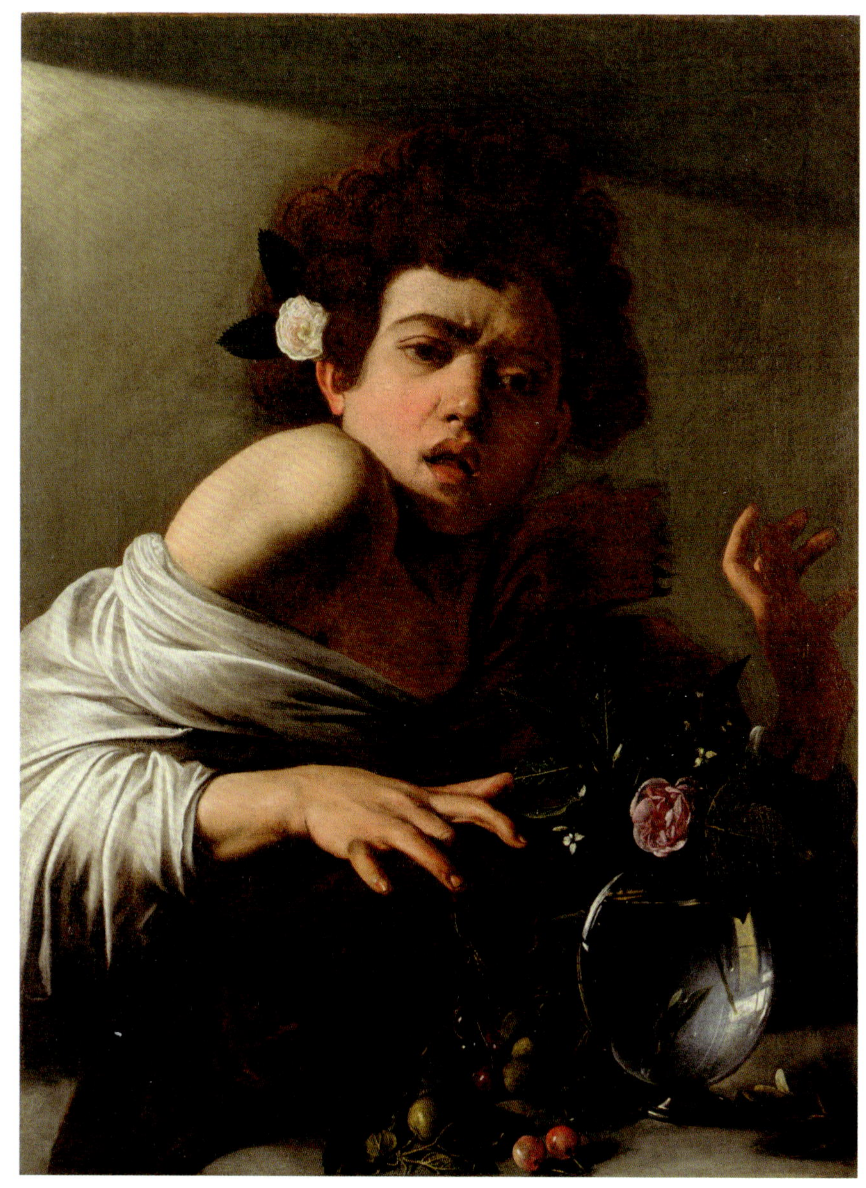

Boy Being Bitten by a Lizard (second version)

Garçon mordu par un lézard (deuxième version)

Knabe, der von einer Eidechse gebissen wird (zweite Fassung)

Chico mordido por una lagartija (segunda versión)

Ragazzo morso da un ramarro (seconda versione)

Jongen die door een hagedis wordt gebeten (tweede versie)

1594/95, Oil on canvas/Huile sur toile, 66 × 49,5 cm, National Gallery, London

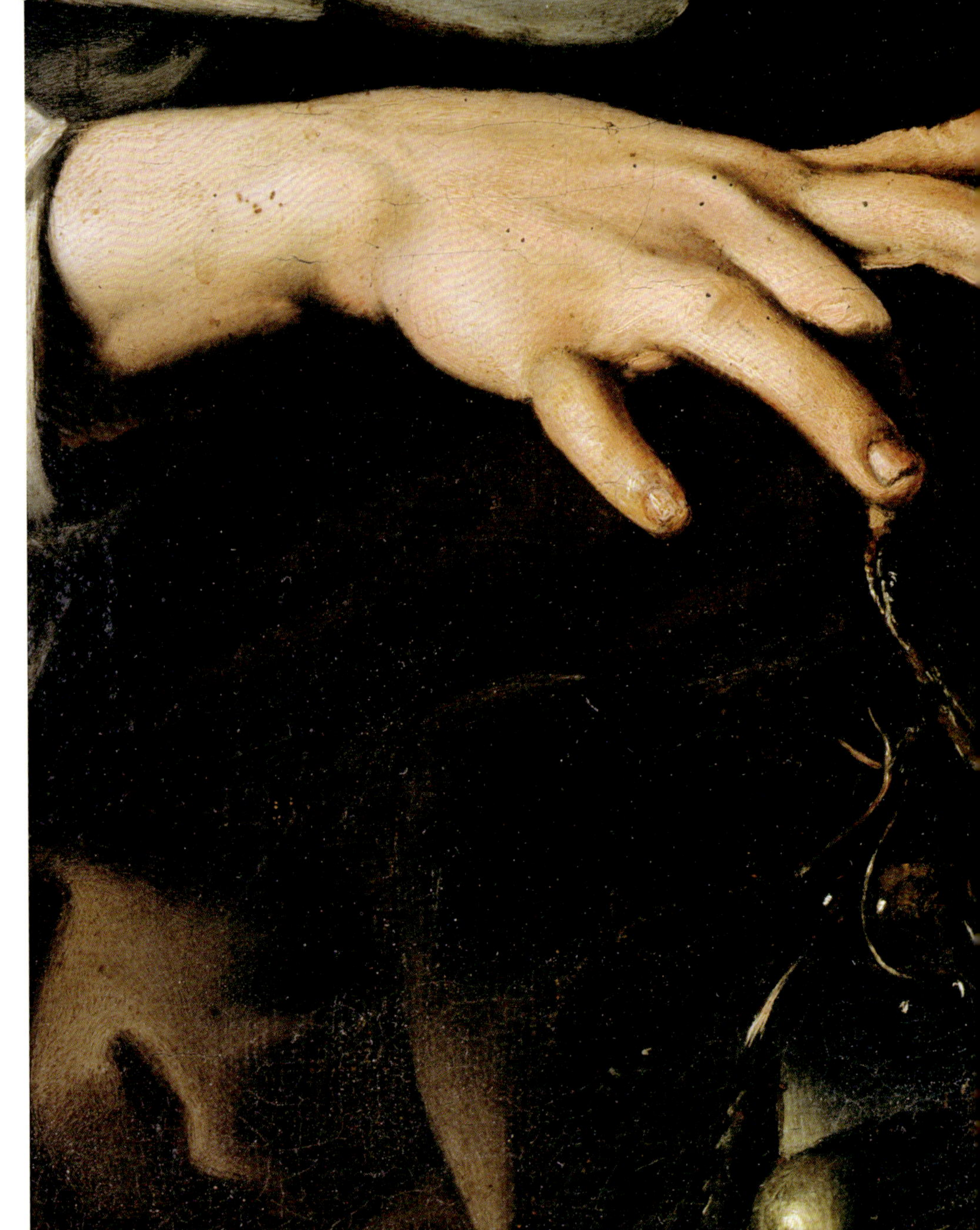

Detail of the
first version

Détail de la
première version

Detail der
ersten Fassung

Detalle de la
primera versión

Dettaglio della
prima versione

Detail uit de
eerste versie

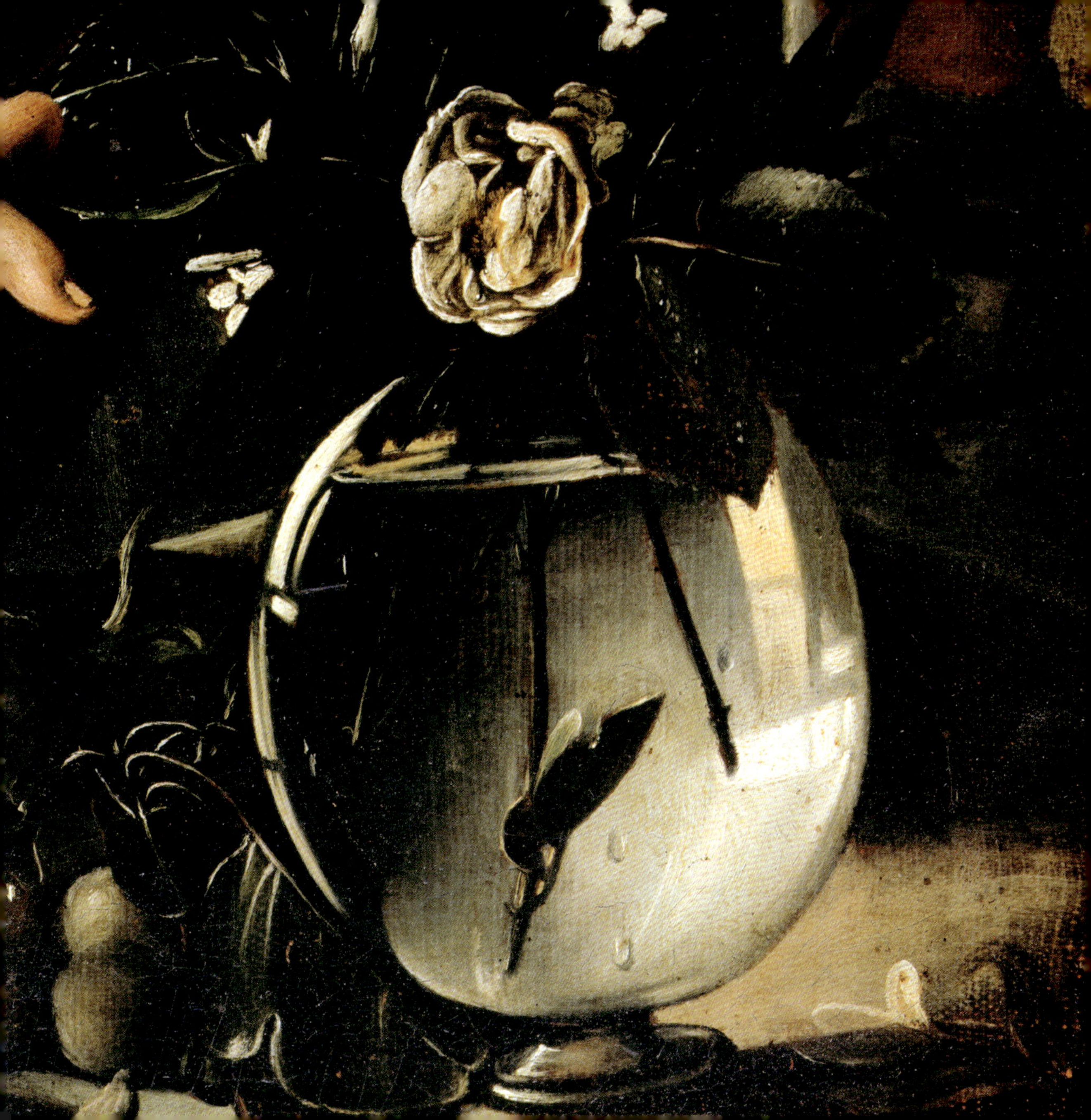

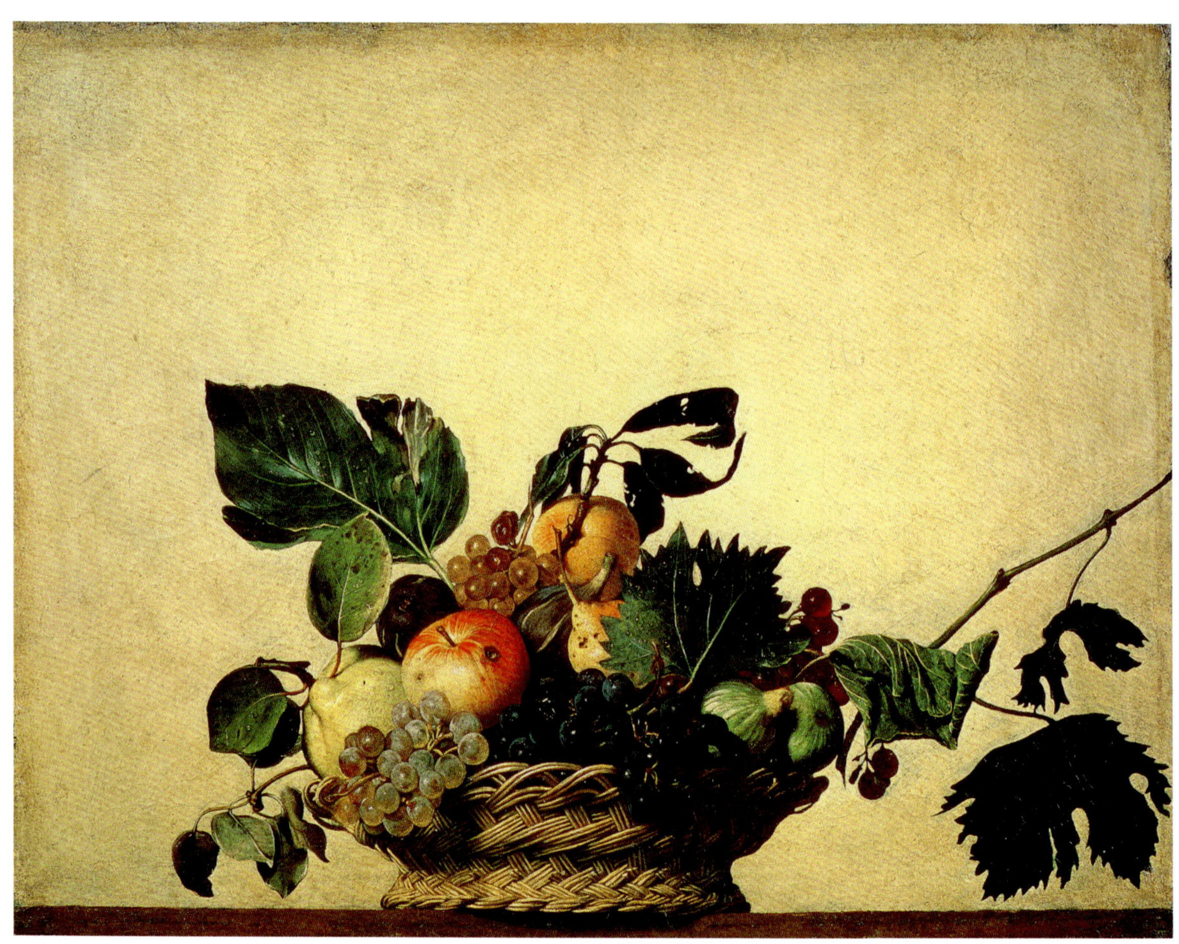

Basket of Fruit

Corbeille de fruits

Der Obstkorb

El cesto de fruta

Canestra di frutta

De fruitmand

c. 1597, Oil on canvas/Huile sur toile, 47 × 62 cm, Pinacoteca Ambrosiana, Milano

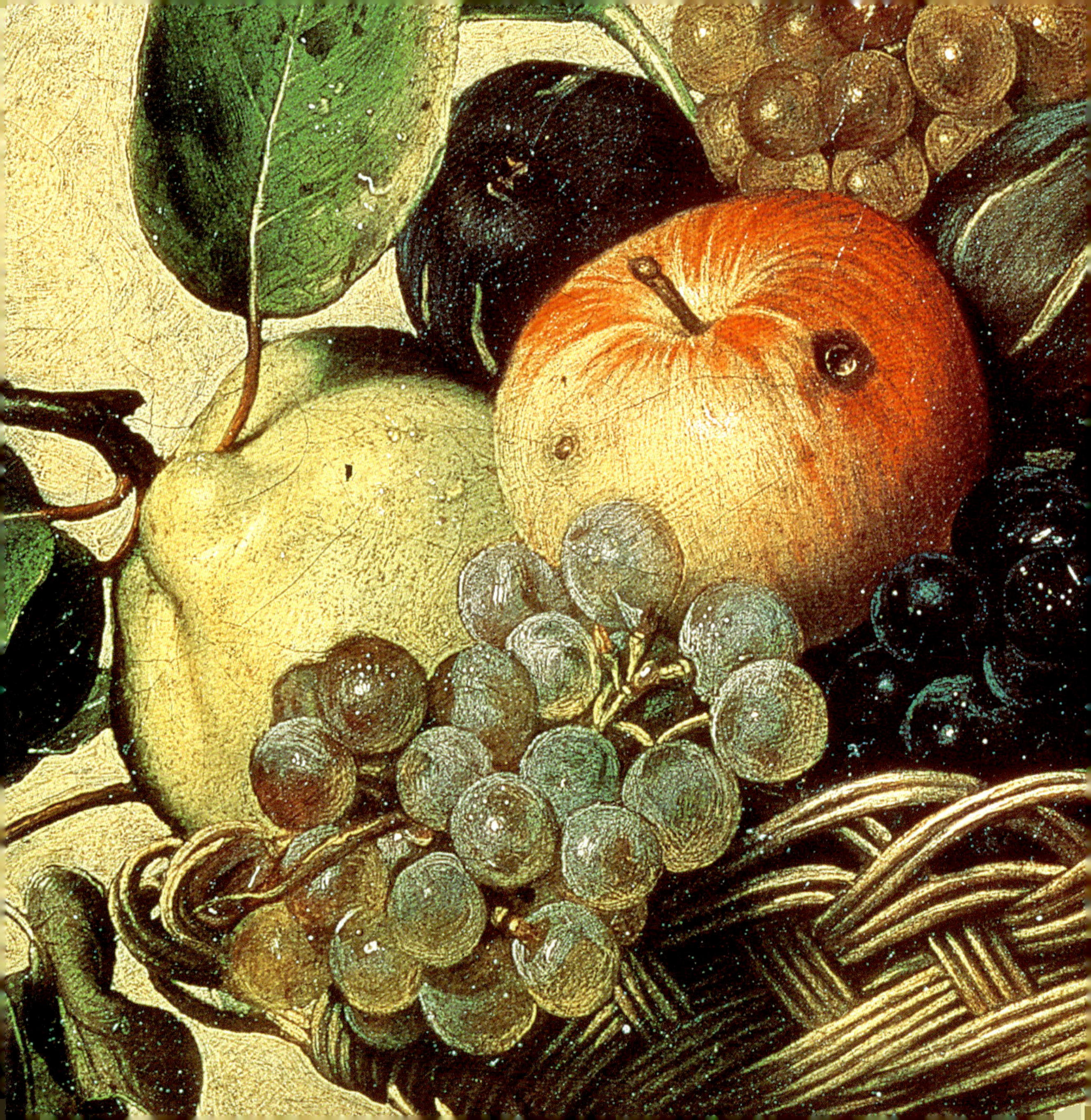

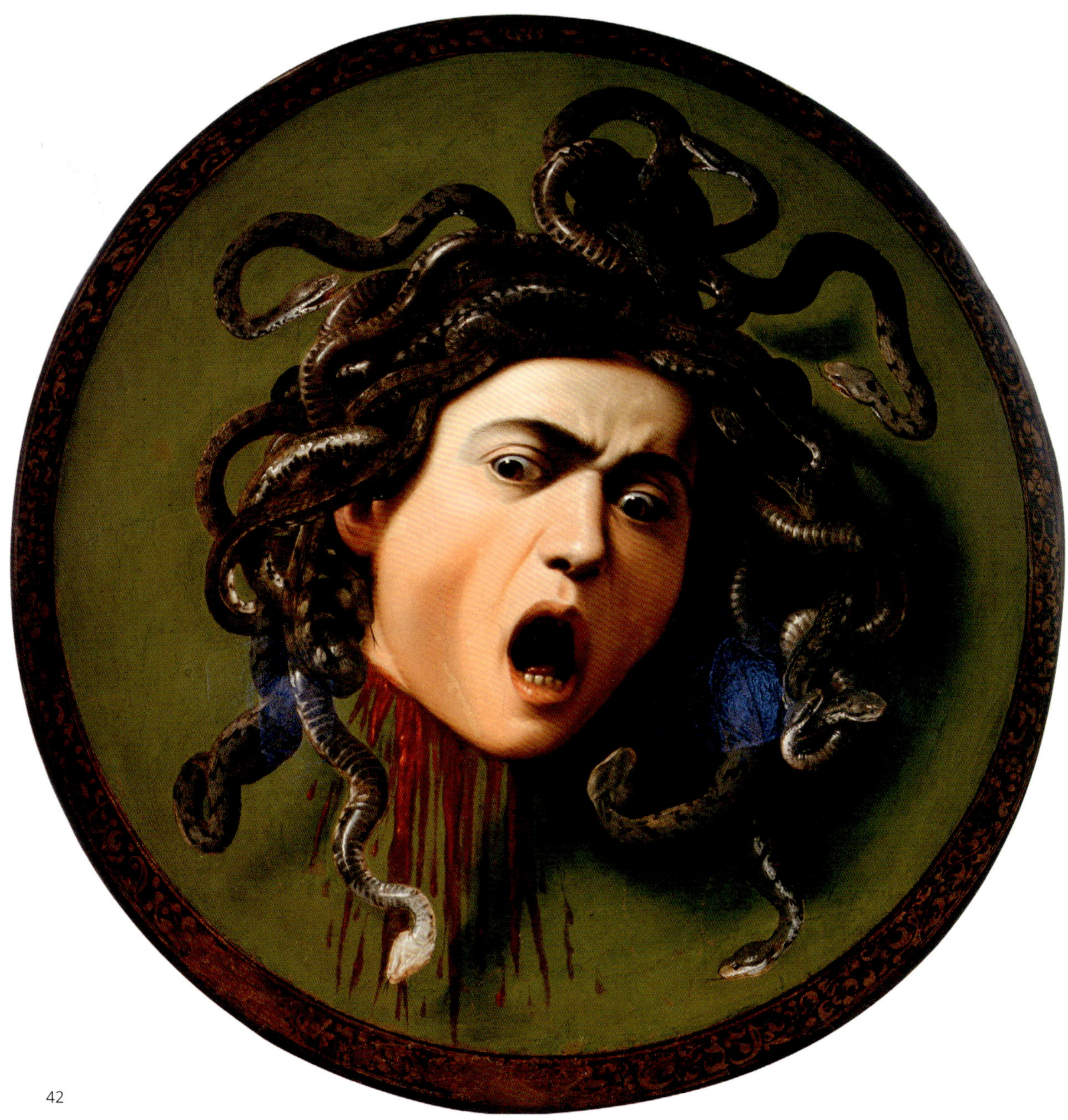

The Head of Medusa

Méduse

Kopf der Medusa

La cabeza de Medusa

Medusa

Medusa

c. 1597/98, Oil on canvas stretched over wood/Huile sur toile marouflée sur un bouclier en bois, 57 cm, Galleria degli Uffizi, Firenze

The snakes are still writhing on her head, her mouth and eyes are still wide open in fear, but Medusa is lost. In the Renaissance, the death of this monster from ancient Greek mythology had become a popular motif, but no one had depicted this scene quite as brutally as Caravaggio. He created this decorative sign for Cardinal del Monte as part of his parade armor.

Des serpents se tordent encore sur sa tête, sa bouche et ses yeux sont dilatés de terreur – mais Méduse est perdue. À la Renaissance, la mort de ce monstre de la mythologie grecque était un sujet en vogue ; cependant, personne n'a représenté la scène de façon aussi brutale que Caravage. Ce tableau est une commande du cardinal del Monte, comme décoration d'un bouclier de parade.

Die Schlangen züngeln noch auf ihrem Haupt, Mund und Augen sind im Schreck geweitet, doch Medusa ist verloren. In der Renaissance war der Tod des Monsters aus der altgriechischen Mythologie ein beliebtes Thema, aber kaum ein Künstler hat die Szene so brutal dargestellt wie Caravaggio. Er schuf diesen Schmuckschild im Auftrag des Kardinals del Monte als Teil einer Paraderüstung.

Las serpientes se agitan todavía sobre su cabeza y la boca y ojos se abren con estupor, pero Medusa está ya perdida. El motivo de la muerte del monstruo de la mitología clásica griega era uno de los favoritos durante el Renacimiento, pero nadie lo pintó de forma tan brutal como Caravaggio. Creó esta obra decorativa, a encargo del Cardenal del Monte, como parte de una armadura de gala.

I serpenti guizzano ancora sulla sua testa, la sua bocca e i suoi occhi sono ancora spalancati per la paura, ma la Medusa è ormai perduta. Durante il Rinascimento, la morte di questo mostro dalla mitologia greca era un motivo popolare, tuttavia nessuno rappresentò la scena in modo così brutale come Caravaggio. Il pittore dipinse questo scudo per il cardinal Del Monte come parte di un'armatura da parata.

De slangen kronkelen nog rond haar hoofd en haar mond en ogen staan wijd open van verschrikking, maar de Medusa is verslagen. In de Renaissance was de dood van dit monster uit de Griekse oudheid een geliefd motief, maar niemand schilderde het zoals Caravaggio. Hij creëerde dit sierschild voor kardinaal Del Monte, als onderdeel van een wapenrusting voor een parade.

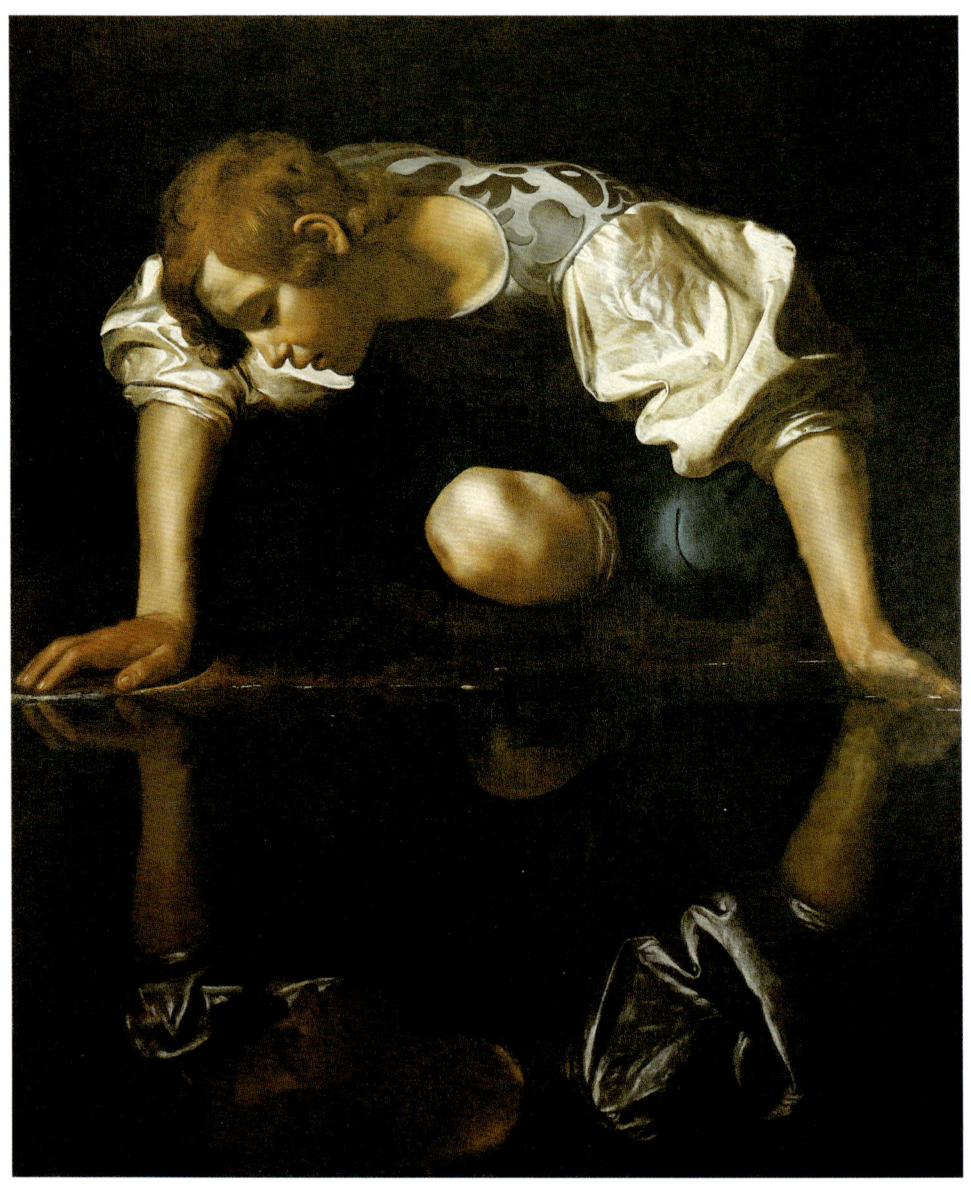

Narcissus

Narcisse

Narziss

Narciso

Narciso

Narcissus

c. 1598/99, Oil on canvas/Huile sur toile, 113,3 × 94 cm, Palazzo Barberini, Roma

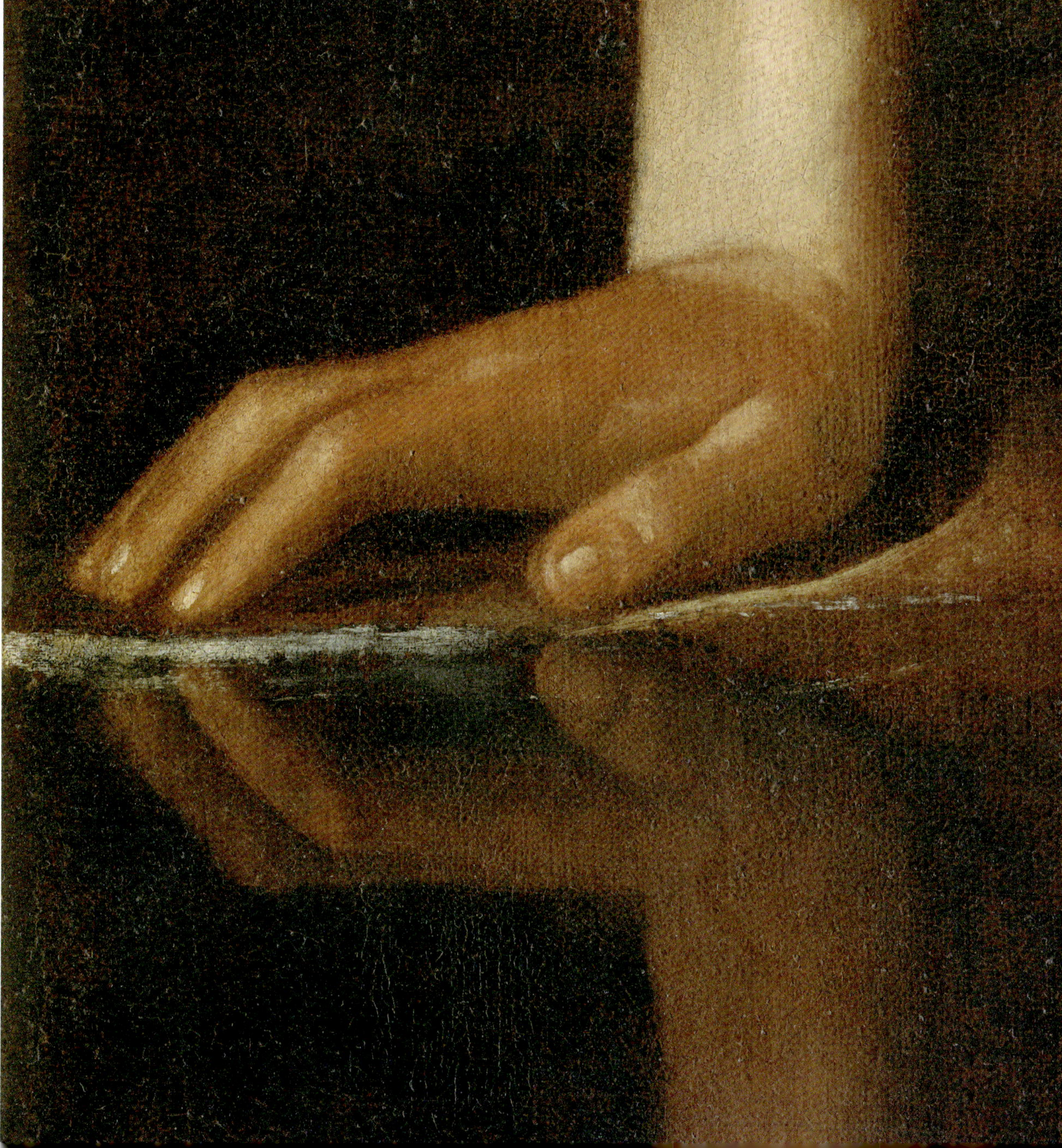

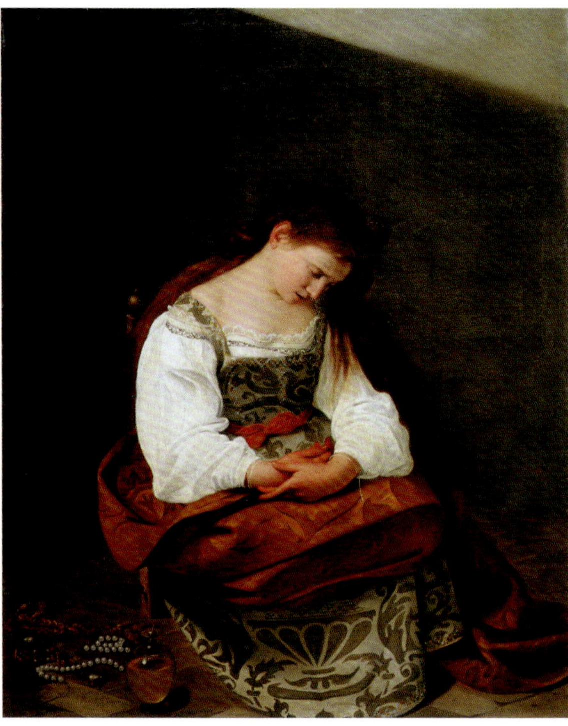

c. 1596, Oil on canvas/Huile sur toile, 122,5 × 98,5 cm,
Palazzo Doria Pamphilj, Roma

Early sacred painting

Cardinal del Monte, who had given
Caravaggio quarters in his Roman
residence, introduced the artist to the
circles of Roman aristocracy, which, in
turn, opened the doors of their private
art collections to the painter. The result
were his first religious paintings such as
the *Penitent Magdalene,* the *Rest on the
Flight into Egypt,* and *Martha and Mary
Magdalene.* He continued to apply the
realism from his secular works as he
turned to religious scenes. The penitent
Magdalene is seated on a low stool,
weeping as she leaves behind her life

Premiers tableaux sacrés

Le cardinal del Monte – qui hébergeait
Caravage dans sa résidence romaine –
l'introduisit dans les cercles de
l'aristocratie, ouvrant ainsi au peintre
les portes des collections de la Ville
Éternelle. Il peignit alors ses premiers
tableaux religieux tels que la *Madeleine
repentante, Le Repos pendant la fuite en
Égypte* et *Marthe et Marie-Madeleine,*
prolongeant dans le domaine sacré le
réalisme de ses œuvres profanes. La
Madeleine repentante est figurée dans
le moment où elle renonce à sa vie
impure de courtisane, pleurant sur un

Frühe sakrale Gemälde

Kardinal del Monte, der Caravaggio in
seiner römischen Residenz wohnen ließ,
führte ihn in die Kreise der römischen
Aristokratie ein, was dem Maler die
Türen zu den Kunstsammlungen der
Stadt öffnete. Es entstanden die ersten
religiösen Gemälde wie die *Büßende
Magdalena,* die *Ruhe auf der Flucht nach
Ägypten* und *Martha und Magdalena.* Den
Realismus seiner profanen Werke führte
er im sakralen Bereich fort. Die büßende
Magdalena hockt im Moment der Abkehr
von ihrem Leben als unkeusche Kurtisane
weinend auf einem niedrigen Schemel,

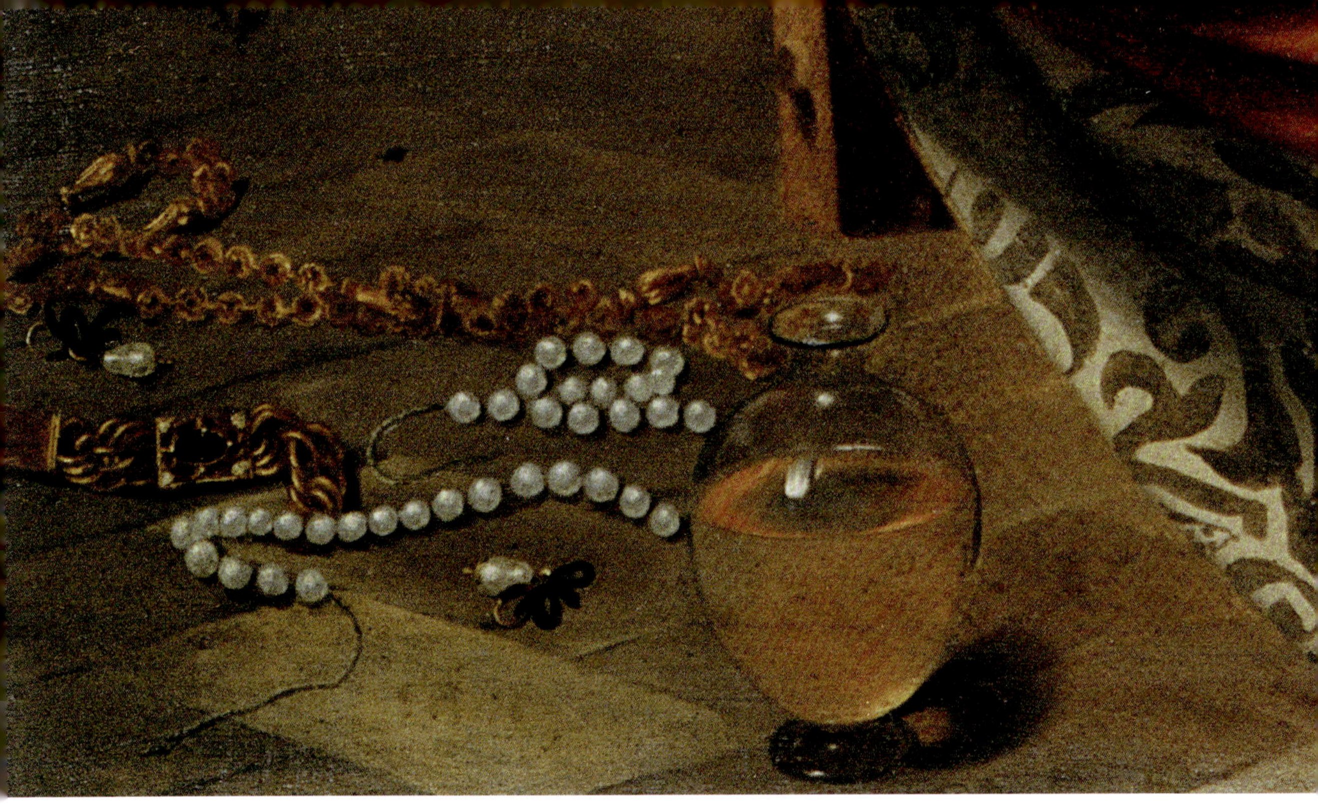

Pinturas sacras tempranas

El Cardenal del Monte, quien permitió
a Caravaggio vivir en su residencia
romana, le presentó en los círculos
aristocráticos romanos, lo cual abrió al
artista las puertas de las colecciones
de arte de la ciudad. Es la época de
las primeras pinturas religiosas como
*Magdalena penitente, Descanso durante la
huida a Egipto* y *Marta y María Magdalena*.
En estos trabajos sacros se continúa
el realismo de sus obras profanas. La
Magdalena penitente reposa sobre
un taburete en el momento de su
renuncia a su vida de cortesana impura,

La pittura sacra degli inizi

Il cardinal del Monte, che accolse
Caravaggio nella sua residenza romana,
presentò l'artista ai circoli dell'aristocrazia
romana, aprendogli così le porte alle
collezioni d'arte della città. In questo
periodo nacquero i primi quadri
religiosi del pittore, come la *Maddalena
penitente*, il *Riposo durante la fuga in
Egitto* e *Marta e Maria Maddalena*, in
cui ritroviamo il realismo delle opere
profane di Caravaggio. La Maddalena
penitente piange seduta su uno sgabello
basso al momento del suo abbandono
della vita da cortigiana; accanto a lei

Vroege sacrale werken

Kardinaal del Monte, die Caravaggio
in zijn Romeinse residentie opnam,
voerde hem in kringen van de Romeinse
adel in, waardoor de schilder toegang
kreeg tot talloze kunstcollecties. In deze
tijd ontstonden zijn eerste religieuze
schilderijen, zoals *Boetende Magdalena*,
de *Rust op de vlucht naar Egypte* en *Martha
bekeert Maria Magdalena*. Het realisme
van zijn profane werken zette hij in zijn
sacrale doeken voort. De boetvaardigde
Magdalena zit op een eenvoudig krukje,
walgend van haar eigen leven als onkuise
courtisane; naast haar liggen sieraden,

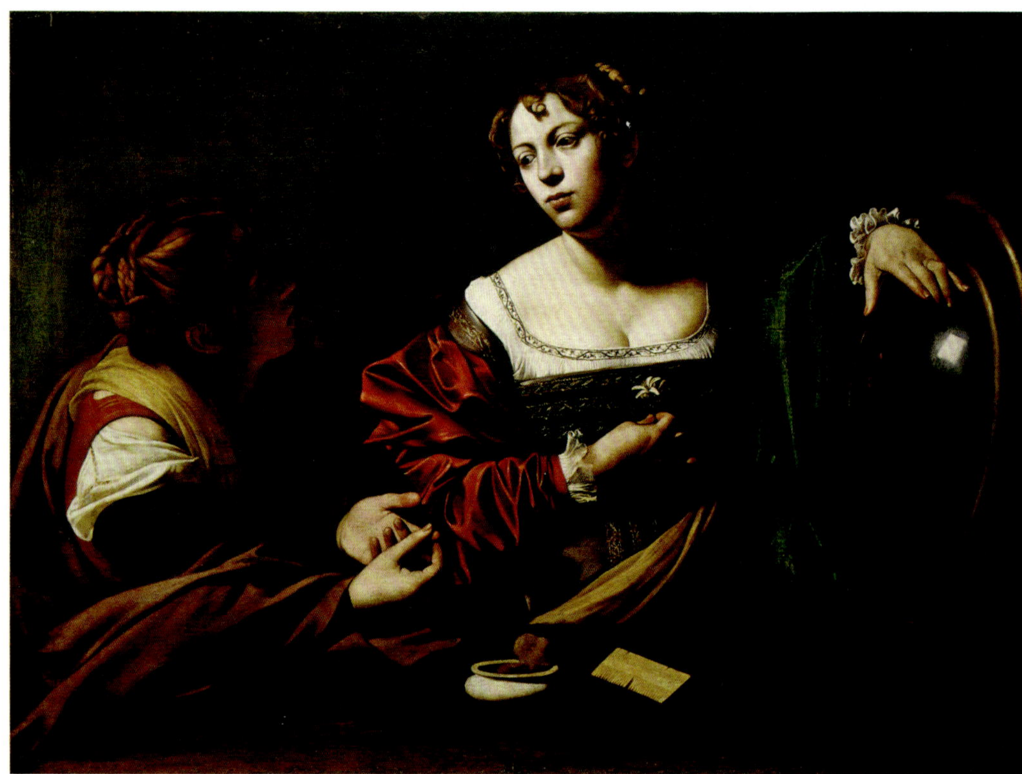

as a courtesan, with precious jewelry lying next to her. None of the usual visual cues of Counter-Reformation depictions of saints are present. There is no crucifix, prayer book, praying hands, etc. The jewelry as the only attribute shown is more a reference to the sin of vanity arising from the lack of chastity. A remarkably profane view of a sacred subject. Equally unconventional are his *Rest on the Flight into Egypt* and the later *Supper at Emmaus.*

siège bas à côté de ses bijoux. Aucun détail iconographique – crucifix, livre de prières, mains jointes, etc. – ne suggère intrinsèquement le thème de la sainte, courant dans les représentations de la Contre-Réforme. La parure abandonnée comme unique attribut renvoie plutôt au péché de vanité qu'à celui d'impureté, représentation sensiblement profane d'un sujet sacré. La même absence de convention se vérifie dans *Le Repos pendant la fuite en Égypte* et *Le Repas à Emmaüs* (plus tardif).

neben ihr liegt kostbarer Schmuck. Keinerlei ikonografische Hinweise wie Kruzifix, Gebetbuch, betende Hände usw. weisen das in der Gegenreformation gängige Bildthema der Heiligen als solches aus. Der Schmuck als einziges Attribut verweist eher auf die Sünde der Eitelkeit denn auf die der mangelnden Keuschheit. Eine bemerkenswert profane Darstellung eines sakralen Themas. Ähnlich unkonventionell sind auch die *Ruhe auf der Flucht nach Ägypten* und das spätere *Emmausmahl.*

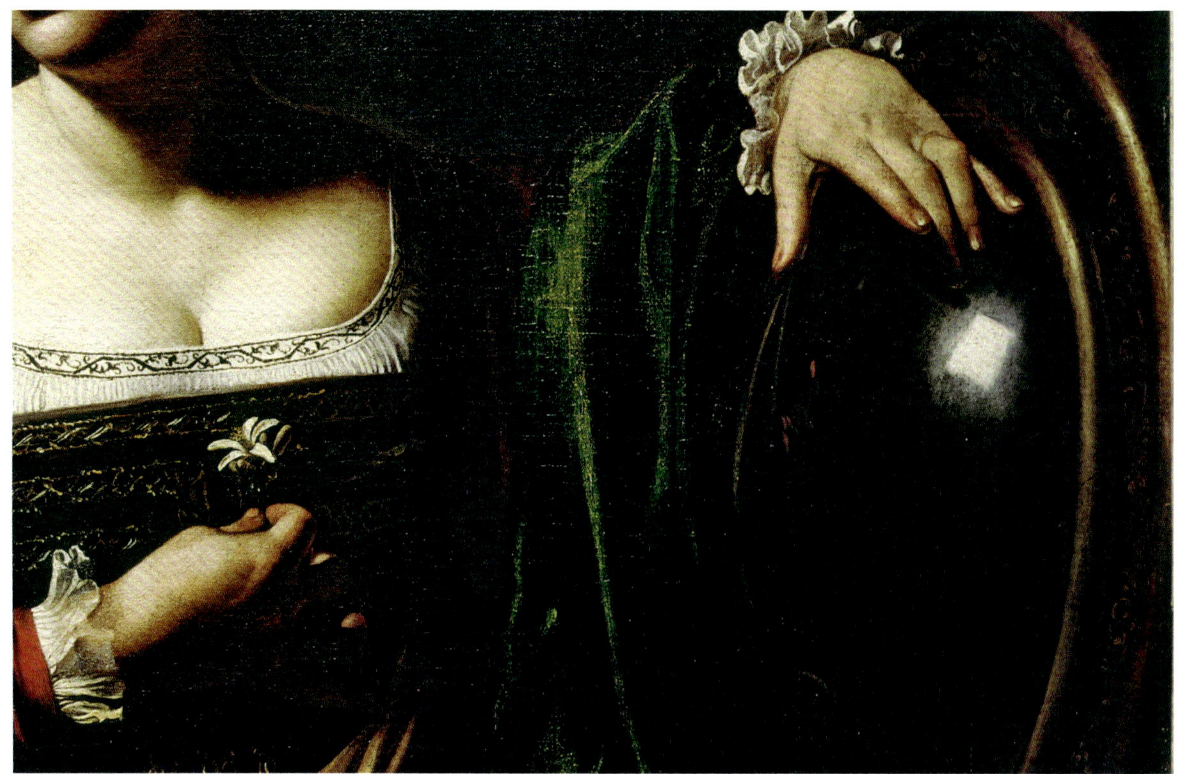

sus preciosas joyas a su lado. No hay
ninguna indicación iconográfica como un
crucifijo, libro de oraciones, manos en
posición de rezo, etc. que identifiquen
el tema de la Santa, habitual durante
la Contrarreforma, como tal. El único
atributo, las joyas, remiten más bien al
pecado de la vanidad que al de la falta
de castidad. Una representación por
tanto notablemente profana de un tema
sacro. También poco convencionales son
el *Descanso durante la huida a Egipto* y la
posterior *Los discípulos de Emaús*.

si osservano gioielli preziosi. Nessun
accenno iconografico, come il crocifisso, il
libro di preghiere o le mani congiunte in
preghiera, richiamano il motivo dei santi
della Controriforma. I gioielli, invece,
unico attributo presente, rimandano
al peccato della vanità e, dunque, alla
mancanza di castità. Si tratta di una
rappresentazione notevolmente profana
di un motivo sacro. Non convenzionali
come quest'opera sono anche il *Riposo
durante la fuga in Egitto* e la *Cena
in Emmaus*.

maar iconografische verwijzingen
als de crucifix, het gebedenboek of
gevouwen handen zijn afwezig in dit
heiligentafereel, dat gedurende de
Contrareformatie zeer geliefd was. Als
enige attribuut verwijzen de sieraden
veeleer naar de zonde van de hoogmoed
dan die van de onkuisheid. Het is een
opmerkelijke profane uitbeelding
van een sacraal thema. Niet minder
onconventioneel zijn de *Rust op de vlucht
naar Egypte* en het latere *Avondmaal
te Emmaüs*.

St Francis Receiving the Stigmata
Extase de saint François
Der hl. Franziskus empfängt die Wundmale
San Francisco recibiendo las llagas
San Francesco d'Assisi in estasi
De heilige Franciscus ontvangt de stigmata
1595, Oil on canvas/Huile sur toile, 92,5 × 127,8 cm, Wadsworth Atheneum, Hartford

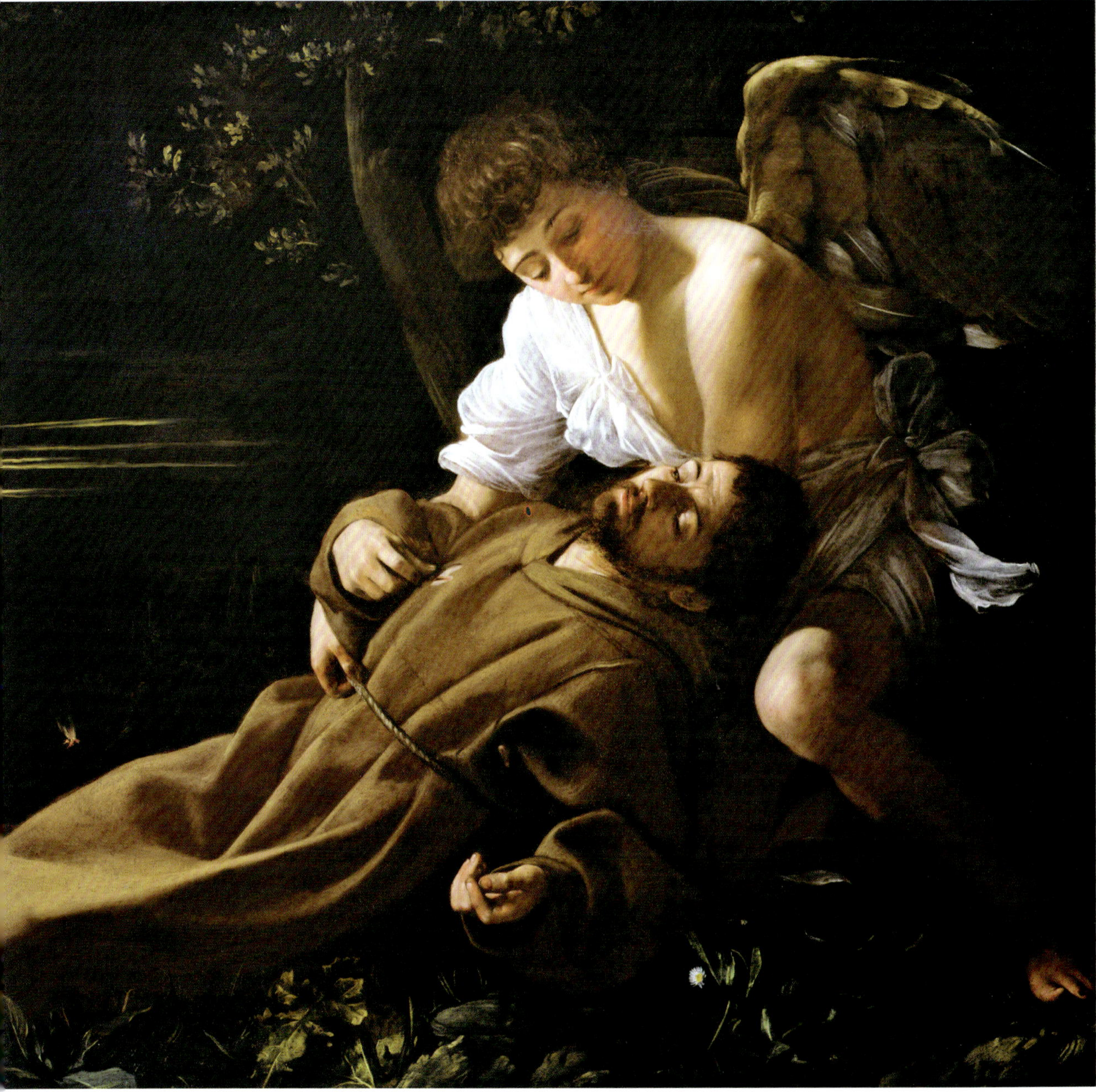

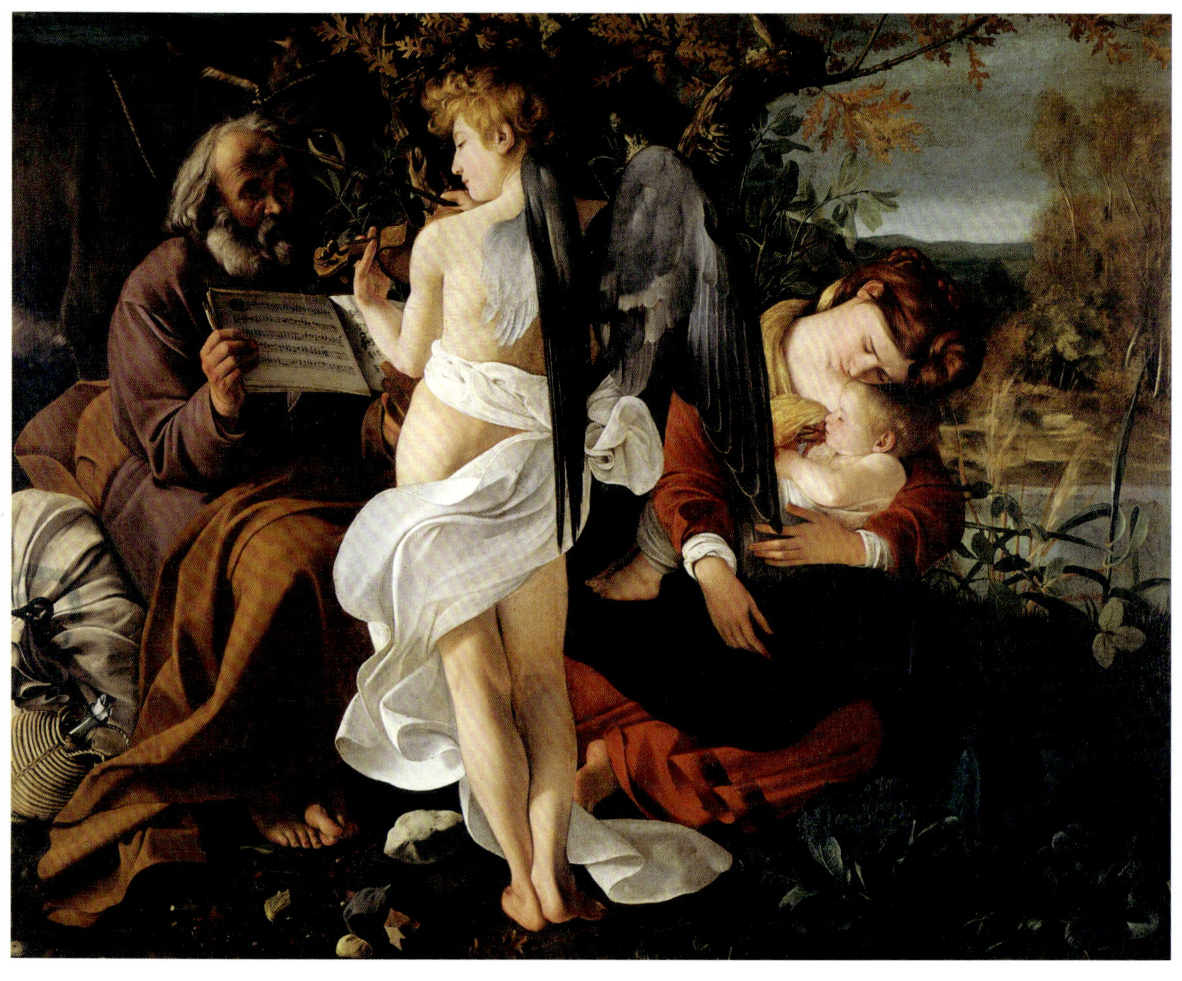

Rest on the Flight to Egypt
Le Repos pendant la fuite en Égypte

Ruhe auf der Flucht nach Ägypten
Un descanso durante la huida a Egipto

Riposo durante la fuga in Egitto
Rust op de vlucht naar Egypte

c. 1596, Oil on canvas/Huile sur toile, 135,5 × 166,5 cm, Palazzo Doria Pamphilj, Roma

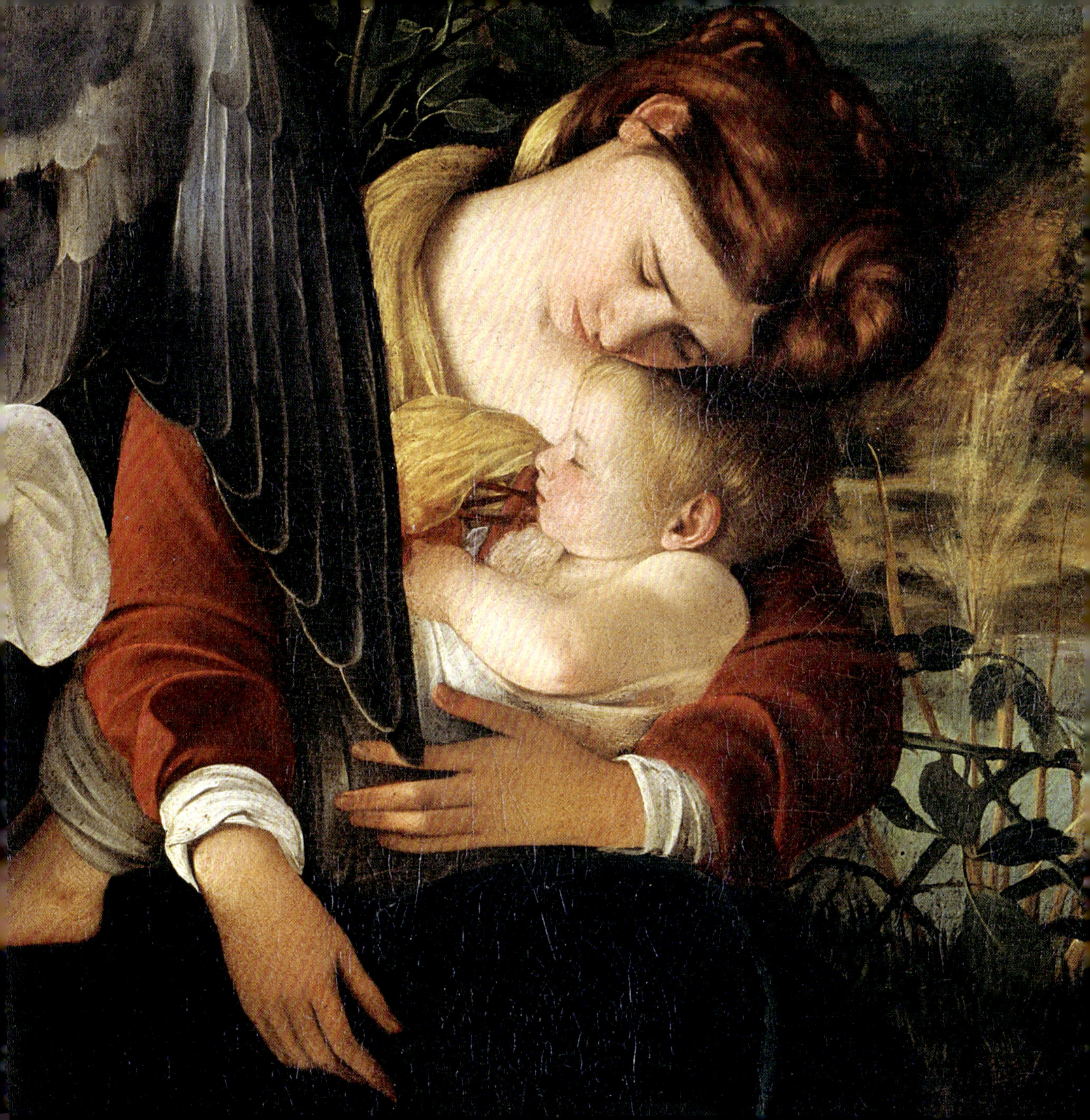

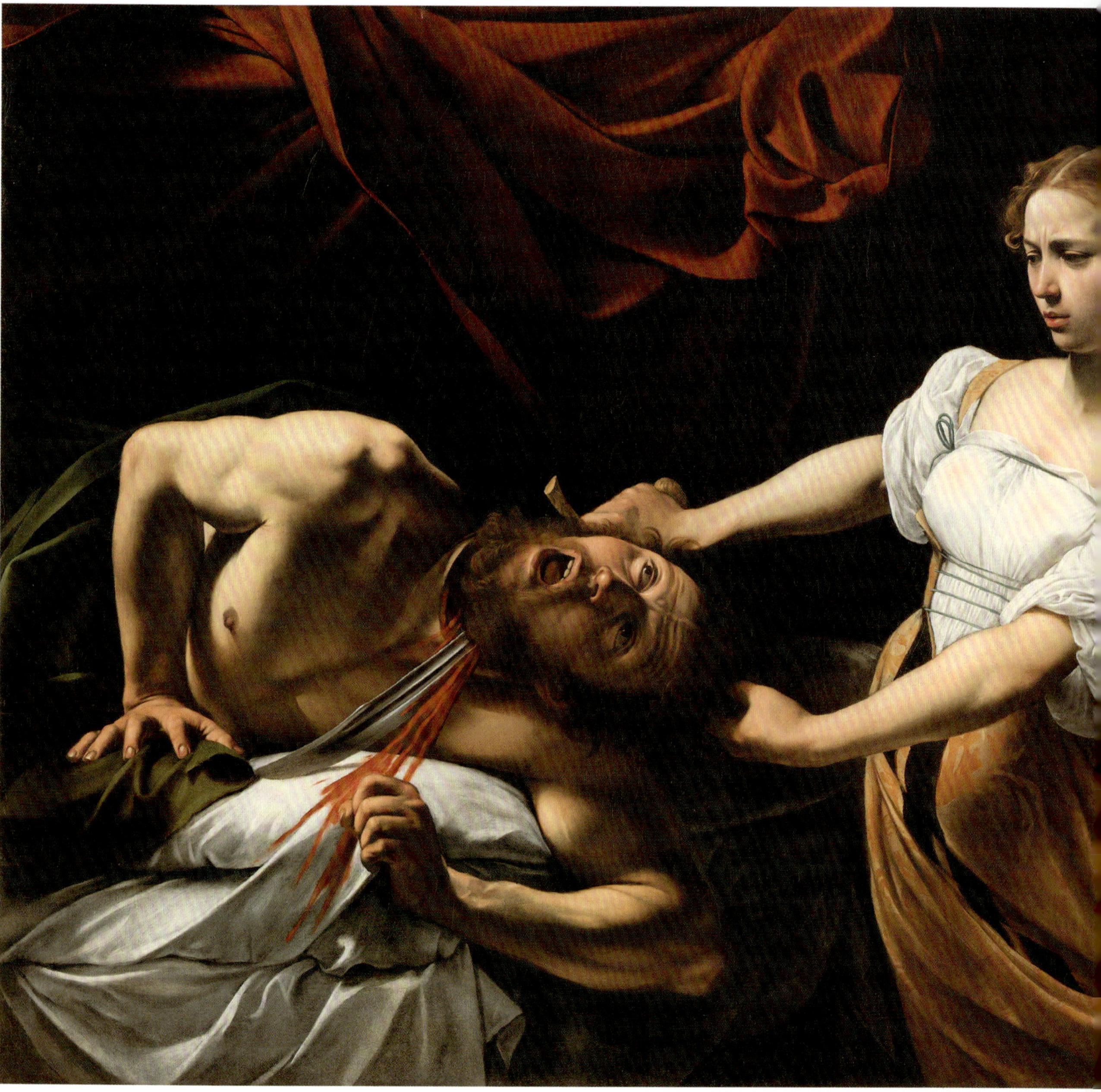

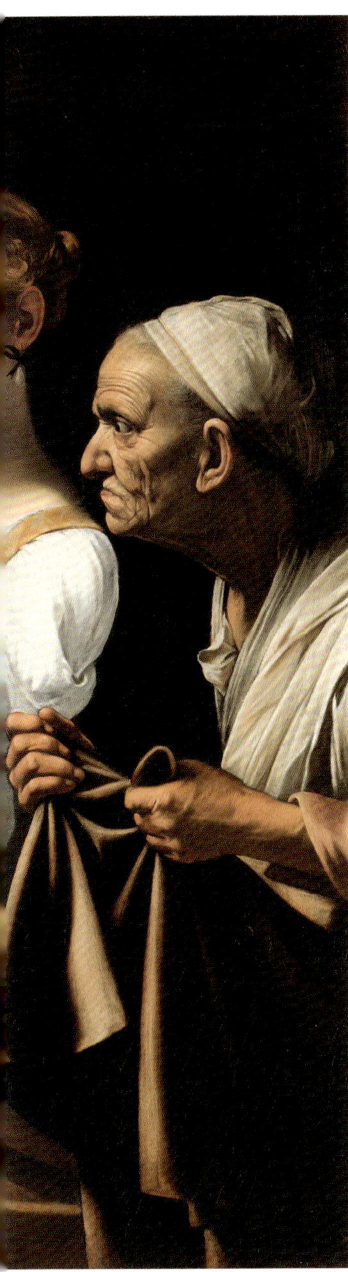

Judith and Holofernes

Judith et Holopherne

Judith und Holofernes

Judith y Holofernes

Giuditta e Oloferne

Judith onthoofdt Holofernes

c. 1599, Oil on canvas/Huile sur toile, 145 × 195 cm, Palazzo Barberini, Roma

This depiction of the beheading of the Assyrian commander by the beautiful Jewish widow Judith hits the viewer with the full force of its drama. The clearly contoured figures stand out sharply against the dark background, a characteristic of Caravaggio's work. In stark contrast are the disgusted expression on the face of the young woman and the grim determination of the wrinkled, old maid waiting to take the head of Holofernes from her mistress. The lighting, dramaturgy, and visual composition here foreshadow the visual language of the Baroque and can be found in the works of numerous later imitators.

La représentation de la décapitation du général assyrien par la belle veuve juive Judith frappe le spectateur par la puissance de son dramatisme. Les personnages nettement définis se détachent fortement sur l'arrière-plan sombre, trait caractéristique des tableaux de Caravage. Le contraste des expressions est également saisissant, entre le visage de la jeune femme et celui de la vieille servante ridée qui attend de recevoir la tête d'Holopherne avec une détermination féroce. La conduite de la lumière, la dramaturgie et la composition de l'image annoncent le langage iconographique du baroque et se retrouveront dans les œuvres des nombreux suiveurs de Caravage.

Die Darstellung der Enthauptung des assyrischen Heerführers durch die schöne jüdische Witwe Judith trifft den Betrachter mit der ganzen Wucht ihrer Dramatik. Die klar konturierten Figuren heben sich scharf vor dem dunklen Hintergrund ab, ein Charakteristikum für Caravaggios Bilder. Im krassen Gegensatz stehen auch der angewiderte Gesichtsausdruck im Gesicht der jungen Frau und die grimmige Entschlossenheit der runzeligen, alten Magd, die bereitsteht, den Kopf des Holofernes entgegenzunehmen. Lichtführung, Dramaturgie und Bildaufbau künden bereits die Bildsprache des Barock an und finden sich in den Werken der zahlreichen späteren Nachahmer Caravaggios wieder.

La representación de la decapitación del general asirio a manos de la bella viuda Judith alcanza al espectador con toda la fuerza de su dramatismo. La figuras, bien delineadas, se perfilan sobre el fondo oscuro, una característica típica de las imágenes de Caravaggio. En claro contraste están también la expresión de repulsión en la cara de la joven y la determinación feroz de la vieja criada, llena de arrugas, que se prepara para recibir la cabeza de Holofernes. El uso de la luz, la dramaturgia y la composición de la imagen anuncian el lenguaje pictórico del Barroco, y pueden encontrarse en las obras de multitud de imitadores de Caravaggio.

La rappresentazione della decapitazione del comandante assiro da parte della bella vedova ebrea Giuditta colpisce lo spettatore con tutta la forza della sua drammaticità. Le figure chiaramente sagomate spiccano nettamente sullo sfondo scuro, come in quasi tutti i quadri di Caravaggio. In netto contrasto sono anche l'espressione disgustata sul volto della giovane donna e la cupa determinazione dell'anziana servitrice, con il viso pieno di rughe, che è pronta a ricevere la testa di Oloferne. L'illuminazione, la drammaturgia e la composizione anticipano il linguaggio plastico del barocco e possono essere ritrovate nelle opere dei numerosi imitatori successivi di Caravaggio.

De dood van de Assyrische legerleider door de schone joodse weduwe Judith wordt in deze versie in al zijn drama ontvouwt. De beide figuren steken tegen de donkere achtergrond af, een kenmerk voor Caravaggio's werk. Een schril contrast vormen ook de uitdrukking van walging op het gezicht van de jonge vrouw en de grimmige vastberadenheid van de oude maagd, die klaarstaat om het hoofd van Holofernes in ontvangst te nemen. De lichtval, het drama en de compositie kondigen reeds de beeldtaal van de barok aan en zijn later in het werk van talrijke navolgers van Caravaggio terug te vinden.

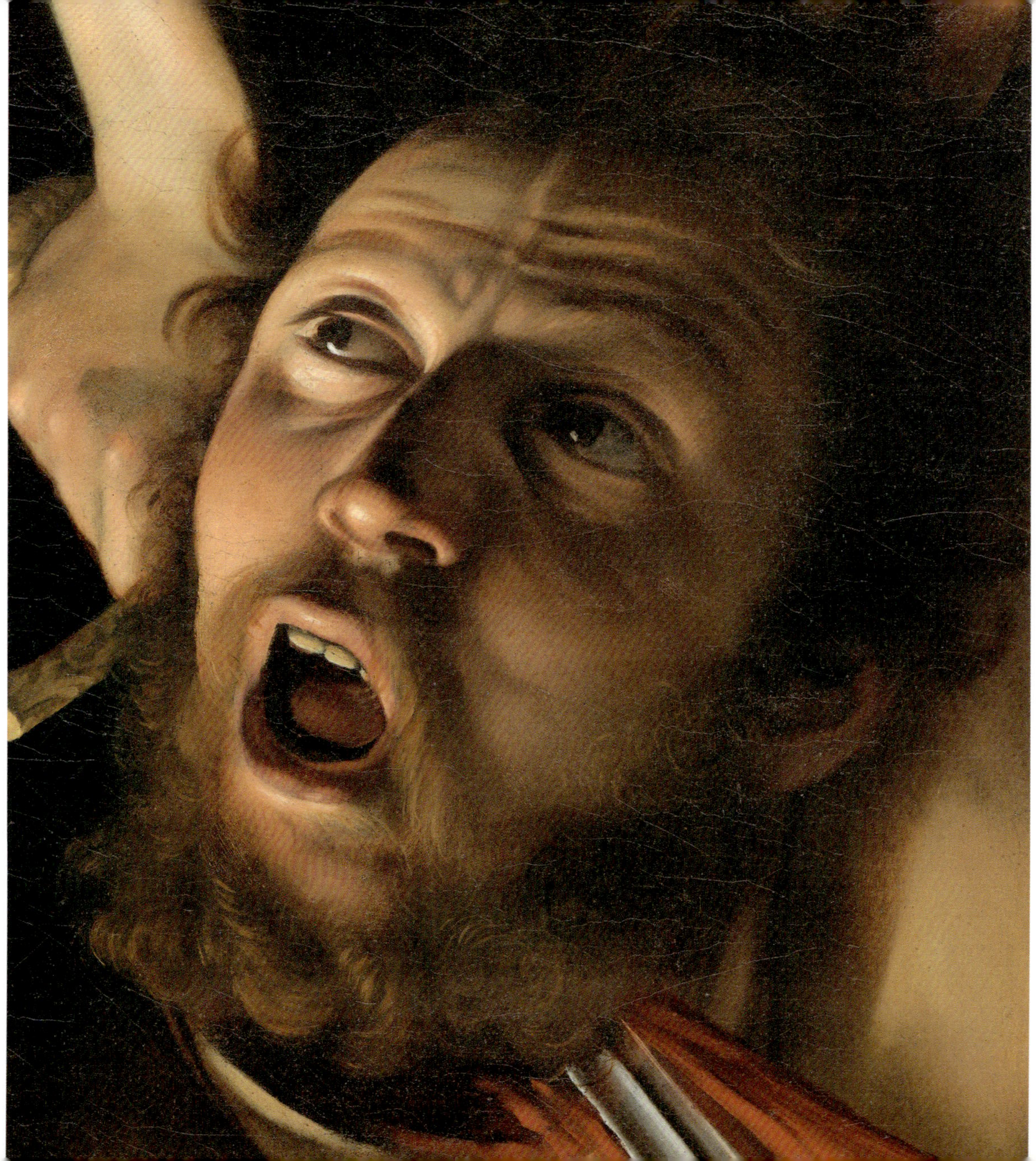

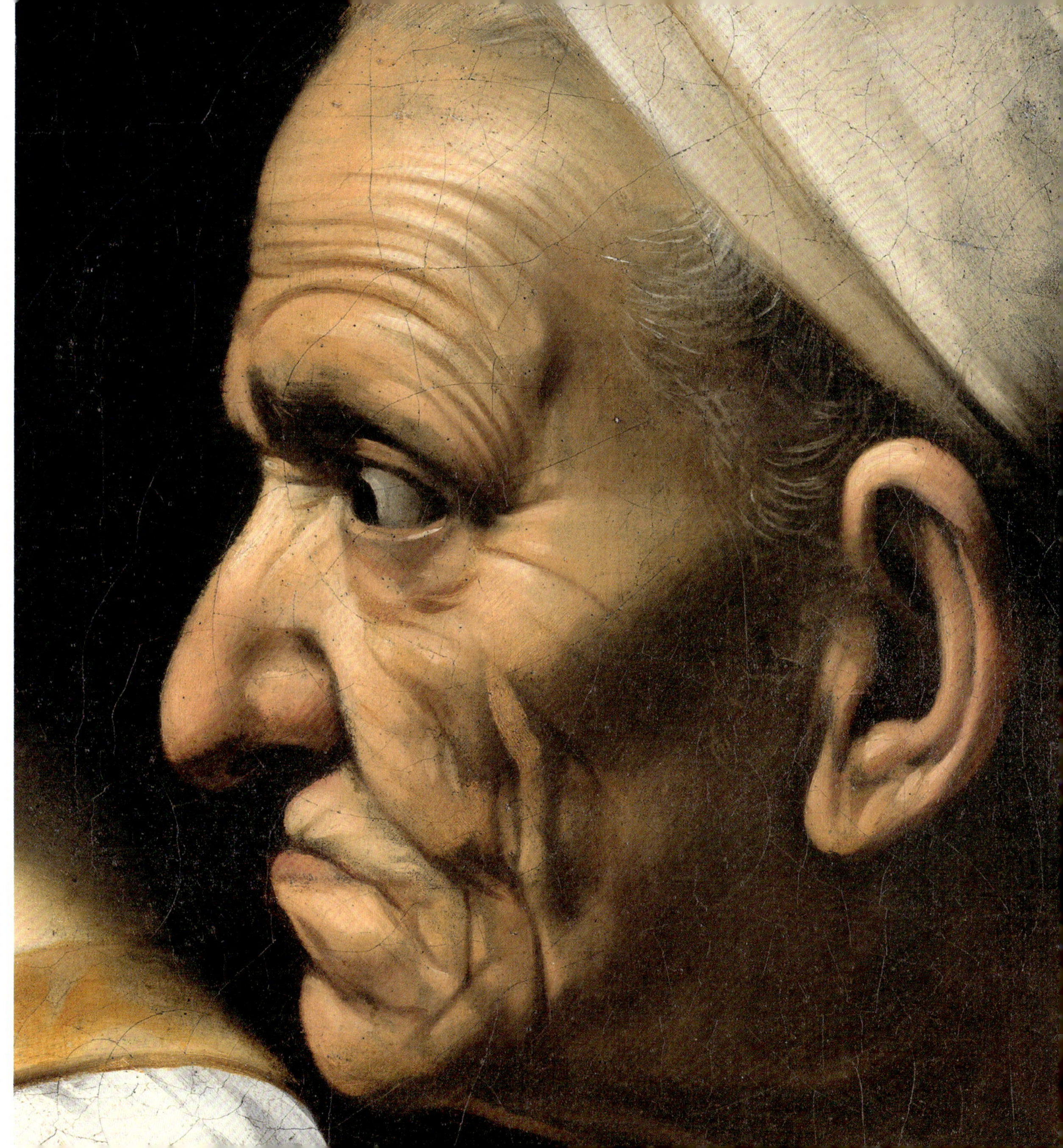

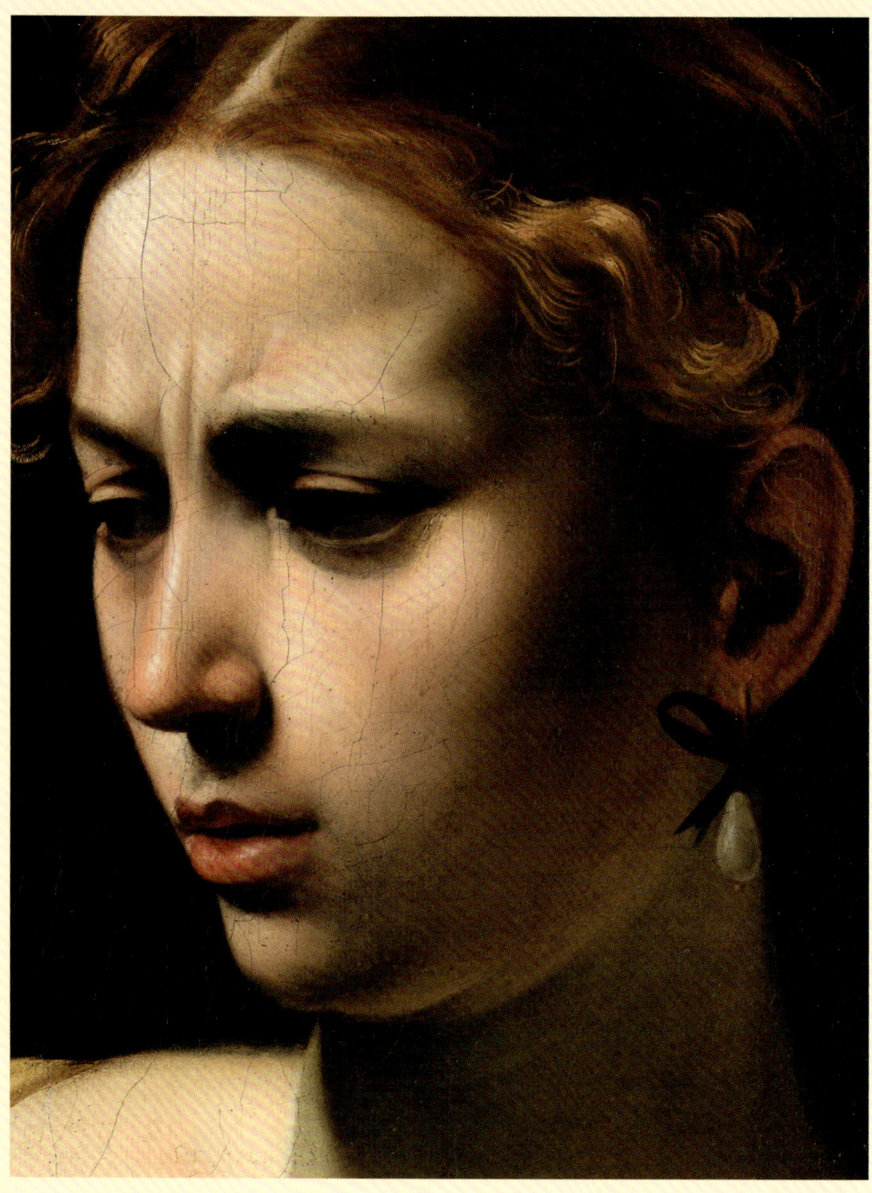

St Catherine of Alexandria (detail)

*Sainte Catherine
d'Alexandrie (détail)*

*Hl. Katharina von
Alexandria (Detail)*

*Santa Catalina de
Alejandría (detalle)*

*Santa Caterina d'Alessandria
(particolare)*

*De heilige Catharina van
Alexandrië (detail)*

see/voir p. 54

Caravaggio's models

Caravaggio took his models from the streets and taverns of Rome. We can recognize his friend Mario Minniti as *The Lutenist*, while Judith is the prostitute Fillide Melandroni, who also posed for other biblical figures as Saint Martha and Saint Catharine. He even allegedly used prostitutes to pose for his paintings of the Virgin. The incorporation of the recognizable physiognomy of real people was not an innovation, but instead common practice in the Renaissance. However, the choice of the models and Caravaggio's refusal to compromise in their portrayal proved to be too much for many of his ecclesiastical clients.

Les modèles de Caravage

Caravage prenait ses modèles dans les rues et les tavernes de Rome. Nous reconnaissons l'ami Mario Minniti dans *Le Joueur de luth* ; la courtisane Fillide Melandroni est le modèle de Judith et d'autres personnages sacrés comme sainte Marthe ou sainte Catherine. Même pour les représentations de Marie, Caravage prend comme modèle une prostituée. L'insertion des visages de personnes identifiables n'était pas une invention de Caravage, mais une pratique courante de l'époque. Reste que le choix des personnes et le réalisme sans compromission dans la représentation allaient toutefois trop loin pour de nombreux commanditaires, surtout ecclésiastiques.

Caravaggios Modelle

Caravaggio holte seine Modelle von der Straße und aus den Tavernen Roms. Seinen Freund Mario Minniti erkennen wir im *Lautenspieler*, für die Judith stand die Dirne Fillide Melandroni Modell, ebenso wie auch für andere biblische Frauengestalten wie die hl. Martha oder hl. Katharina. Sogar für Mariendarstellungen soll eine Prostituierte als Modell gedient haben. Das Einbauen von wiedererkennbaren Physiognomien realer Personen war keine Erfindung Caravaggios, sondern eine übliche Praxis in der Renaissance. Die Wahl der Personen und Kompromisslosigkeit in der Darstellung Caravaggios ging jedoch vielen der vor allem kirchlichen Auftraggeber zu weit.

Los modelos de Caravaggio

Caravaggio escogía sus modelos de entre la calle y las tabernas de Roma. Reconocemos a su amigo Mario Minniti en *El tañedor de laúd*, la prostituta Fillide Melandroni Modell posó para Judith, así como para otras figuras femeninas bíblicas como Santa Marta o Santa Catalina. Incluso para algunas imágenes marianas habría posado una prostituta. La introducción de aspectos fisionómicos reconocibles de personas reales no era una invención de Caravaggio, sino más bien una práctica común en el Renacimiento. La elección de las personas y el extremismo de la representación de Caravaggio iba sin embargo demasiado lejos para muchos de sus clientes eclesiásticos.

I modelli di Caravaggio

Caravaggio trasse i suoi modelli dalle strade e dalle taverne di Roma: il suo amico Mario Minniti è il volto del *Suonatore di liuto* e la prostituta Fillide Melandroni fu la modella per Giuditta, nonché per altre figure bibliche come Santa Marta o Santa Caterina. Anche per le rappresentazioni di Maria Caravaggio fece probabilmente servire come modello una prostituta. L'incorporazione di fisionomie riconoscibili di persone reali non era un'invenzione di Caravaggio, bensì una pratica comune nel Rinascimento. Tuttavia, la scelta dei soggetti e la riluttanza al compromesso nelle rappresentazioni di Caravaggio andarono troppo oltre per molti dei principali committenti ecclesiastici.

Caravaggio's modellen

Caravaggio vond zijn modellen op de straten en in de kroegen van Rome. Zijn vriend Mario Minniti herkennen we als *luitspeler,* de prostituee Fillide Melandroni stond model voor Judith en voor andere Bijbelse vrouwenfiguren, onder wie de heiligen Martha en Catharina. Zelfs voor de uitbeelding van Maria gebruikte hij waarschijnlijk een prostituee. Het opnemen van herkenbare fysieke trekjes van echte personen was geen uitvinding van Caravaggio, maar in de Renaissance heel gebruikelijk. Maar Caravaggio's modelkeuze en compromisloze uitwerking ervan ging veel kerkelijke opdrachtgevers te ver.

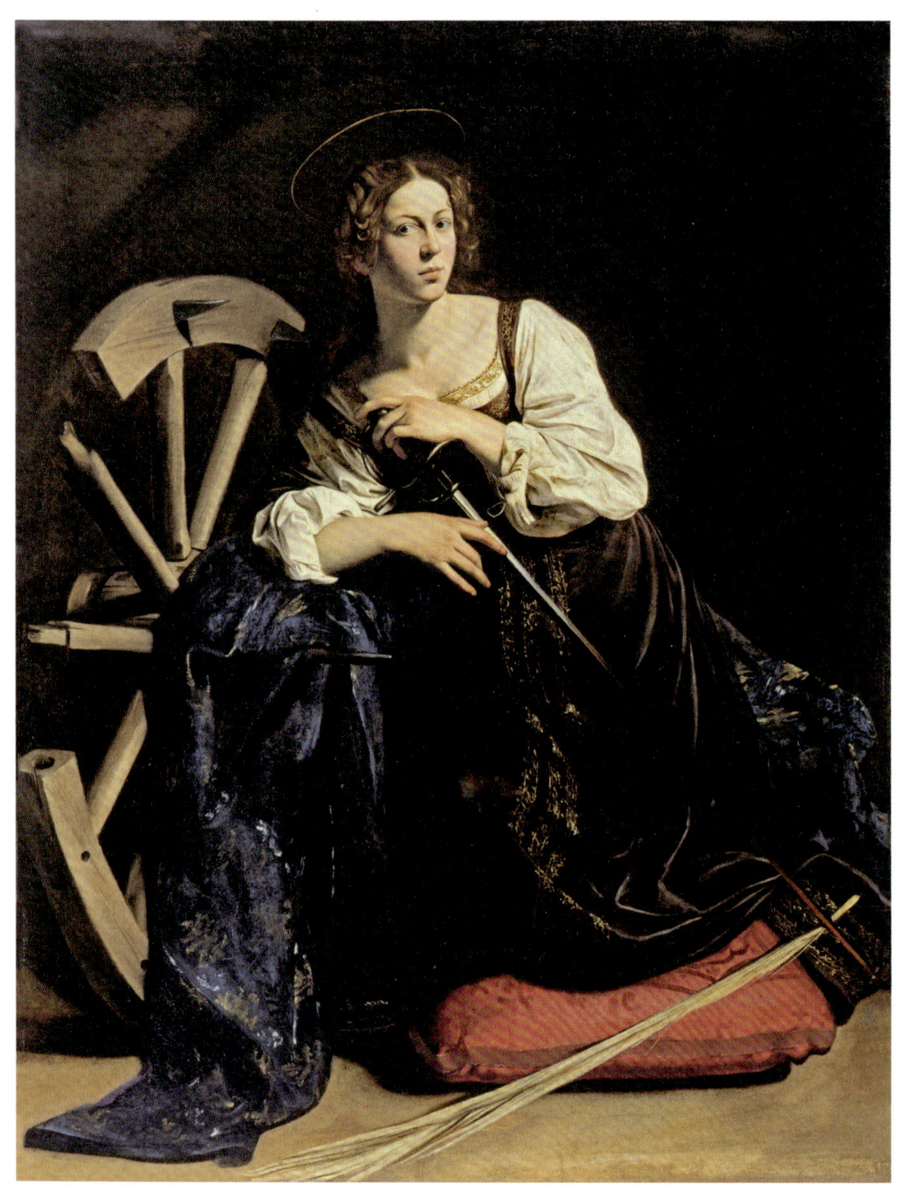

St Catherine of Alexandria

Sainte Catherine d'Alexandrie

Hl. Katharina von Alexandria

Santa Catalina de Alejandría

Santa Caterina d'Alessandria

*De heilige Catharina
van Alexandrië*

1598, Oil on canvas/Huile sur toile,
173 × 133 cm, Museo Thyssen-
Bornemisza, Madrid

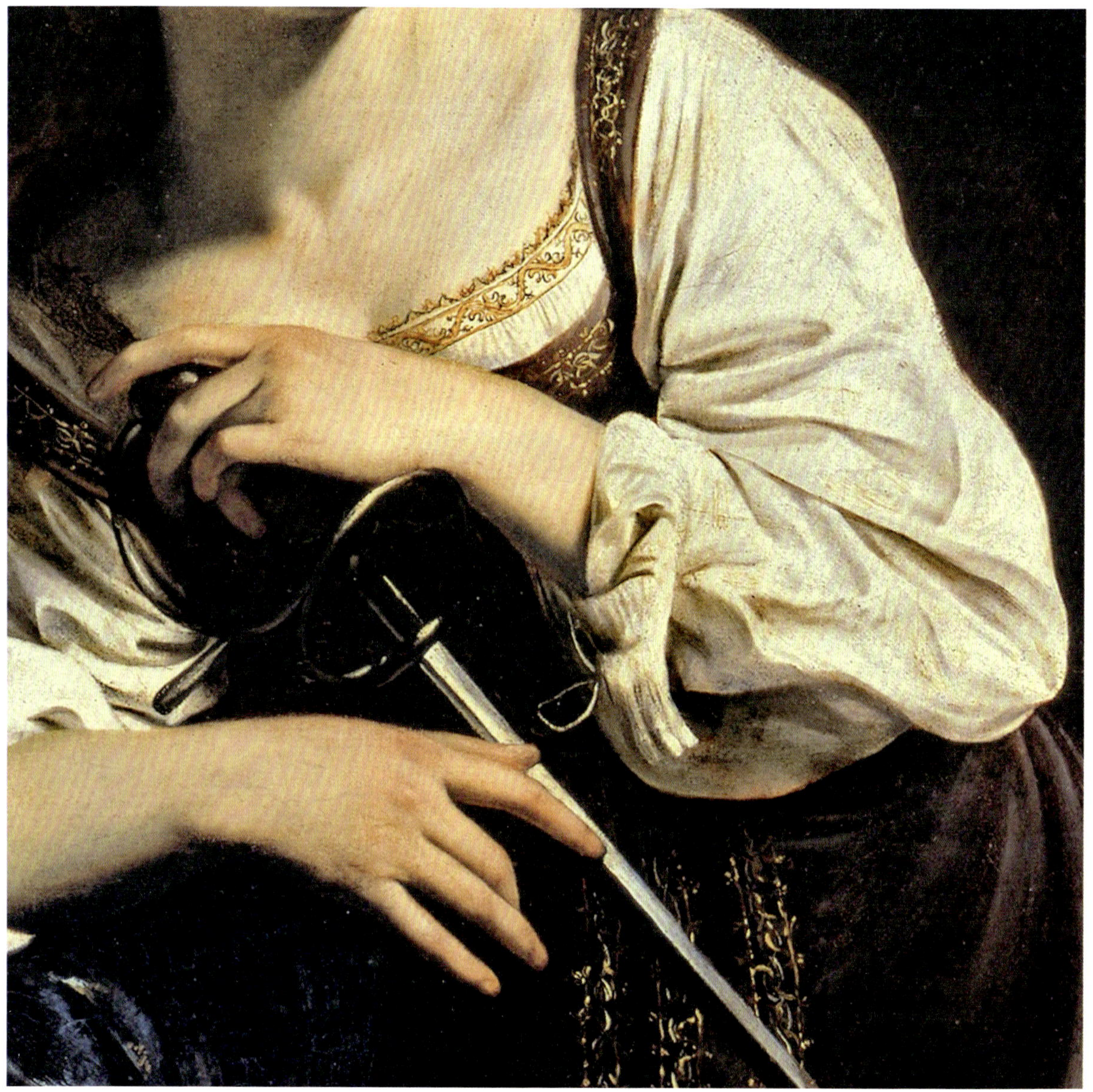

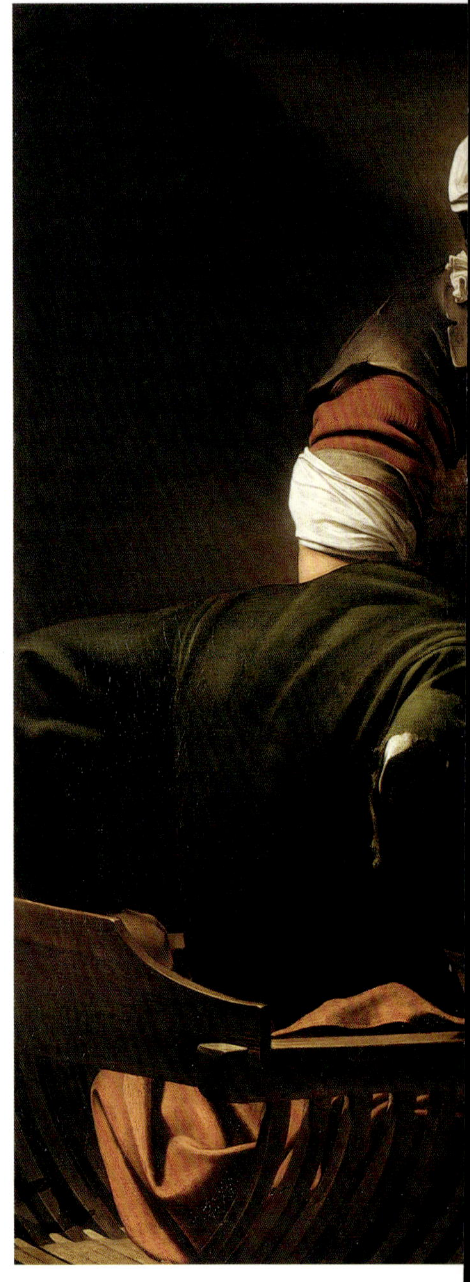

Supper at Emmaus
Le Repas à Emmaüs
Das Emmausmahl
Los discípulos de Emaús
Cena in Emmaus
Het avondmaal te Emmaüs
1601, Oil on canvas/Huile sur toile, 141 × 196,2 cm, National Gallery, London

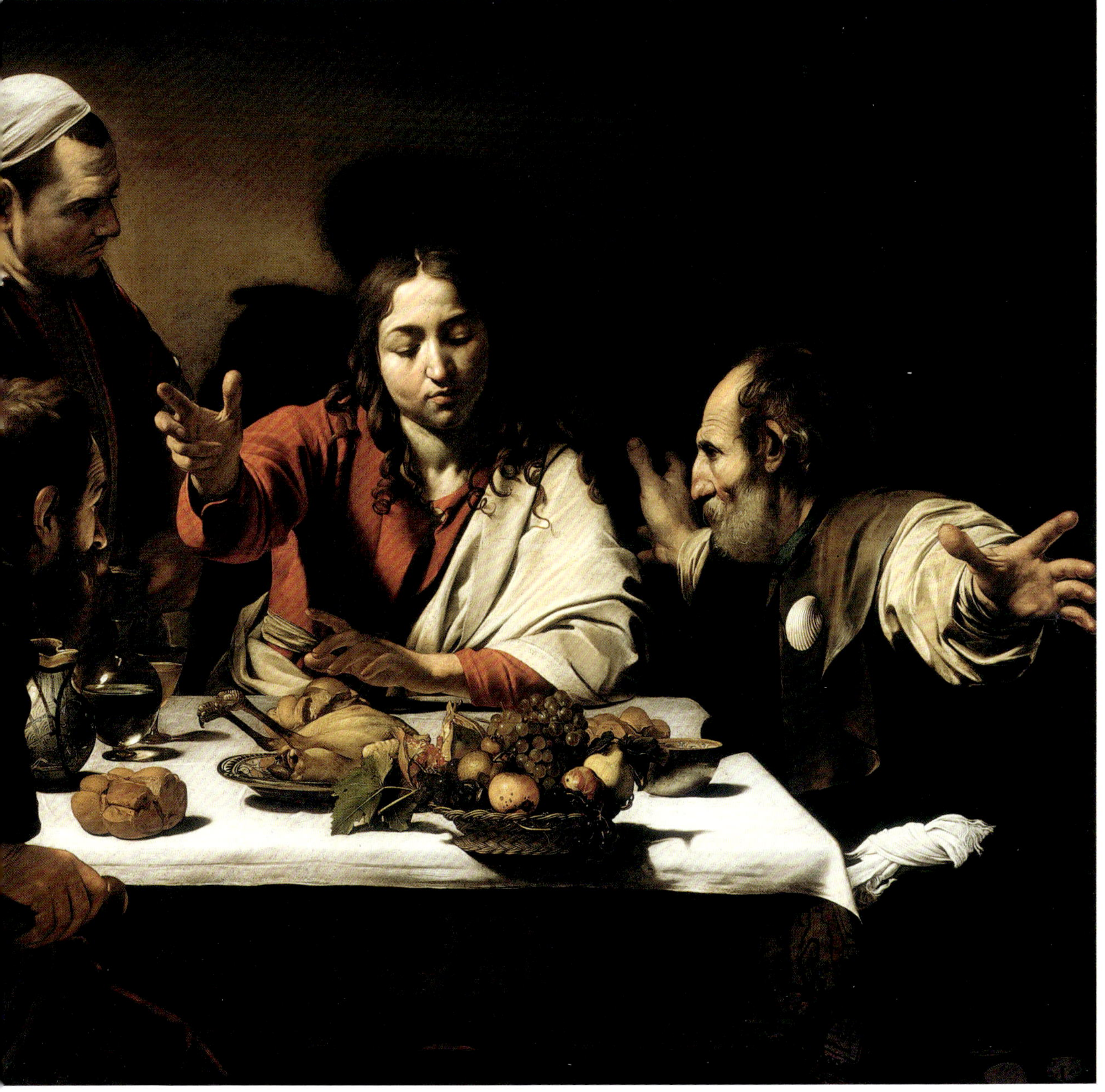

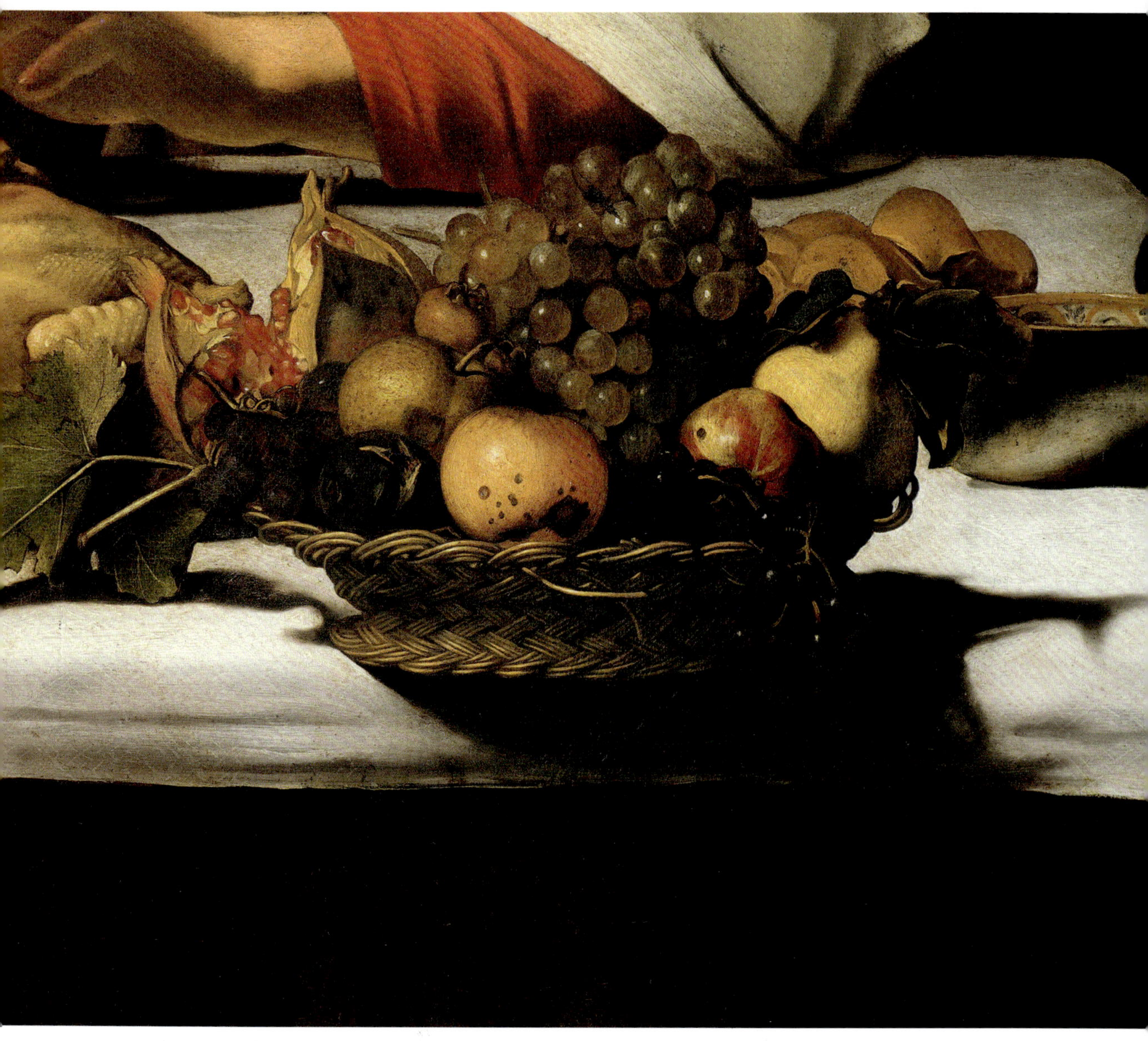

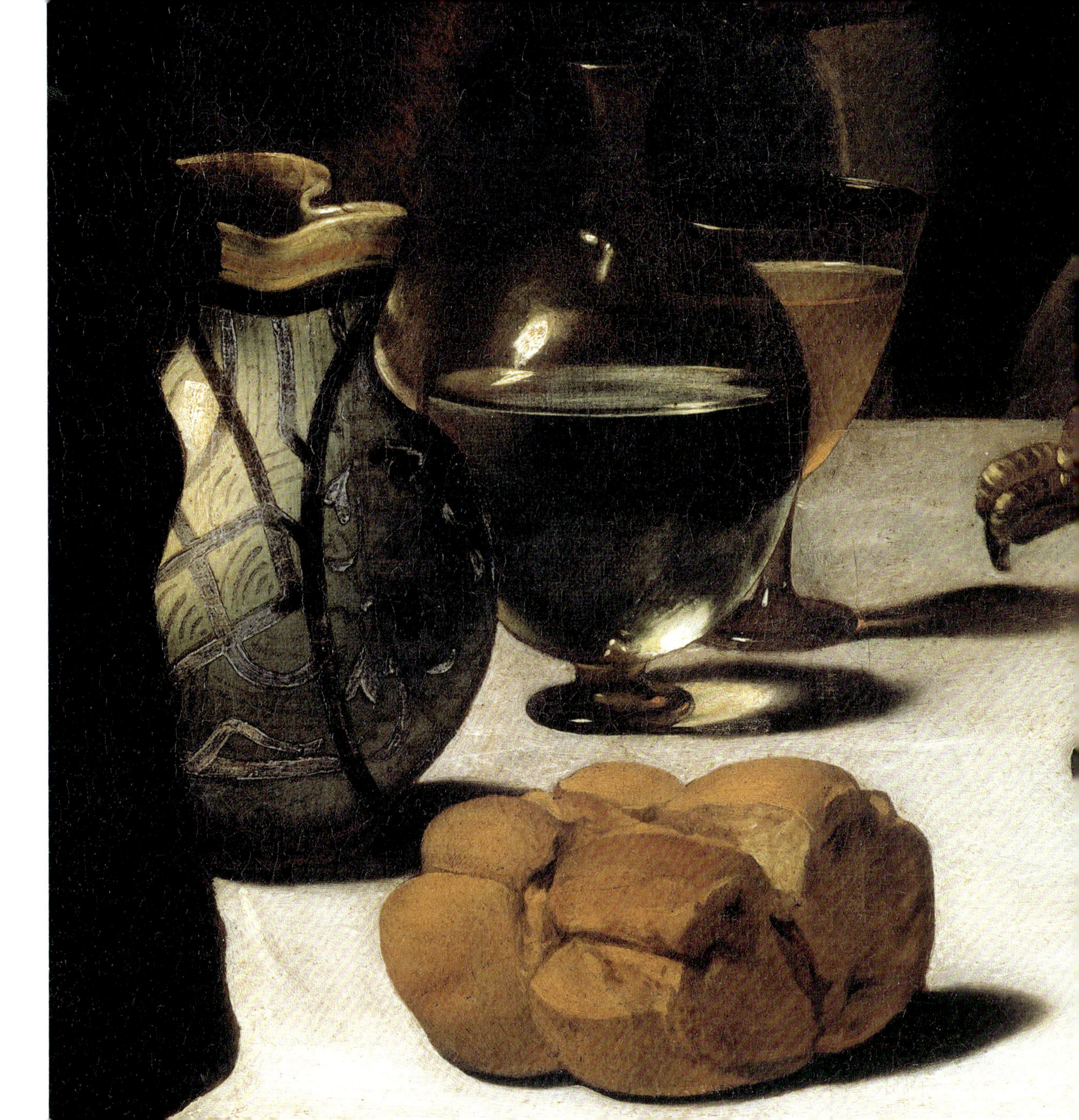

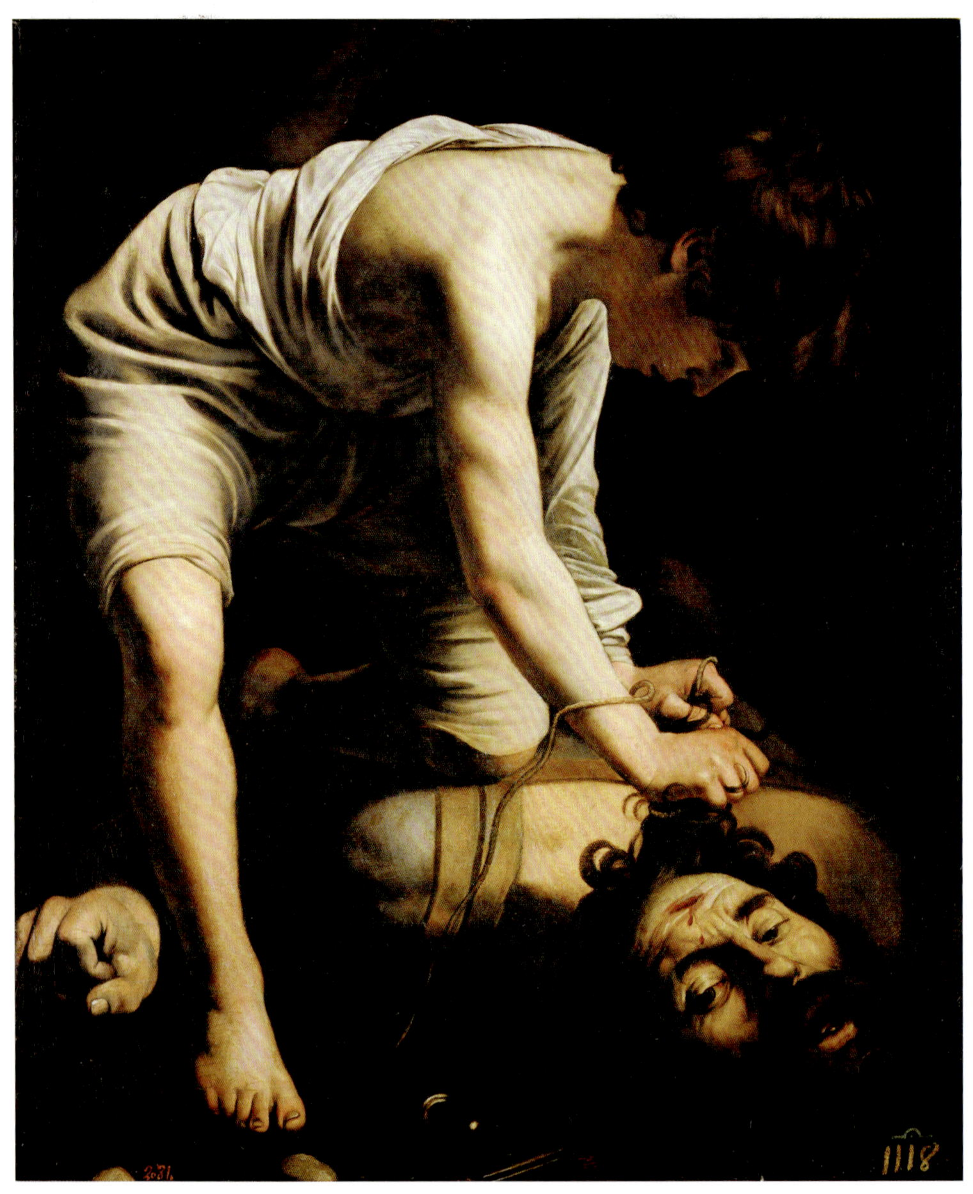

**David Defeating
Goliath**

David et Goliath

David besiegt Goliath

David y Goliat

Davide e Golia

David verslaat Goliath

c. 1599/1600, Oil on
canvas/Huile sur toile,
110,4 × 91,3 cm, Museo
del Prado, Madrid

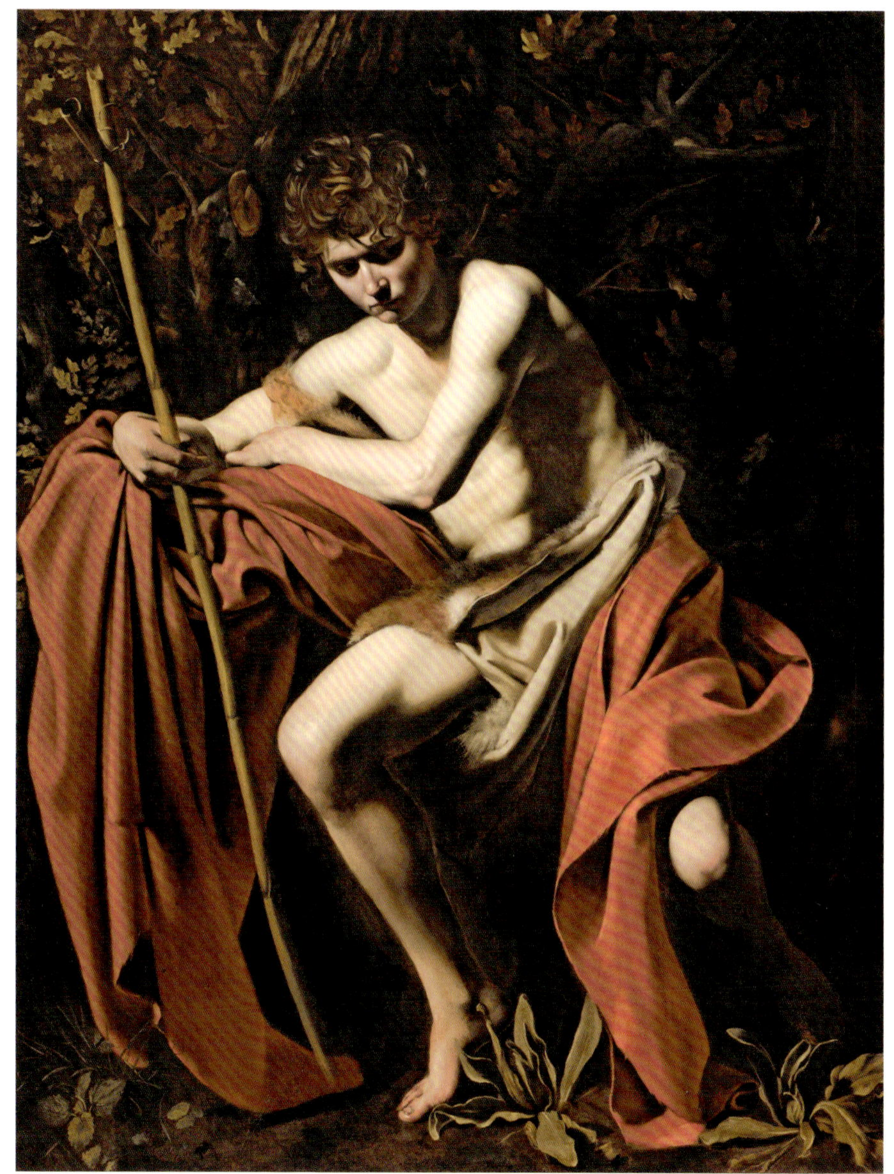

John the Baptist

*Saint Jean-Baptiste
dans le désert*

Johannes der Täufer

San Juan Bautista

San Giovanni Battista

Johannes de Doper

c. 1602/03, Oil on canvas/Huile sur
toile, 173 × 133 cm,
The Nelson-Atkins Museum of Art,
Kansas City

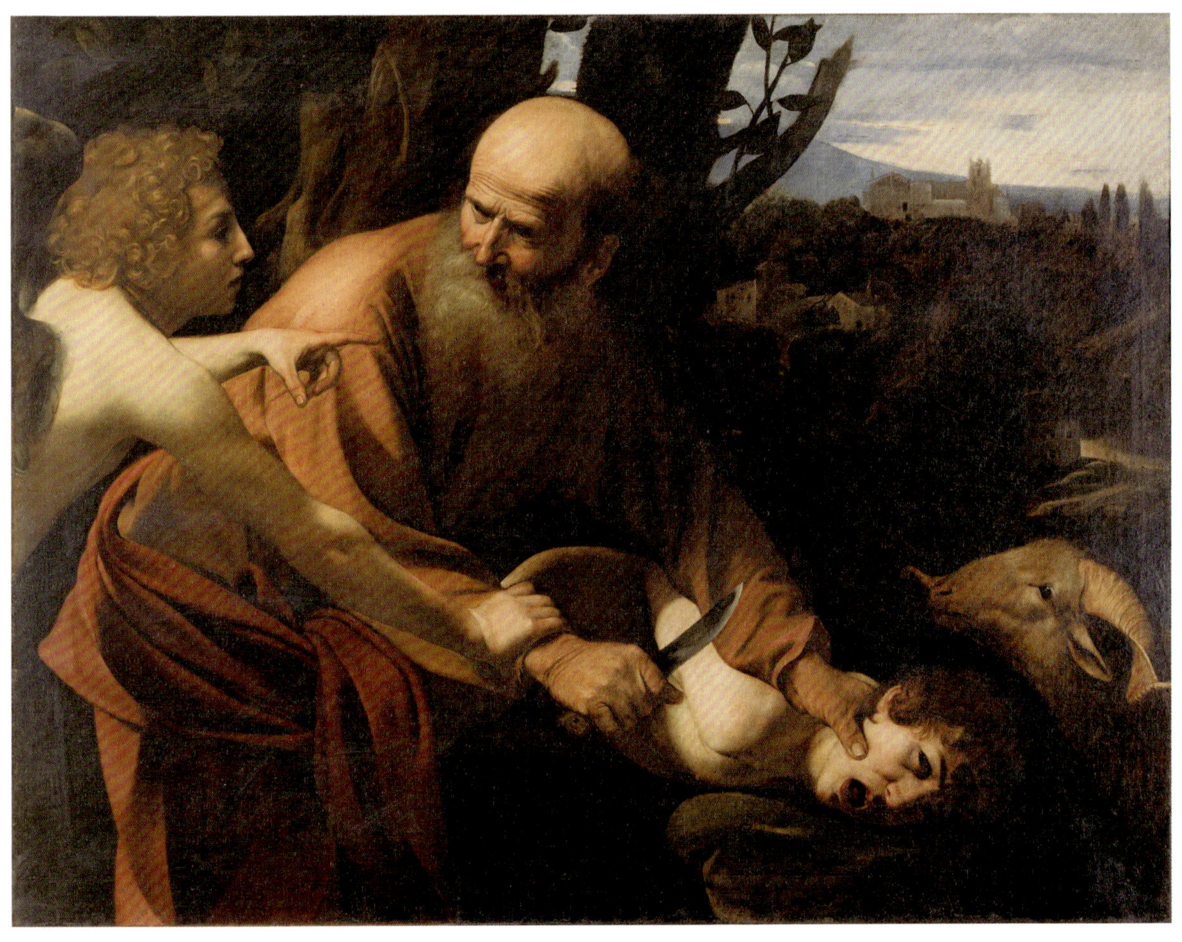

The Sacrifice of Isaac

Le Sacrifice d'Isaac

Opferung Isaaks

El sacrificio de Isaac

Sacrificio di Isacco

Het offeren van Isaak

c. 1598–1603, Oil on canvas/Huile sur toile, 104 × 135 cm, Galleria degli Uffizi, Firenze

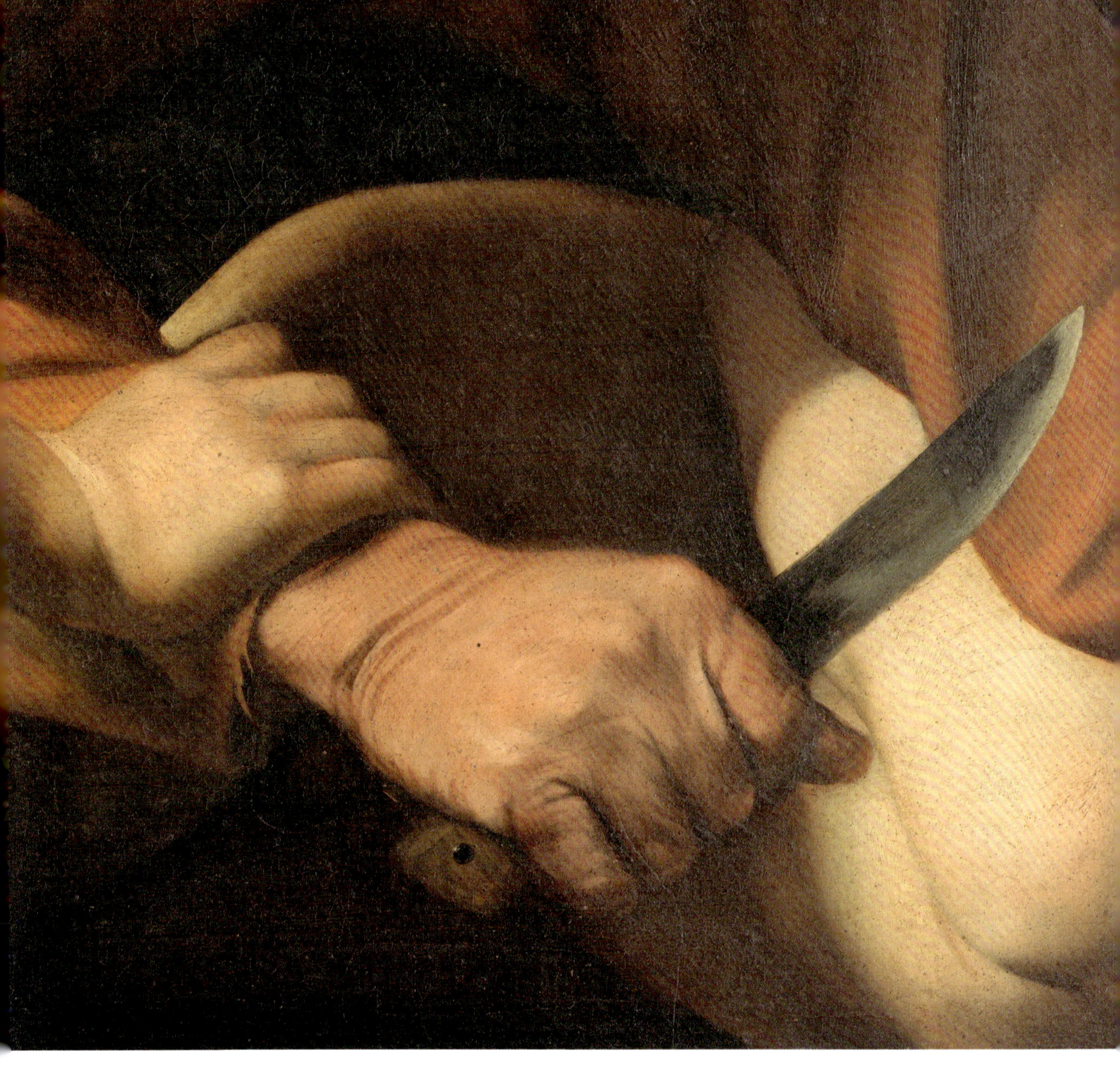

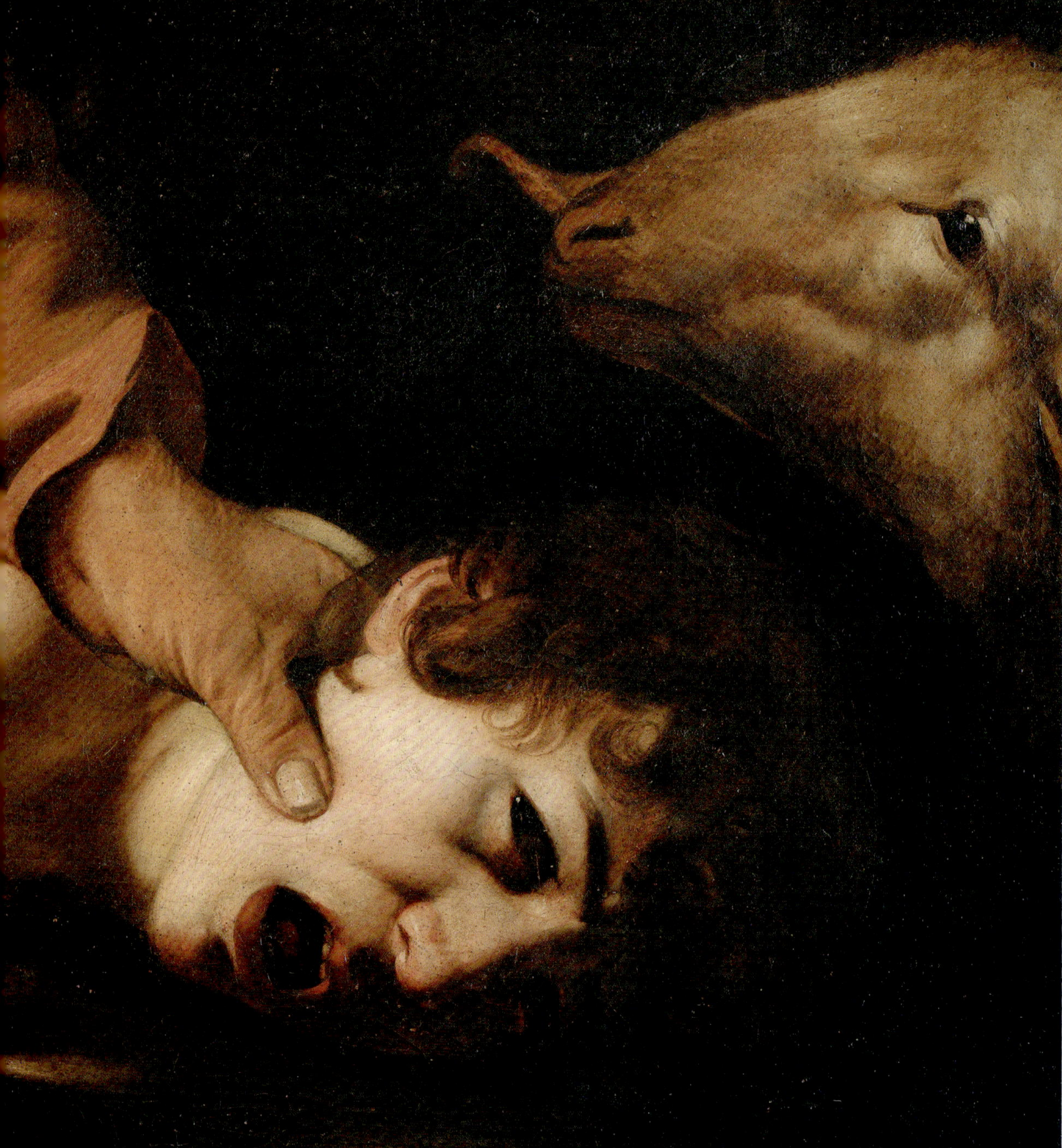

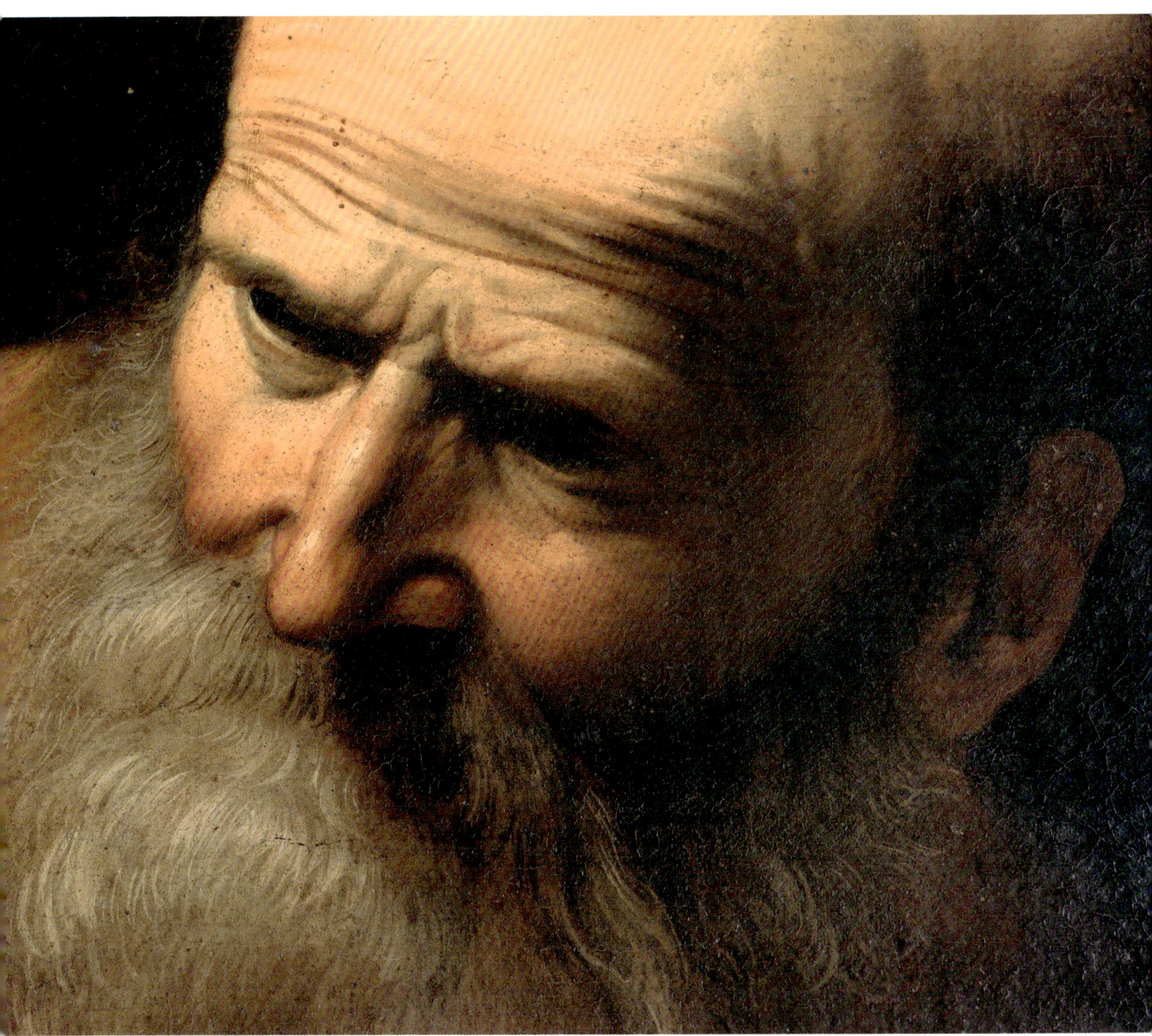

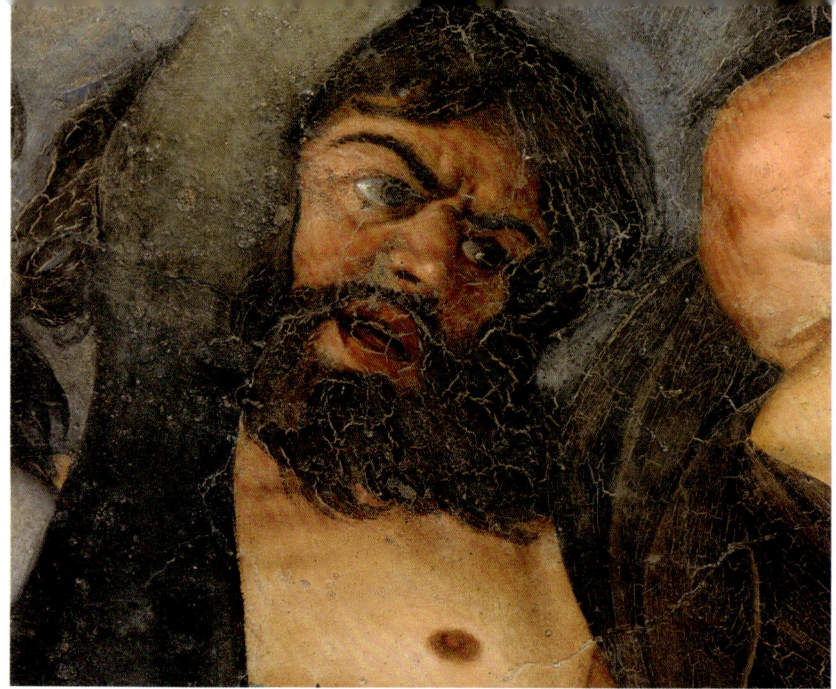

c. 1597, Fresco/Fresque, Villa Aurora, Roma

Major commissions in Rome

By 1600, Caravaggio had become a much sought-after artist in Rome. For the ceiling of the Villa Aurora, Caravaggio painted his only large-scale fresco *Jupiter, Neptune, and Pluto*. To gain more fame, however, artists in Rome needed commissions that would be made available to a wider public audience. By 1599, Caravaggio's time had come. Caravaggio signed on to create an altarpiece and two side images for the burial chapel of French cardinal Mathieu Cointrel (known in Italian as Matteo Contarelli) at the Church of San Luigi dei Francesi. A short time later, he received his second major commission for the Cappella Cerasi in the church of Santa Maria del Popolo.

Les grandes commandes romaines

En 1600, Caravage est bien établi à Rome comme peintre à succès. Sur le plafond d'un casino de la villa del Monte, il peint une grande fresque – *Jupiter, Neptune et Pluton* – seule peinture murale du maître. Mais pour acquérir plus de gloire, un artiste de l'époque doit réaliser des œuvres accessibles à un plus vaste public. Caravage y parvient en 1599 : il s'engage alors à peindre un retable et deux panneaux latéraux pour la chapelle funéraire du cardinal français Matthieu Cointerel (« Matteo Contarelli » en italien), dans l'église Saint-Louis-des-Français. Peu après, le peintre obtient une deuxième grande commande pour la chapelle Cerasi, à Santa Maria del Popolo.

Die großen römischen Aufträge

Bis 1600 etablierte sich Caravaggio in Rom als vielgefragter Künstler. Für die Decke der Villa Aurora malte Caravaggio das großformatige Fresko *Jupiter, Neptun und Pluto*, das einzige Caravaggios. Um mehr Ruhm zu erlangen, benötigte man als Künstler in Rom jedoch Aufträge, die einem größeren öffentlichen Publikum zugänglich waren. 1599 war es soweit. Caravaggio verpflichtete sich, ein Altar- und zwei Seitenbilder für die Grabkapelle des französischen Kardinals Mathieu Cointrel (ital. Matteo Contarelli) in San Luigi dei Francesi zu erstellen. Kurze Zeit später erhielt er sein zweites großes Auftragswerk für die Cappella Cerasi der Kirche Santa Maria del Popolo.

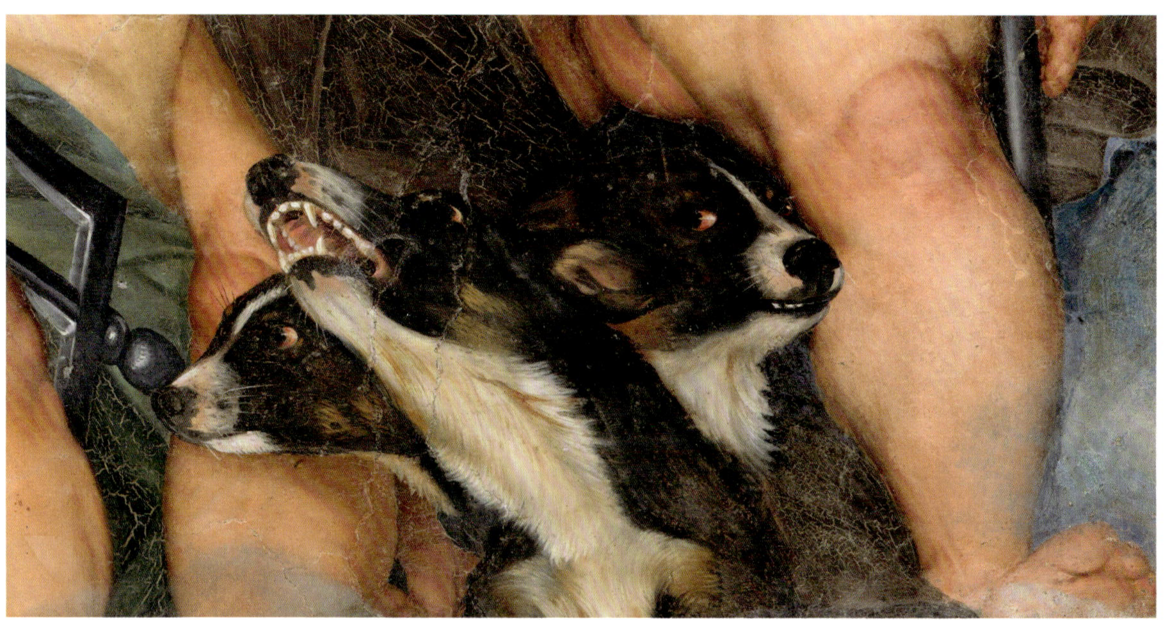

Los grandes encargos romanos

Hacia 1600 Caravaggio estaba ya
establecido en Roma como artista
aclamado. Realizó el fresco a gran
formato, el único de Caravaggio, *Júpiter,
Neptuno y Plutón* para el techo de la Villa
Aurora. Para obtener más fama como
artista sin embargo se necesitaba recibir
de Roma el tipo de encargos accesibles
a un público más amplio. En 1599 llegó el
momento. Caravaggio se comprometió
a realizar una pintura para el altar y dos
para los laterales de la capilla ardiente
del cardenal francés Mathieu Cointrel
(en italiano Matteo Contarelli) en San
Luigi dei Francesi. Poco tiempo después
recibió su segundo gran encargo para
la Cappella Cerasi de la iglesia de Santa
Maria del Popolo.

Le grandi commissioni romane

Nel 1600 Caravaggio era ormai a Roma
un artista molto ricercato. Dipinse per
il soffitto della Villa Aurora l'affresco di
grandi dimensioni di *Giove, Nettuno e
Plutone,* l'unica pittura murale eseguita
dall'artista. Per guadagnare più fama
nella città eterna, un artista doveva però
ottenere commissioni accessibili a un
pubblico più vasto. Per Caravaggio tale
momento giunse nel 1599, quando si
impegnò a creare una pala d'altare e
due tele laterali per la cappella funebre
del cardinale francese Mathieu Cointrel
(italianizzato, Matteo Contarelli) nella
Chiesa di San Luigi dei Francesi. Poco
tempo dopo ricevette il suo secondo
incarico importante per la Cappella Cerasi
nella Basilica di Santa Maria del Popolo.

De grote Romeinse opdrachten

Tot 1600 maakte Caravaggio als
veelgevraagd kunstenaar naam in
Rome. Voor het plafond van de Villa
Aurora schilderde hij het grote fresco
Jupiter, Neptunus en Pluto, zijn enige
plafondschildering. Om in Rome als
kunstenaar roem te vergaren had
Caravaggio echter opdrachten nodig voor
werken die een groter publiek bereikten.
In 1599 was het zover: Caravaggio kreeg
het verzoek om een altaarstuk met twee
flankerende doeken te schilderen voor de
grafkapel van de Franse kardinaal Mathieu
Cointrel (in het Italiaans: Matteo Contarelli)
in de kerk San Luigi dei Francesi. En kort
erna kreeg hij opdracht een doek te
vervaardigen voor de Cappella Cerasi in de
Santa Maria del Popolo.

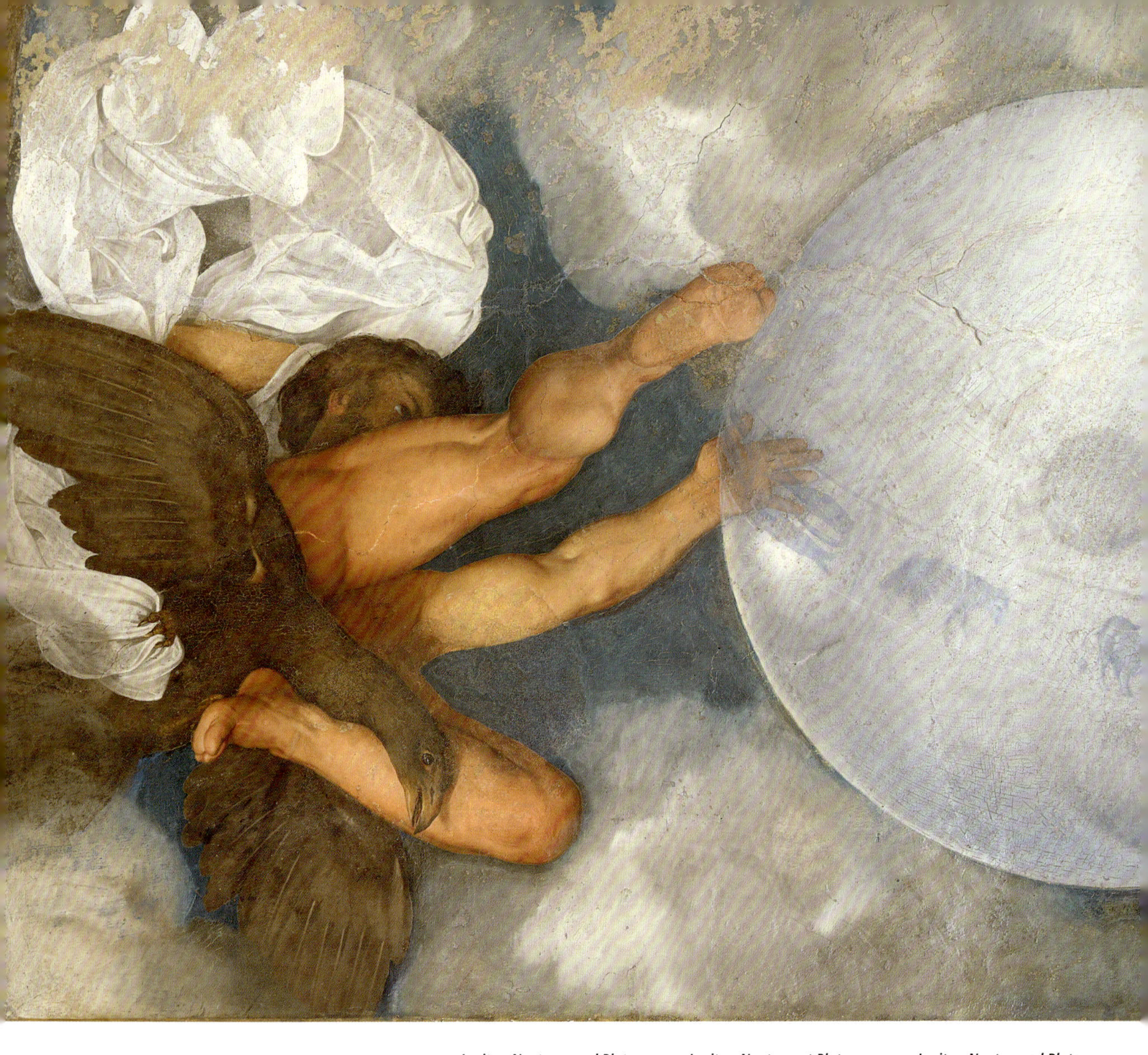

Jupiter, Neptune, and Pluto   **_Jupiter, Neptune et Pluton_**   **_Jupiter, Neptun und Pluto_**

c. 1597, Fresco/Fresque, 316 × 152 cm, Villa Aurora, Roma

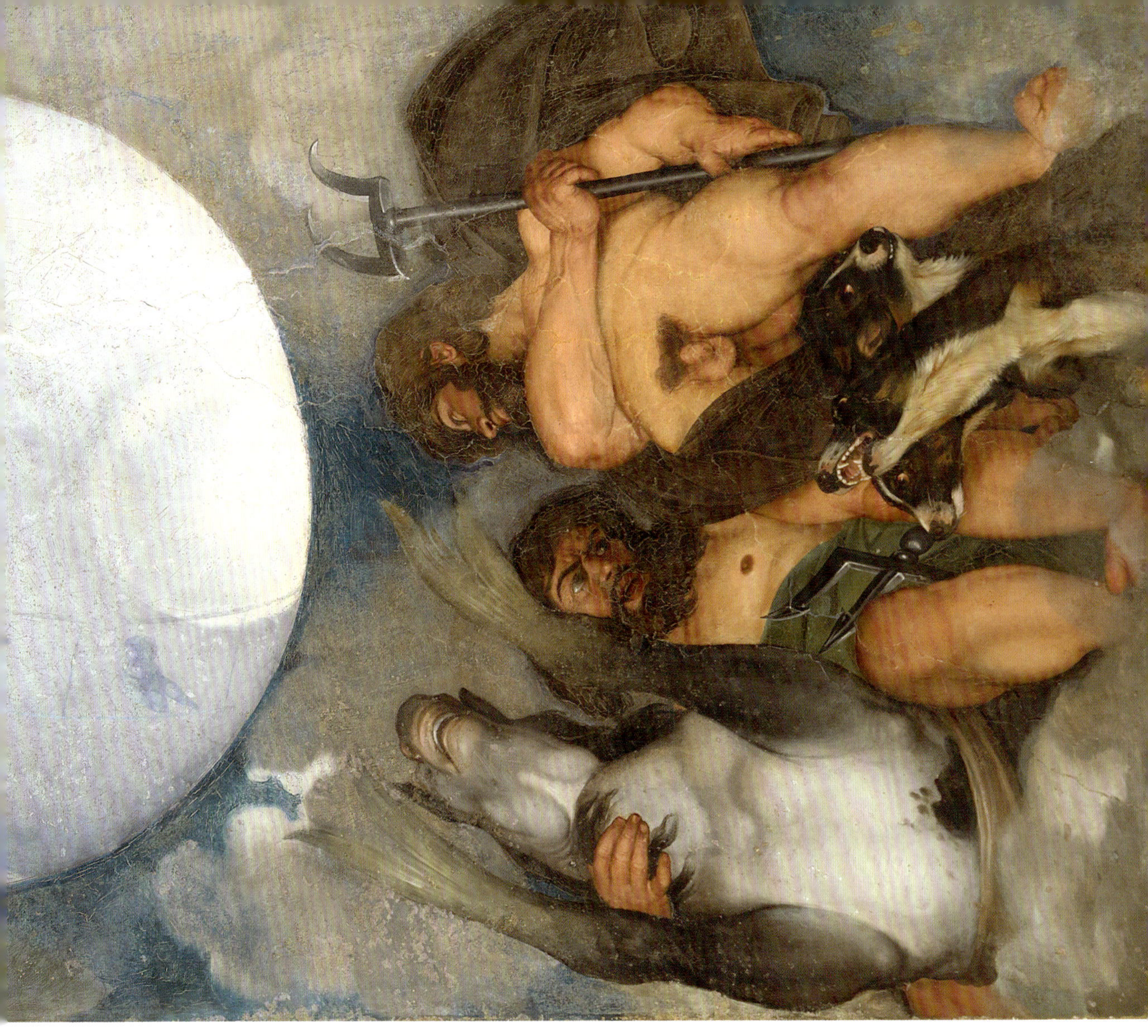

Júpiter, Neptuno y Plutón   *Giove, Nettuno e Plutone*   *Jupiter, Neptunus en Pluto*

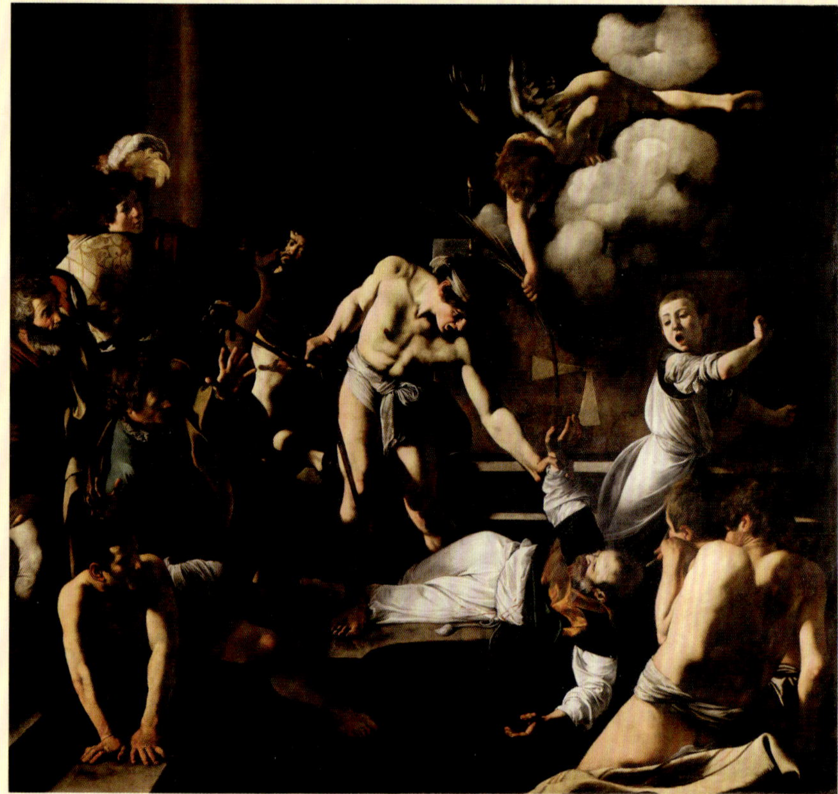

1599–1600, Oil on canvas/Huile sur toile, 323 × 343 cm, Chiesa di San Luigi dei Francesi, Roma

The Cappella Contarelli in San Luigi dei Francesi

Caravaggio's *Martyrdom of St Matthew*, completed in 1600, caused quite a sensation. The image is staged theatrically around the martyr and his executioner in the center and draws the viewer directly into the event. The effective chiaroscuro puts a spotlight on the executioner and the realistic representation of the drama creates a snapshot of a single moment in time

La chapelle Contarelli, à Saint-Louis-des-Français

Vers 1600, l'achèvement du *Martyre de saint Matthieu* fait sensation. À la manière d'une mise en scène théâtrale, la composition du tableau tourbillonne autour du groupe central (le martyr et son bourreau), impliquant ainsi très directement le spectateur dans l'événement. L'instantané de l'impressionnant effet de clair-obscur – le bourreau semble éclairé

Die Cappella Contarelli in San Luigi dei Francesi

Caravaggios um 1600 vollendetes *Martyrium des hl. Matthäus* war eine Sensation. Gleich einer theatralischen Inszenierung dreht sich der Bildaufbau um die mittige Figurengruppe des Märtyrers und seines Henkers und bezieht den Betrachter so direkt mit in das Geschehen ein. Die durch das effektvolle Hell-Dunkel – wie in einem Schlaglicht erscheint der Henker –

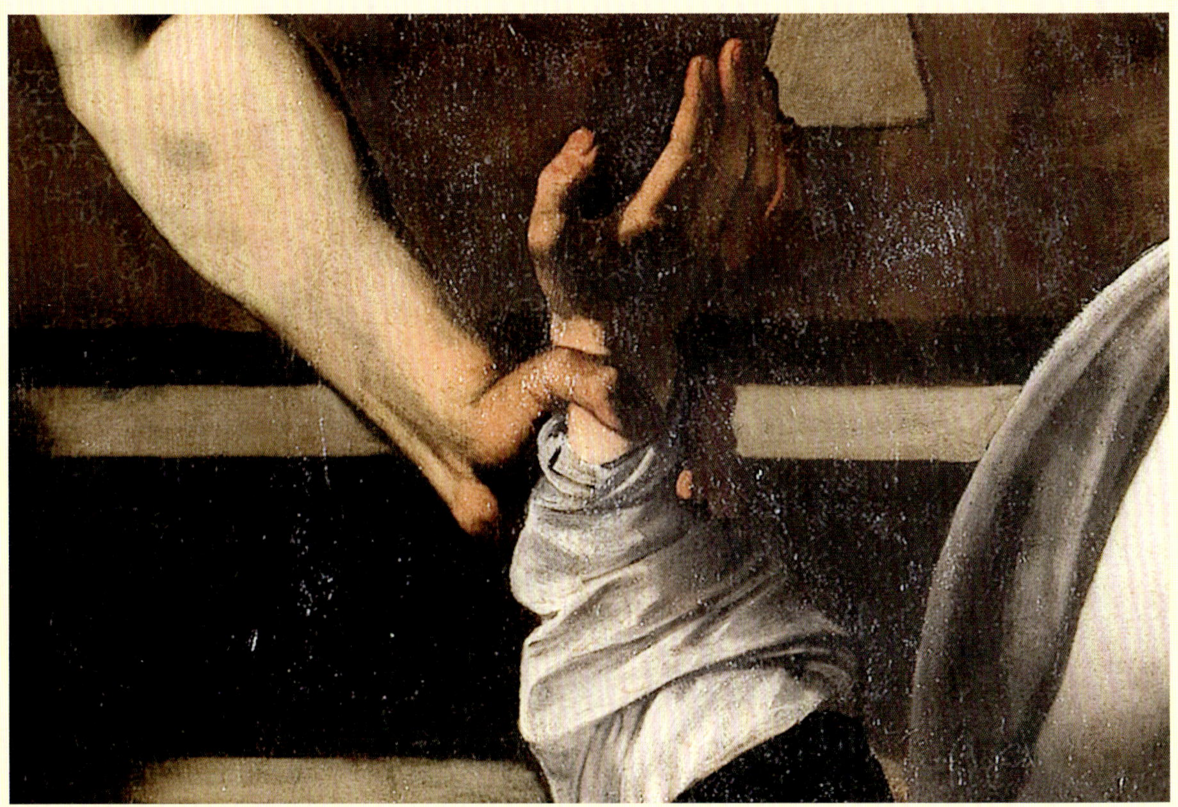

La Capilla Contarelli en
San Luigi dei Francesi

Los trabajos terminados por Caravaggio
alrededor del 1600 sobre el *Martitio de
San Mateo* fueron una sensación. Con
una tremenda sensibilidad teatral, la
composición pictórica gira en torno al
grupo de figuras del mártir y su verdugo,
introduciendo así directamente al
espectador en la escena. La instantánea,
con su efectivo uso del chiaroscuro –el
verdugo parece estar casi bajo un

La Cappella Contarelli nella
Chiesa di San Luigi dei Francesi

Il lavoro di Caravaggio *Martirio di
San Matteo* completato nel 1600 creò
molto scalpore. Proprio come una messa
in scena teatrale, la composizione
del quadro ruota intorno al gruppo
di figure centrale composto dal
martire e dal suo carnefice e rende
l'osservatore direttamente partecipe
dell'azione. L'efficace chiaroscuro (il
carnefice è illuminato da un fascio di

De Cappella Contarelli in de
San Luigi dei Francesi

De werken die Caravaggio rond 1600
over het *Martyrium van de heilige
Matteüs* schilderde, waren een sensatie.
Als in een theatrale enscenering
draait de compositie van de centrale
figurengroep rond de martelaar en
zijn beulen, waardoor de beschouwer
direct bij het gebeuren wordt betrokken.
Dankzij de efficiënte inzet van helder en
donker – de beul lijkt in het licht van een

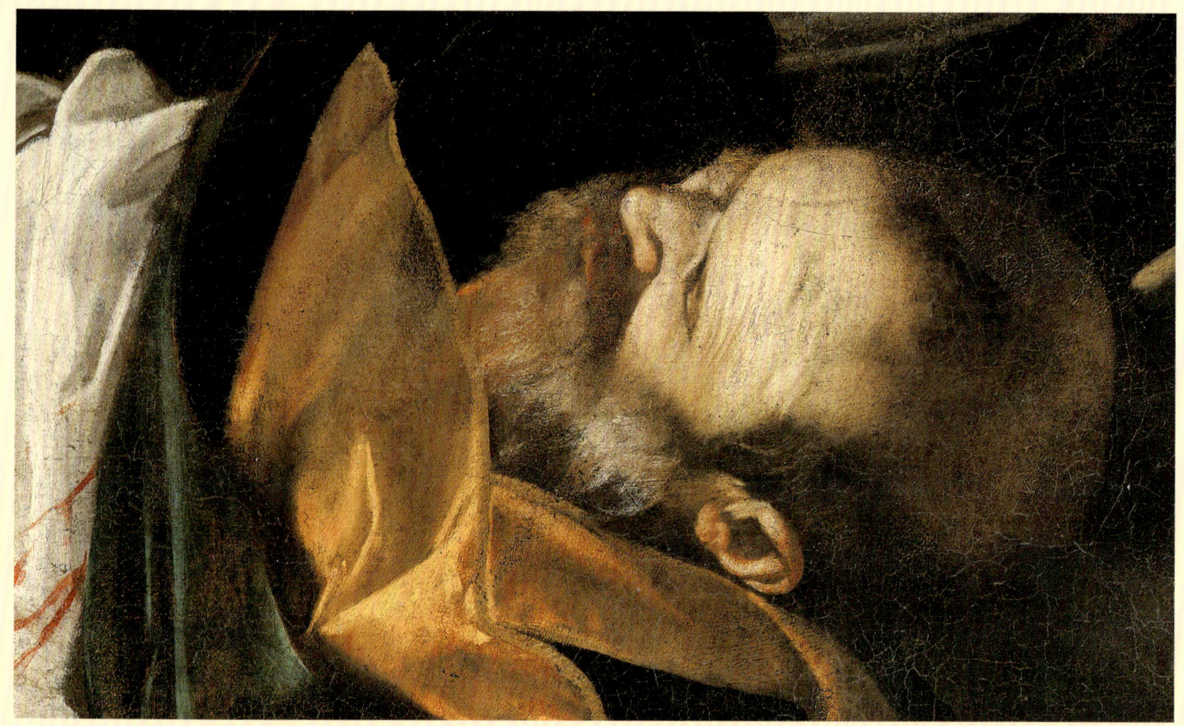

that takes the theme to an entirely new emotional level. Instead of the formal elevation of the saint and his martyrdom, Caravaggio links the event with the cruelty of real life. He takes the saint down from his pedestal and represents him in his moment of humiliation.

In *The Calling of St Matthew*, Caravaggio again makes innovative use of light. It does not fill the room diffusely, as was the case in earlier works, but instead plays a role in how the scene is laid out. Jesus enters from the right beckoning the tax collector Matthew with a gesture reminiscent

par un projecteur – et la représentation réaliste, sans équivalent dans le dramatisme, élèvent le sujet à un niveau d'émotion jamais atteint. Au lieu d'exalter formellement le saint et son martyr, Caravage rattache l'événement sacré à la cruauté profane de la vie réelle. Il fait descendre le saint de son piédestal en le représentant au moment même de son humiliation.

La Vocation de saint Matthieu révèle aussi le traitement novateur apporté par Caravage dans la conduite de la lumière. Elle ne remplit plus l'espace de façon diffuse – comme dans les

und die realistische Darstellung an Dramatik kaum zu überbietende Momentaufnahme hebt das Bildthema auf ein neues emotionales Niveau. Statt der formalen Überhöhung des Heiligen und seines Martyriums verknüpft Caravaggio das heilige Geschehen mit dem grausam Profanen des wahren Lebens. Er holt den Heiligen von seinem Podest und stellt ihn im Moment der Erniedrigung dar.

Auch in der *Berufung des hl. Matthäus* zeigt sich Caravaggios neuartiger Umgang mit der Lichtführung im Bild. Es erfüllt nicht, wie in früheren Werken,

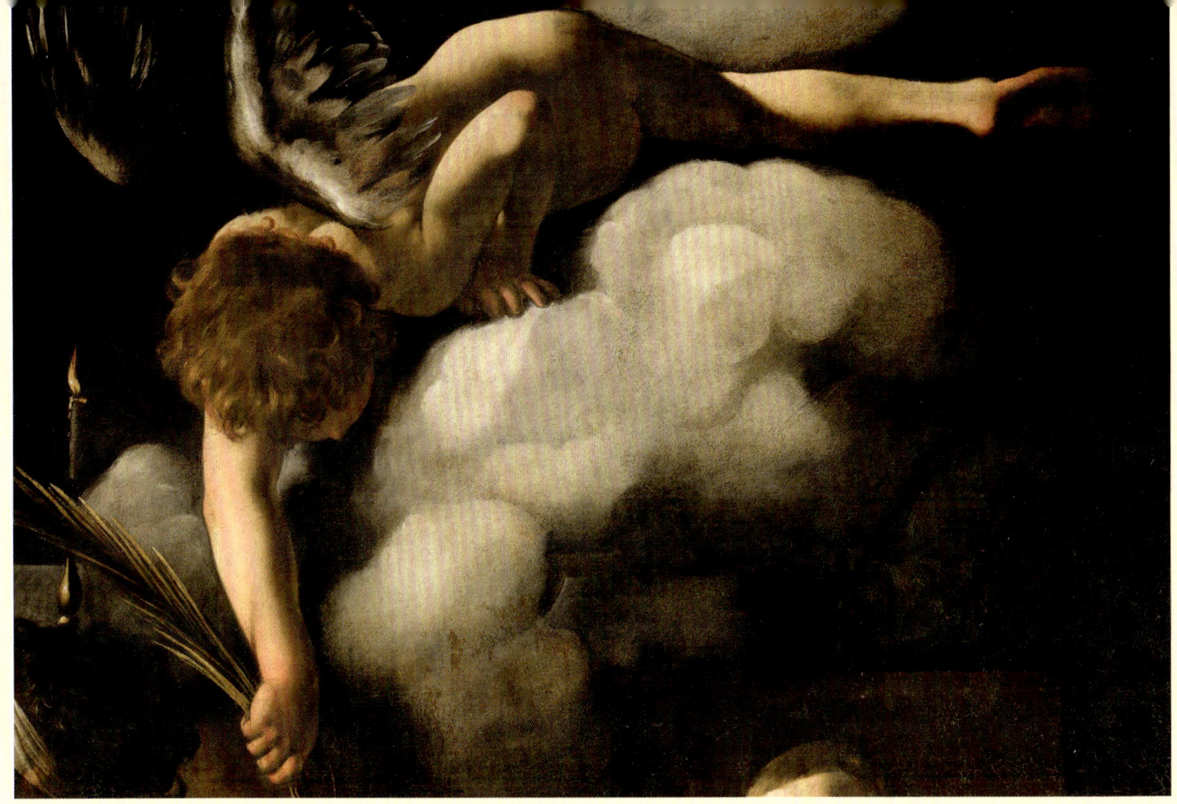

foco – y su representación realista del
dramatismo, es casi insuperable y eleva
el tema a nuevas cotas emocionales. En
lugar de la elevación formal del santo y
su martirio Caravaggio conjunta el hecho
sagrado con lo cruelmente profano de la
vida real. Baja al santo de su pedestal y lo
presenta en un momento de humillación.

También en *La vocación de San Mateo*
queda patente la manera novedosa
de Caravaggio a la hora de trabajar
la iluminación de la imagen. No
llena –como en trabajos más tempranos–
de manera difusa el espacio, sino
que sirve de forma consciente para

luce) e la rappresentazione realistica
di questa scena drammatica, quasi
fosse un'istantanea, portano il motivo
del quadro ad un livello emotivo tutto
nuovo. Invece dell'elevazione formale
del santo e del suo martirio, Caravaggio
collega l'evento sacro alla crudele
profanità della vita reale. Fa scendere il
santo dal suo piedistallo e lo rappresenta
nel momento dell'umiliazione.

Anche nella *Vocazione di San Matteo*
si può osservare il nuovo uso della
luce da parte di Caravaggio. Come in
opere precedenti, essa non è diffusa,
ma viene utilizzata consapevolmente

schijnwerper te staan – en de realistische
uitbeelding van een dramatische
momentopname heeft het schilderij
een ongekend emotionele uitstraling.
In plaats van de formele uitlichting van
de apostel en zijn martyrium verbindt
Caravaggio het heilige gebeuren met de
wrede profaanheid van het echte leven.
Hij haalt de heilige van zijn voetstuk
en beeldt hem op een moment van
vernedering uit.

Ook uit *De roeping van de heilige
Matteüs* blijkt de nieuwe wijze waarop
Caravaggio lichten donkerpartijen
benaderde. De ruimte baadt niet – zoals

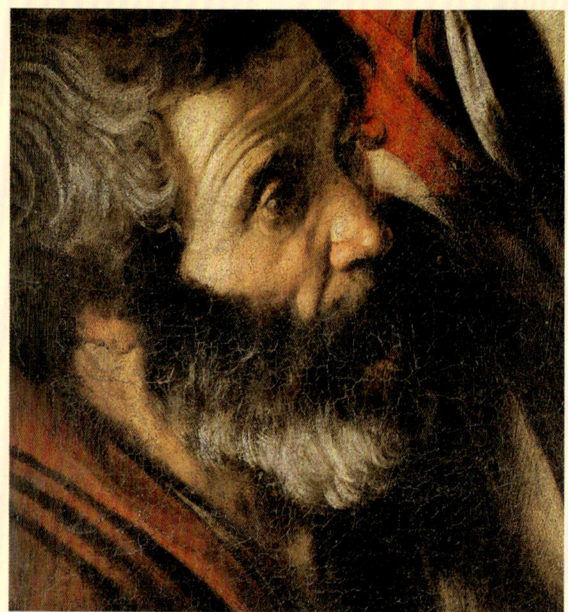 

of Michelangelo's Adam in the famous creation scene in the Sistine Chapel. The sharply defined beam of light follows the action and puts the spotlight on the beckoning gesture and the questioning reaction of the future disciple.

The first version of Caravaggio's depiction of the angelic inspiration of St Matthew's writing of his gospel was rejected by the client for being too primitive. In the second version, the painter took more account of the sensitivities of his client, dressing the saint in an elegant gown, with an appropriate halo adorning his head, and with fingers both delicate and in motion. The facial expression in this second version does not express disbelief, but instead understanding.

œuvres antérieures – mais sert de façon consciente au développement de la structure iconographique. Le Christ entre par la droite et indique le publicain d'un geste impérieux (rappelant celui de Dieu dans la fresque célèbre de *La Création d'Adam*, peinte par Michel-Ange à la chapelle Sixtine). Le rayon de lumière fortement accentué épouse l'événement en éclairant à la fois le geste d'intimation et la réaction dubitative du futur disciple.

La représentation de Matthieu écrivant son évangile sous l'inspiration d'un ange a été précédée d'une première version refusée par le commanditaire qui la trouvait trop « primitive ». Dans la version définitive, le peintre a mieux tenu compte de la sensibilité de son

diffus den Raum, sondern dient bewusst der Entwicklung des Bildaufbaus. Von rechts tritt Christus ein und weist mit gebieterischer Geste, die an Michelangelos Adam in der berühmten Schöpfungsszene in der Sixtinischen Kapelle erinnert, auf den Zöllner Matthäus. Der scharf akzentuierte Lichtstrahl folgt dem Geschehen und erhellt den Berufungsgestus ebenso wie die fragende Reaktion des zukünftigen Jüngers.

Seiner Darstellungen des Evangelisten Matthäus, der von einem Engel inspiriert sein Evangelium niederschreibt, ging eine erste, abgelehnte Fassung voraus, die dem Auftraggeber zu primitiv war. In der zweiten Fassung nahm der Maler mehr

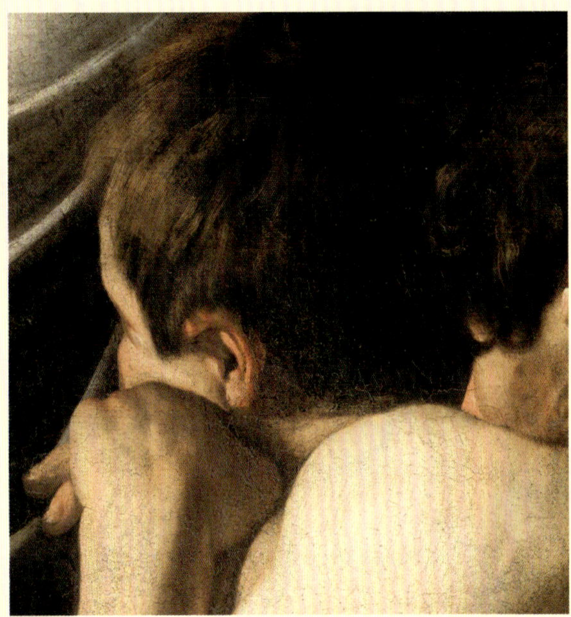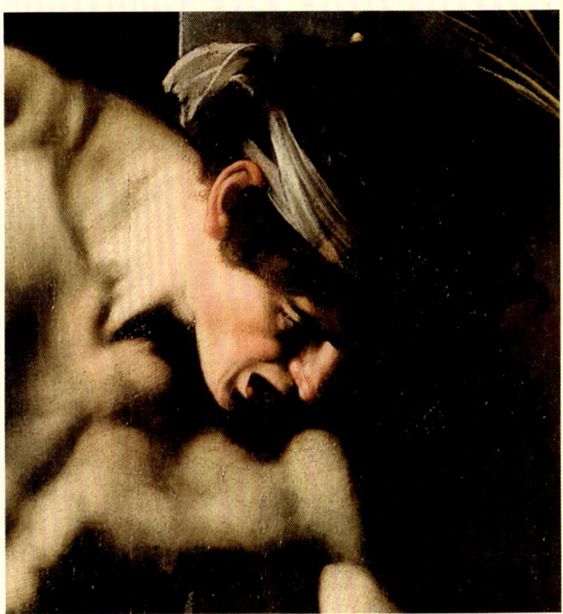

desarrollar la composición de la imagen. Cristo aparece por la parte derecha y señala con gesto imperativo, que recuerda al Adán de Miguel Ángel en la famosa creación de la Capilla Sixtina, al recaudador Mateo. El rayo de luz, fuertemente acentuado, sigue a la acción e ilumina tanto el llamamiento como la reacción incrédula del futuro discípulo.

Su pintura del evangelista Mateo, escribiendo su evangelio inspirado por el ángel, estaba precedida de otra primera versión, rechazada por el cliente por considerarla demasiado primitiva. En esta segunda versión el pintor trabaja con más consideración hacia la sensibilidad de su cliente: el santo aparece envuelto en un elegante paño, la correspondiente aureola adorna su

per lo sviluppo della composizione del quadro. Da destra entra Cristo che, con un gesto imperioso che ricorda quello della famosa *Creazione di Adamo* di Michelangelo nella Cappella Sistina, indica il pubblicano Matteo. Il fascio di luce ben definito dà direzione di lettura all'avvenimento e illumina il gesto della vocazione e l'espressione sbigottita del futuro discepolo.

La sua raffigurazione dell'evangelista Matteo, che scrive il suo vangelo ispirato da un angelo, fu preceduta da una prima versione, che fu respinta dal committente in quanto ritenuta troppo primitiva. Nella seconda versione il pittore prese in maggiore considerazione la sensibilità del suo committente: il santo indossa una veste elegante, la sua

eerder – in een diffuus licht, maar speelt een rol in de opbouw van de compositie. Christus treedt van rechts naar voren en wijst gebiedend – vergelijkbaar met Michelangelo's *Schepping van Adam* in de Sixtijnse Kapel – naar de tollenaar Matteüs. Het scherp afgetekende licht volgt het gebeuren en verlicht zowel het roepingsgebaar als de vragende blik op het gezicht van de evangelist in spe.

De uitbeelding van Matteüs, door een engel geïnspireerd tot het schrijven van zijn evangelie, werd voorafgegaan door een eerste versie, die in de ogen van de opdrachtgever te primitief was. In de tweede versie hield de schilder rekening met de gevoeligheden van zijn mecenas: de heilige is in een voornaam gewaad gehuld, rond zijn hoofd schijnt

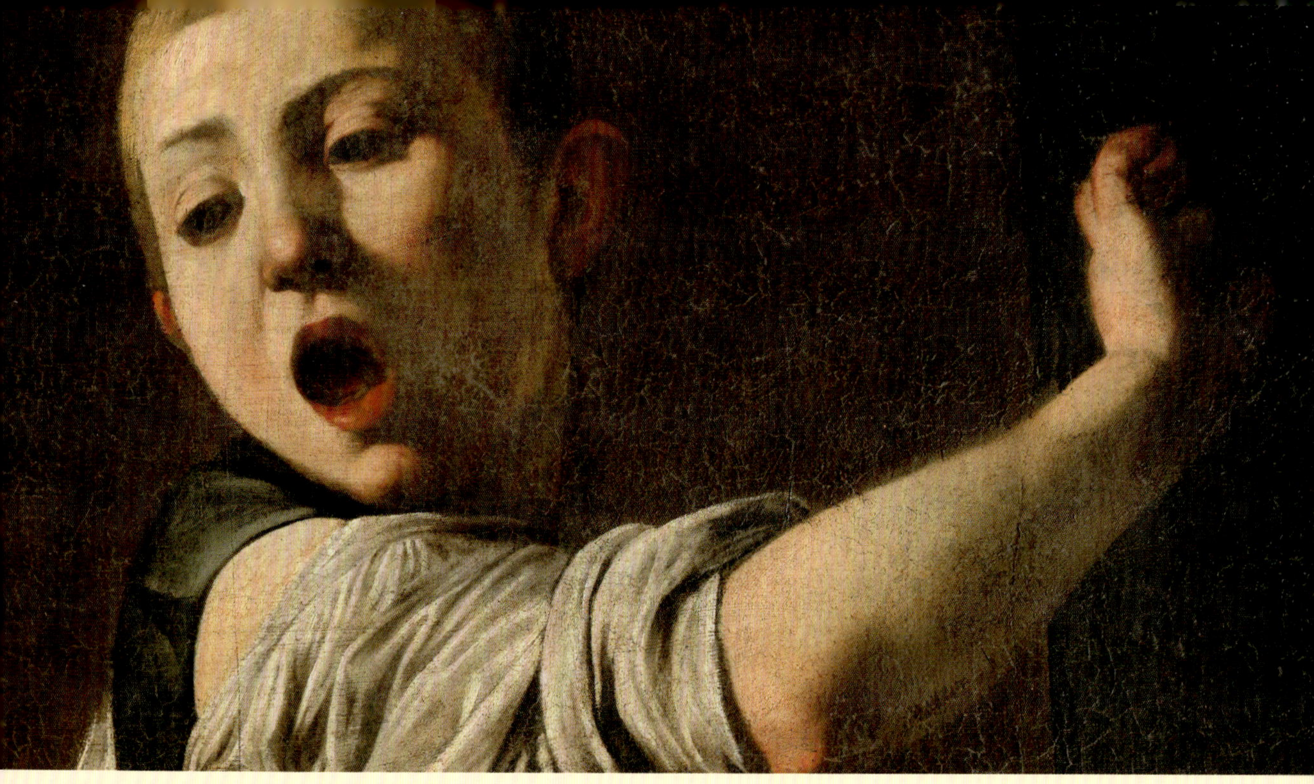

The three large format paintings remain in San Luigi in exactly the same spots where the painter originally hung them. They signal Caravaggio as one of the pioneers of the Baroque together with Annibale Carracci (1560–1609).

client : le saint est environné d'un ample manteau très distingué, une auréole conforme à son statut orne sa tête, et ses doigts paraissent déliés et agiles. L'expression du visage n'exprime pas l'étonnement incrédule, mais atteste la compréhension.

Les trois panneaux se trouvent à leur place initiale, à Saint-Louis-des-Français, où ils ont été accrochés en présence du peintre. Ils montrent Caravage en précurseur du baroque, à l'instar de Carrache (1560–1609).

Rücksicht auf die Empfindsamkeit seines Auftraggebers: Der Heilige ist in ein vornehmes Tuch gehüllt, ein standesgemäßer Heiligenschein schmückt sein Haupt und seine Finger wirken feingliedrig und beweglich. Der Gesichtsausdruck spricht nicht von ungläubigem Staunen, sondern bekundet Verstehen.

Die drei großformatigen Gemälde befinden sich in San Luigi noch immer an genau der Stelle, an der sie in der Gegenwart des Malers aufgehängt wurden, und zeichnen Caravaggio, zusammen mit Annibale Carracci (1560–1609), als Wegbereiter des Barock aus.

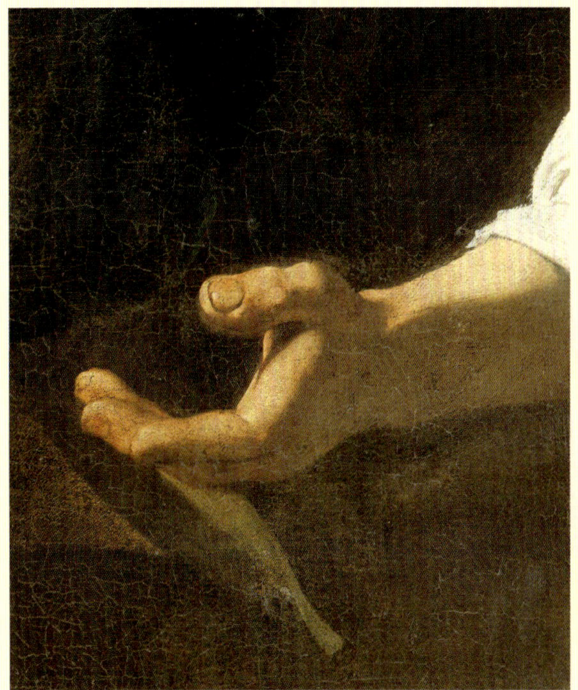 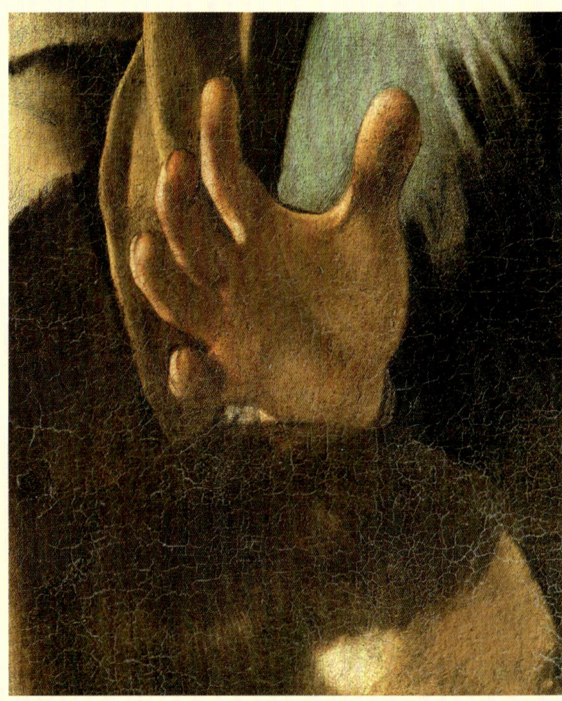

cabeza y sus dedos dan una impresión delicada y viva. La expresión facial no transmite un asombro incrédulo, sino más bien entendimiento manifiesto.

Estas tres pinturas cuelgan en San Luigi todavía exactamente en el mismo lugar en el que se colocaron en vida el pintor, y muestran a Caravaggio, junto a Annibale Carracci (1560–1609), como iniciadores del Barroco.

testa è adornata da una classica aureola e le sue dita sembrano muoversi in modo delicato e agile; il suo volto non esprime incredulità ma comprensione.

Le tre grandi tele sono conservate tuttora nella Chiesa di San Luigi nel punto esatto in cui furono appese alla presenza del pittore, e mostrano come Caravaggio, insieme a Annibale Carracci (1560–1609), fosse un precursore del Barocco.

de halo, zoals het een heilige betaamt, en zijn vingers zijn verfijnd en behendig. De gelaatsuitdrukking is niet die van ongelovige verbazing maar van toonbaar begrip.

De drie schilderijen op groot formaat bevinden zich in de San Luigi nog altijd op de plek waar ze in aanwezigheid van de schilder werden opgehangen en getuigen van de pioniersrol van Caravaggio, die samen met Annibale Carracci (1560–1609) tot de wegbereider van de barok wordt gerekend.

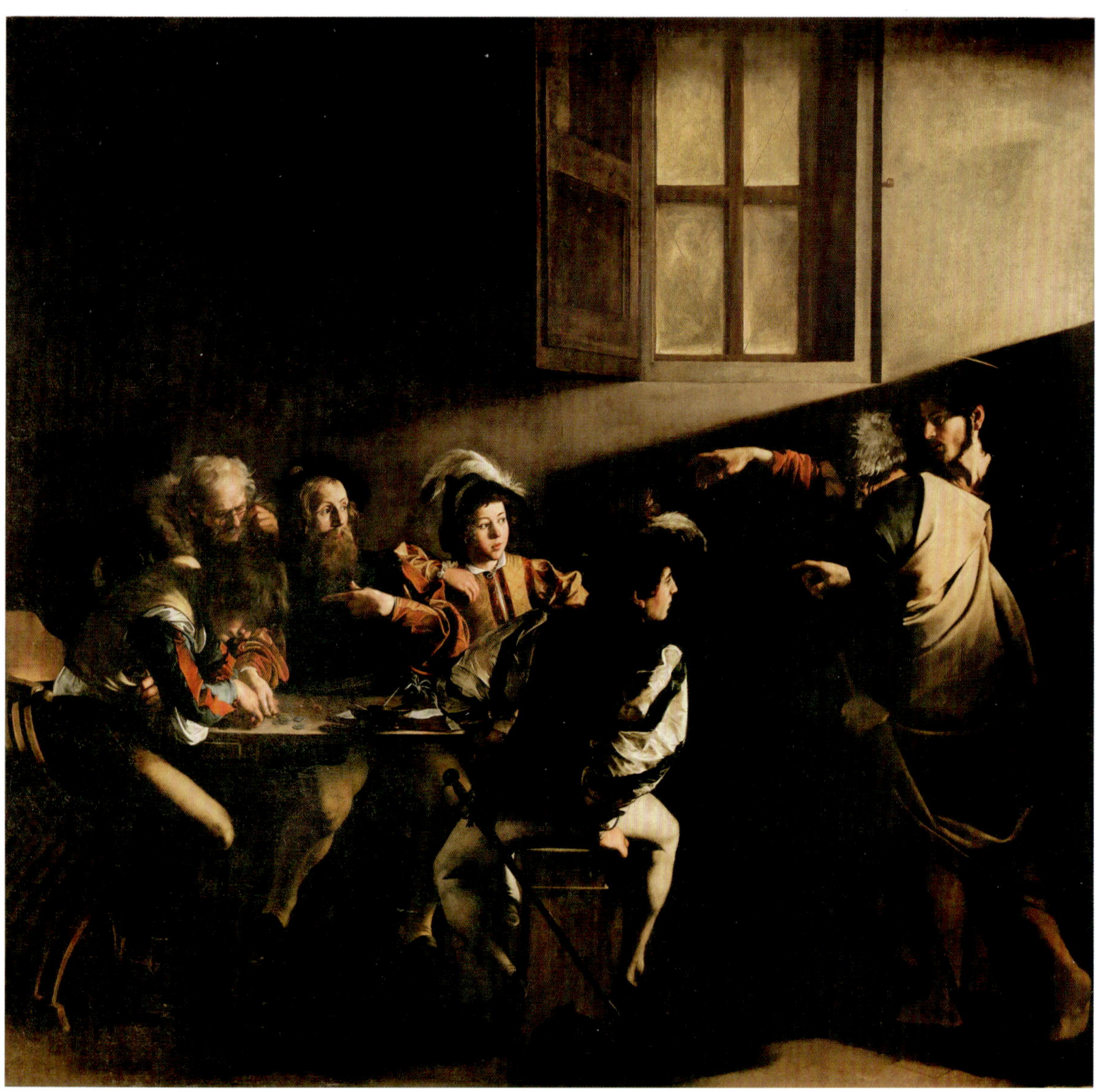

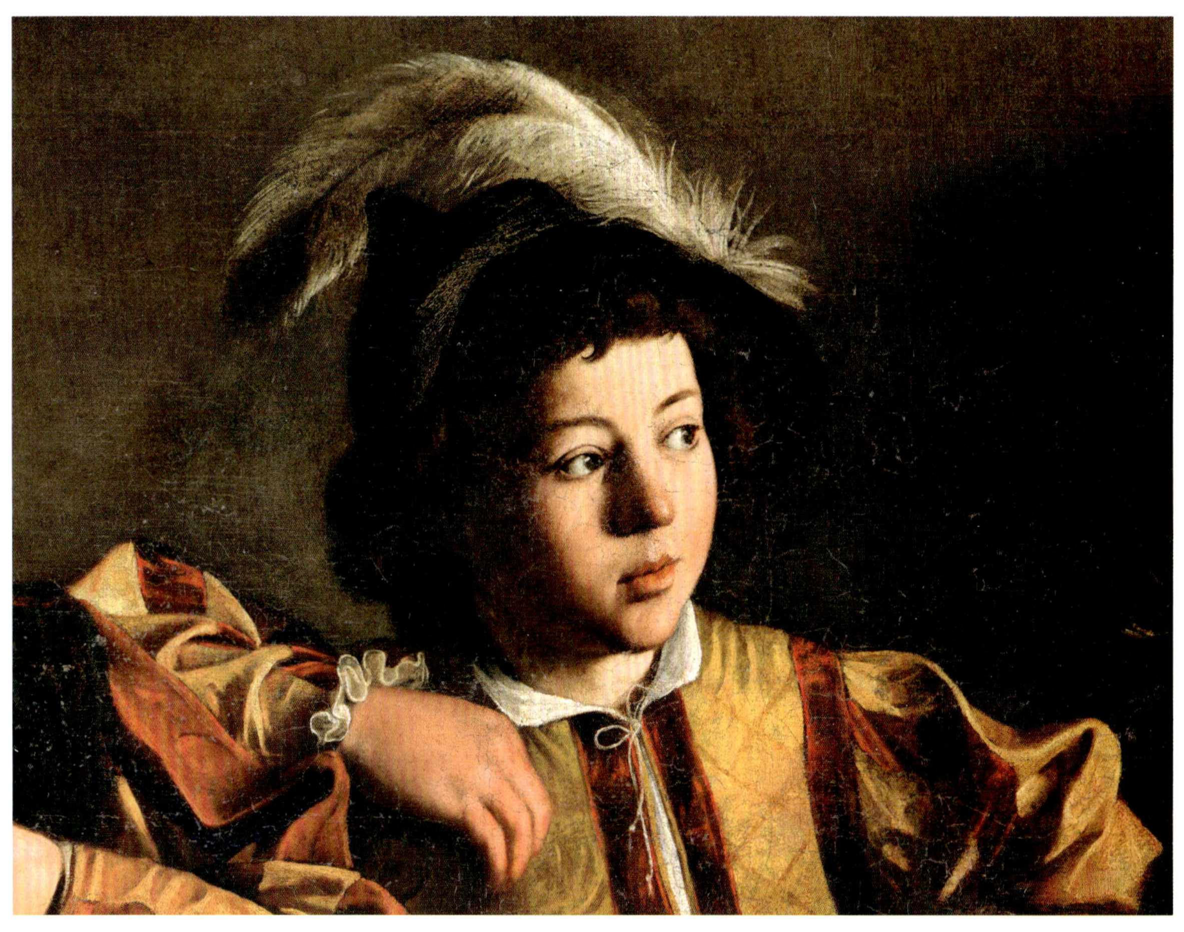

The Calling of St Matthew

La Vocation de saint Matthieu

Die Berufung des hl. Matthäus

La vocación de San Mateo

Vocazione di San Matteo

De roeping van de heilige Matteüs

1599/1600, Oil on canvas/Huile sur toile, 322 × 340 cm, Chiesa di San Luigi dei Francesi, Roma

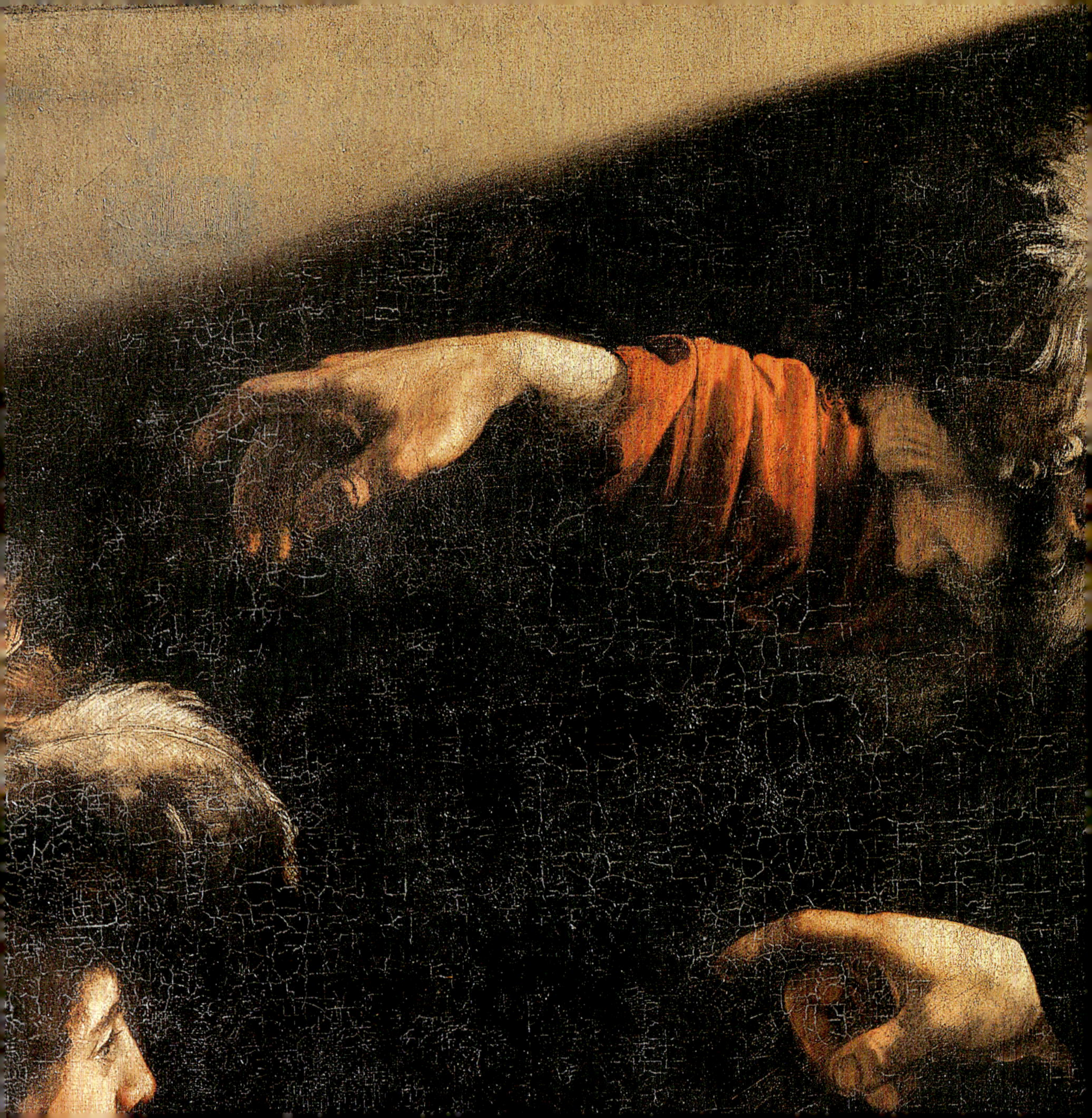

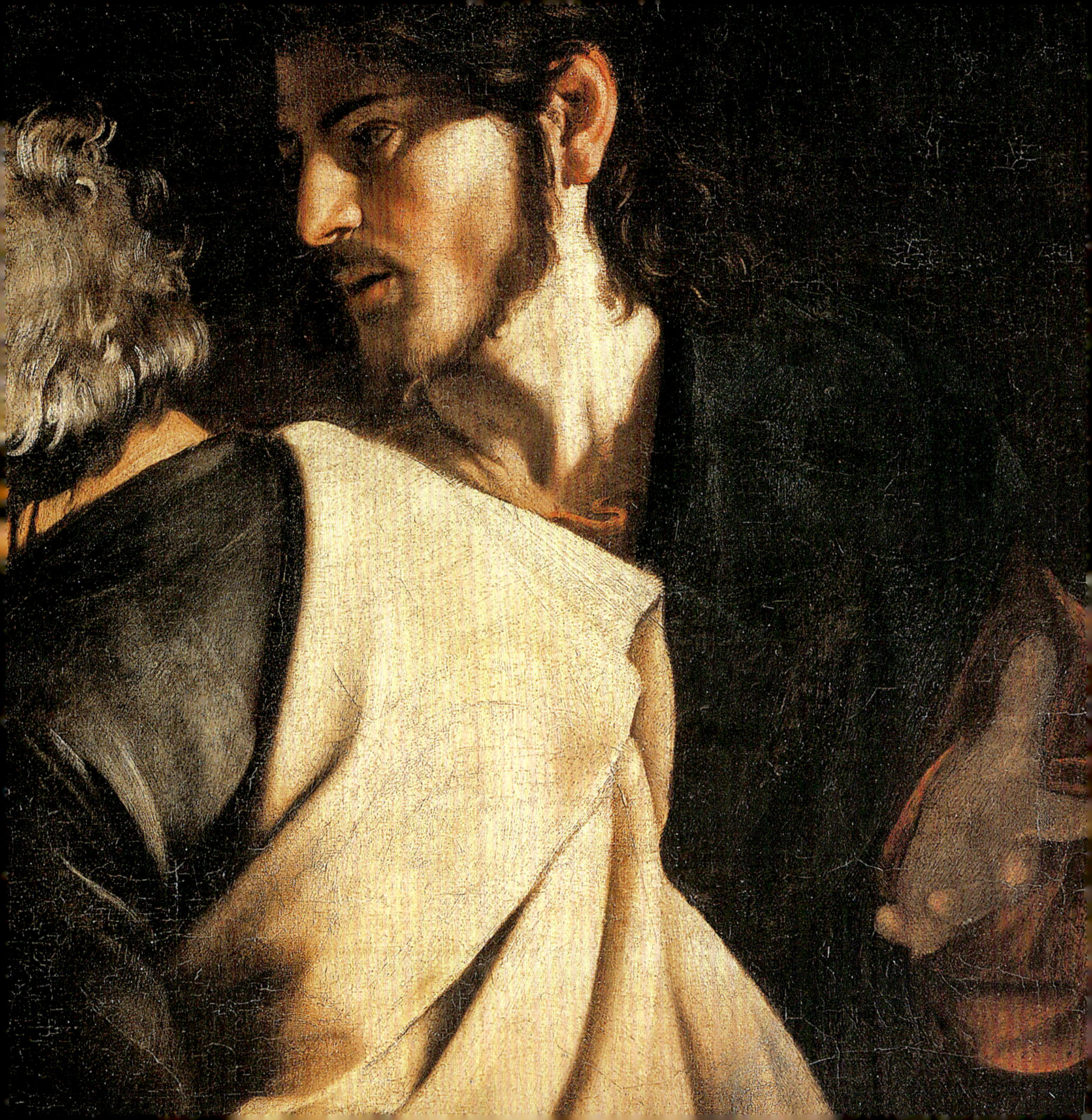

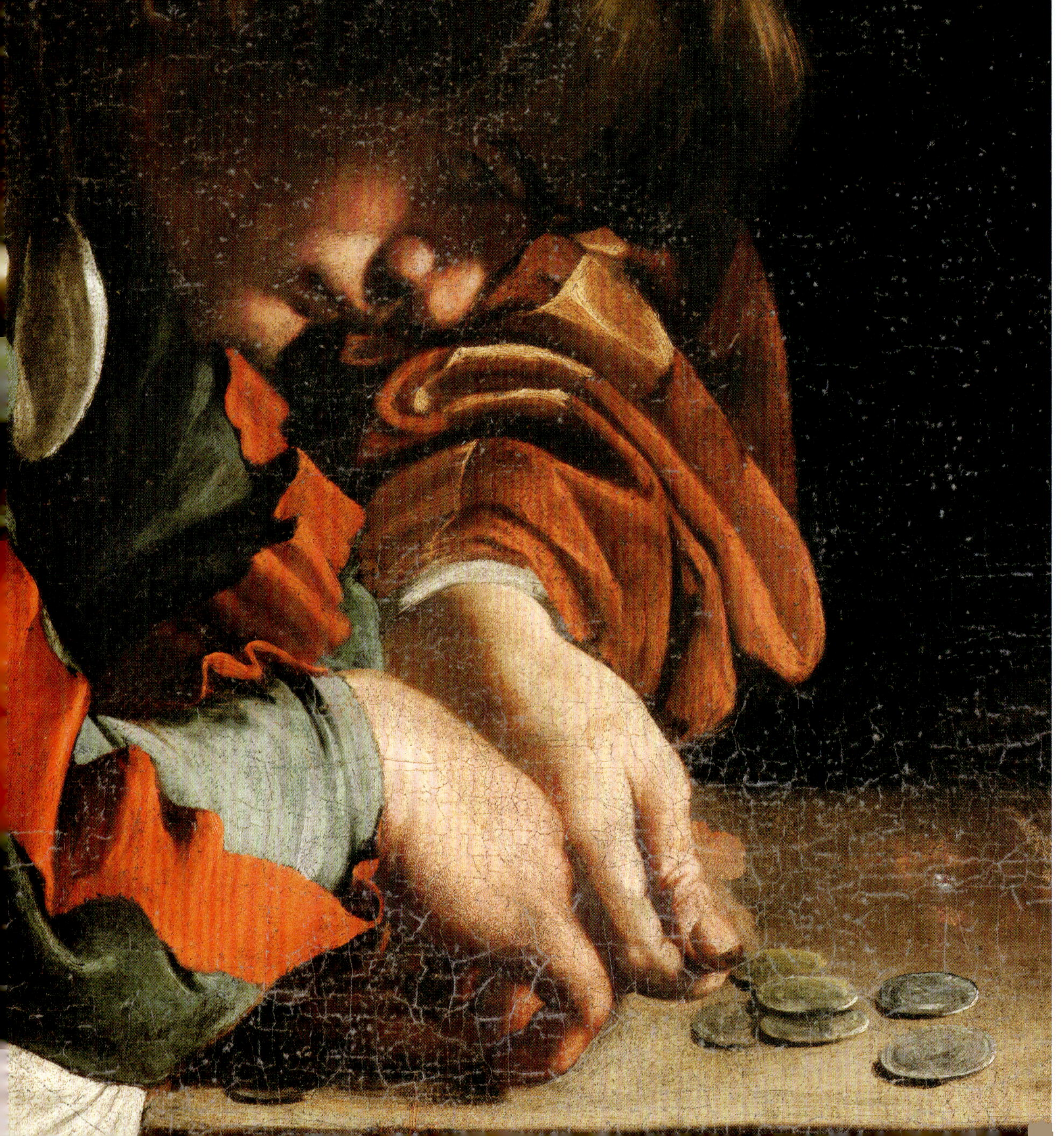

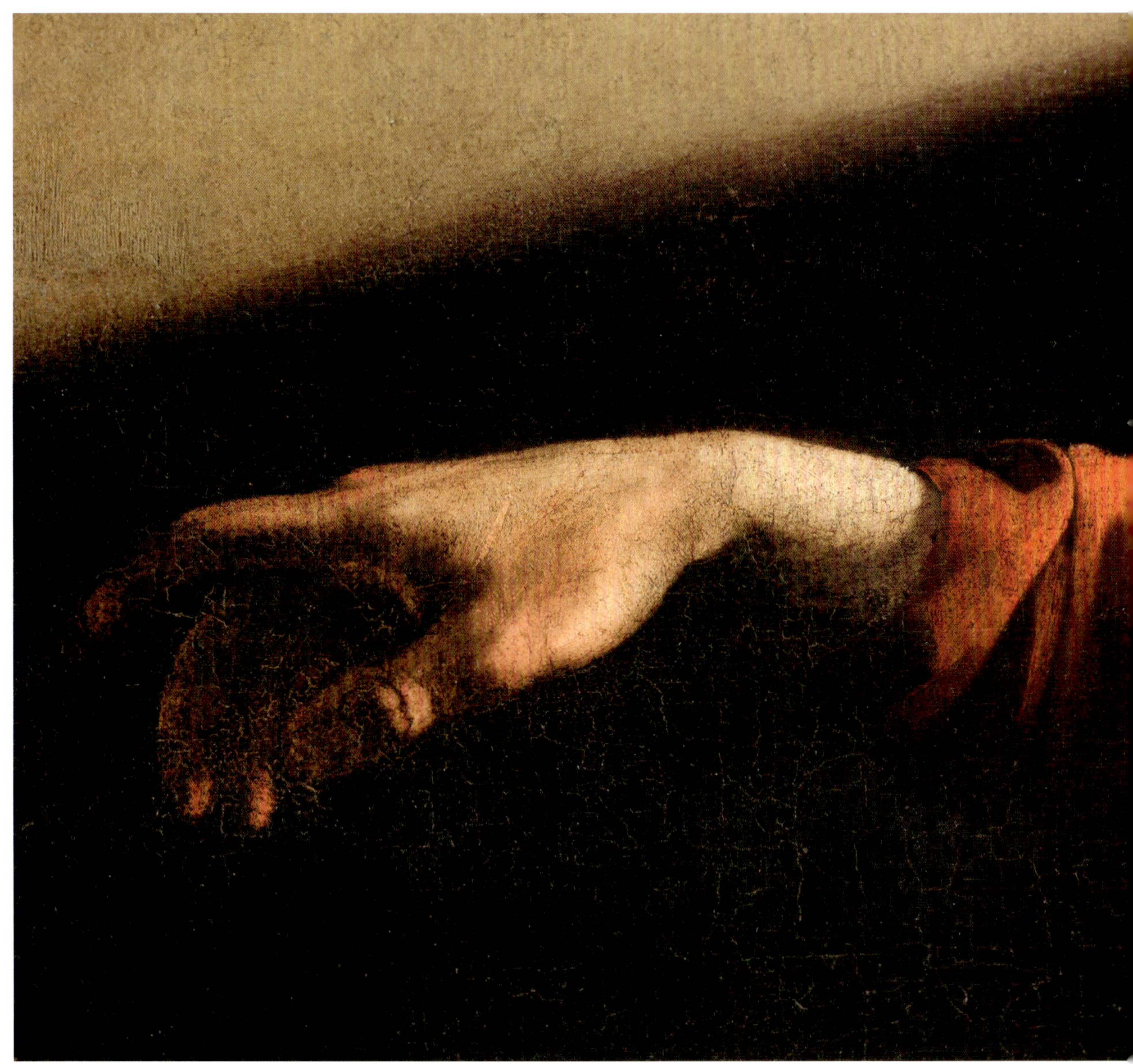

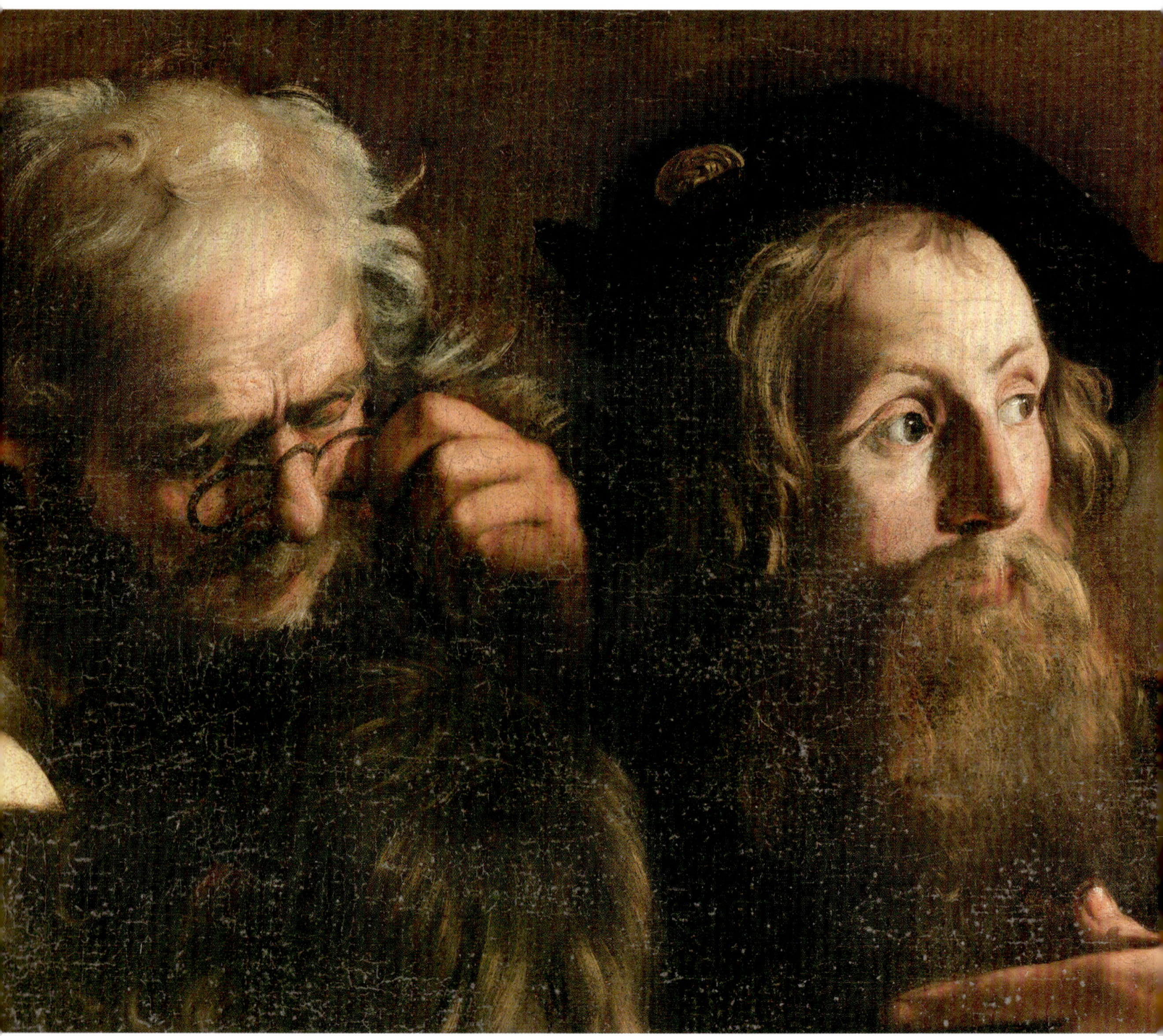

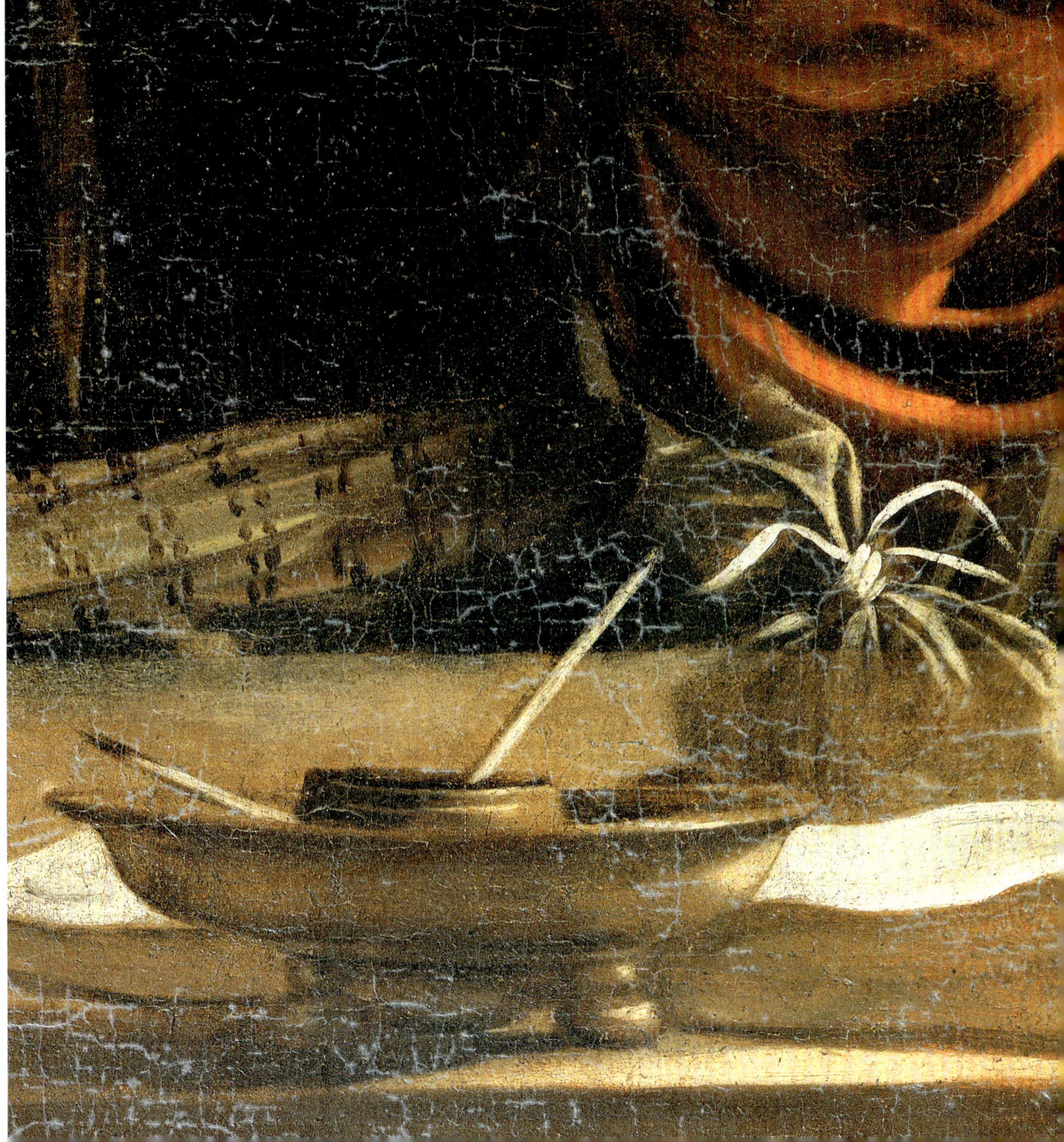

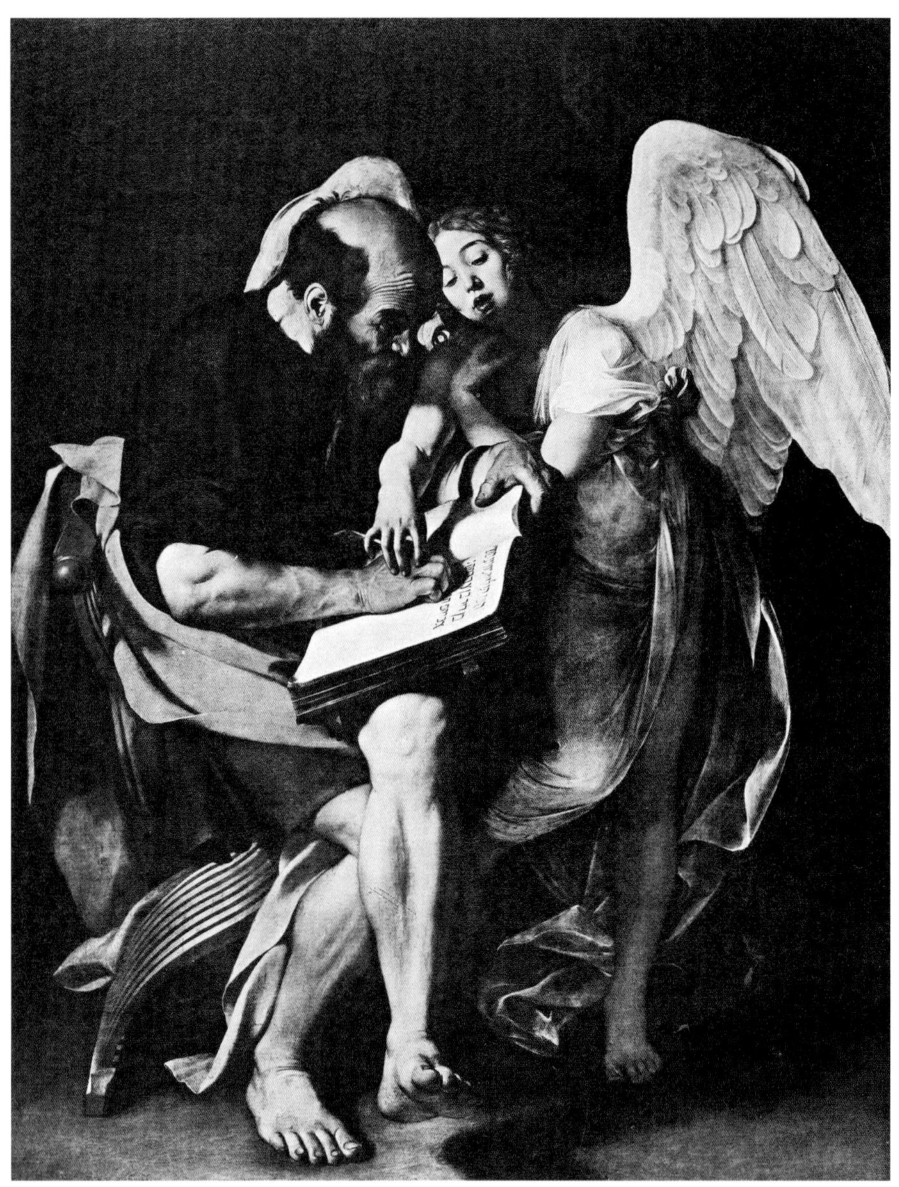

The Inspiration of St Matthew
(first, rejected version)

Saint Matthieu et l'Ange
(première version)

Inspiration des Matthäus
(erste, abgelehnte Fassung)

La inspiración de Mateo
(primera versión, rechazada)

San Matteo e l'angelo
(prima versione respinta)

De heilige Matteüs en de engel
(eerste, afgewezen versie)

c. 1598, Oil on canvas/Huile sur toile, 232 × 183 cm, burnt/brûlé 1945

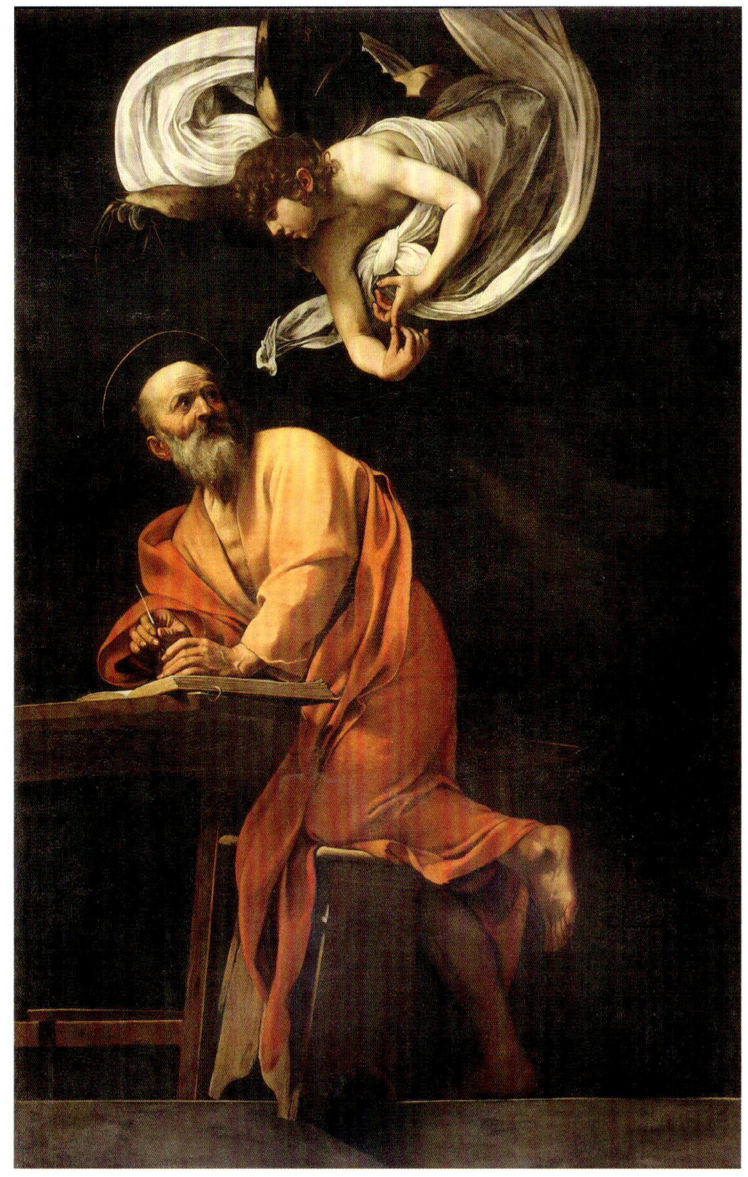

St Matthew with the Angel (second version)
Saint Matthieu et l'Ange (deuxième version)
Der hl. Matthäus mit dem Engel (zweite Fassung)
San Mateo con el ángel (segunda versión)
San Matteo e l'angelo (seconda versione)
De heilige Matteüs en de engel (tweede versie)

*1602, Oil on canvas/Huile sur toile, 292 × 186 cm,
Chiesa di San Luigi dei Francesi, Roma*

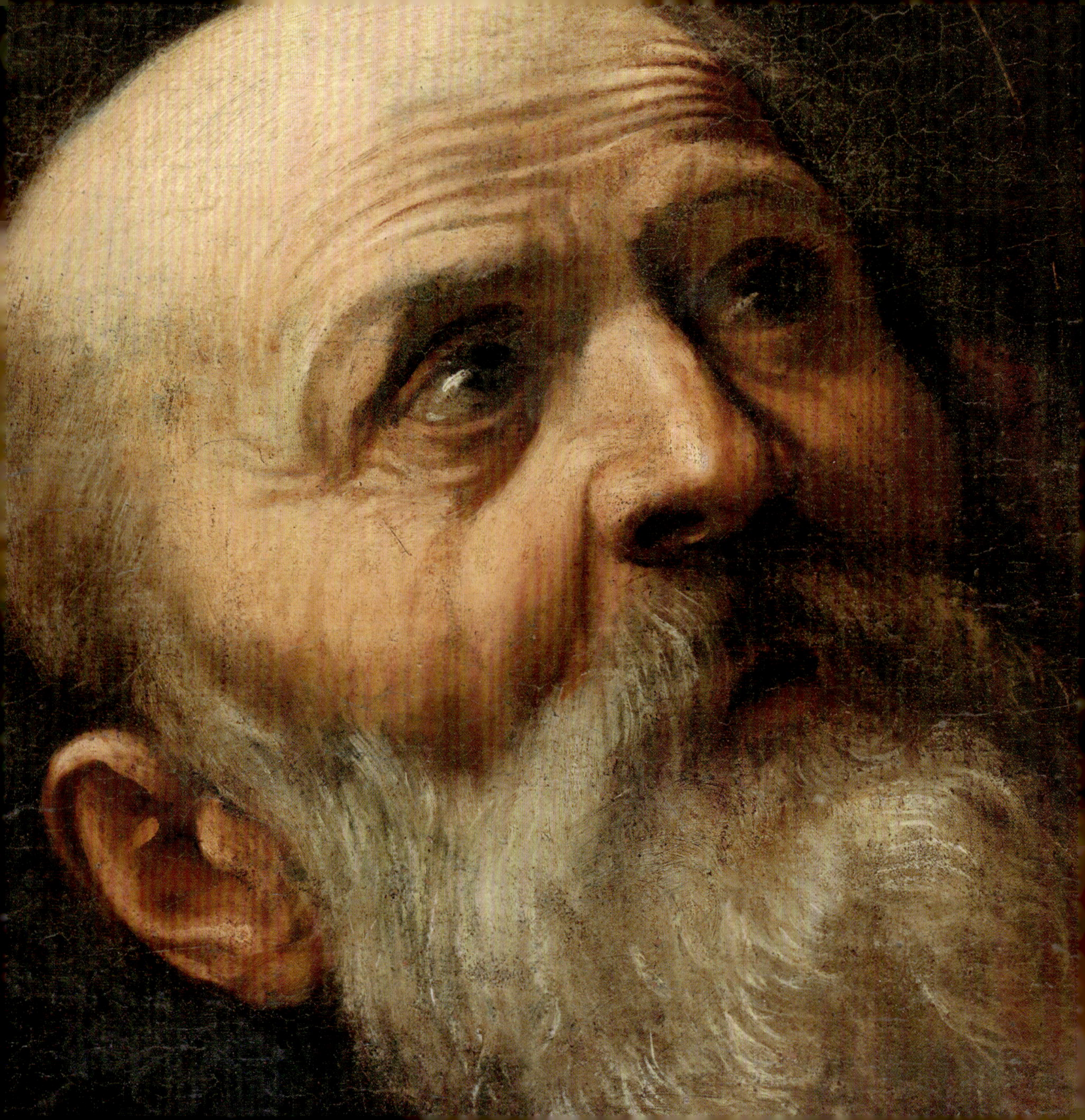

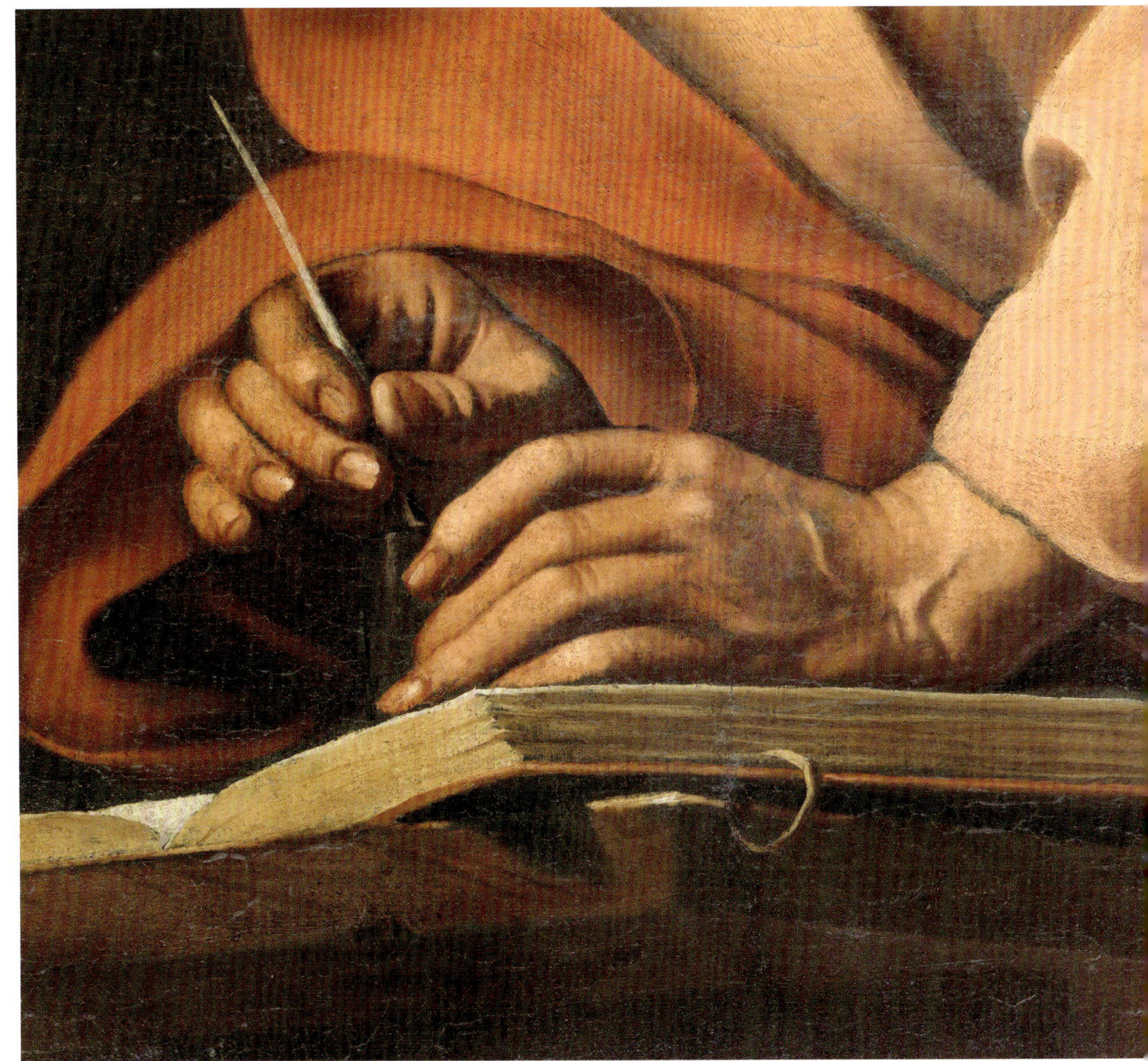

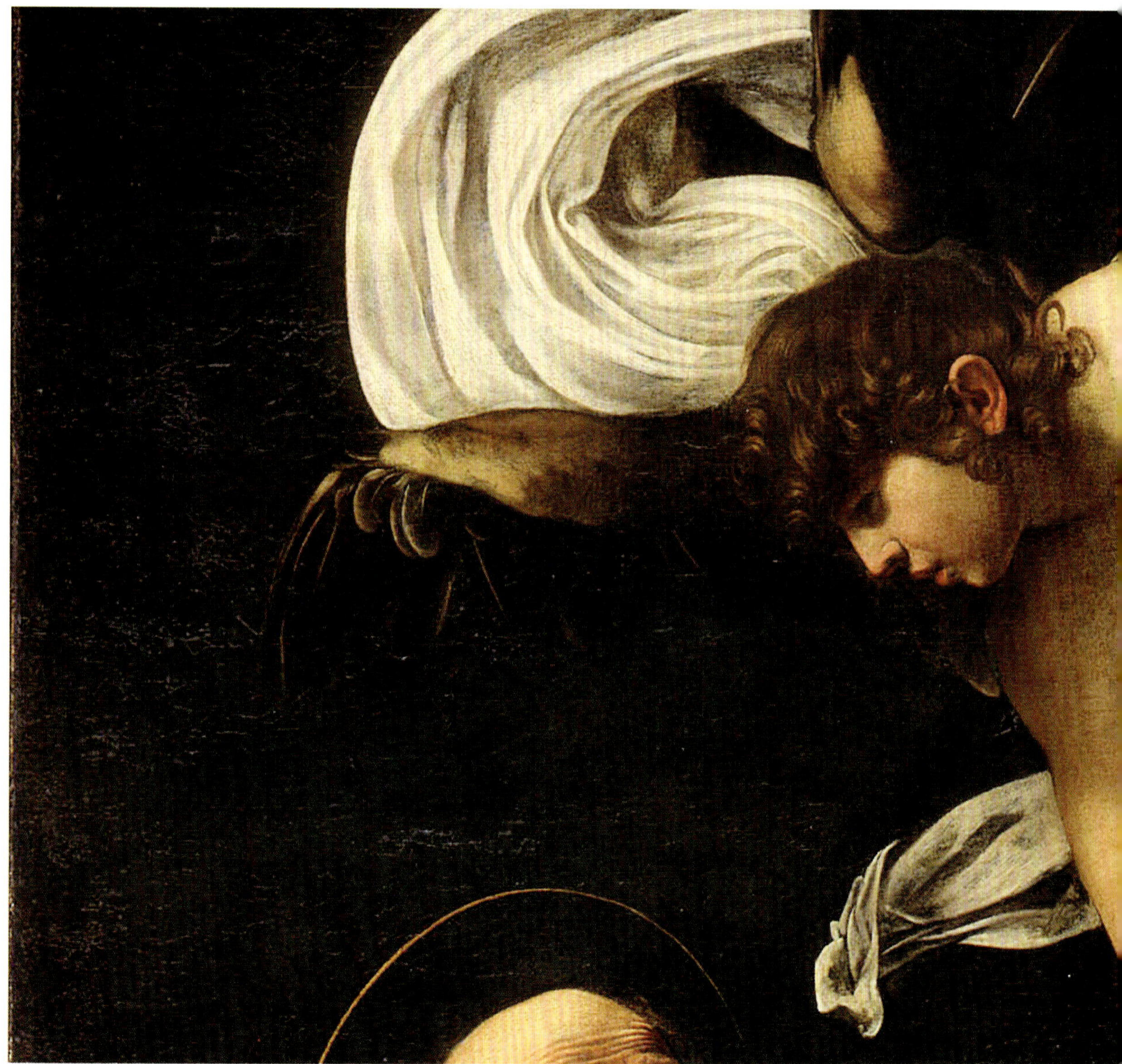

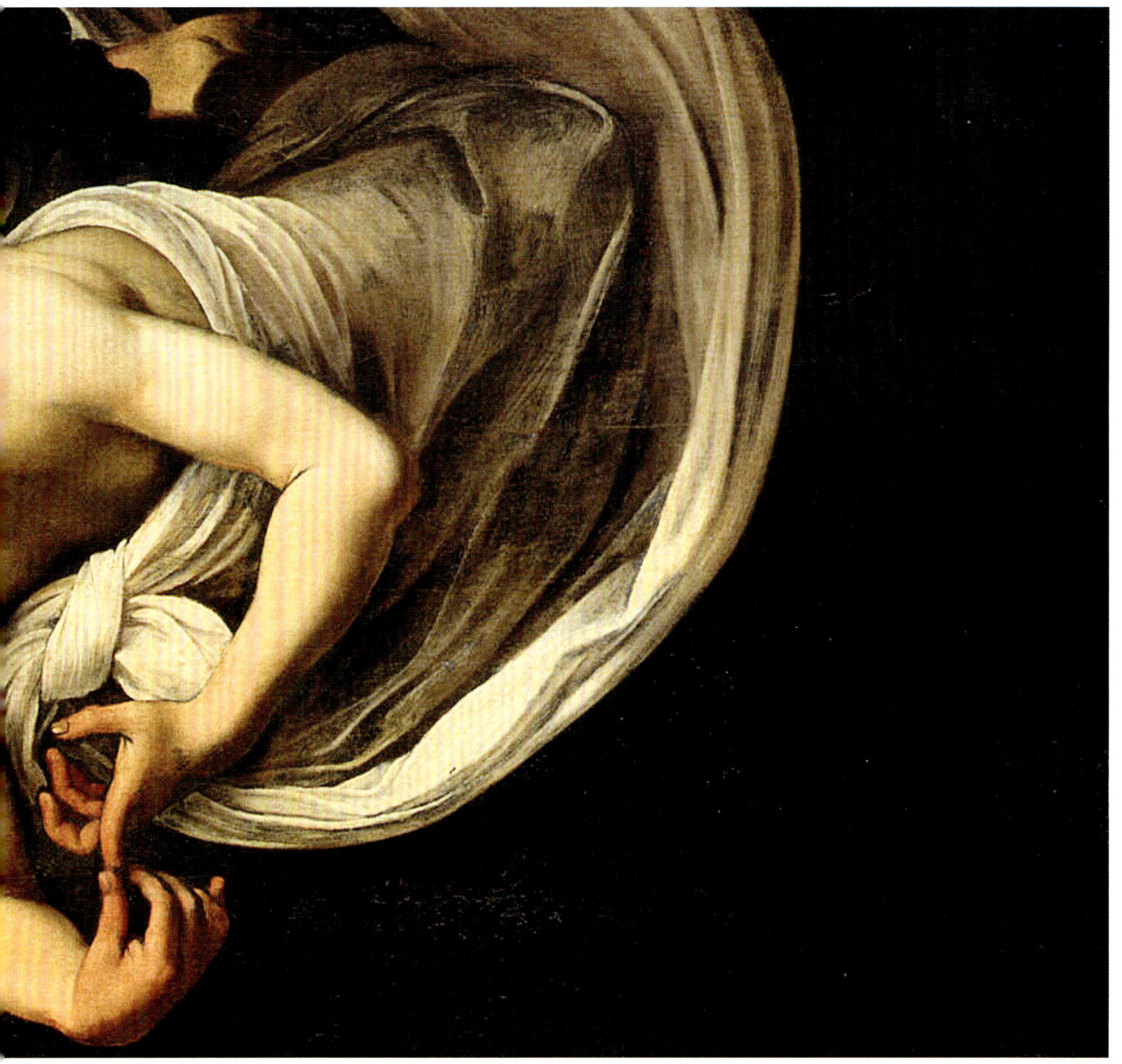

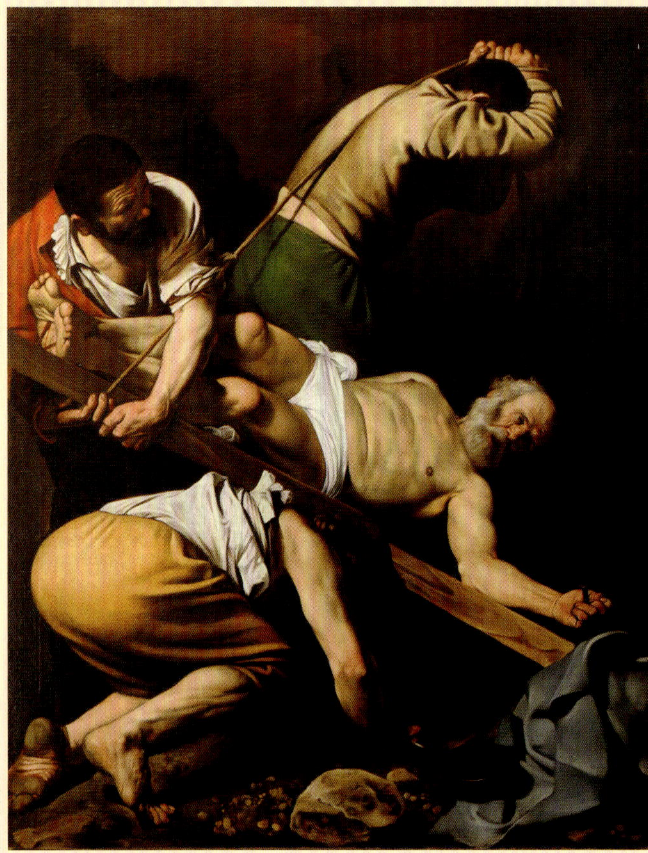

The Cappella Cerasi in Santa Maria del Popolo

The Conversion of St Paul and *The Crucifixion of St Peter* are in the same style as the Matthew paintings in the Cappella Contarelli. They were commissioned by the pope's treasurer general Tiberio Cerasi, who had also commissioned Bologna-born Annibale Carracci to paint the altarpiece for his

La chapelle Cerasi, à Santa Maria del Popolo

La Conversion de saint Paul et *Le Crucifiement de saint Pierre* suivent immédiatement – également sur le plan stylistique – le cycle de la chapelle Contarelli. Le commanditaire Tiberio Cerasi, trésorier général du Saint-Siège, avait commandé en même temps au Bolognais Annibal Carrache (1560–1609)

Die Cappella Cerasi in Santa Maria del Popolo

Die *Bekehrung des hl. Paulus* und die *Kreuzigung des hl. Petrus* folgen – auch stilistisch – unmittelbar auf den Zyklus der Cappella Contarelli. Ihr Auftraggeber, der päpstliche Generalschatzmeister Tiberio Cerasi, hatte gleichzeitig den Bologneser Annibale Carracci damit beauftragt, eine *Himmelfahrt*

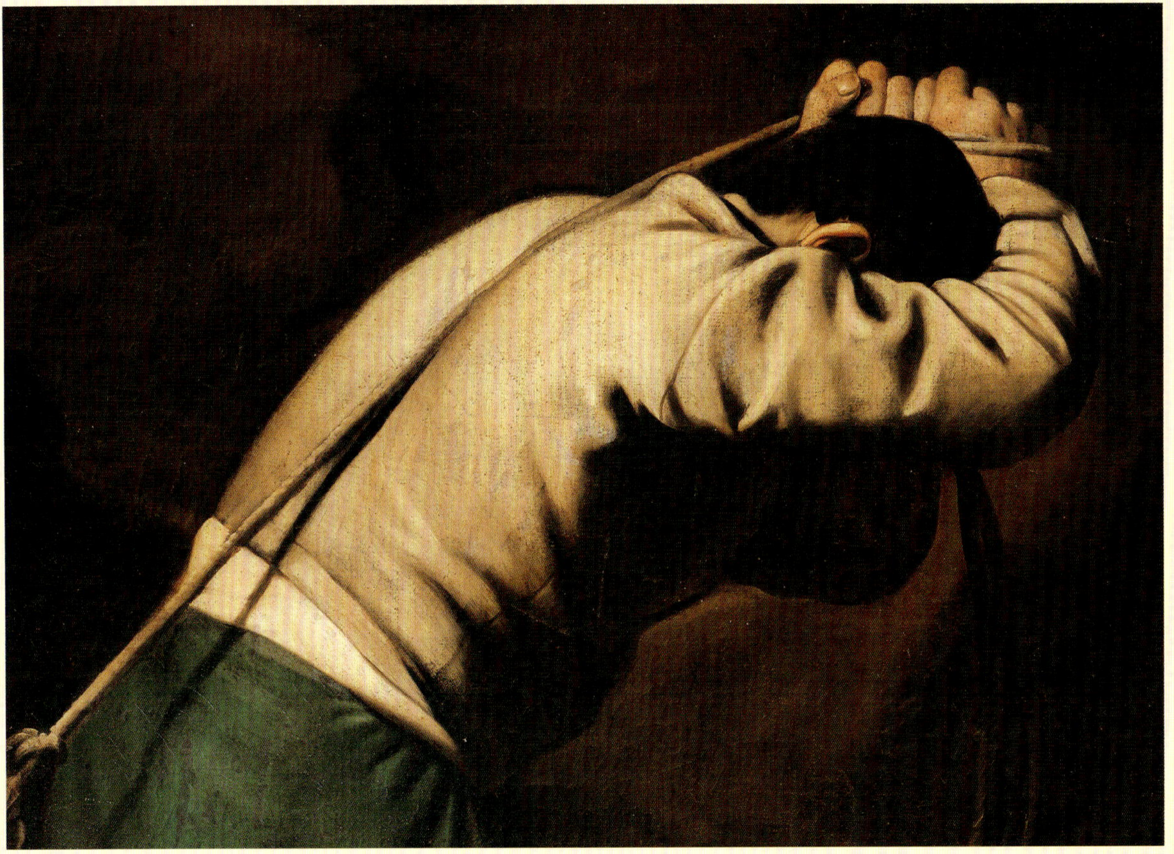

La Capilla Cerasi
en Santa María del Popolo

La vocación de San Pablo y *La crucifixión de San Pedro* constituyen la inmediata continuación –también estilística– del ciclo de la Capilla Contarelli. El encargo vino de la mano del tesorero general del papado Tiberio Cerasi, que había encargado a la vez a Annibale Carracci de Bolonia pintar una *Ascensión de María*

La Cappella Cerasi
a Santa Maria del Popolo

La *Conversione di San Paolo* e la *Crocefissione di San Pietro* seguono direttamente, anche dal punto di vista stilistico, al ciclo della Cappella Contarelli. Il loro committente, il tesoriere generale pontificio Tiberio Cerasi, aveva allo stesso tempo incaricato il bolognese Annibale Carracci della

De Cappella Cerasi
in de Santa Maria del Popolo

De bekering van de heilige Paulus en *De kruisiging van de heilige Petrus* worden – ook stilistisch – direct gevolgd door de cyclus in de Cappella Contarelli. De opdrachtgever, de pauselijke schatmeester Tiberio Cerasi, had tegelijkertijd de Bolognese schilder Annibale Carracci gevraagd om een

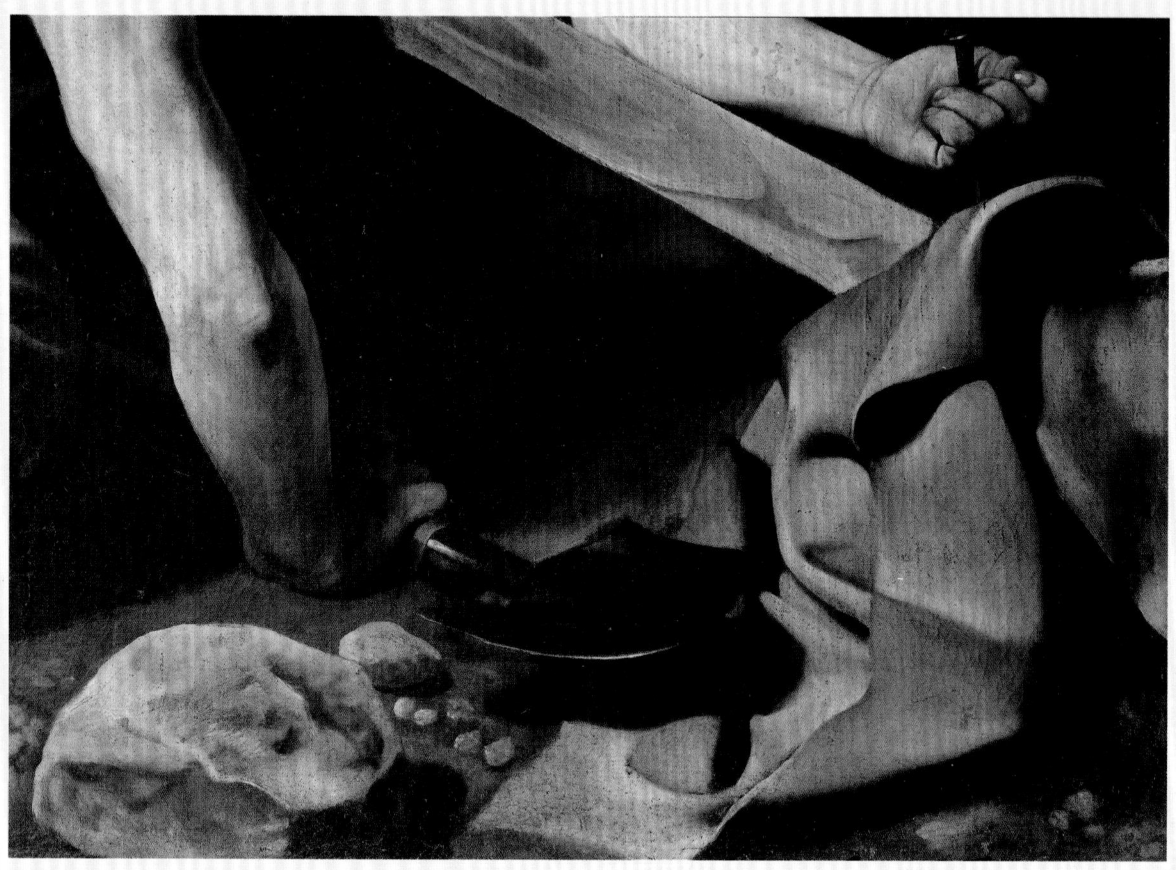

funeral chapel depicting the *Assumption of Mary* (c. 1600). Unlike Carracci's work, which received the client's approval, Cerasi rejected Caravaggio's pieces for the side walls and forced him to create a new version that was only finished after Cerasi's death in 1601 and installed in 1605.

le retable de sa chapelle funéraire, avec la représentation d'une *Assomption* (v. 1600). À la différence de l'œuvre de Carrache agréée par Cerasi, ce dernier refusa les panneaux latéraux imaginés par Caravage et lui imposa la réalisation d'une nouvelle version, qui ne fut terminée qu'après la mort de Cerasi (1601) et installée en 1605.

Mariens (ca. 1600) für den Altar seiner Begräbniskapelle anzufertigen. Anders als Carraccis Werk, das die Zustimmung des Auftraggebers gefunden hatte, lehnte Cerasi Caravaggios Werke für die Seitenwände ab und nötigte ihn zu einer neuen Version, die erst nach Cerasis Tod (1601) fertiggestellt und 1605 installiert wurde.

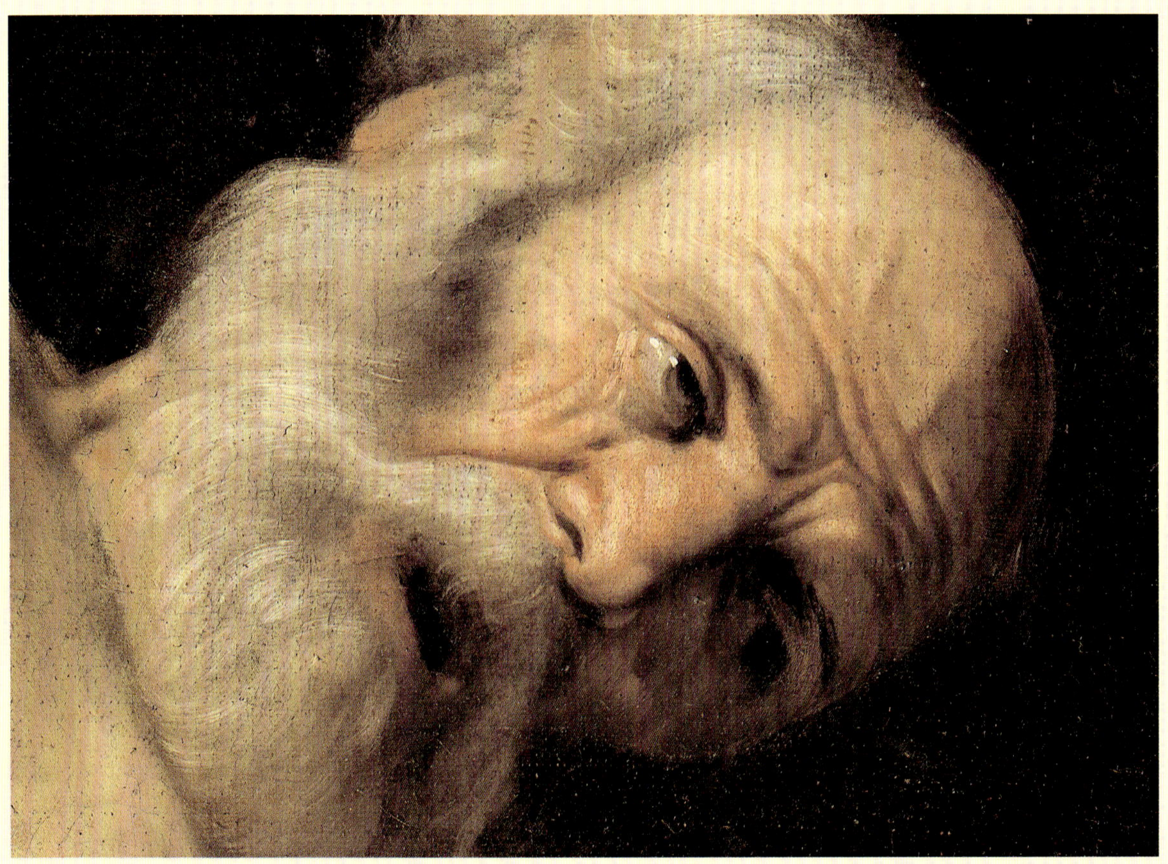

(ca. 1600) para su capilla ardiente. Si bien la obra de Carracci ganó la aprobación del cliente, Cerasi rechazó los trabajos de Caravaggio para los muros laterales y le invitó a realizar una nueva versión, que fue concluida e instalada en 1605, ya después de la muerte de Cerasi (1601).

rappresentazione di un'*Assunzione della Vergine* (1600 circa) per l'altare della sua cappella funebre. A differenza dell'opera di Carracci, che incontrò l'approvazione del committente, Cerasi respinse le opere di Caravaggio per le tele laterali e lo costrinse a crearne una nuova versione, che fu tuttavia completata solo dopo la morte di Cerasi (1601) e venne collocata nella cappella nel 1605.

Hemelvaart van Maria (ca. 1600) voor het altaar van zijn grafkapel te vervaardigen. Anders dan het werk van Carracci, dat Cerasi's goedkeuring kon wegdragen, wees de mecenas Caravaggio's werken voor de zijwanden af en vroeg hem nieuwe versies te maken, die pas na Cerasi's dood (1601) werden voltooid en in 1605 werden opgehangen.

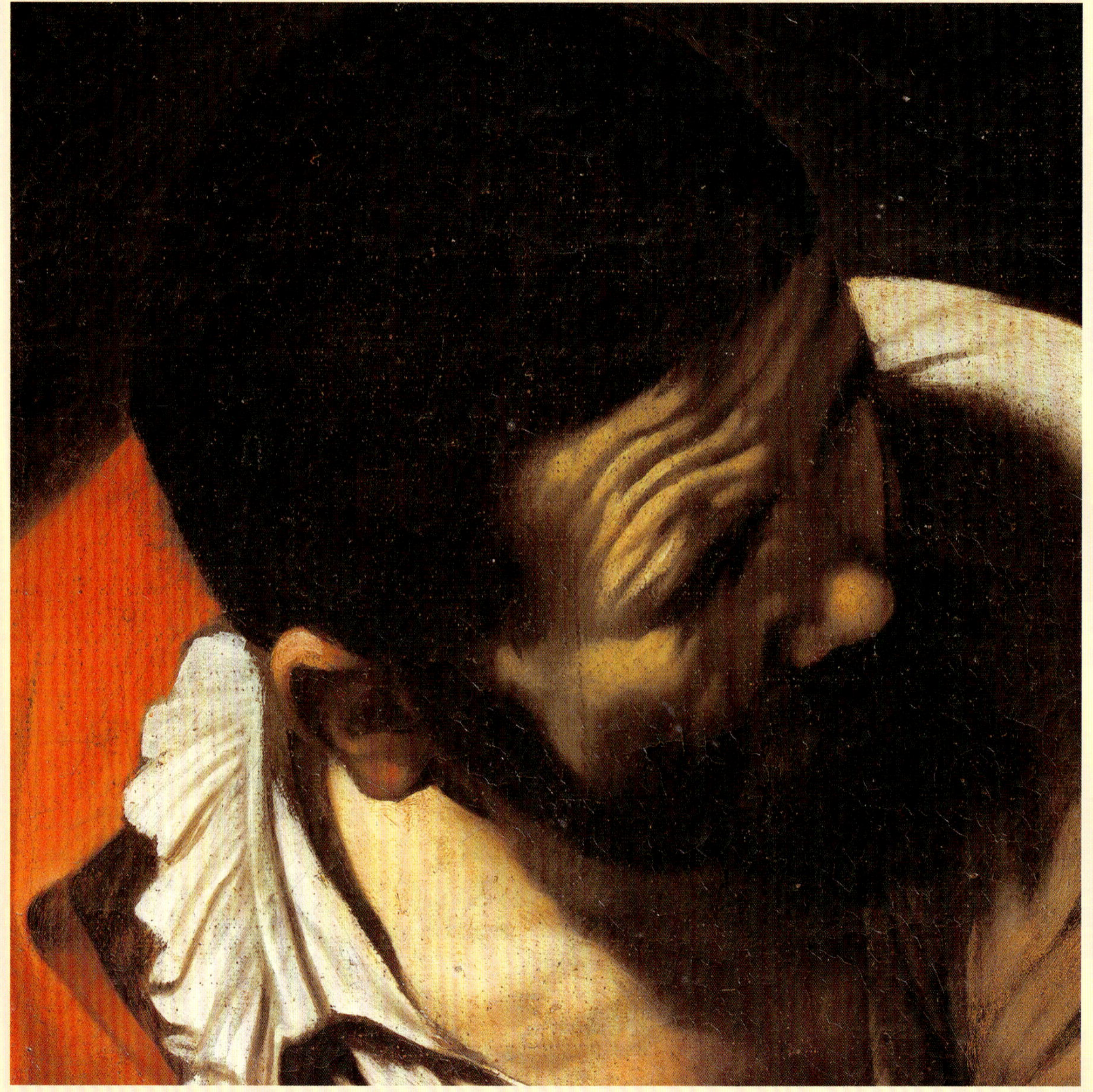

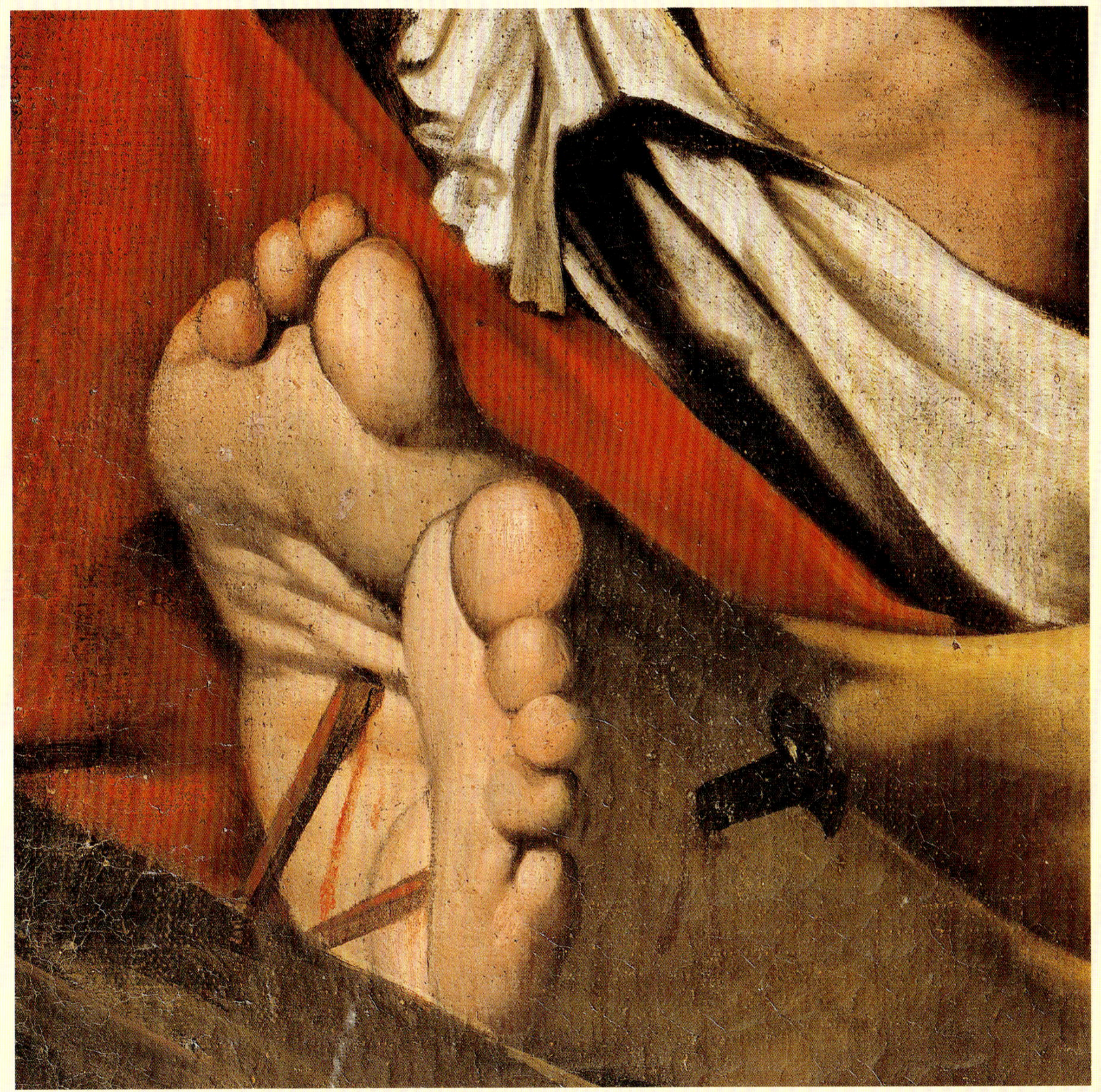

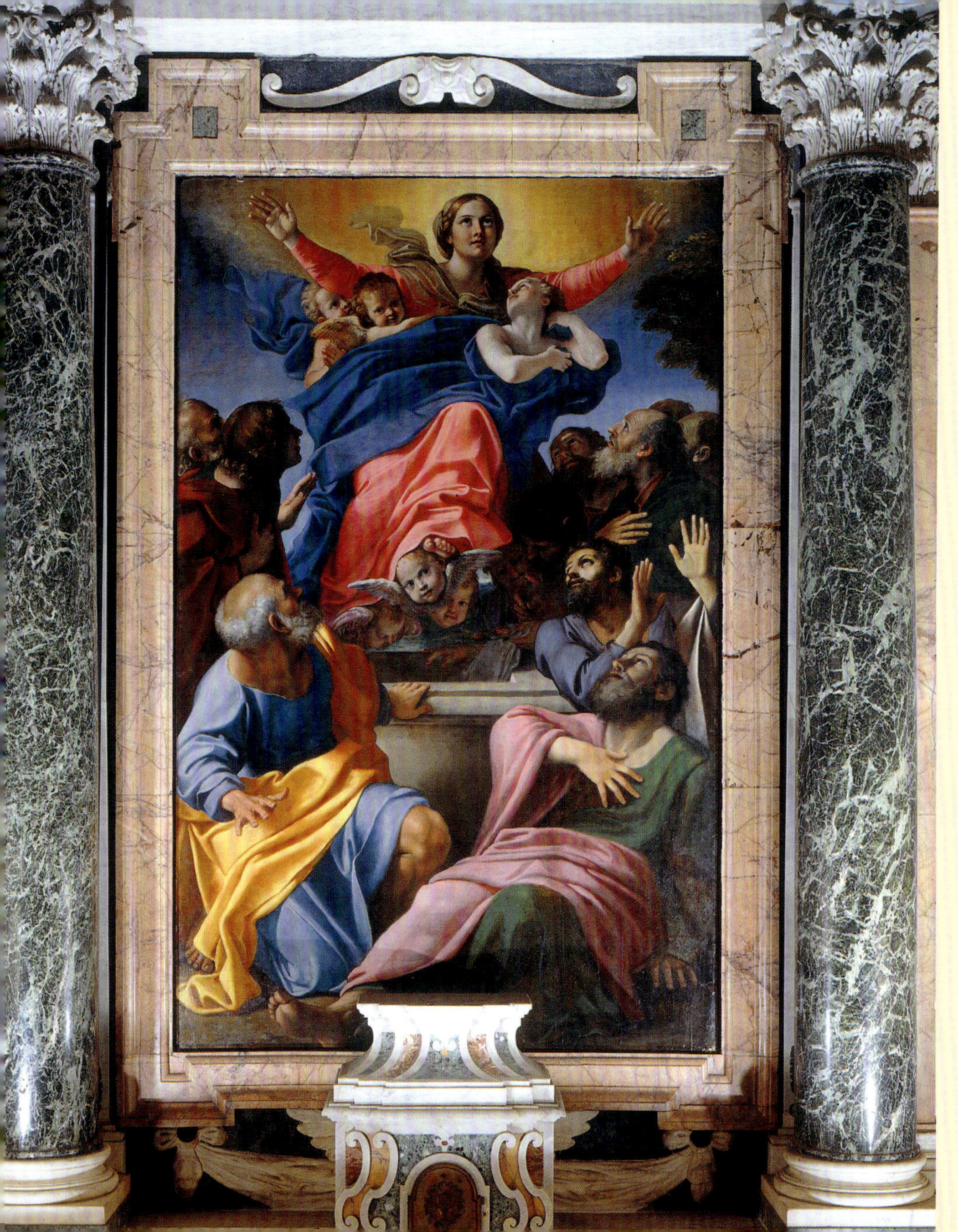

Annibale Carracci
(1560–1609)

**The Assumption
of Mary**

**L'Assomption
de la Vierge**

Himmelfahrt Mariens

La ascensión de María

**Assunzione
della Vergine**

**De hemelvaart
van Maria**

*c. 1600, Oil on canvas/
Huile sur toile,
245 × 155 cm, Basilica di
Santa Maria del Popolo,
Roma*

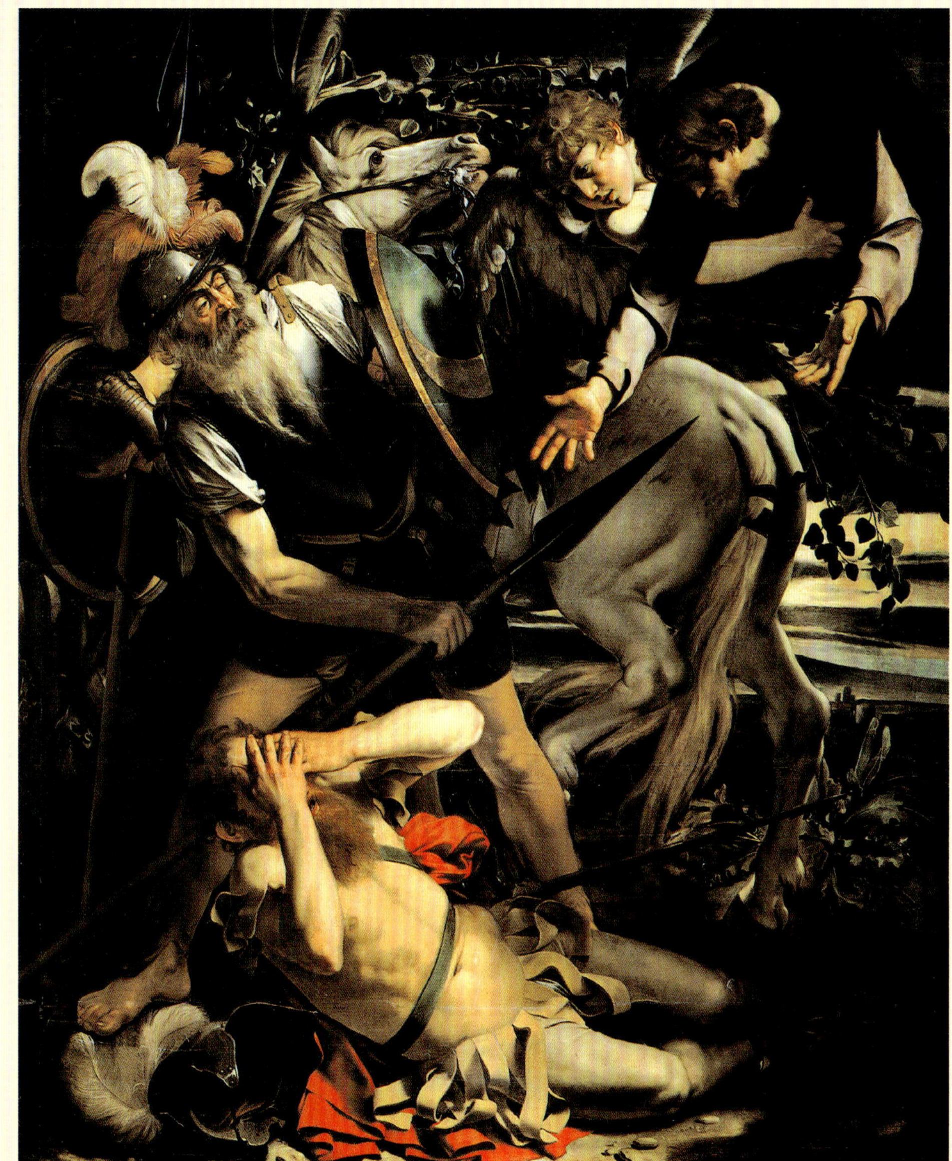

The Conversion of Paul
(first, rejected version)

*La Conversion de saint
Paul* **(première version)**

Bekehrung des Paulus
**(erste, abgelehnte
Fassung)**

*La conversión de
San Pablo* **(primera
versión, rechazada)**

*Conversione di
San Paolo* **(prima
versione respinta)**

*De bekering van
Paulus* **(eerste,
afgewezen versie)**

*c. 1599–1600, Oil on
wood/Huile sur bois,
237 × 189 cm, Palazzo
Chigi-Odescalchi, Roma*

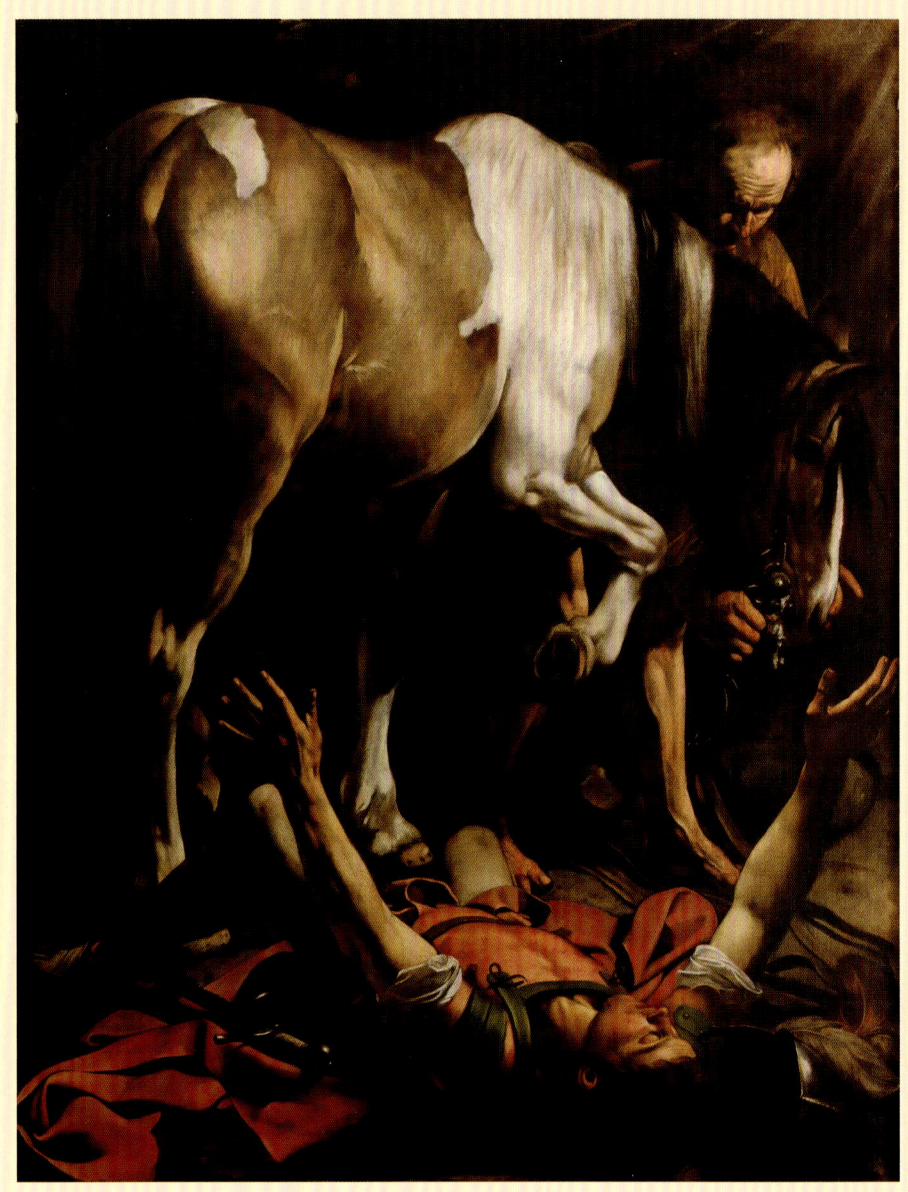

The Conversion of Paul

*La Conversion de saint Paul
sur le chemin de Damas*

Bekehrung des Paulus

La conversión de San Pablo

Conversione di San Paolo

De bekering van Paulus

*c. 1604, Oil on canvas/Huile sur
toile, 230 × 175 cm, Basilica di
Santa Maria del Popolo, Roma*

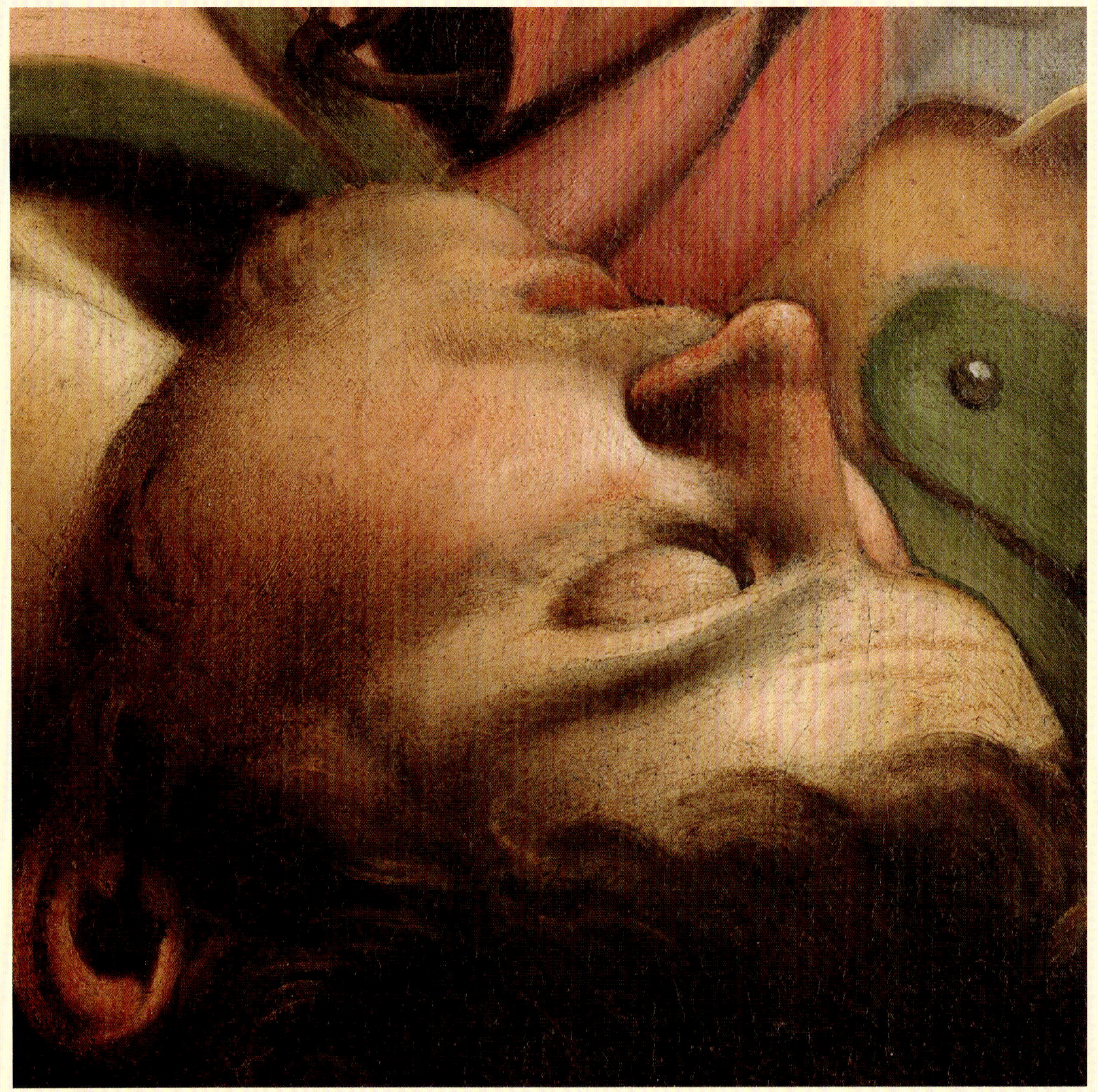

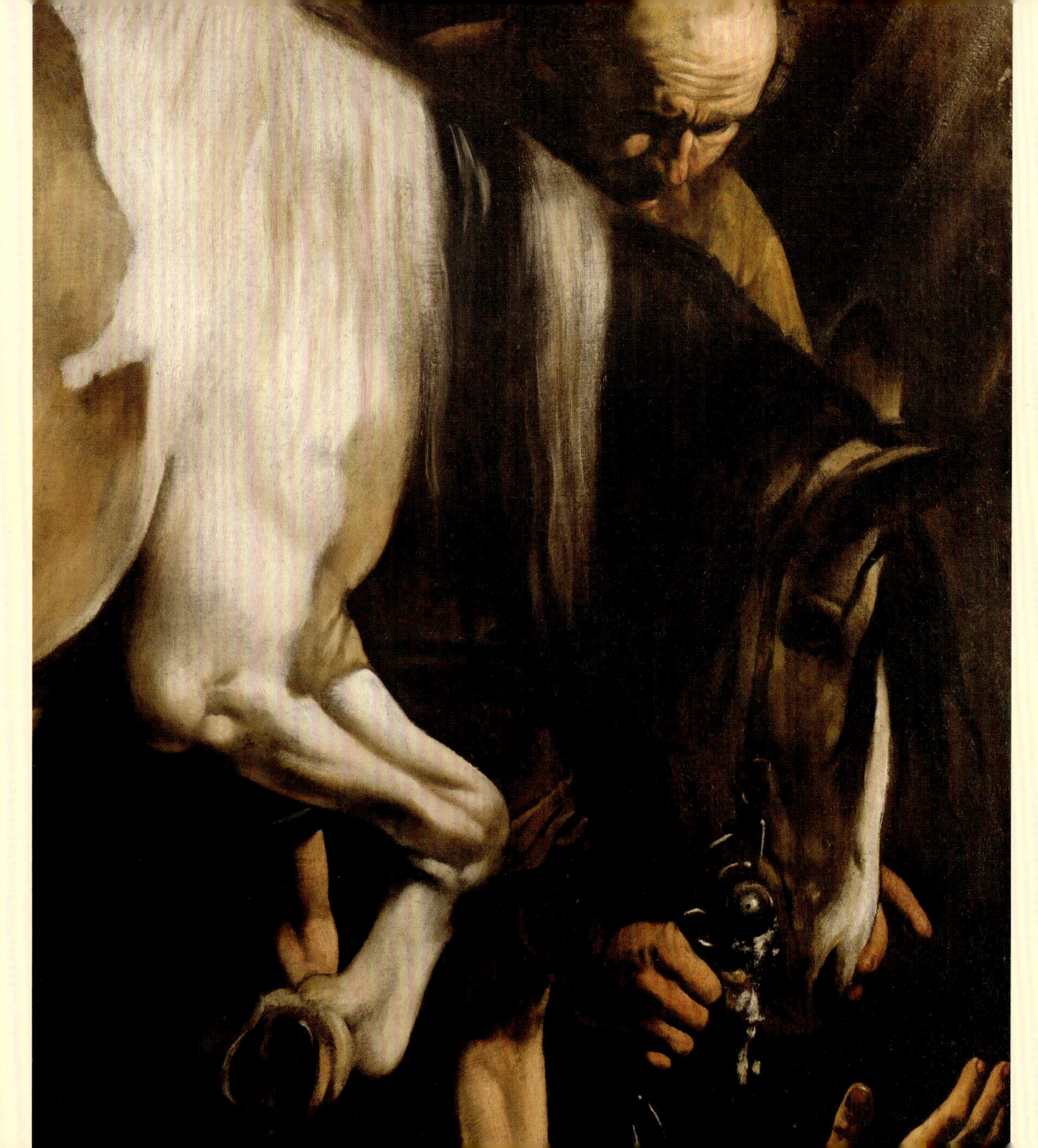

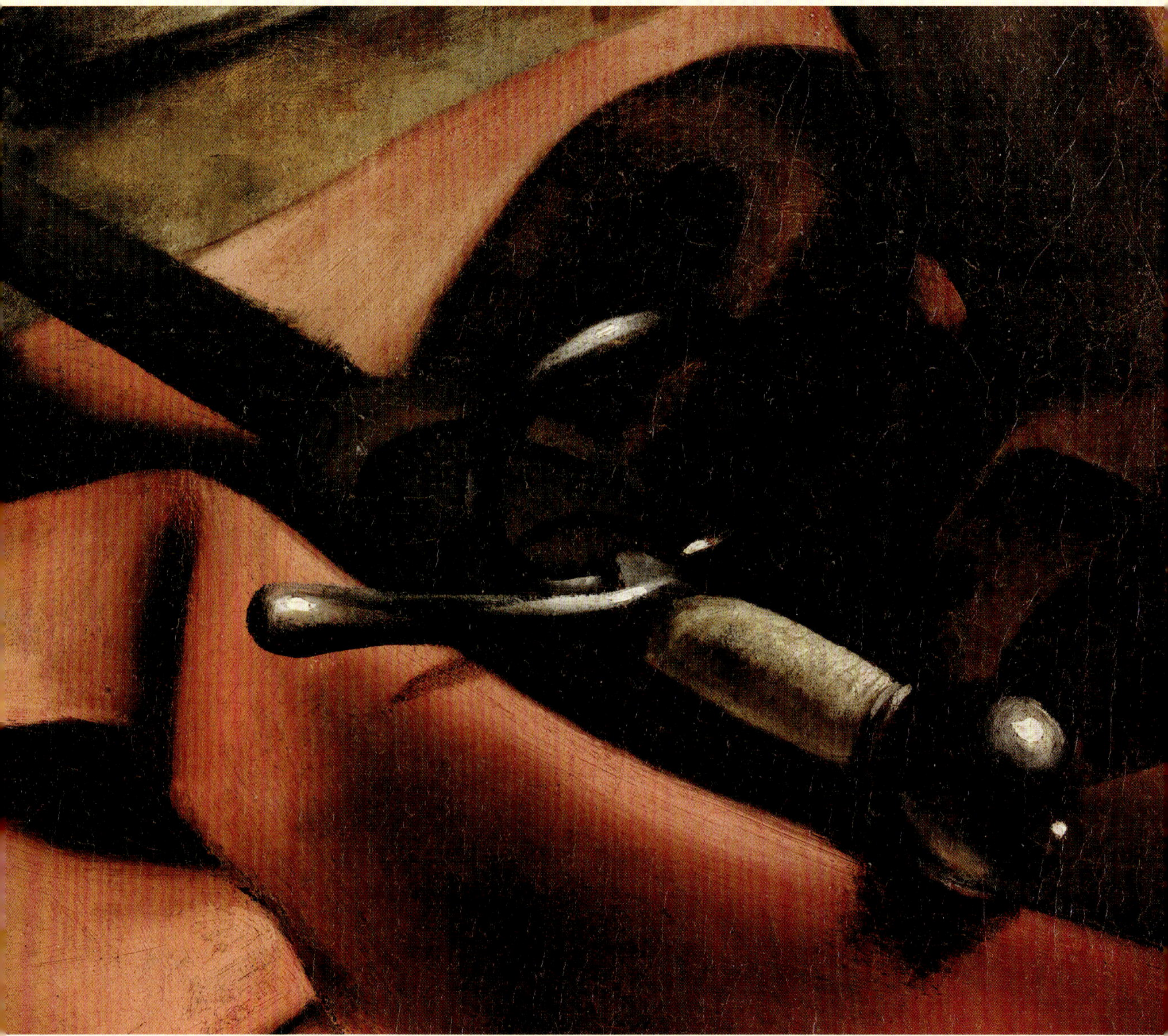

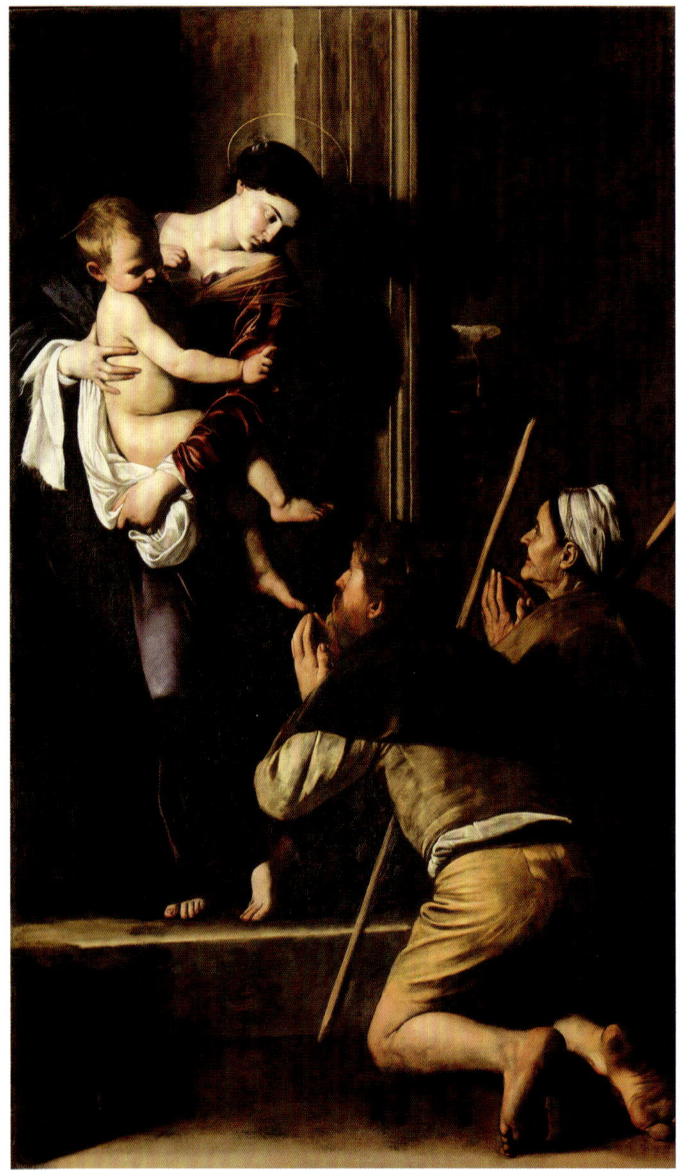

Madonna di Loreto or **The Pilgrims' Madonna**

La Madone des pèlerins ou **La Vierge de Lorette**

Madonna di Loreto oder **Madonna der Pilger**

Madonna de Loreto o **Madonna de los peregrinos**

Madonna di Loreto o **Madonna dei pellegrini**

Madonna di Loreto of **Madonna van de pelgrims**

*1604/05, Oil on canvas/Huile sur toile, 260 × 150 cm,
Chiesa Sant'Agostino, Roma*

The so-called *Pilgrim's Madonna* was created for chapel of the
Santa Casa in the central Italian town of Loreto. This Virgin
radiates an extraordinary humanity, which earned her the
ridicule of critics and the veneration of ordinary believers.

La Madone des pèlerins célébrant la Vierge de Lorette – objet
d'un pèlerinage très populaire – rayonne d'une humanité
extraordinaire, ce qui lui valut en son temps les moqueries
de la critique et la vénération des simples fidèles.

Die sogenannte *Madonna der Pilger* für die Kapelle der
Santa Casa des mittelitalienischen Pilgerortes Loreto
strahlt außergewöhnliche Menschlichkeit aus – was ihr
bei den Kritikern Spott und bei den einfachen Gläubigen
Verehrung einbrachte.

La conocida como *Madonna de los peregrinos* realizada para
la Capilla de la Santa Casa, en el lugar de peregrinación
medieval Loreto, irradia una humanidad extraordinaria, lo
que le cosechó el escarnio de los críticos y la admiración de
los sencillos creyentes.

La cosiddetta *Madonna dei Pellegrini* dipinta per la cappella
della Santa Casa di Loreto, meta di pellegrinaggio sita
nel centro Italia, emana una straordinaria umanità che le
valse il biasimo delle cerchie di critici e l'ammirazione dei
credenti comuni.

De *Madonna van de pelgrims* voor de kapel van de Santa
Casa in het Centraal-Italiaanse pelgrimsoord Loreto straalt
een bijzondere menselijkheid uit – wat de schilder bij critici
op spot en bij het gewone publiek op bewondering kwam
te staan.

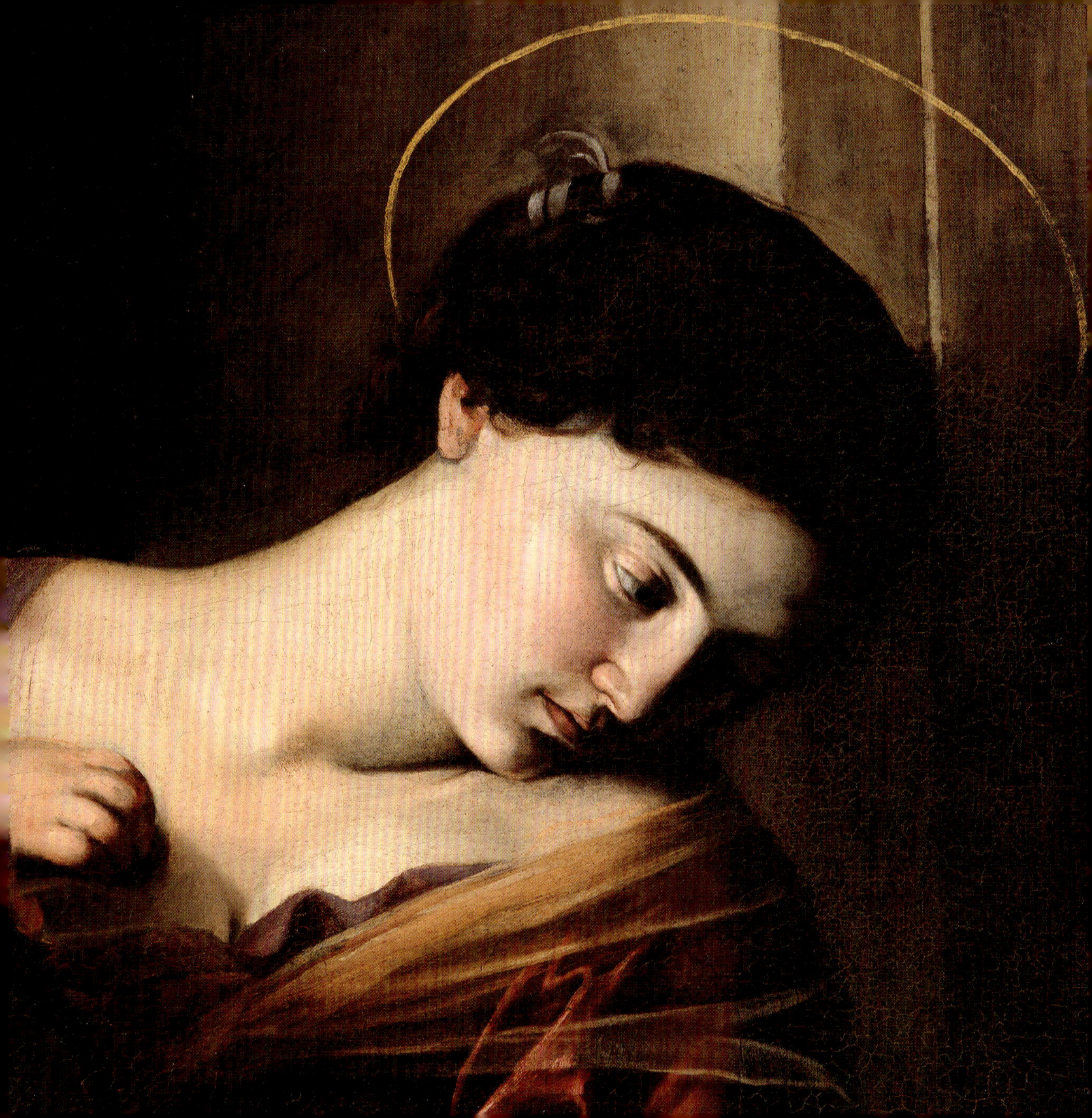

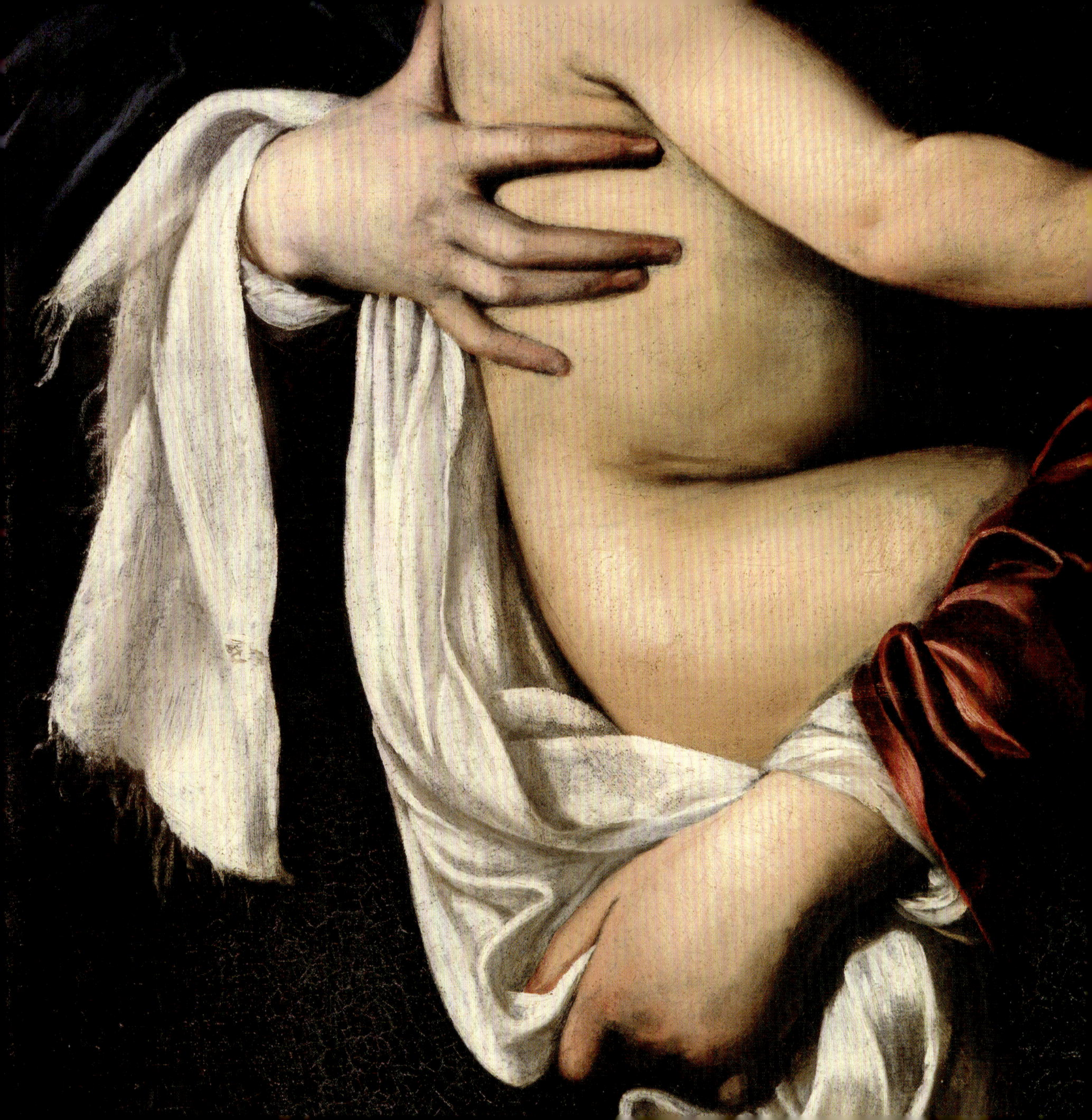

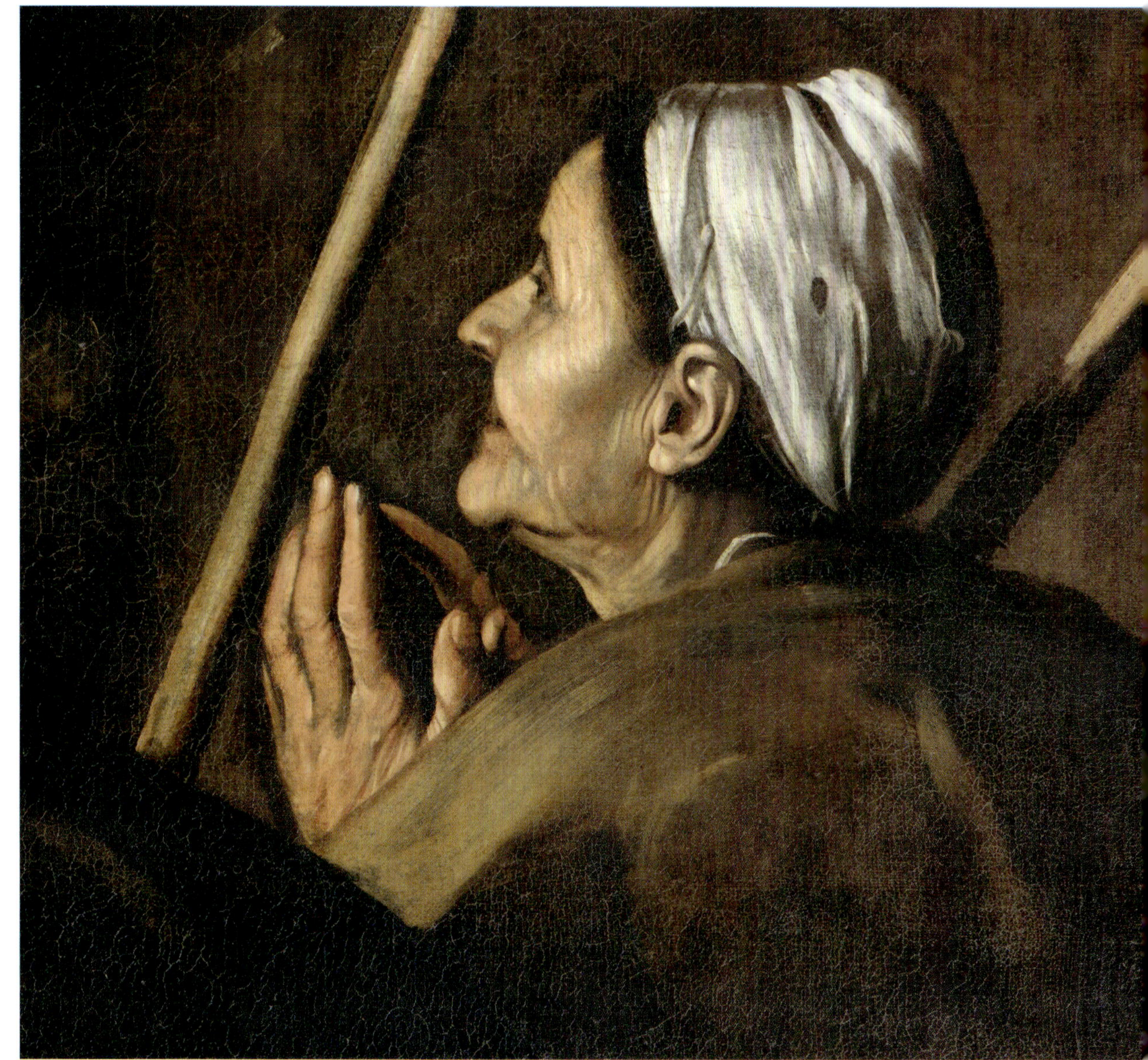

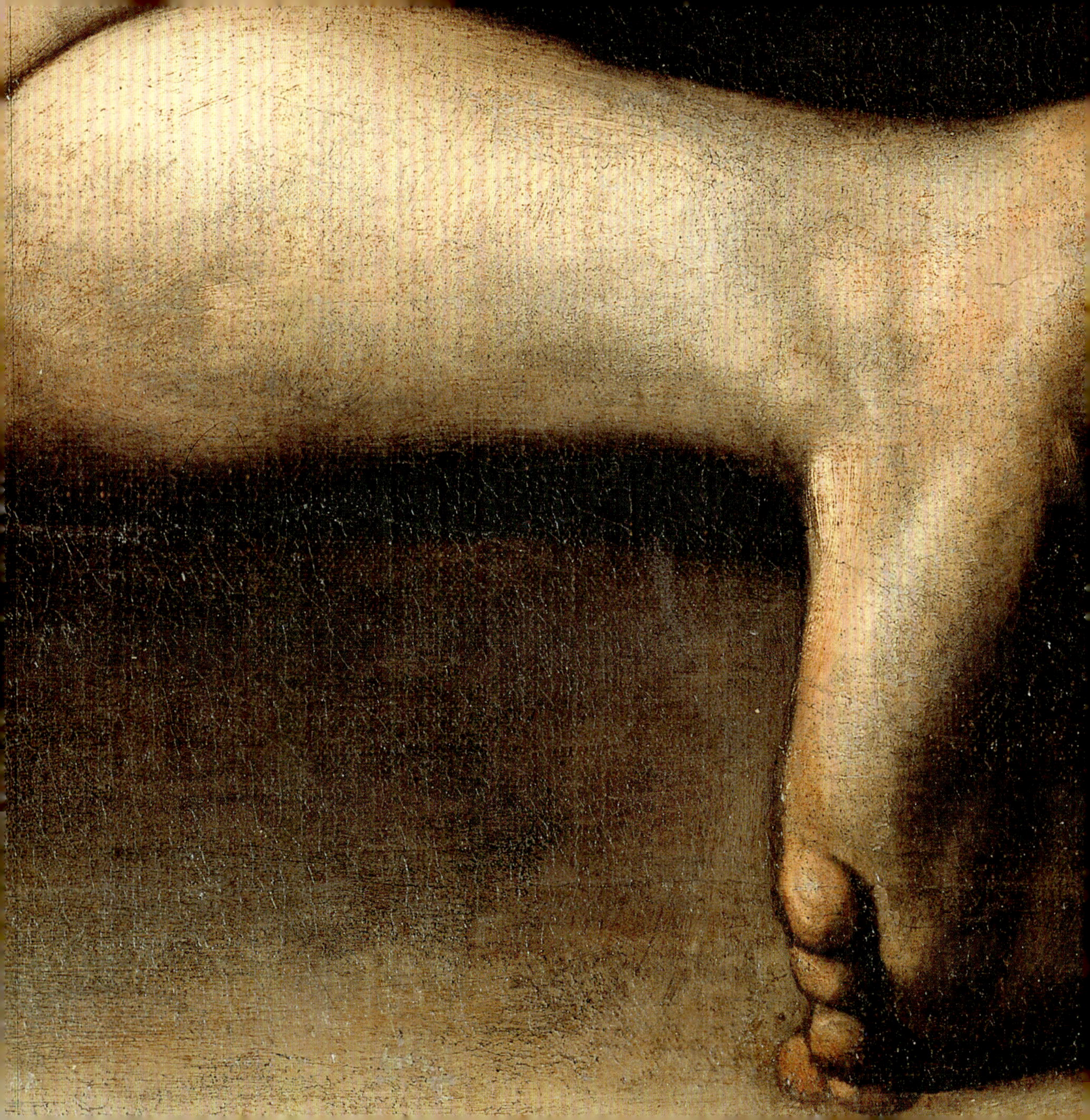

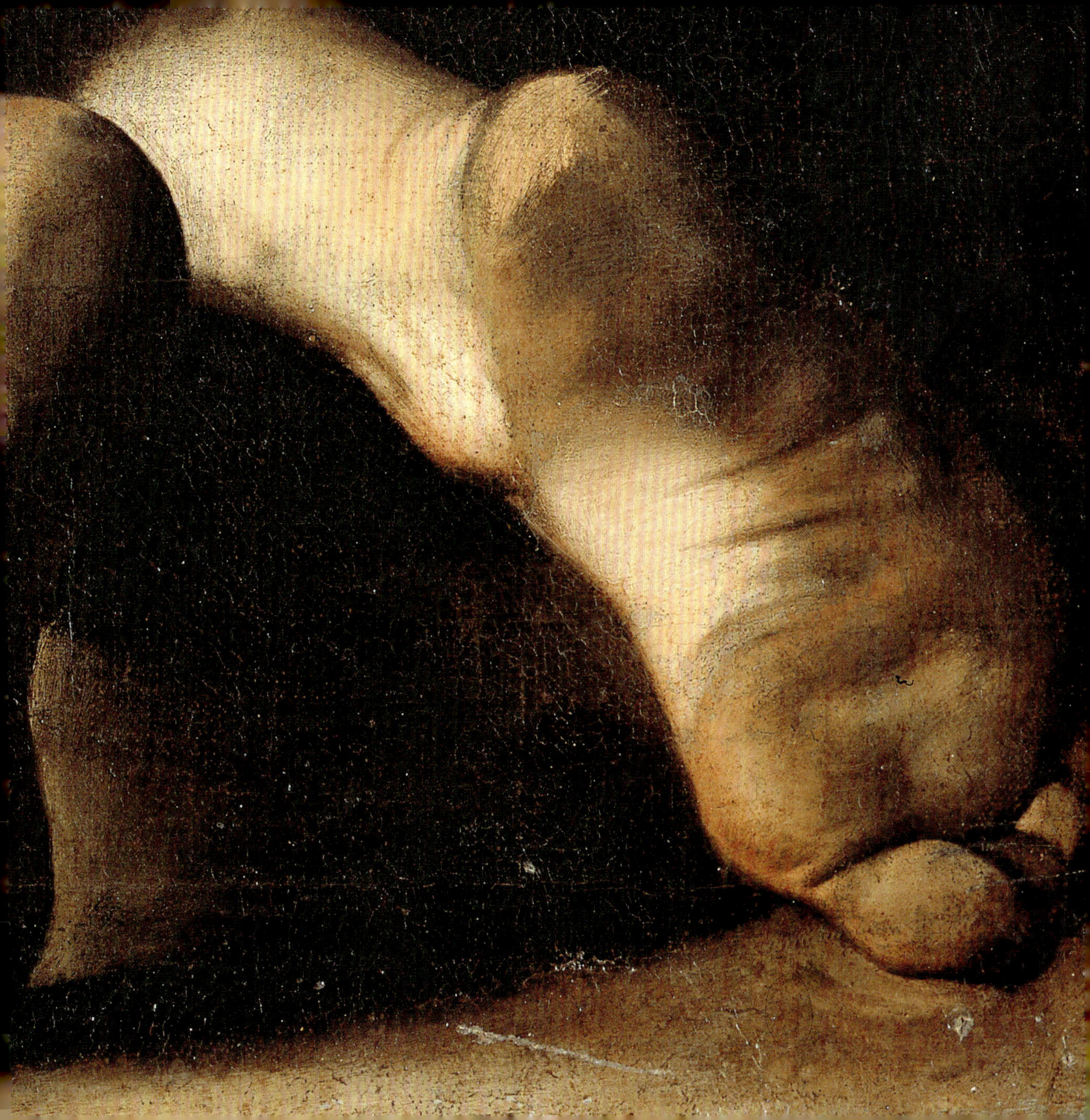

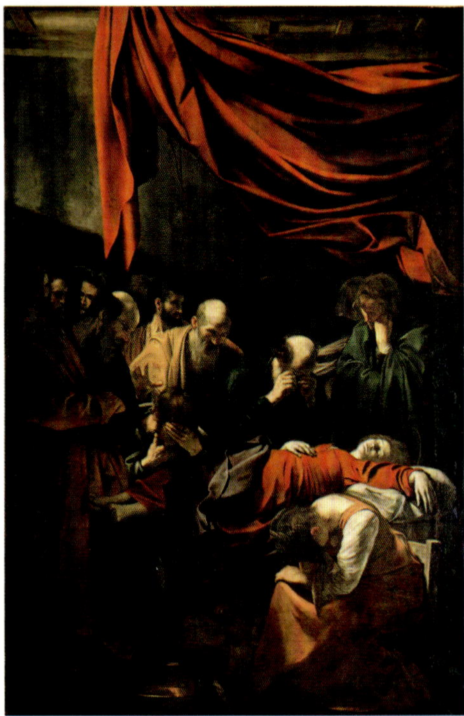

1605/06, Oil on canvas/Huile sur toile, 369 × 245 cm, Musée du Louvre, Paris

Later Roman commissions

Although Caravaggio had powerful clients such as the Marchese Vincenzo Giustiniani and Cardinal Scipione Borghese who helped him with his problems with the law, he continually got in trouble and had to flee to Genoa for a few weeks in 1604. His *Death of the Virgin* triggered further scandals. Caravaggio was accused of having used a prostitute as a model and that the flesh tones of Mary were too close to those of a real dead woman.

Travaux romains tardifs

Malgré de puissants protecteurs comme le marquis Vincenzo Giustiniani et le cardinal Scipion Borghèse, qui l'aidaient aussi dans ses démêlés avec la justice, Caravage eut des ennuis réitérés et dut se réfugier à Gênes quelques semaines, en 1604. *La Mort de la Vierge* fut l'occasion d'un nouveau scandale : on reprocha à Caravage d'avoir pris comme modèle une courtisane, mais on blâma aussi la carnation trop réaliste du corps sans vie de Marie.

Späte römische Aufträge

Obwohl Caravaggio mächtige Auftraggeber hatte, wie den Marchese Vincenzo Giustiniani und den Kardinal Scipione Borghese, die ihm auch bei Problemen mit der Justiz halfen, geriet er mit dem Gesetz immer wieder in Konflikt und musste 1604 für einige Wochen nach Genua fliehen. Auch der *Tod der Jungfrau* löste wieder Skandale aus. Man warf Caravaggio vor, eine Dirne als Modell gewählt zu haben und das Inkarnat der Maria ähnele zu realistisch dem einer Toten.

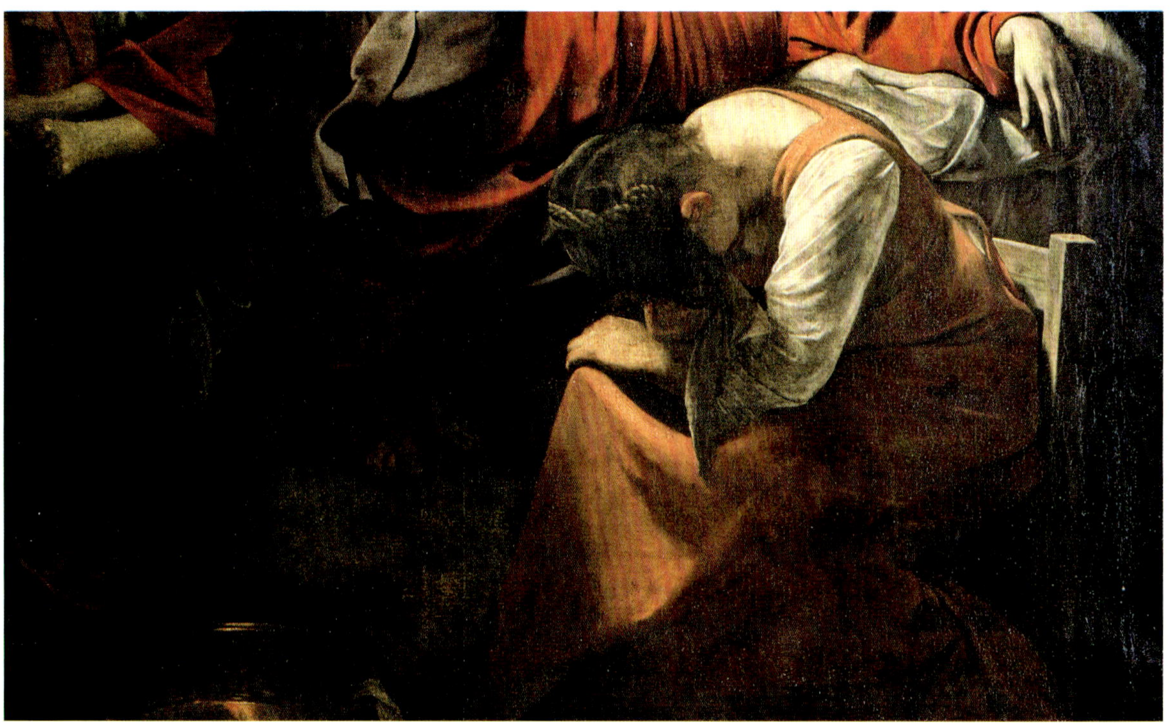

Los encargos romanos tardíos

Si bien Caravaggio tenía clientes poderosos, como el marqués Vincenzo Giustiniani y el Cardenal Scipione Borghese, que también le ayudaban en sus problemas con la justicia, siguió teniendo conflictos con la ley que le llevaron a tener que ausentarse a Génova varias semanas en 1604. También la *Muerte de la Virgen* estuvo rodeada por el escándalo. Se recriminaba a Caravaggio haber escogido a una prostituta como modelo, y que la representación de María se acercaría de manera demasiado realista a la de una muerta.

Le commissioni romane più tarde

Sebbene avesse potenti committenti, come il marchese Vincenzo Giustiniani e il cardinale Scipione Borghese, che lo aiutarono con i suoi problemi con la giustizia, Caravaggio ebbe un nuovo guaio con la legge e nel 1604 dovette fuggire per alcune settimane a Genova. Anche la *Morte della Vergine* tornò a creare uno scandalo, in quanto si rimproverava a Caravaggio di aver scelto una prostituta come modello e di aver dipinto l'incarnato di Maria in modo troppo realistico e simile a quello di un morto.

Late Romeinse opdrachten

Hoewel Caravaggio invloedrijke opdrachtgevers had, onder wie markies Vincenzo Giustiniani en kardinaal Scipione Borghese (die hem ook bij zijn conflicten met de wet hielp), raakte Caravaggio steeds opnieuw in de problemen en moest in 1604 enkele weken naar Genua vluchten. Ook *De dood van de Maagd* lokte een schandaal uit, omdat men Caravaggio verweet een prostituee als model te hebben gekozen en omdat de huidskleur van Maria te veel aan die van een lijk deed denken.

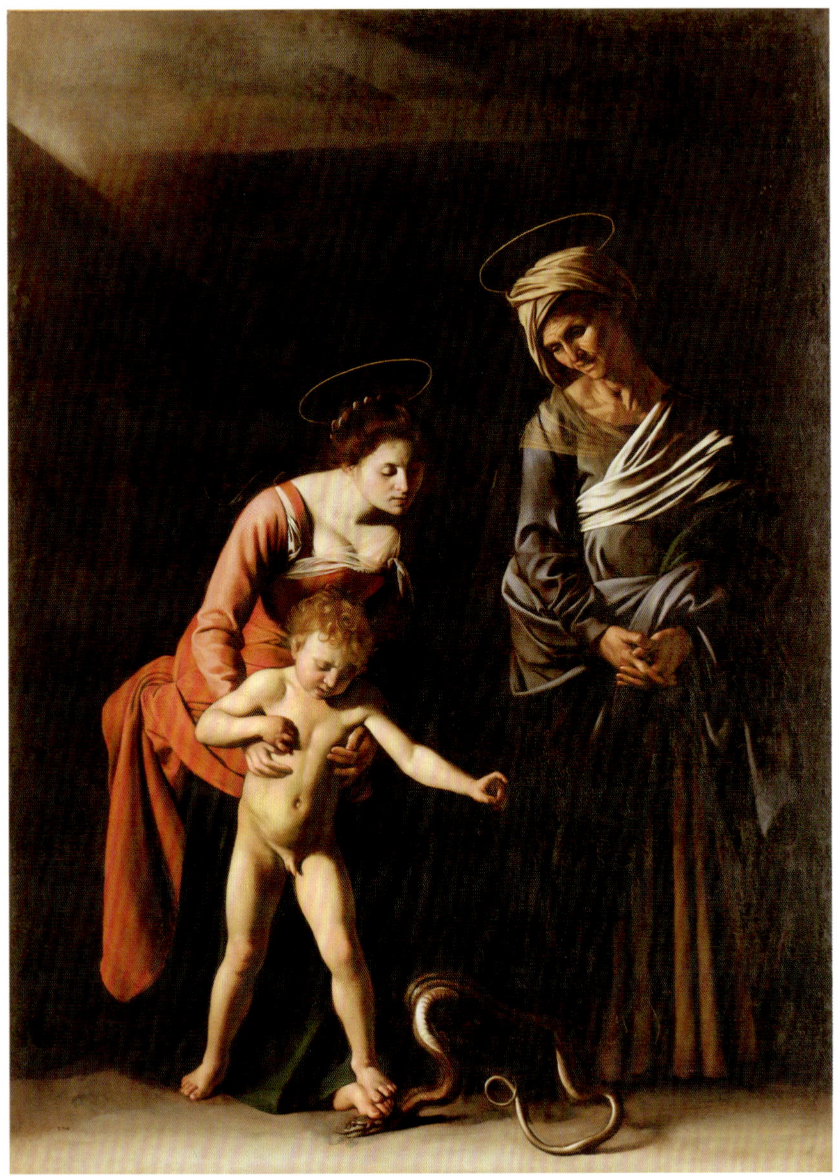

Madonna dei Palafrenieri or *Madonna with Snake*

La Madone des palefreniers ou *La Madone au serpent*

Madonna dei Palafrenieri oder *Madonna mit der Schlange*

Madonna con el niño y Santa Ana o *Madonna de los palafreneros*

Madonna dei Palafrenieri o *Madonna della Serpe*

Madonna dei Palafrenieri of *Madonna met de slang*

1605/06, Oil on canvas/Huile sur toile, 292 × 211 cm, Galleria Borghese, Roma

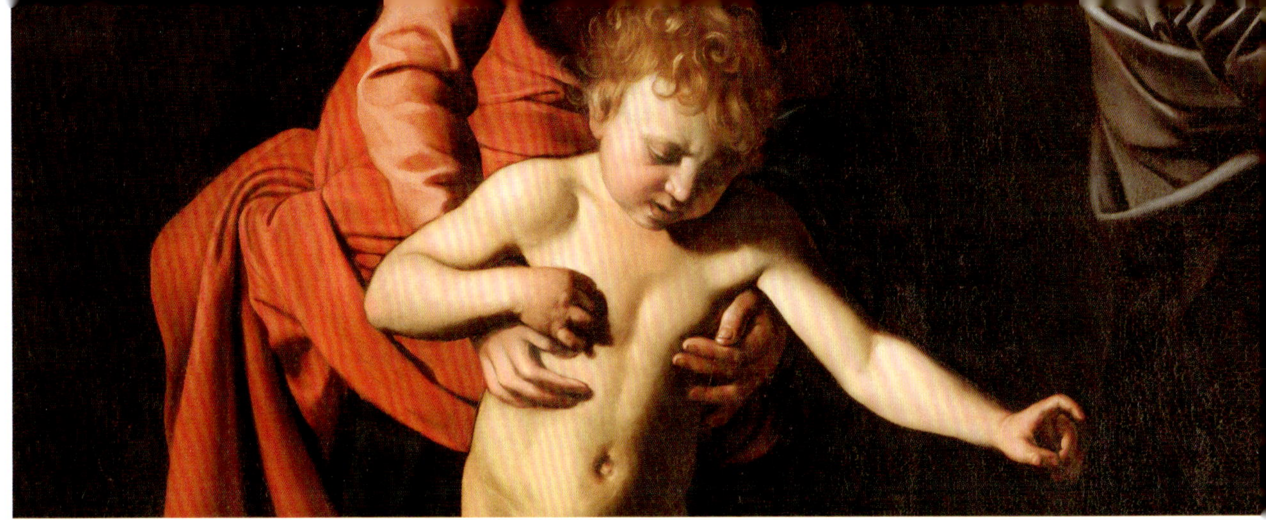

In 1605, Caravaggio finally received a long-coveted commission from the Vatican: the Brotherhood of the Palafrenieri commissioned a painting for St Peter's Basilica. What should have been the high point of his career ended in a catastrophe, however. Caravaggio's realistic depiction of the Virgin Mary, crushing the head of the snake, symbolizing original sin, with the help of the Infant Jesus went too far for the clients. They did not find an allegory of such an important doctrine compatible with the natural nakedness of the Infant Jesus, the almost humiliating depiction of St Anne as an old grandmother, let alone the fact that allegedly a notorious prostitute had once again posed for this portrait of Mary.

En 1605, Caravage obtint du Vatican la commande attendue : un retable pour la chapelle de l'archiconfraternité des Palefreniers, à Saint-Pierre-de-Rome. Mais ce qui aurait pu être l'apogée de sa carrière aboutit à une catastrophe. La représentation de la Vierge écrasant avec l'aide de l'Enfant Jésus un serpent symbole du péché originel allait trop loin dans son réalisme profane (non pour les destinataires mais pour les cardinaux de la fabrique). Une allégorie religieusement si importante n'était compatible ni avec la nudité naturelle d'un Jésus enfant, ni avec la vieillesse presque humiliante de sainte Anne – pour ne rien dire du modèle choisi pour la représentation de la Vierge : une courtisane connue à Rome.

1605 erhielt Caravaggio endlich den ersehnten Auftrag aus dem Vatikan: Die Bruderschaft der Palafrenieri bestellte ein Gemälde für den Petersdom. Was der Höhepunkt seiner Karriere hätte sein können, endete in einer Katastrophe. Caravaggios Darstellung der Gottesmutter, die mit der Hilfe des Jesuskindes der Schlange, dem Sinnbild der Erbsünde, den Kopf zerdrückt, ging den Auftraggebern in ihrem profanen Realismus zu weit. Eine Allegorie von solcher Wichtigkeit war nicht vereinbar mit der natürlichen Nacktheit eines Jesuskindes, der fast schon herabwürdigenden Greisenhaftigkeit der hl. Anna, geschweige denn mit der Vermutung, dass für die Maria wieder eine stadtbekannte Dirne Modell gestanden haben sollte.

En 1605 Caravaggio recibió por fin el ansiado encargo del Vaticano: la hermandad de los palafreneros le encargó una pintura para la basílica de San Pedro. Lo que podía haber constituido el culmen de su carrera acabó siendo una catástrofe. La representación de la madre de Dios aplastando, con la ayuda del niño Jesús, la cabeza de la serpiente, símbolo del pecado original, iba demasiado lejos en su profano realismo para sus clientes. Una alegoría de tal importancia no podía conjugarse con la desnudez naturalista del niño Jesús, la casi denigrante senilidad de Santa Ana, por no hablar del hecho de que la modelo que posó para María había sido nuevamente una conocida prostituta de la ciudad.

Nel 1605 Caravaggio ricevette finalmente la desiderata commissione da parte del Vaticano: l'Arciconfraternita dei Parafrenieri Pontifici gli incaricò un dipinto per la Basilica di San Pietro. Tuttavia, quello che avrebbe dovuto rappresentare il culmine della sua carriera finì in disastro. La rappresentazione di Caravaggio della Vergine Maria che schiaccia con l'aiuto di Gesù Bambino la testa del serpente, simbolo del peccato originale, si scostava troppo dai desideri del committente a causa del suo realismo secolare. Un'allegoria di tale importanza non era compatibile con la nudità naturale del Bambino Gesù e la quasi dispregiativa senilità di Santa Anna, per non parlare poi del fatto che il modello per la raffigurazione di Maria era stato a quanto pare una prostituta molto nota in città.

In 1605 kreeg Caravaggio dan eindelijk een opdracht van het Vaticaan: de broederschap van de Palafrenieri bestelde een schilderij voor de Sint-Pieter. Maar wat het hoogtepunt van zijn carrière had moeten zijn, werd een ramp. Caravaggio's uitbeelding van de moeder gods, die samen met het Jezuskind de kop van de slang – zinnebeeld van de erfzonde – vertrapt, ging de opdrachtgevers in zijn profane realisme te ver. Deze verheven allegorie mocht niet worden uitgedrukt in de natuurlijke naaktheid van het Jezuskind en de bijna onwaardige ouderdom van de heilige Anna; en de wetenschap dat een bekende prostituee opnieuw model had gestaan voor Maria, was helemaal onaanvaardbaar.

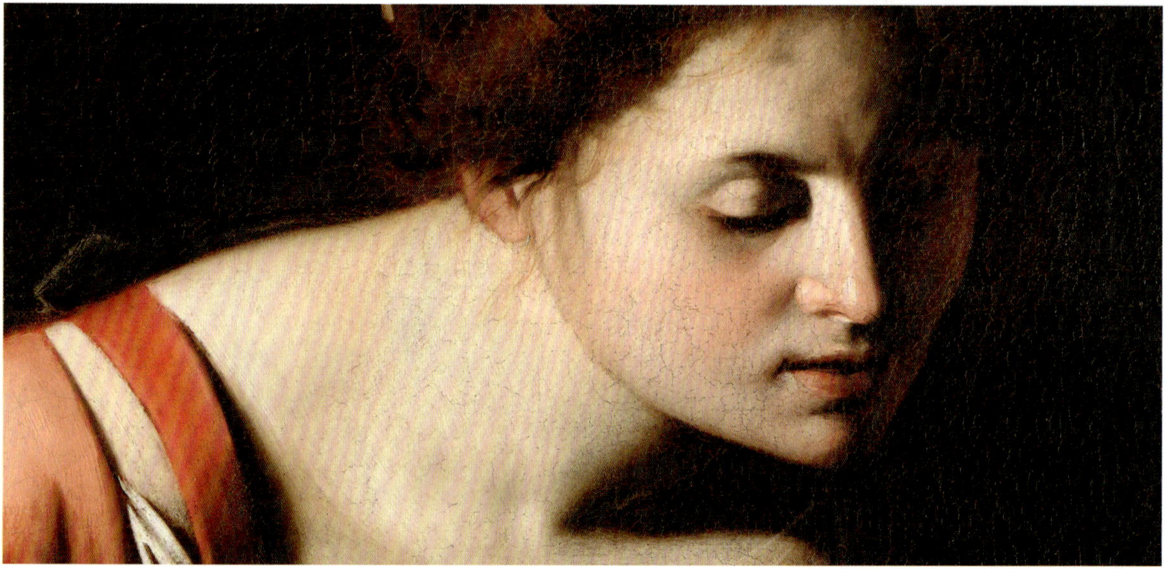

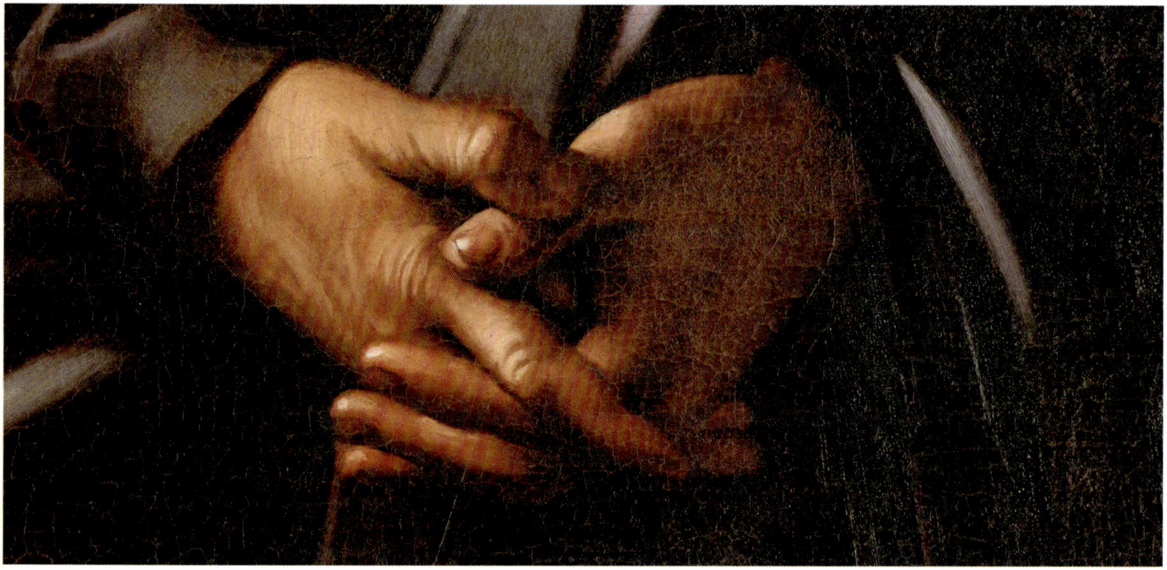

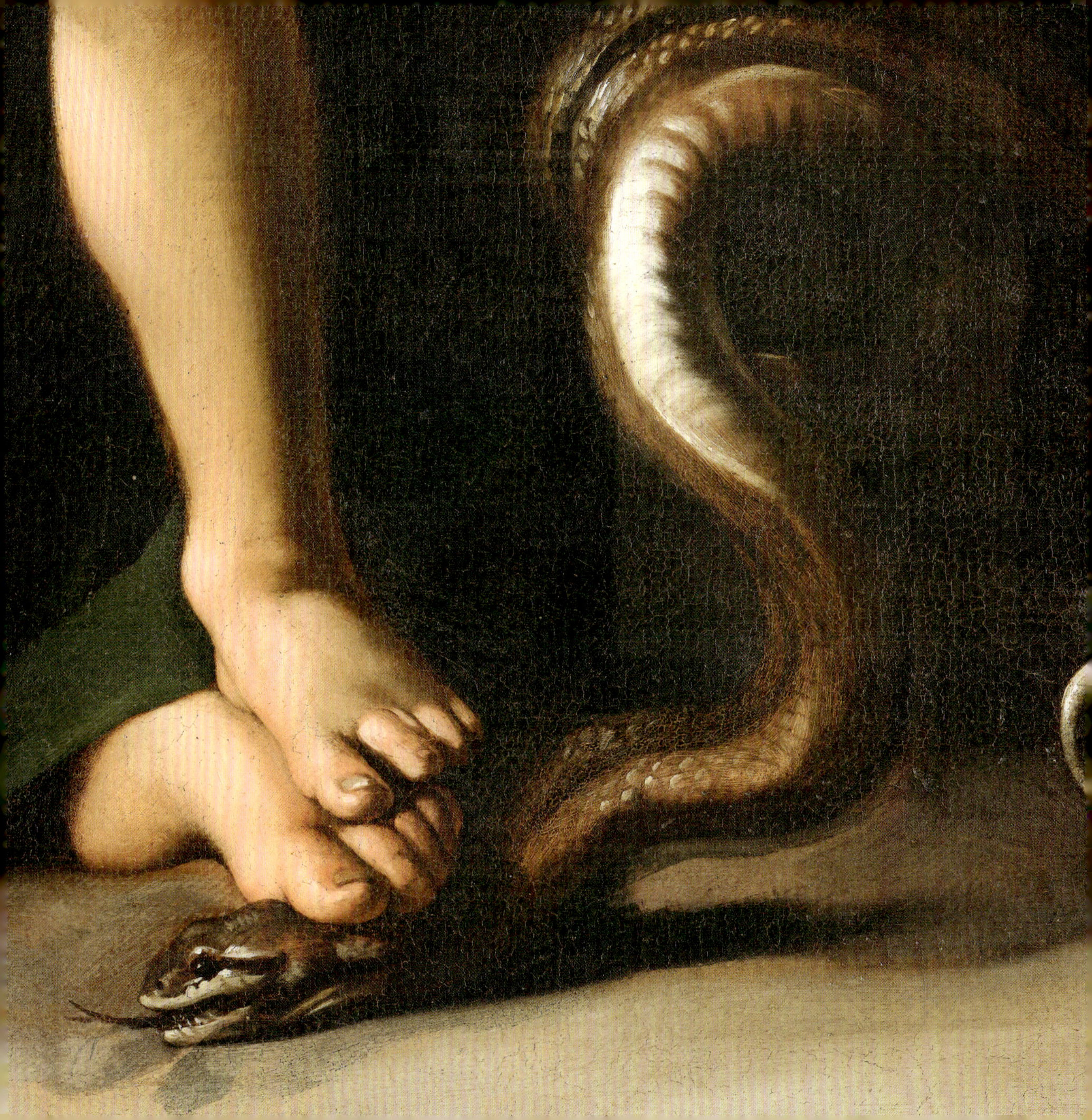

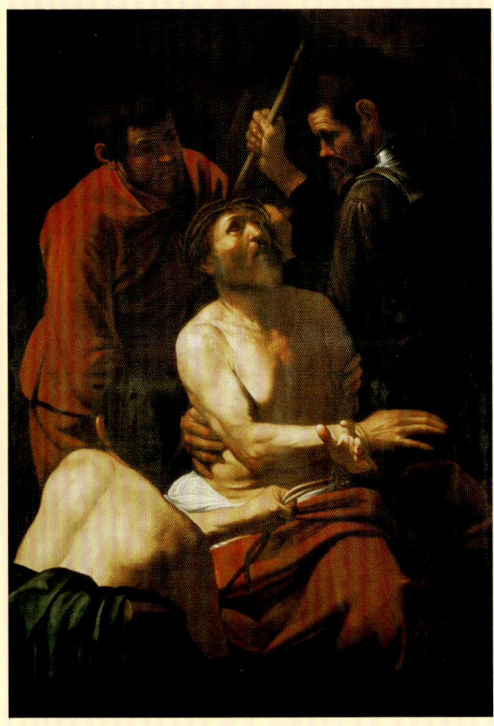

How Caravaggio created his works

Contemporary sources reveal little about how Caravaggio realized his use of light. We do not know, for example, if he used a camera obscura. There are no drawings, no sketchbooks, however it can be assumed that the artist sketched and made preparatory drawings. He probably also did not paint exclusively from live models. In many of his paintings, Caravaggio copied gestures and Details from the works of his great predecessors and competitors, including the sculpture of antiquity, Michelangelo (1475–1564), Raphael (1483–1520), and

La manière picturale de Caravage

Les sources contemporaines livrent peu d'indications à ce sujet : comment travaillait-il ses mises en scène lumineuses ? Utilisait-il une *camera oscura* ? Il n'existe de lui aucun dessin, aucun carnet de croquis – même si l'on peut penser qu'il réalisait esquisses et dessins préparatoires. Il n'est pas exclu non plus qu'il ait peint des modèles, avant et après. Dans bon nombre de ses tableaux, Caravage a repris des gestes et des détails tirés des œuvres de ses grands prédécesseurs et de ses concurrents – dont des sculptures

Caravaggios Malweise

Zeitgenössische Quellen geben wenig Aufschluss darüber, wie Caravaggio seine Lichtinszenierungen realisiert haben könnte, ob er beispielsweise eine Camera Obscura verwendete. Es existieren keine Zeichnungen, keine Skizzenbücher, gleichwohl ist davon auszugehen, dass der Künstler skizzierte und vorbereitende Zeichnungen anfertigte. Auch wird er nicht ausschließlich nach und vor Modellen gemalt haben. In vielen seiner Gemälde hat Caravaggio Gesten und Details aus den Werken seiner großen Vorgänger und Konkurrenten

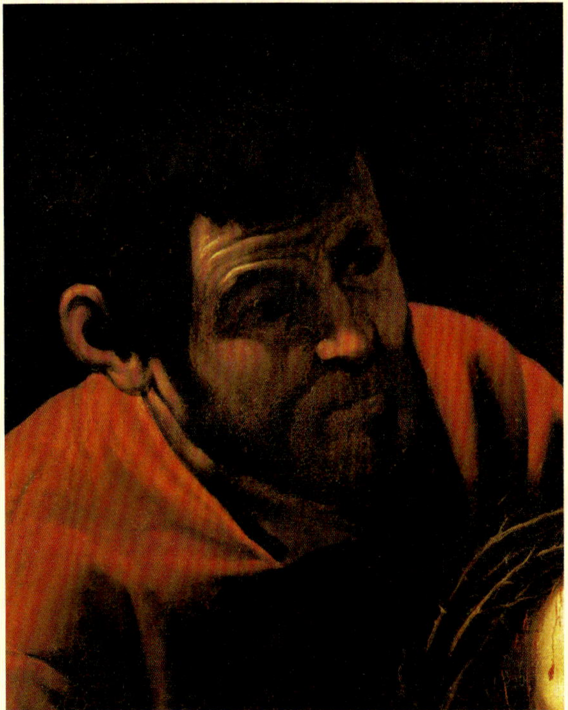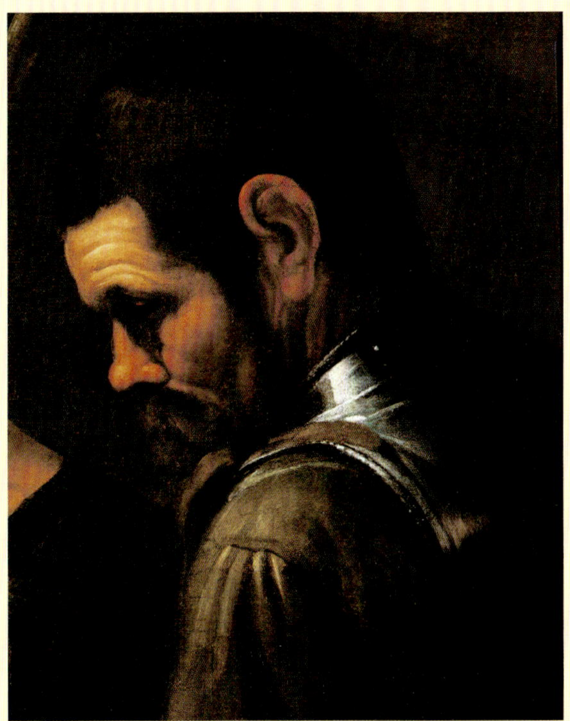

La técnica pictórica de Caravaggio

Las fuentes contemporáneas no nos aportan demasiado sobre cómo podría Caravaggio haber realizado sus escenas de luz, si por ejemplo utilizaba una cámara oscura. No nos han llegado dibujos ni cuadernos de bocetos, si bien hay que suponer que el artista bocetaba y realizaba dibujos preparatorios. Tampoco habrá pintado siempre basándose en modelos. En muchas de sus obras Caravaggiose apropia de gestos y Detalles de los trabajos de sus más grandes predecesores y competidores, entre ellos esculturas antiguas y trabajos

La tecnica pittorica di Caravaggio

Fonti contemporanee di Caravaggio rivelano poco sul modo in cui l'artista dipingeva la luce, ad esempio se si servisse o meno di una camera oscura. Non sono stati rinvenuti né disegni né schizzi, tuttavia si può presumere che il pittore abbozzasse le composizioni e creasse disegni preparatori. Inoltre, si ritiene che non abbia dipinto solo esclusivamente alla presenza di modelli o ispirandosi ad essi. In molti dei suoi dipinti Caravaggio adottò gesti e dettagli tratti dalle opere dei suoi grandi predecessori e concorrenti, tra

Caravaggio's schilderstijl

Bronnen uit de tijd van Caravaggio bieden weinig inzicht in de manier waarop de schilder de lichtval in zijn doeken ensceneerde en of hij mogelijk een camera obscura gebruikte. Er zijn geen tekeningen of schetsboeken, hoewel wordt aangenomen dat hij voorbereidende studies maakte. Ook schilderde Caravaggio niet altijd naar levensechte modellen, want in veel van zijn doeken heeft hij gebaren en Details uit werken van voorgangers en concurrenten overgenomen, waaronder klassieke beeldhouwwerken en

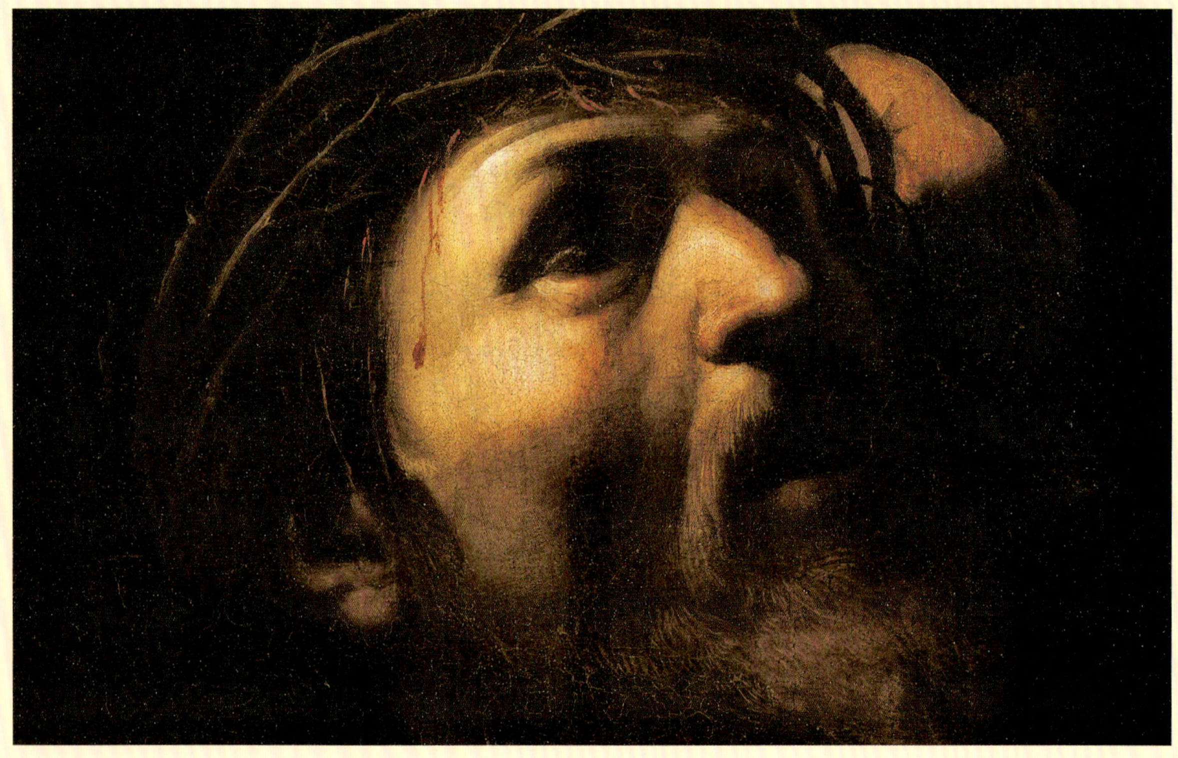

Titian. He also used motifs in works by his contemporaries such as Agostino (1557–1602) and Annibale Carracci. He followed the Venetian tradition and only pained in oil. The provocative naturalness that made his paintings famous is often limited to telling physical Details, such as a saint having the same careworn features of a Roman beggar. Caravaggio's martyrs also did not patiently suffer their fates. In the *Crown of Thorns,* the pain inflicted on Jesus is at the fore, as is the case with the *Scourging of Christ, Ecce Homo,* and

antiques et des tableaux de Michel-Ange (1475–1564), de Raphaël (1483–1520) et de Titien. Il reprit aussi des motifs de ses contemporains comme Annibal Carrache et Girolamo Savoldo (c. 1480/85–1548). Comme les Vénitiens, il travaillait exclusivement à l'huile. Le naturalisme provocant qui a rendu ses tableaux célèbres se borne souvent à des détails physiques expressifs : tel saint a, par exemple, les mêmes traits de visage qu'un mendiant romain. Les martyrs ne sont pas des victimes transfigurées par la douleur : dans *Le Couronnement d'épines,*

übernommen, unter ihnen antike Skulpturen, die Werke Michelangelos (1475–1564), Raffaels (1483–1520) und Tizians. Motive übernahm er auch von seinen Zeitgenossen wie Agostino (1557–1602) und Annibale Carracci. Nach venezianischem Vorbild malte er ausschließlich mit Ölfarben. Die provokative Natürlichkeit, die seine Bilder berühmt machte, beschränkt sich oft auf prägnante körperliche Details, so besitzt ein Heiliger die gleichen verhärmten Gesichtszüge wie ein römischer Bettler. Die Märtyrer

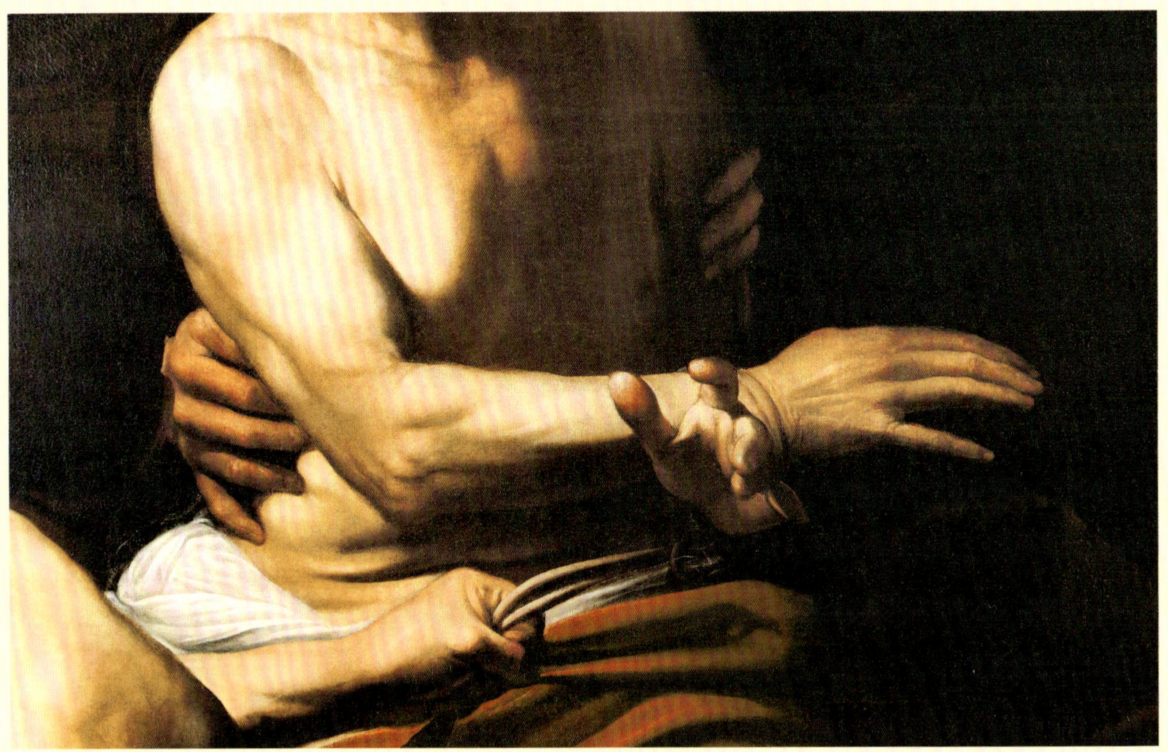

de Miguel Ángel (1475–1564), Rafael (1483–1520) y Tiziano. También utilizó temas de sus contemporáneos como Agostino (1557–1602) y Annibale Carracci. Siguiendo el ejemplo veneciano, pintó exclusivamente al óleo. El polémico naturalismo que hizo famosas sus pinturas se concentra a menudo en Detalles corporales muy específicos, por ejemplo un santo que posee los mismos rasgos demacrados de un mendigo romano. Los mártires no eran sufridores idealizados. En *la Coronación de espinas* el sufrimiento ocupa un

le quali sculture antiche e le opere di Michelangelo (1475–1564), Raffaello (1483–1520) e Tiziano. Trasse inoltre da artisti a lui contemporanei, come Agostino (1557–1602) e Annibale Carracci, anche alcuni dei motivi dei suoi quadri. Seguendo il modello veneziano, dipinse esclusivamente con colori ad olio. La naturalezza provocante che ha reso famosi i suoi quadri si limitava spesso a dettagli fisici specifici. Era così che un santo presentava gli stessi tratti del viso di un mendicante romano. I martiri non erano figure sofferenti

Details van Michelangelo (1475–1564), Rafaël (1483–1520) en Titiaan. Hij "stal" ook motieven van tijdgenoten als Agostino (1557–1602) en Annibale Carracci. Naar Venetiaans voorbeeld werkte hij uitsluitend met olieverf. Het provocerende naturalisme dat zijn schilderijen beroemd maakte, beperkte zich vaak tot opvallende lichamelijke Details: zo heeft een heilige dezelfde getergde gelaatstrekken als die van een Romeinse bedelaar. Caravaggio's martelaars waren niet lijdzaam en verheven. In *De doornenkroning van*

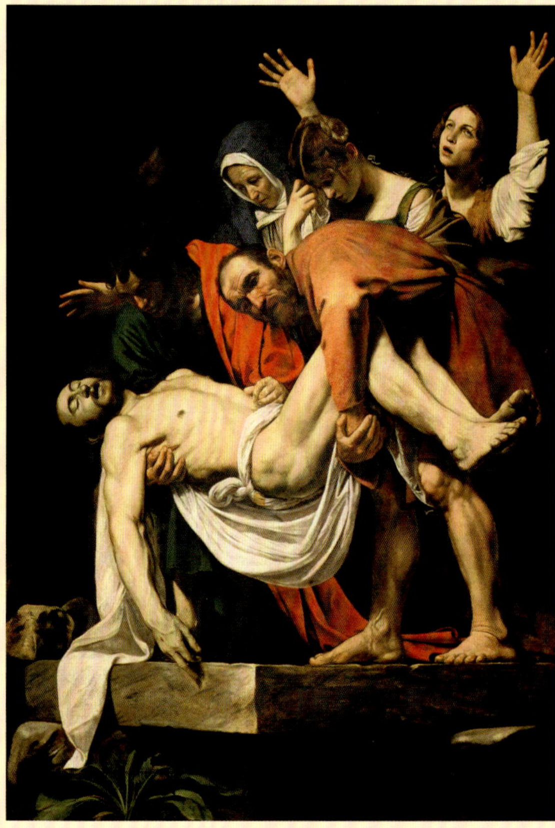

another depiction of *The crowning with thorns.* Caravaggio's style was more than just the stark lighting of blindingly bright bodies against deep shadows. He also depicted suffering in all its real agony. Such experiences were not foreign to his time, but they had never been shown in art quite this way before.

la torture est au premier plan, et cela vaut aussi pour *La Flagellation,* l'*Ecce homo,* un autre *Couronnement d'épines.* Le style caravagesque ne comporte pas seulement le traitement de la lumière, les corps clairs se détachant sur des ombres profondes, mais également le réalisme de la douleur. Cela n'était pas étranger à son époque, mais nouveau pour l'art de celle-ci.

sind keine verklärten Dulder. In der *Dornenkrönung* steht die Qual im Vordergrund, das gilt auch für die *Geißelung Christi,* den *Ecce Homo* und eine weitere *Dornenkrönung.* Zum caravaggesken Stil gehört nicht nur die krasse Lichtführung, die blendend hellen Körper vor tiefen Schatten, sondern auch der Realismus des Leidens. Das alles war seiner Zeit nicht fremd, jedoch für die Kunst seiner Zeit neu.

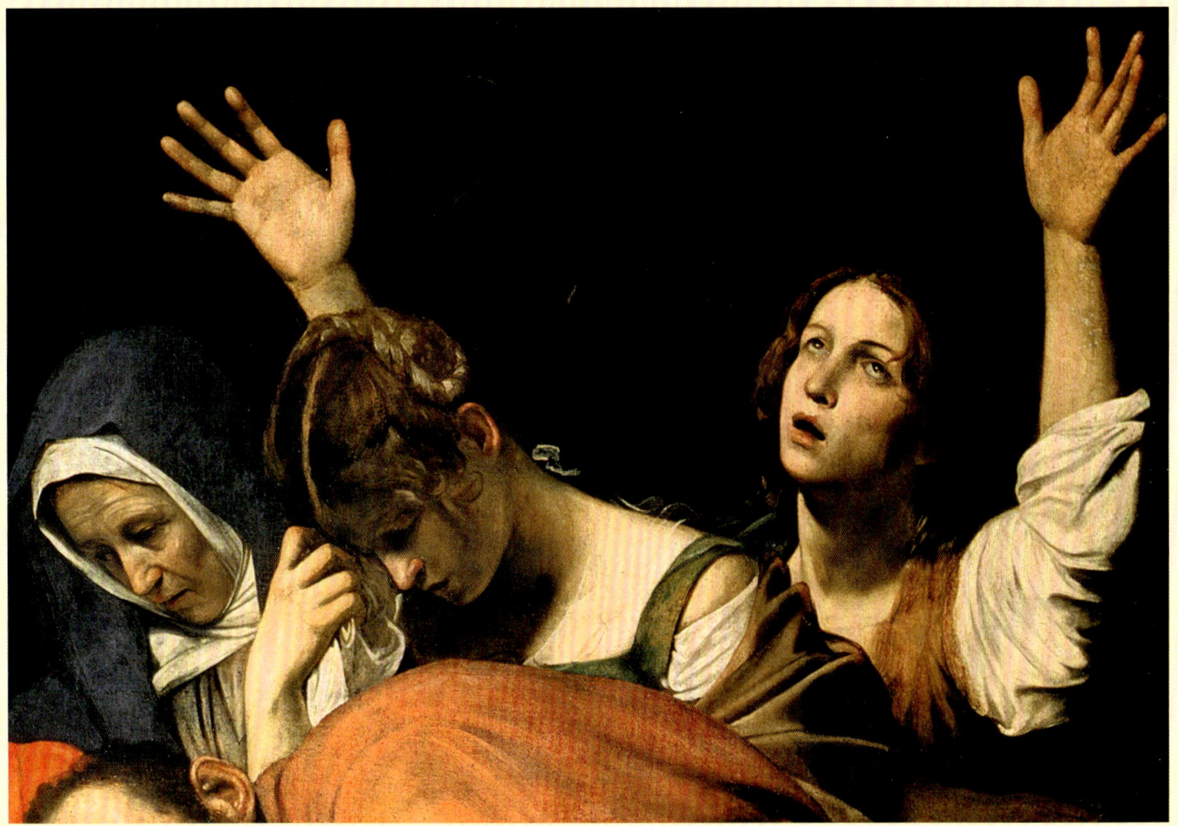

lugar prominente, lo cual es aplicable también a *La flagelación de Cristo,* el *Ecce Homo* y otra *Coronación de espinas.* Parte esencial del estilo de Caravaggio era no solo el drástico uso de la iluminación, con cuerpos refulgentes sobresaliendo de sombras profundas, sino también el realismo del sufrimiento. Esto no era completamente extraño a su época, pero sí era novedoso para el arte del período.

trasfigurate: l'agonia è in primo piano sia nell'*Incoronazione di spine* che nella *Flagellazione di Cristo,* nell'*Ecce Homo* e in un'altra *Incoronazione di spine.* Allo stile caravaggesco appartengono infatti non solo i forti contrasti di luce ed ombra o gli accecanti corpi illuminati che emergono dal buio più profondo, ma anche il realismo della sofferenza, non estranea al tempo dell'artista, ma sì nuova per l'arte dell'epoca.

Christus staat het lijden op de voorgrond, en dat geldt ook voor *De geseling van Christus, Ecce Homo* en een andere *Doornenkroning.* De stijl van Caravaggio werd niet alleen gekenmerkt door de enscenering van de lichtval en fel uitgelichte lichamen naast diepe schaduwen, maar ook door het realisme van het lijden. Voor zijn tijd was dit niet nieuw, voor de kunst wel.

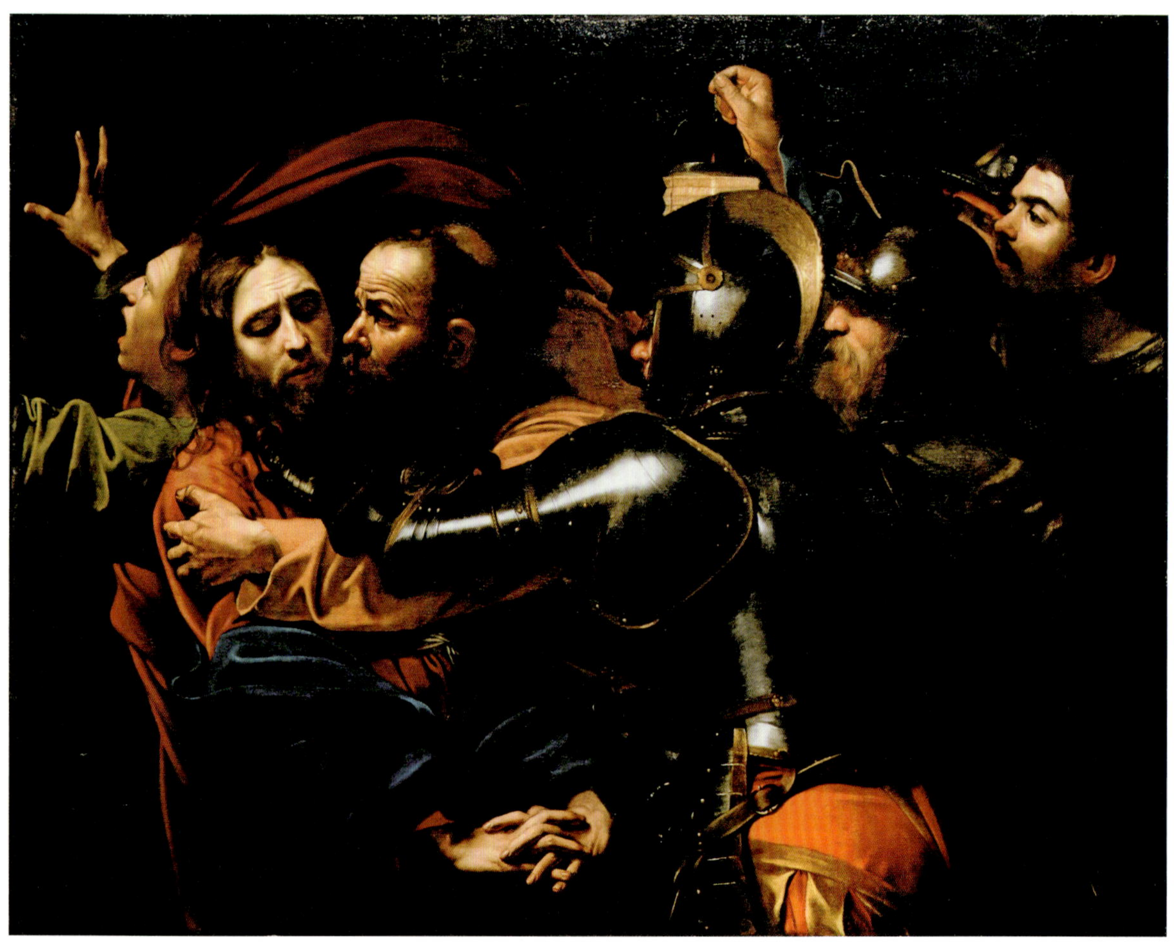

The Arrest of Jesus
L'Arrestation du Christ
Gefangennahme Christi
El prendimiento de Cristo.
Cattura di Cristo
De Gevangenneming van Christus

1602, Oil on canvas/Huile sur toile, 133,5 × 169,5 cm, National Gallery of Ireland, Dublin

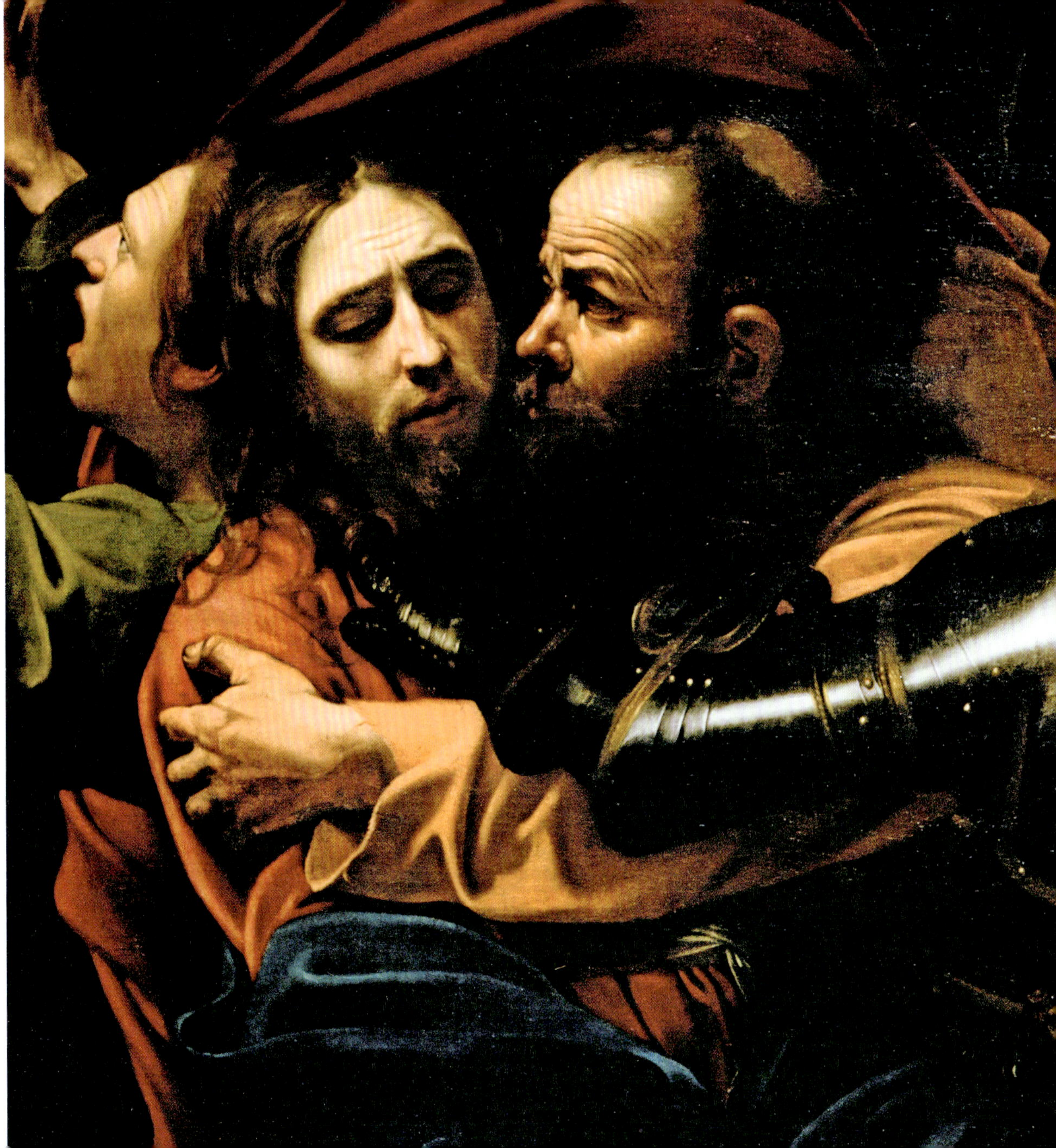

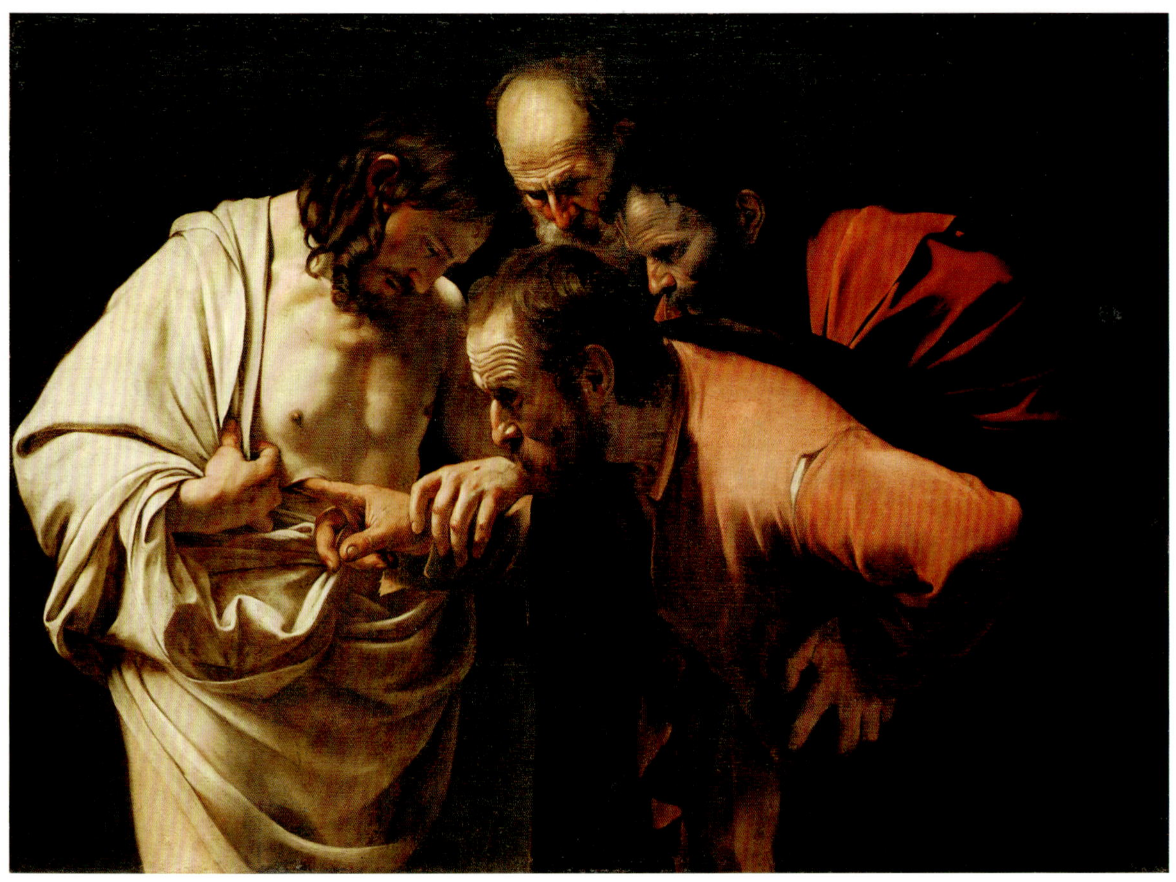

Doubting Thomas

L'Incrédulité de saint Thomas

Der ungläubige Thomas

La incredulidad de Santo Tomás Apostol

Incredulità di San Tommaso

De ongelovige Thomas

c. 1603, Oil on canvas/Huile sur toile, 107 × 146 cm, Bildergalerie, Potsdam

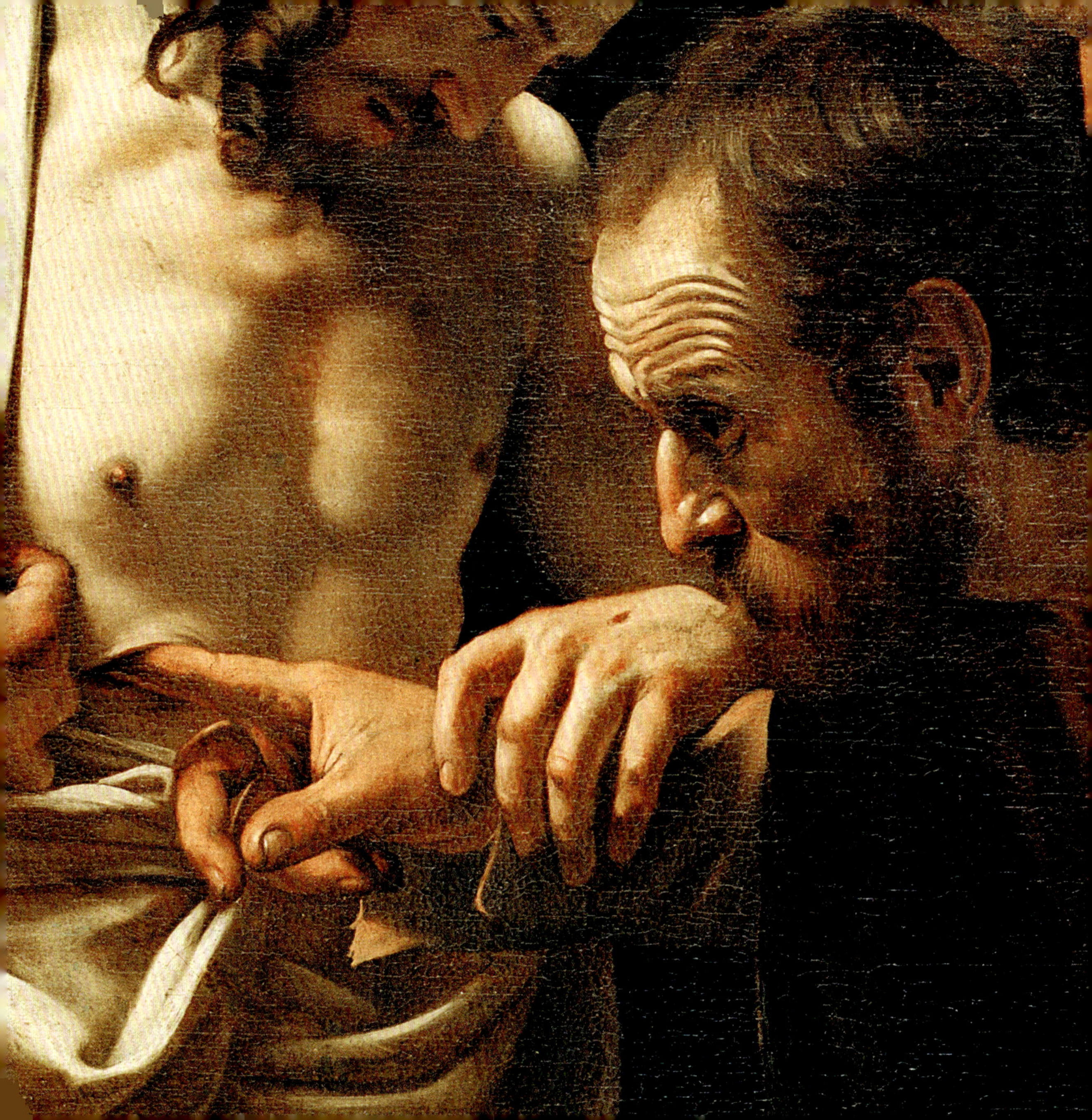

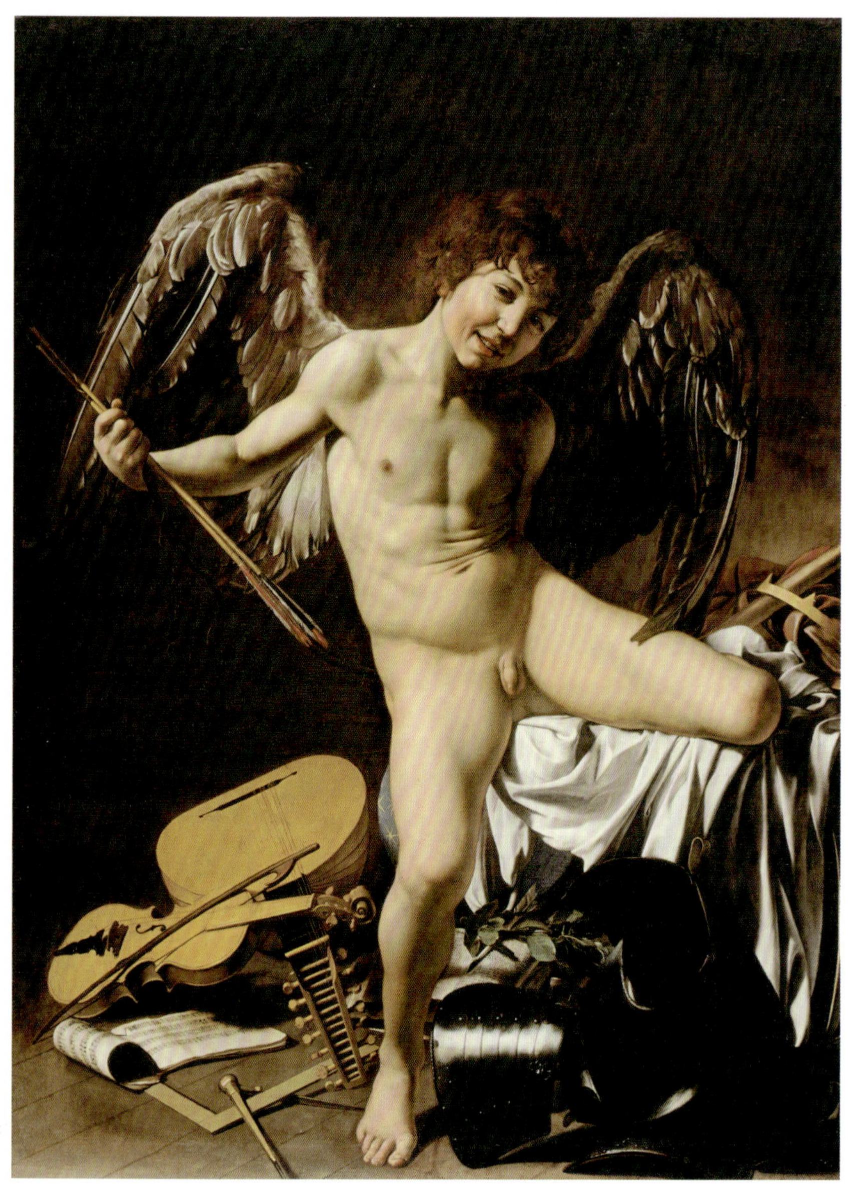

Amor Victorious

L'Amour victorieux

Amor als Sieger

Amor victorioso

Amor Vincit Omnia

Amor als overwinnaar

*1602, Oil on canvas/Huile sur toile,
156 × 113 cm, Gemäldegalerie, Berlin*

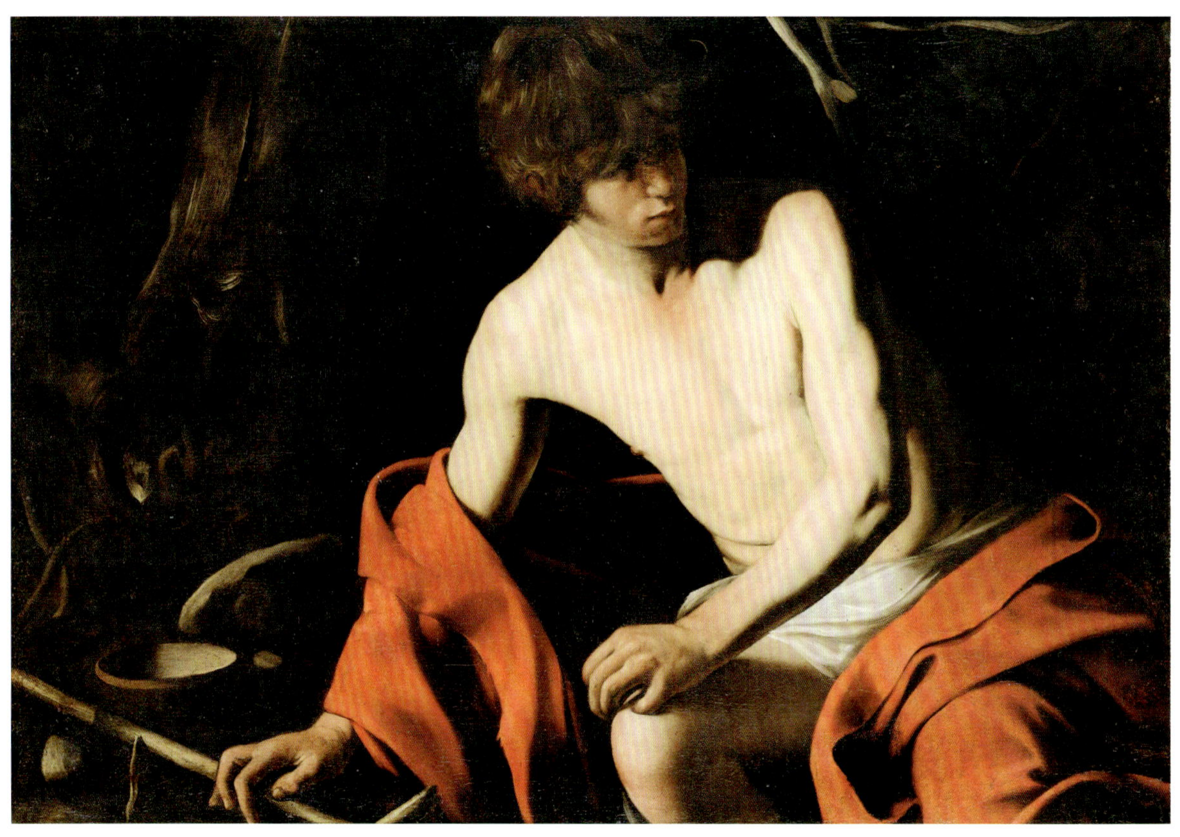

John the Baptist

Saint Jean-Baptiste

Johannes der Täufer

San Juan Bautista

San Giovanni Battista

Johannes de Doper

c. 1604, Oil on canvas/Huile sur toile, 94 × 131 cm, Palazzo Barberini, Roma

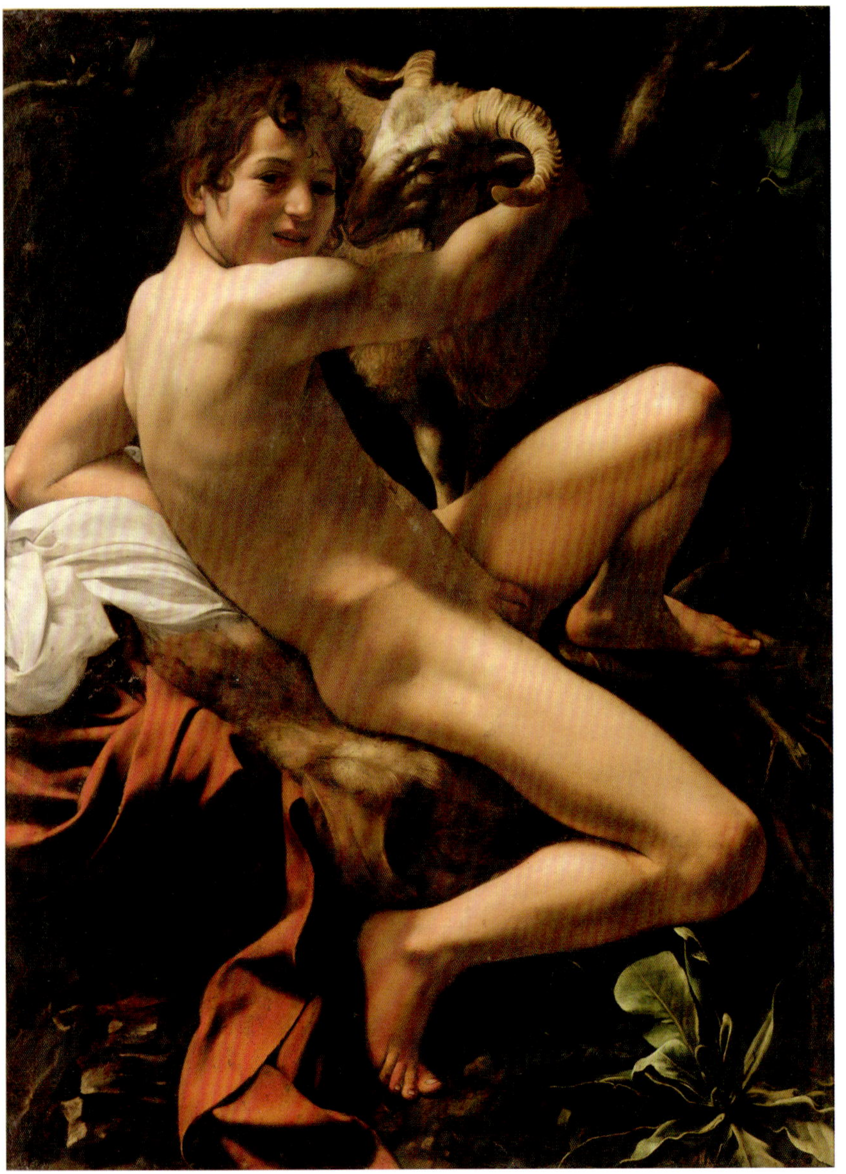

*1602, Oil on canvas/Huile sur toile,
132 × 97 cm, Palazzo Doria Pamphilj,
Roma*

Caravaggio presents John with such sensuality that came across as provocatively profane and even erotic, such that it has been interpreted as a secular painting of a shepherd or of some figure from mythology. Although the fusion of biblical and secular character is not unusual and was inspired by Michelangelo's Ignudi, the subliminal eroticism really pushed the boundaries of representing a saint in his boyhood.

Caravage représente le personnage avec une telle sensualité que ce jeune garçon, perçu comme érotique et provocant, a été différemment interprété : par exemple, comme un simple berger ou un personnage purement mythologique. La fusion de figures bibliques et profanes n'a rien d'inhabituel – dans la veine des Ignudi de Michel-Ange –, mais l'érotisme subliminal est extrêmement scabreux pour la représentation d'un saint dans la fleur de l'adolescence.

Caravaggio präsentiert seine Figur des Johannes mit einer solchen Sinnlichkeit, dass der als provozierend profan und erotisch empfundene Knabe unterschiedlich gedeutet wurde, z.B. als Schäfer oder rein mythologische Gestalt. Zwar ist die Verschmelzung von biblischer und profaner Figur nichts ungewöhnliches – angeregt von Michelangelos Ignudi – die unterschwellige Erotik ist jedoch für die Darstellung eines Heiligen im Knabenalter äußerst delikat.

Caravaggio presenta su figura de San
Juan con una sensualidad tal que el
muchacho de provocadora profanidad
y cierto erotismo fue interpretado
de formas diversas, por ejemplo
como pastor o una figura puramente
mitológica. Es cierto que la mezcla de
figura bíblica y profana no es nada fuera
de lo habitual –inspirada en los Ignudi
de Miguel Ángel–, pero el erotismo
subyacente es ciertamente delicado
especialmente para la representación
de un santo en edad juvenil.

Caravaggio rappresenta la figura di
San Giovanni Battista in modo così
sensuale che essa è stata interpretata
più volte come un ragazzo profano
erotico e provocante, ad esempio come
un pastore o una figura puramente
mitologica. Sebbene la fusione della
figura biblica e di quella secolare non
fosse insolita (ispirata agli ignudi di
Michelangelo), l'erotismo subliminale
era un elemento estremamente delicato
nel caso della rappresentazione di un
santo nella sua fanciullezza.

Caravaggio presenteert Johannes met
zo veel zinnelijkheid dat de knaap,
die als provocerend profaan en
erotisch werd gezien, heel verschillend
is geïnterpreteerd, bijvoorbeeld
als schaapsherder of als puur
mythologische figuur. Hoewel de
versmelting van Bijbelse en profane
figuren niets nieuws was (naar het
voorbeeld van Michelangelo's ignudi),
lag de onderliggende erotiek in deze
uitbeelding van een heilige als jongeling
zeer gevoelig.

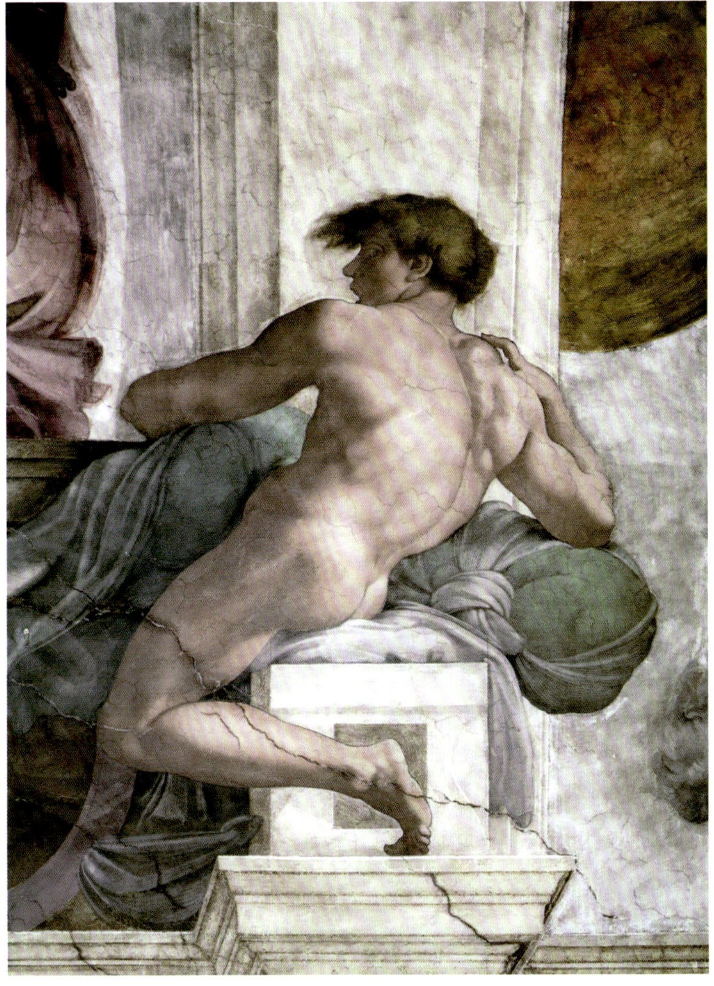

Michelangelo Buonarroti (1475–1564)

*Naked Youth Over
Persian Sibyl*

*Jeune homme nu (ignudo)
près de la sibylle Persique*

*Nackter Jüngling (Ignudo)
über Persischer Sibylle*

*Joven desnudo (Ignudo)
sobre Sibila persa*

*Ignudo sopra alla
Sibilla Persica*

*Naakte jongeling (ignudo)
boven Perzische sibylle*

c. 1511/12, Fresco/Fresque, Cappella Sistina, Roma

135

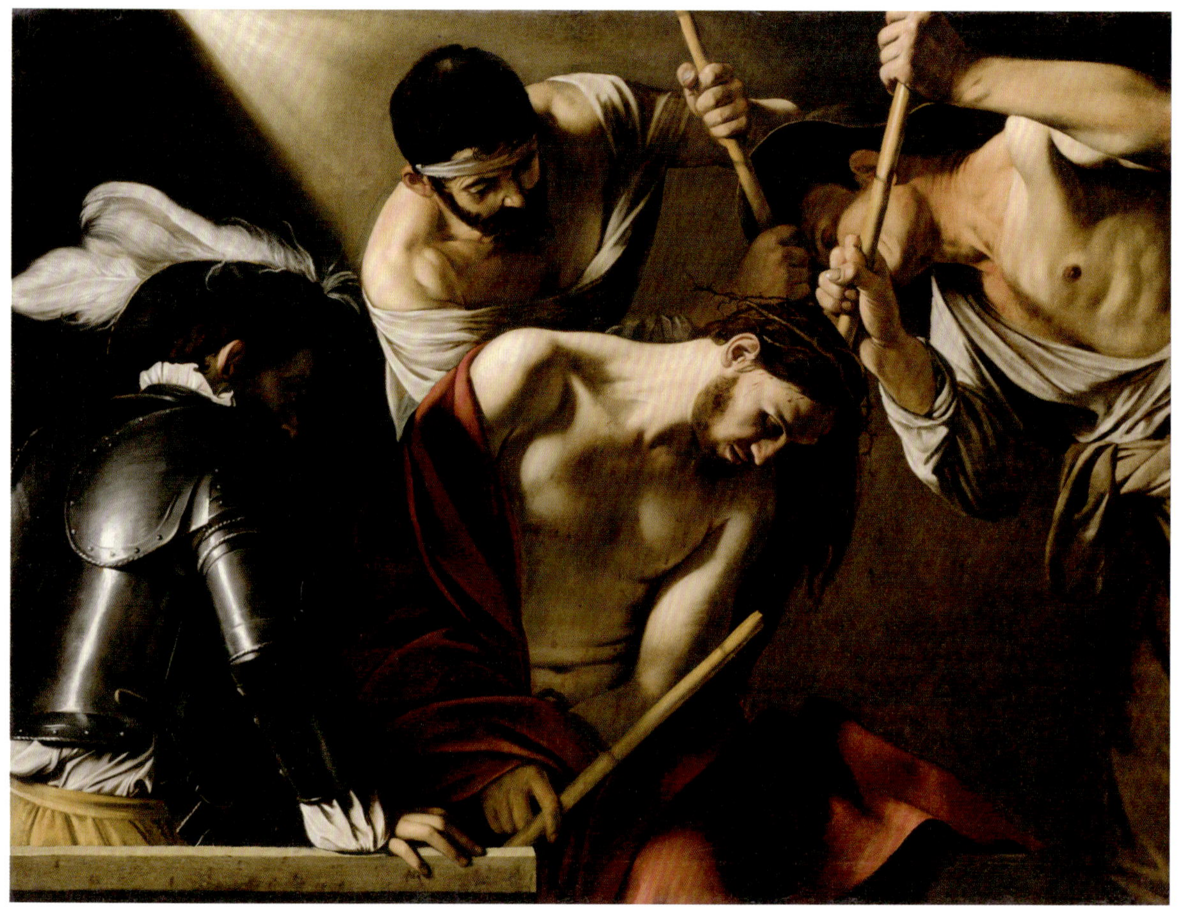

The Crown of Thorns
Le Couronnement d'épines
Dornenkrönung Christi
La coronación de espinas
Incoronazione di spine
De Doornenkroning van Christus

c. 1602/03, Oil on canvas/Huile sur toile, 127 × 165,5 cm,
Kunsthistorisches Museum, Wien

Caravaggio (attr.)

Portrait of a Man (Scipione Borghese?)
Portrait d'un homme (Scipion Borghese?)
Bildnis eines Mannes (Scipione Borghese?)
Retrato de un hombre (Scipione Borghese?)
Ritratto di gentiluomo (Scipione Borghese?)
Mannenportret (mogelijk Scipione Borghese)

c. 1600, Oil on canvas/Huile sur toile, 77 × 69 cm, Museo Civico Pinacoteca Crociani, Montepulciano

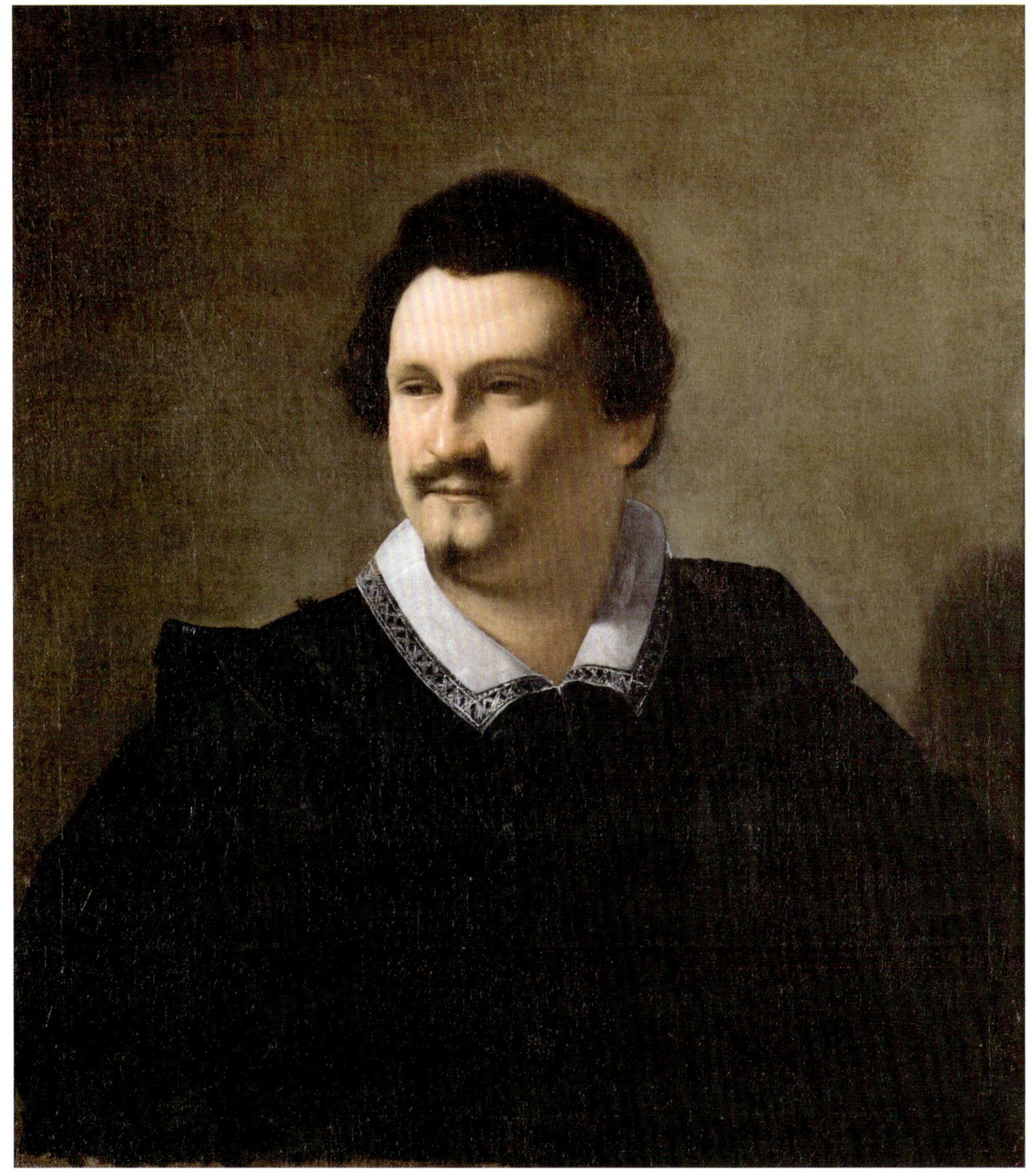

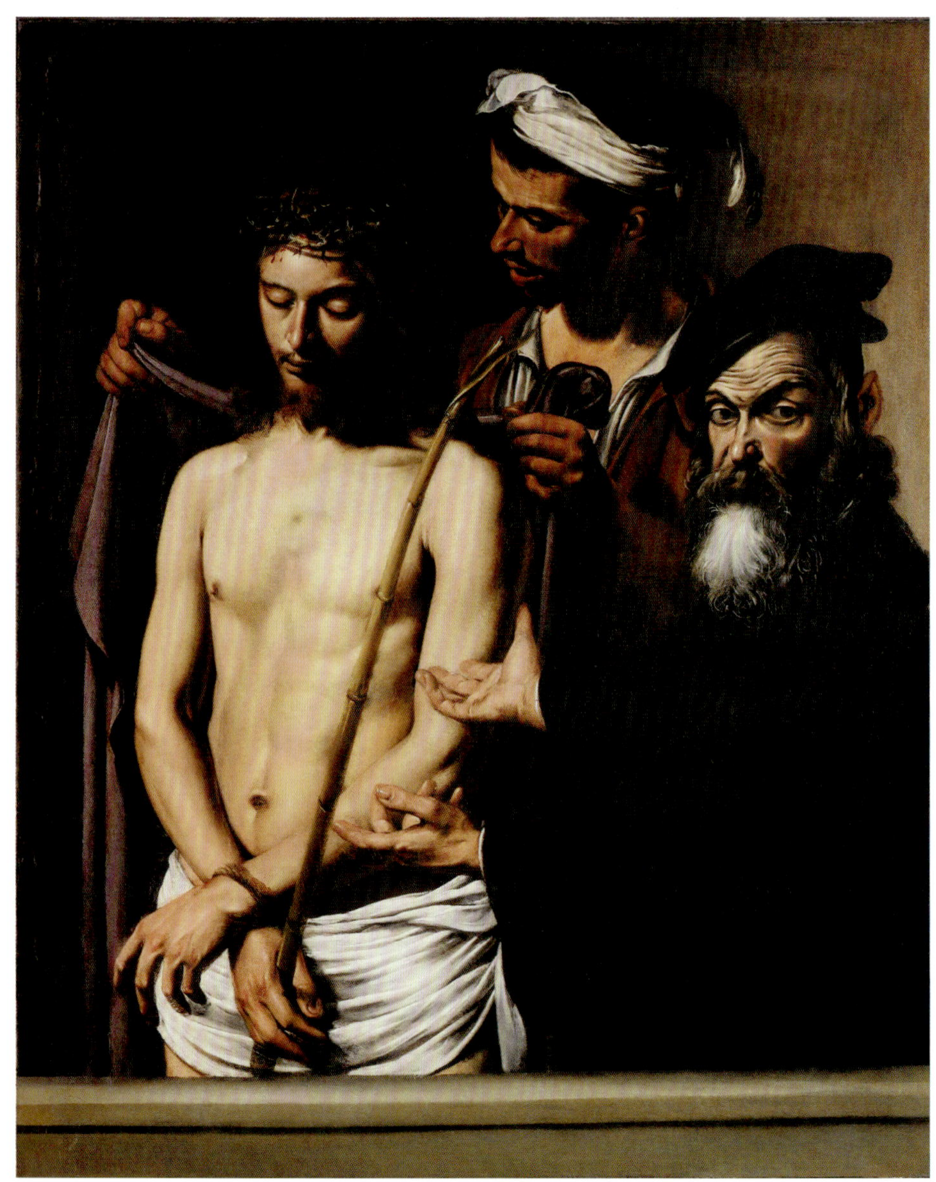

Ecce Homo

c. 1605, Oil on canvas/
Huile sur toile, 128 × 103 cm,
Palazzo Bianco, Genova

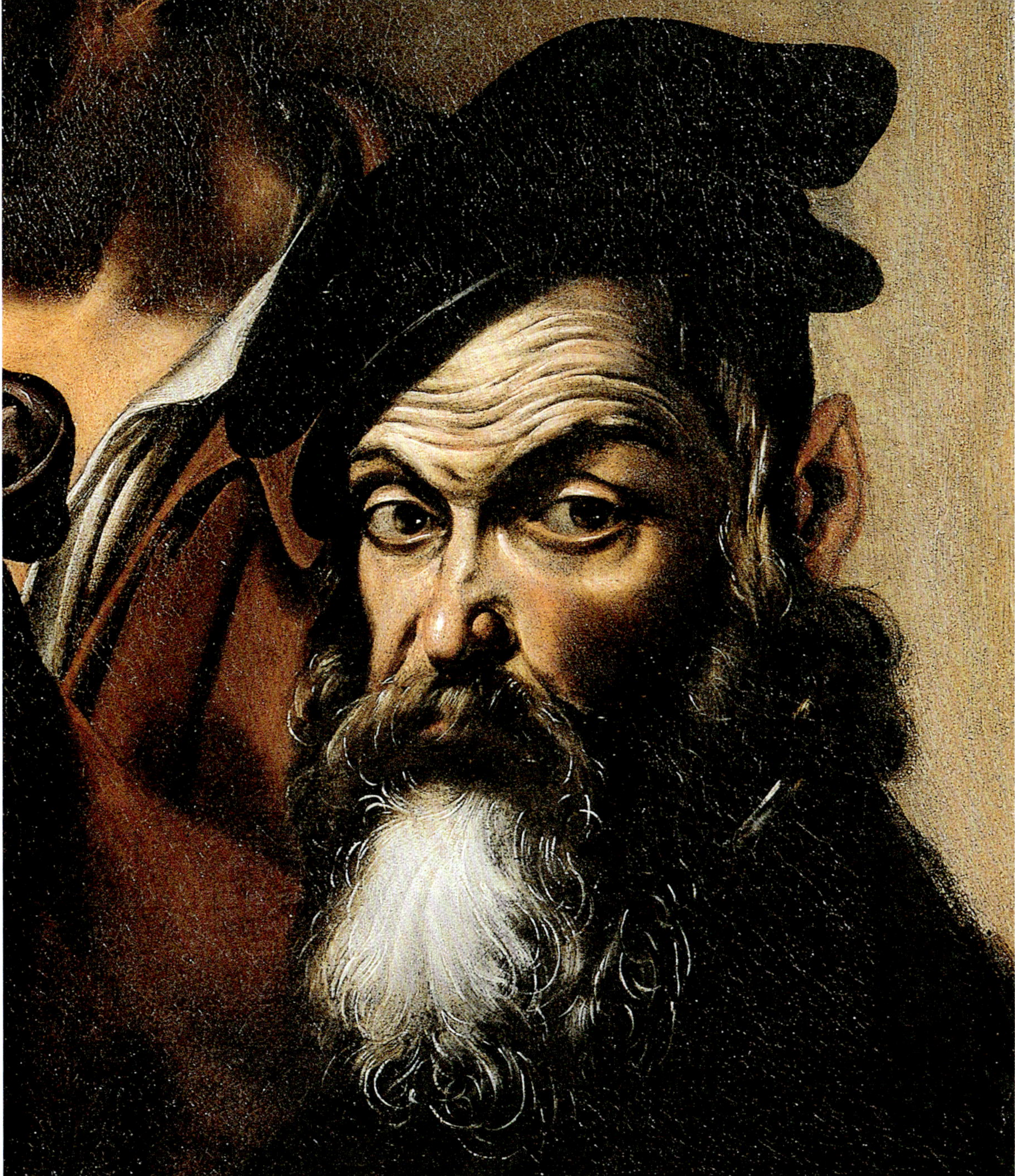

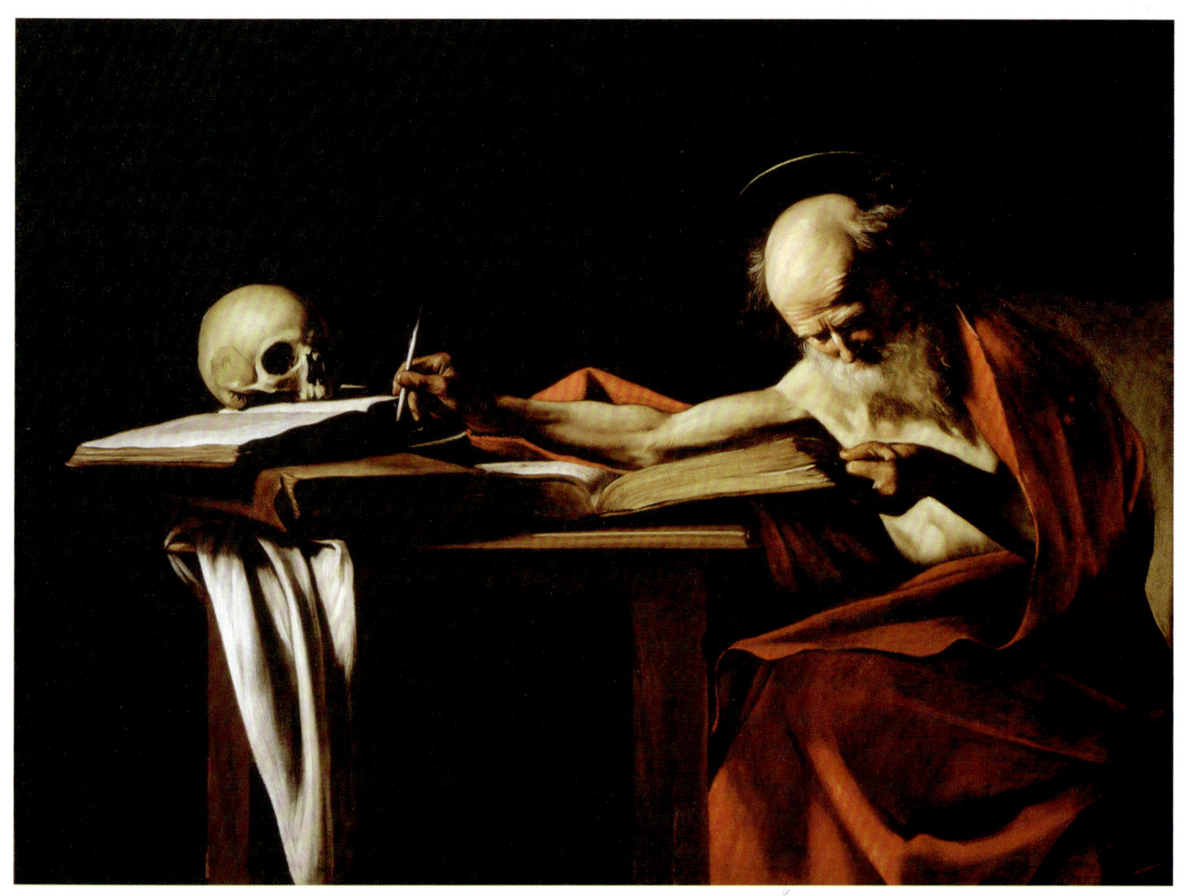

St Jerome Writing

Saint Jérôme écrivant

Der schreibende hl. Hieronymus

San Jerónimo escribiendo

San Girolamo scrivente

De schrijvende Sint-Hiëronymus

1606, Oil on canvas/Huile sur toile, 112 × 157 cm, Galleria Borghese, Roma

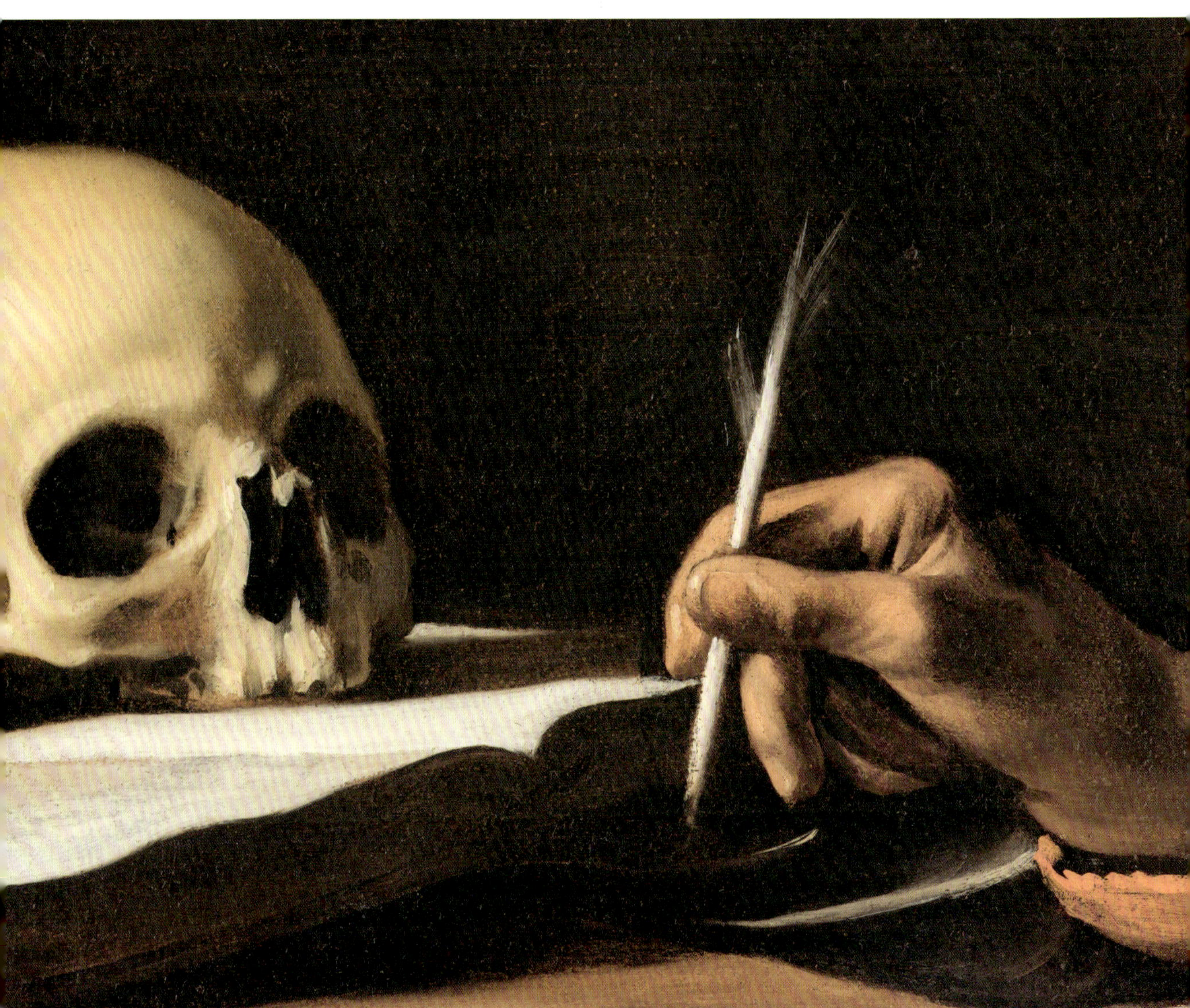

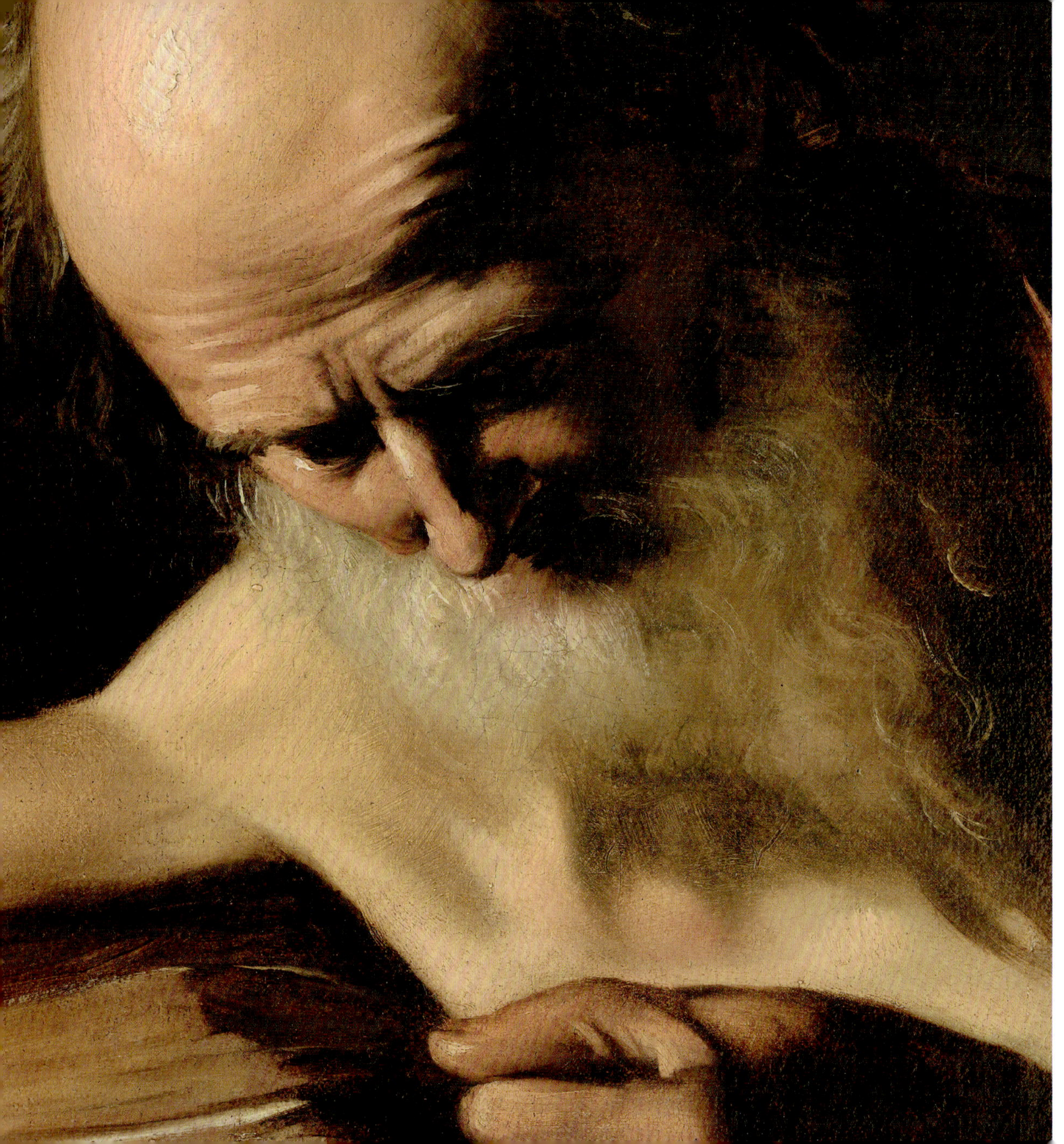

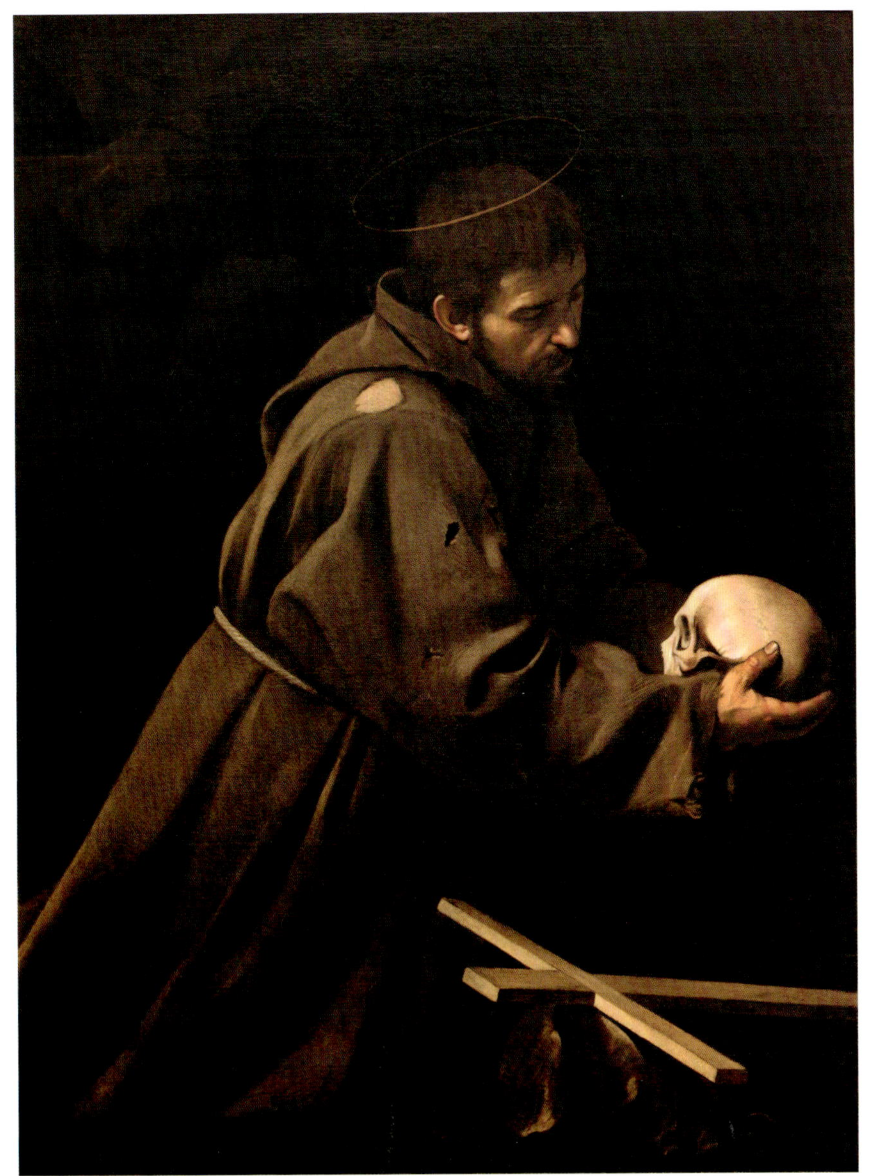

St Francis Meditating
Saint François en méditation
Der hl. Franziskus in Meditation
San Francisco meditando
San Francesco in meditazione
De heilige Franciscus in meditatie

1606, Oil on canvas/Huile sur toile,
128,2 × 97,4 cm, Chiesa di Santa Maria
della Concezione dei Cappuccini, Roma

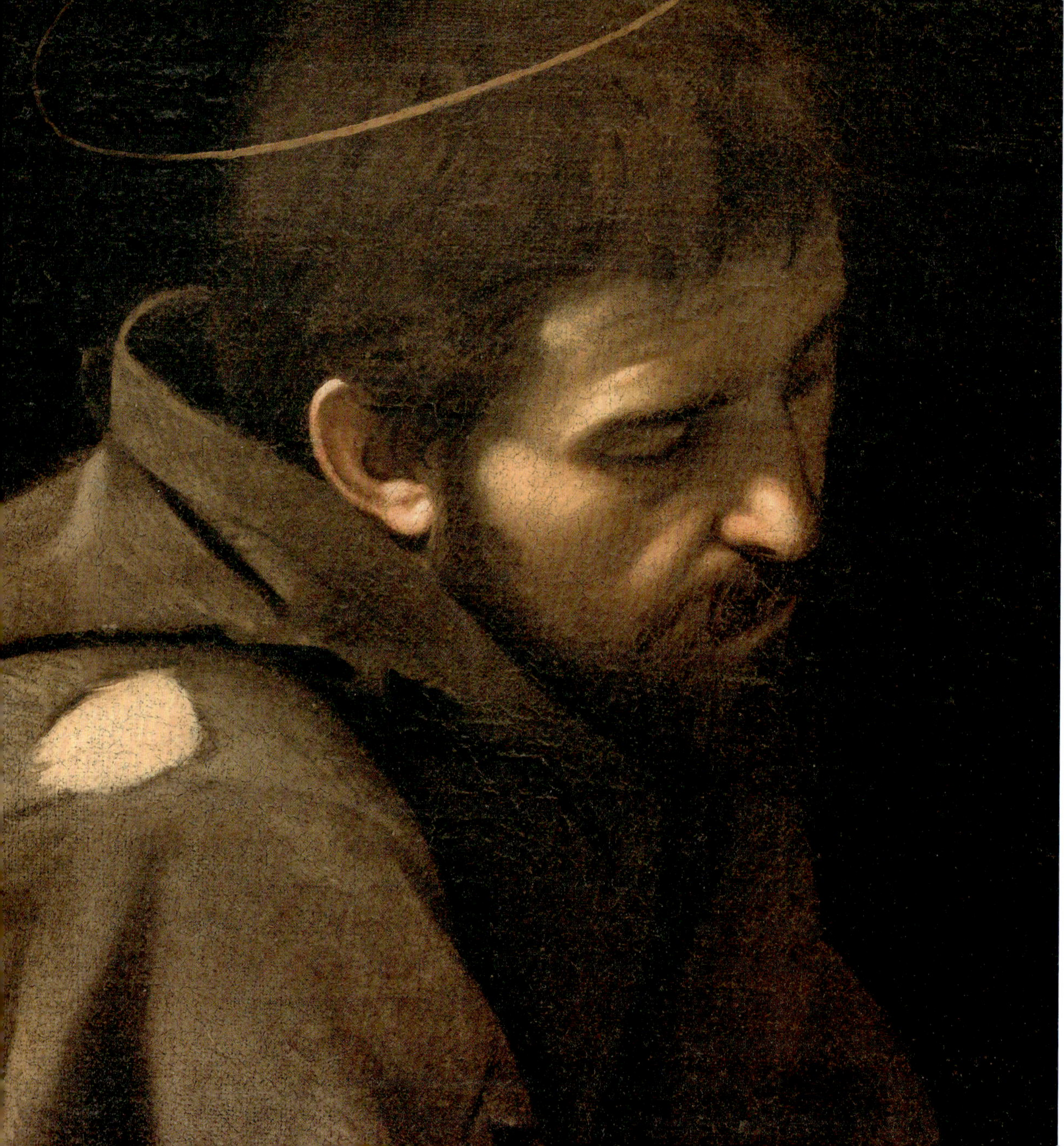

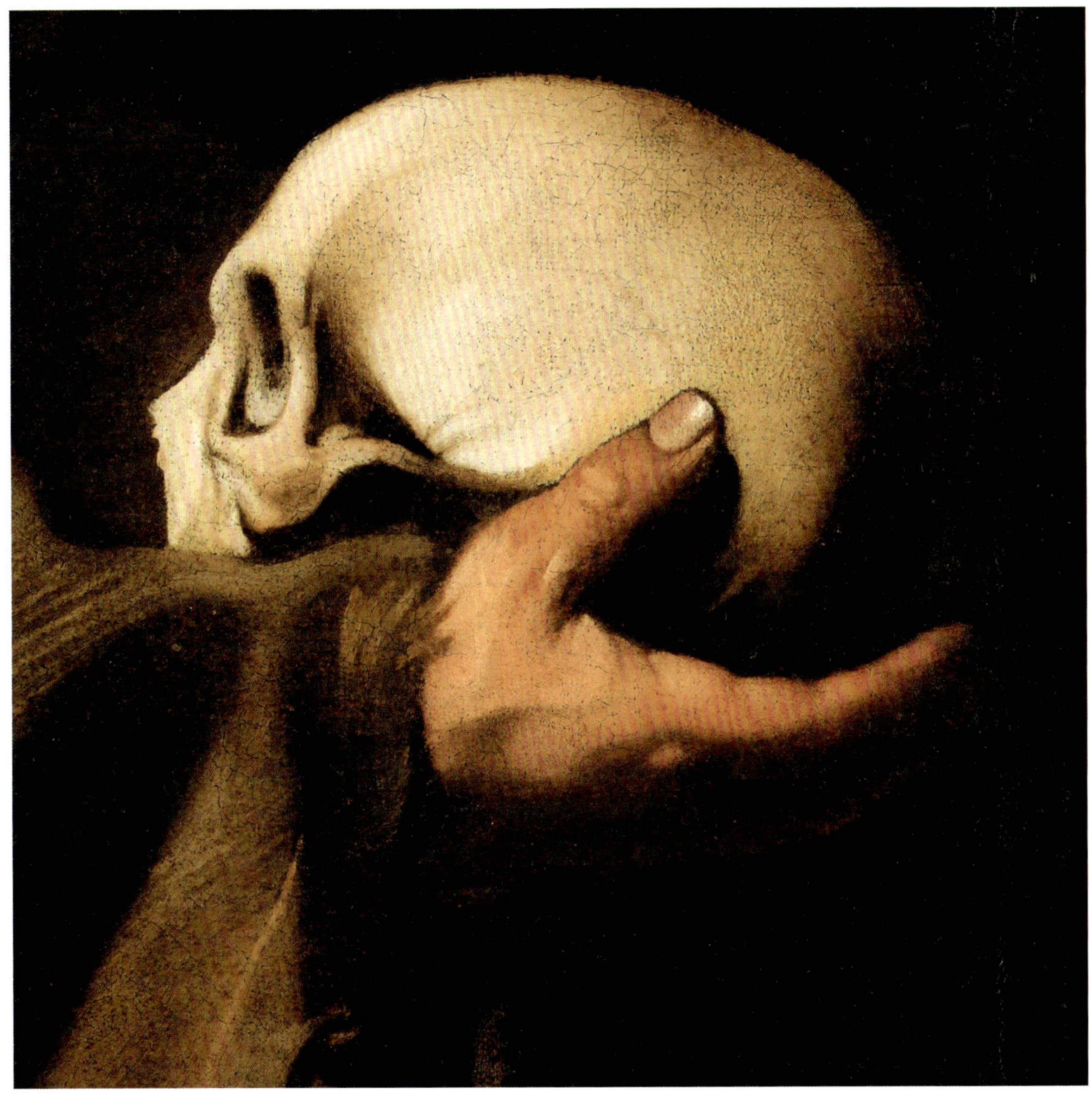

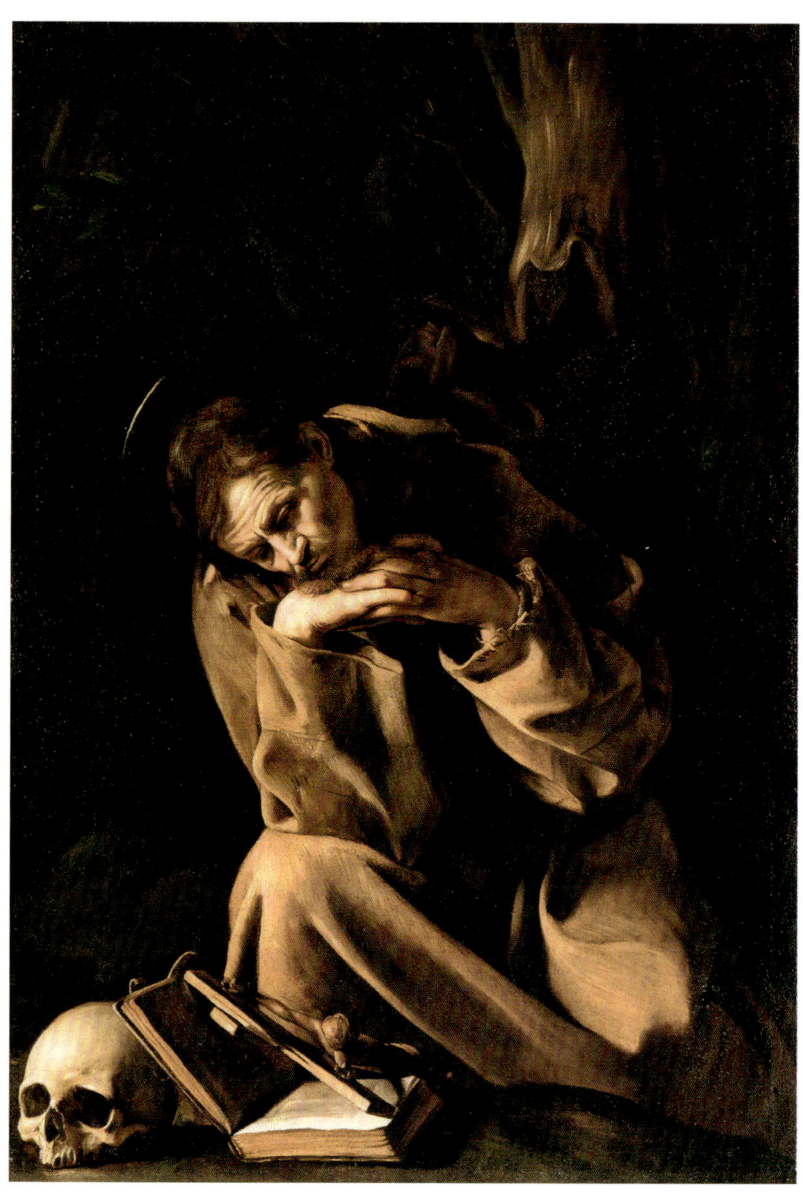

St Francis in Prayer

Saint François en méditation sur le crucifix

Der hl. Franziskus im Gebet

San Franciso en oración

San Francesco in meditazione

De heilige Franciscus in gebed

1606, Oil on canvas/Huile sur toile, 130 × 90 cm, Museo Civico "Ala Ponzone", Cremona

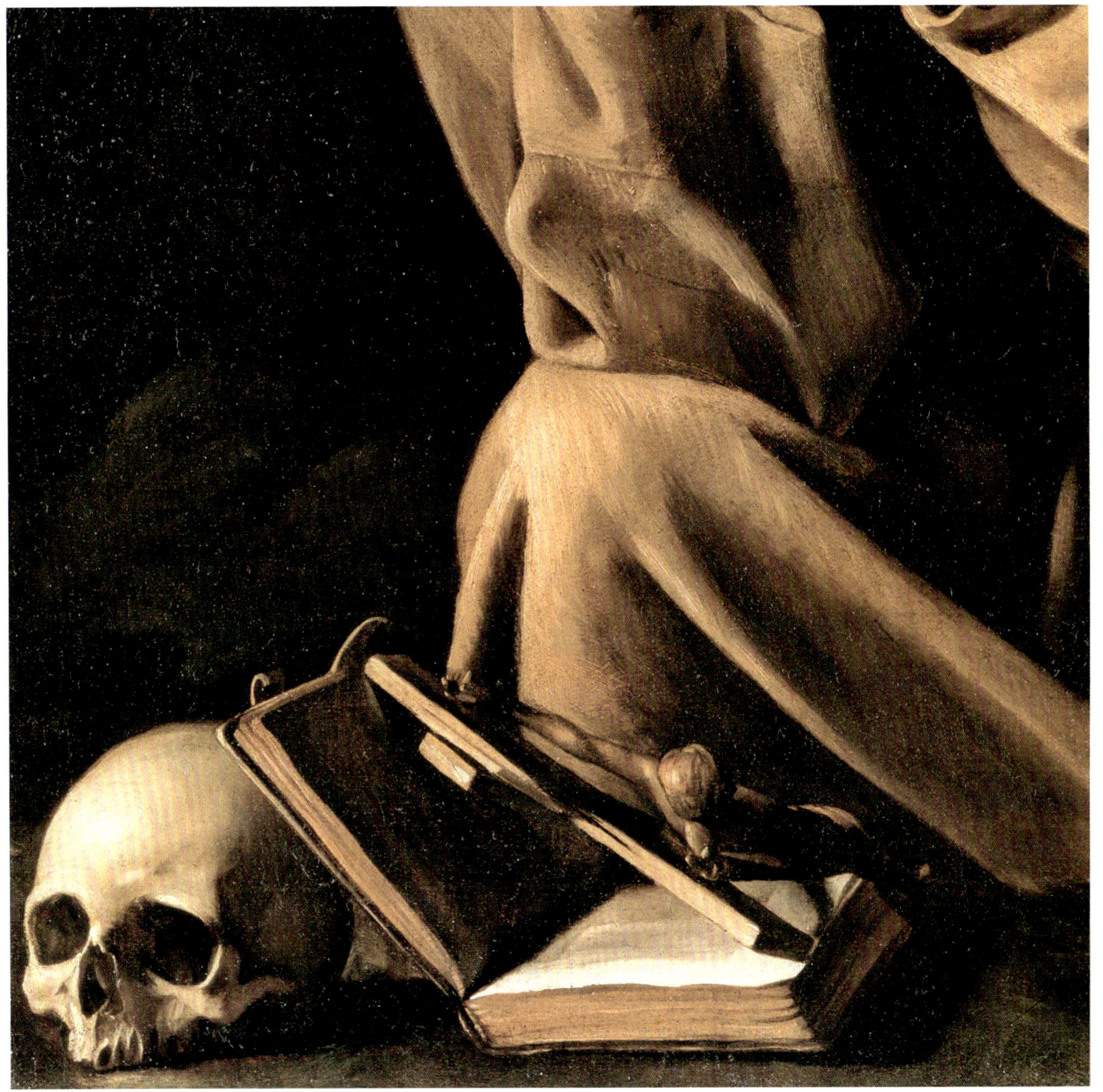

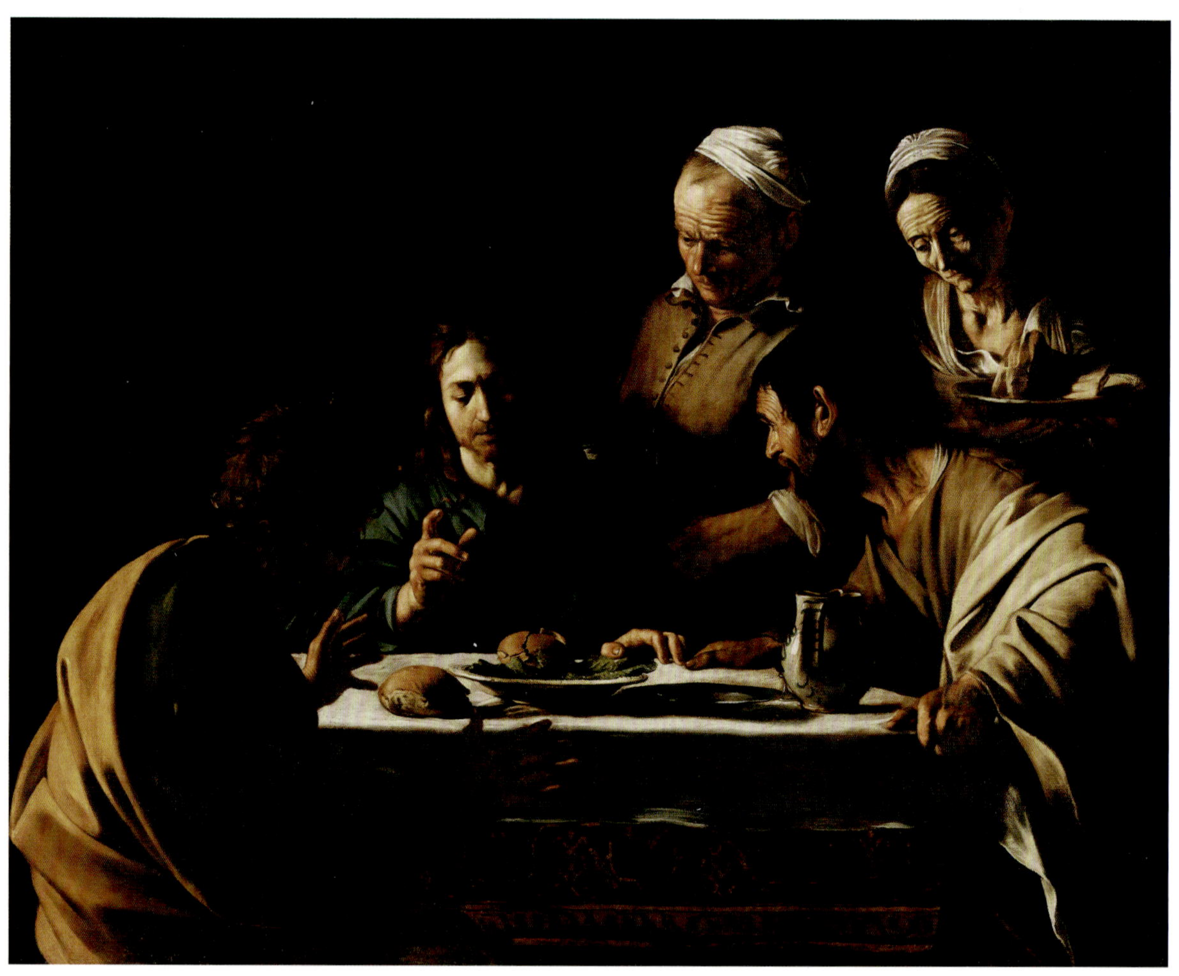

The Supper at Emmaus   *Das Emmausmahl*   *Cena in Emmaus*

Le Repas à Emmaüs   *Los discípulos de Emaús*   *Het avondmaal te Emmaüs*

1606, Oil on canvas/Huile sur toile, 141 × 175 cm, Pinacoteca di Brera, Milano

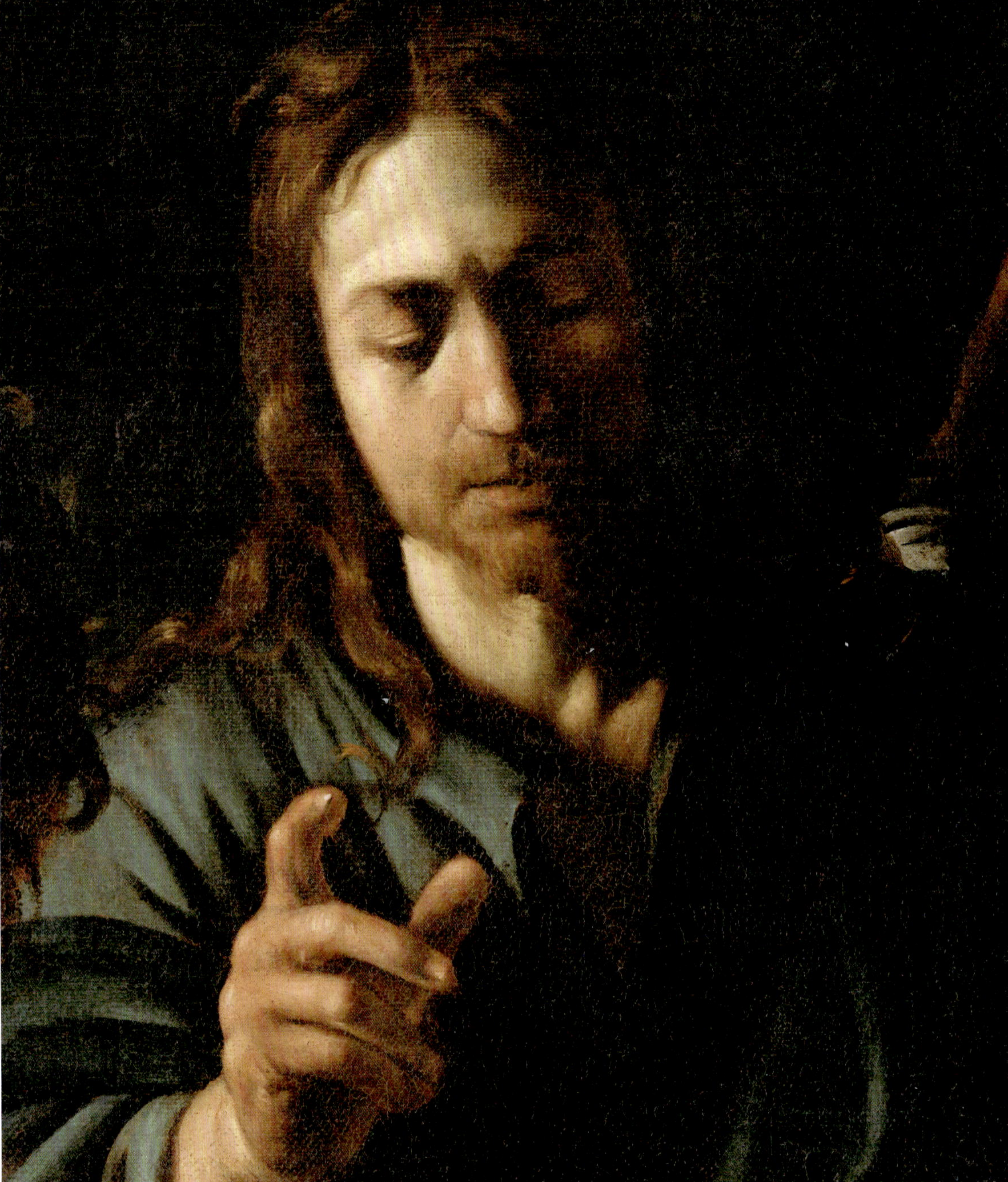

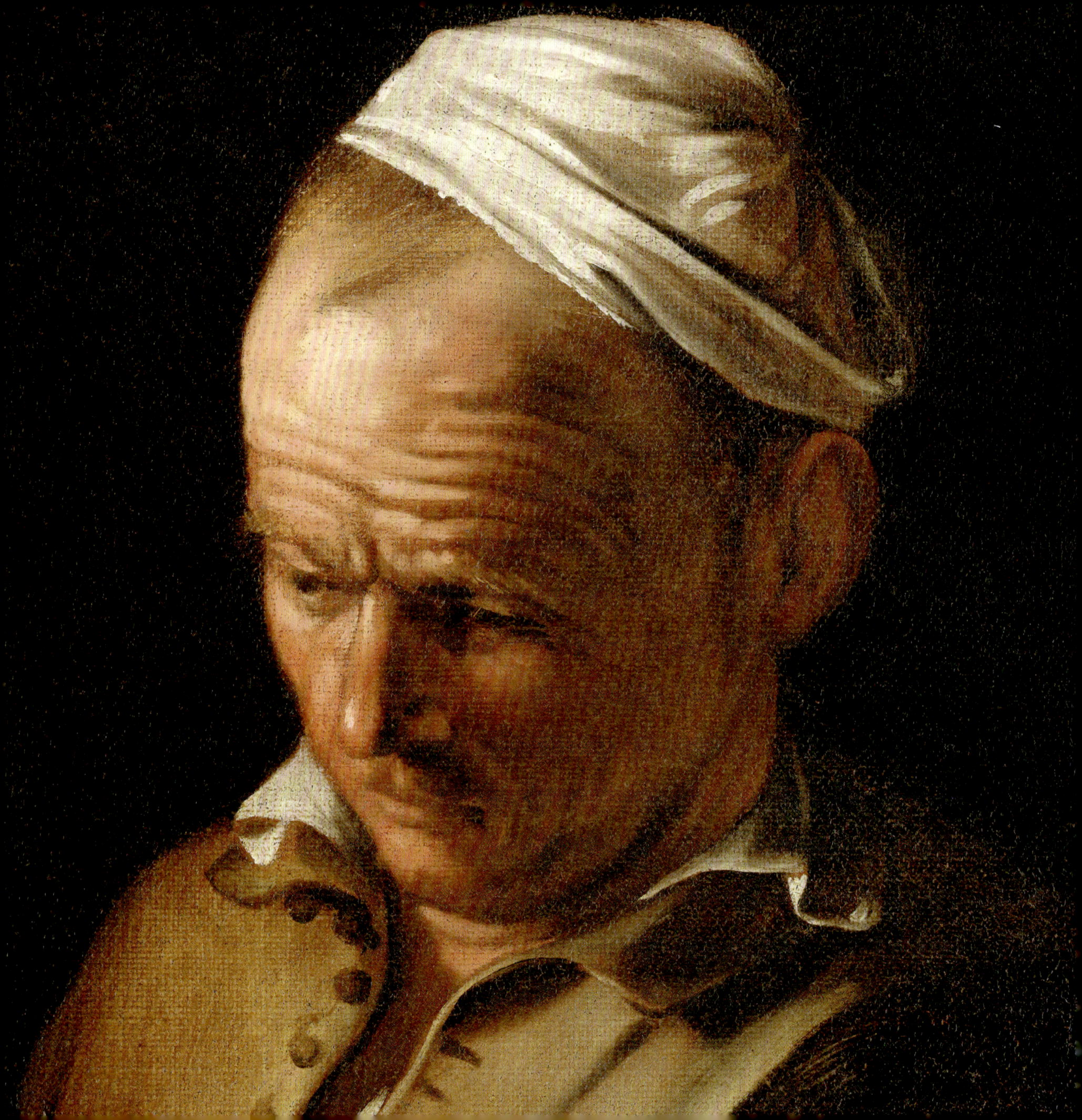

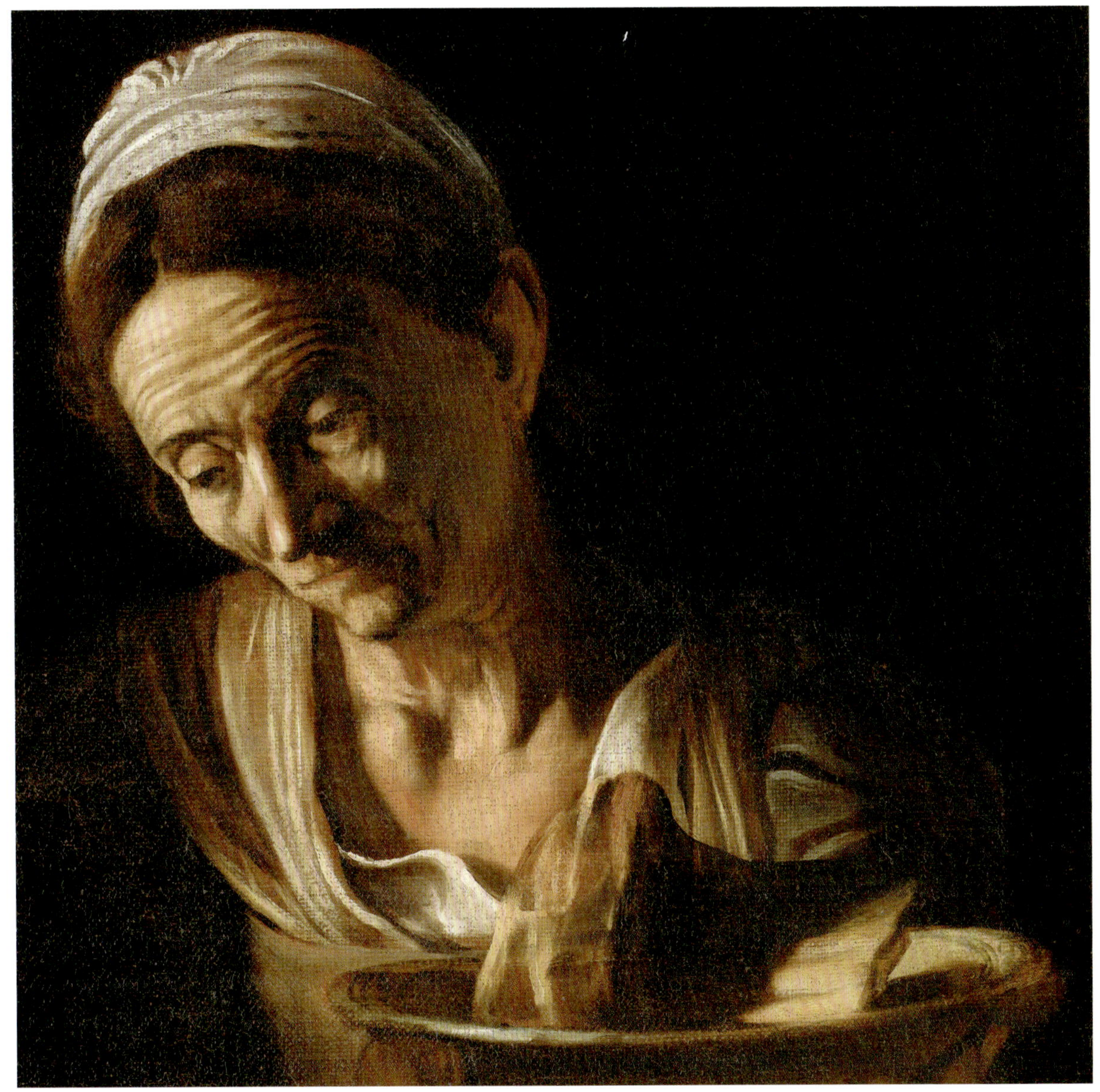

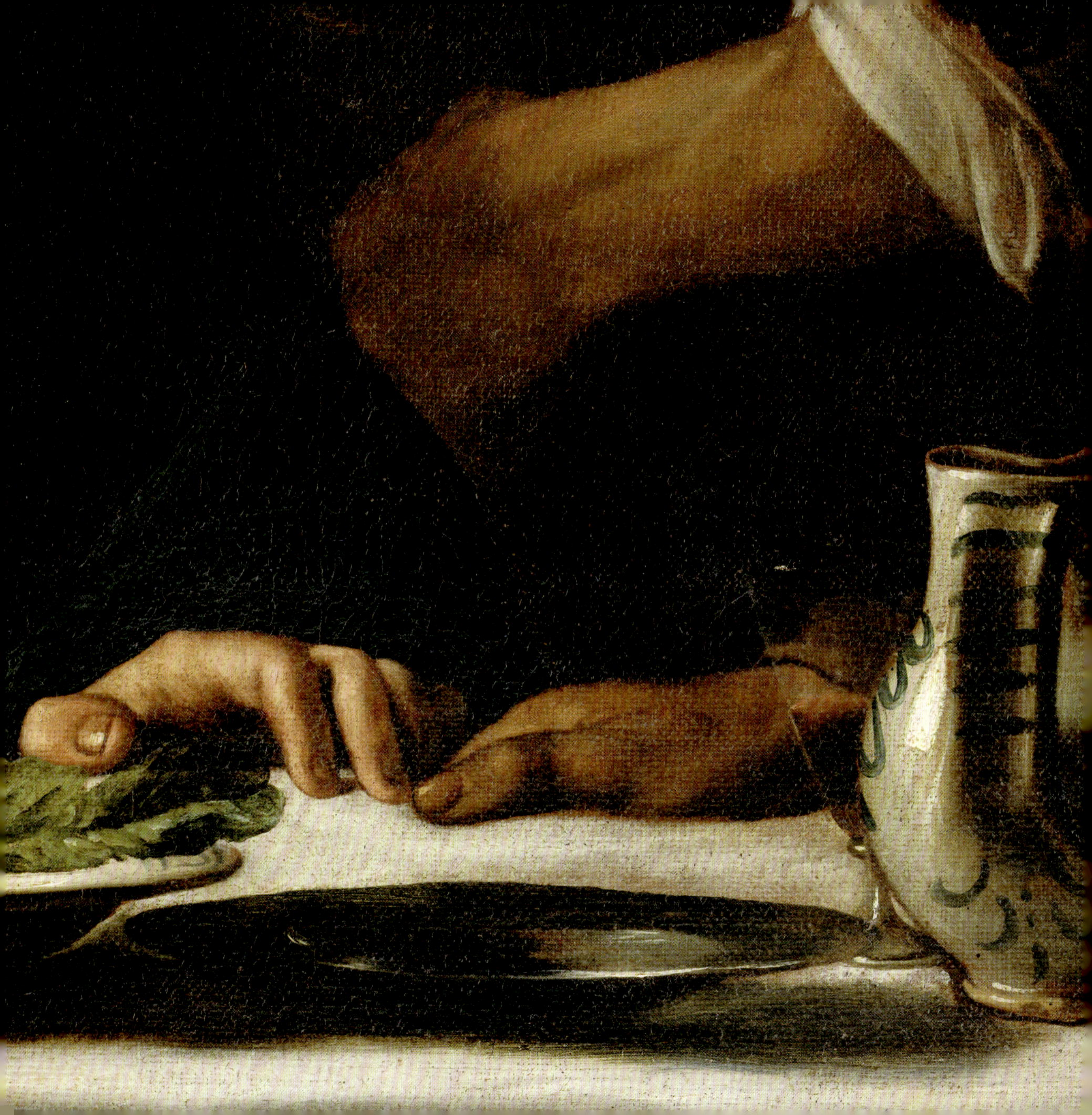

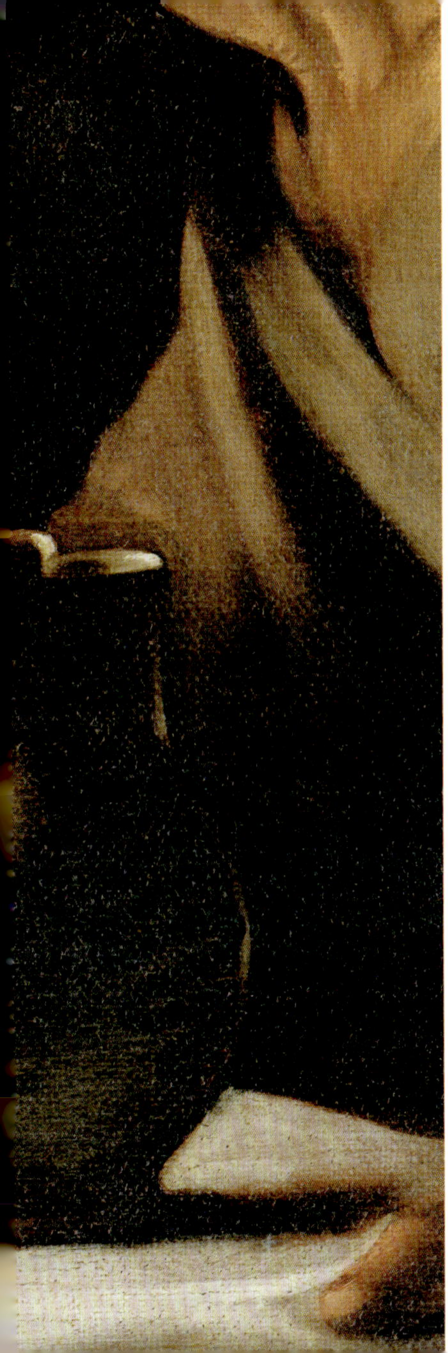

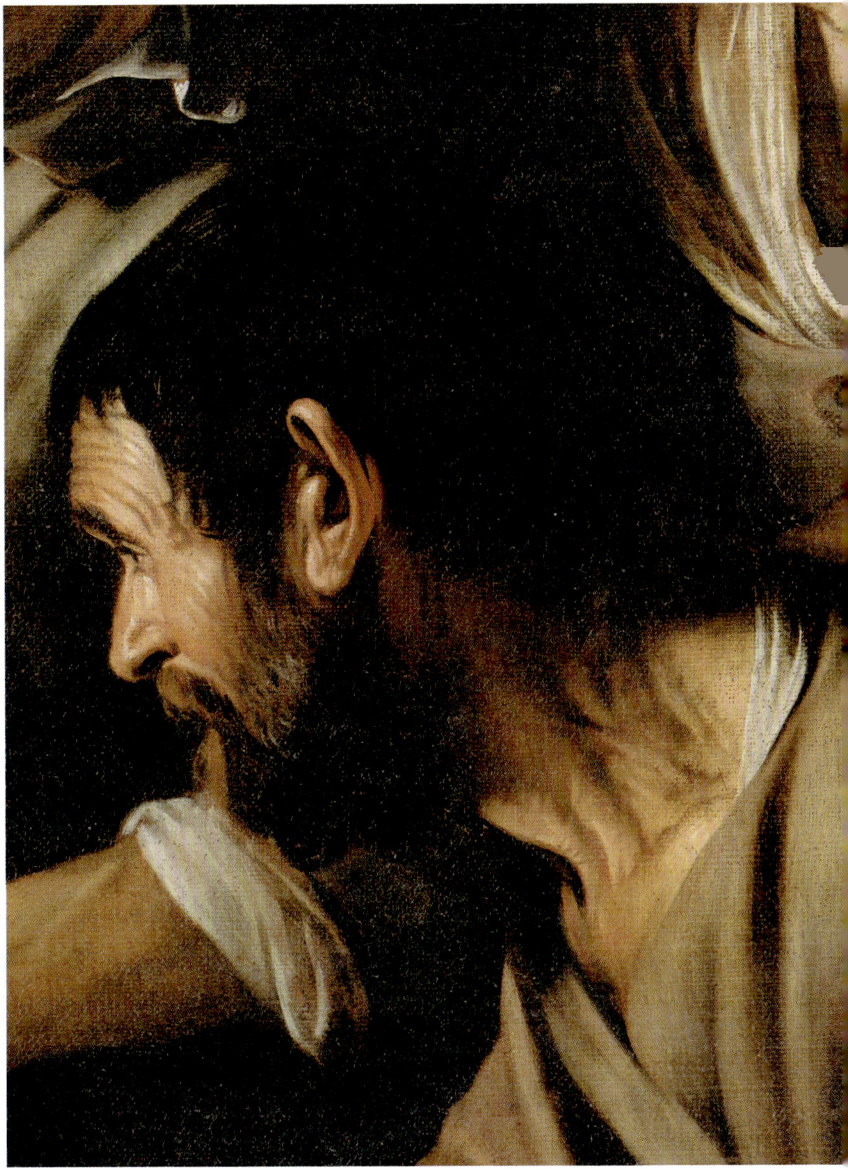

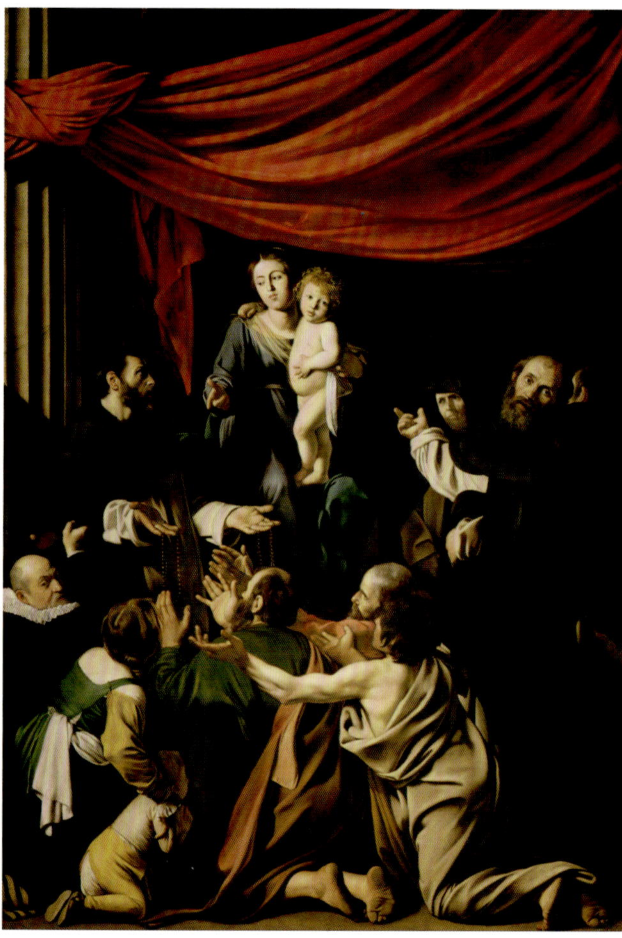

Our Lady of the Rosary

La Madone du rosaire

Rosenkranzmadonna

Madonna del Rosario

Madonna del Rosario

Madonna met de rozenkrans

c. 1606, Oil on canvas/Huile sur toile, 364,5 × 249,5 cm,
Kunsthistorisches Museum, Wien

Escape to Naples

On 29 May 1606, Caravaggio killed a man
in a fight and was wanted for murder. He
managed to escape Rome and hid out on
lands owned by the Colonna family. This
is where he painted a second version of
the *Supper at Emmaus.* But Caravaggio

Fuite à Naples

Le 29 mai 1606, Caravage tue un homme
au cours d'une rixe. Inculpé de meurtre,
il réussit à s'enfuir de Rome pour aller
se mettre à l'abri sur les terres de la
puissante famille Colonna. Il y réalise
une seconde version du *Repas à Emmaüs.*

Flucht nach Neapel

Am 29. Mai 1606 tötete Caravaggio im
Streit einen Mann und wurde wegen
Mordes gesucht. Es gelang ihm, aus Rom
zu entkommen und auf den Besitzungen
der Familie Colonna unterzutauchen.
Hier malte er eine zweite Version des

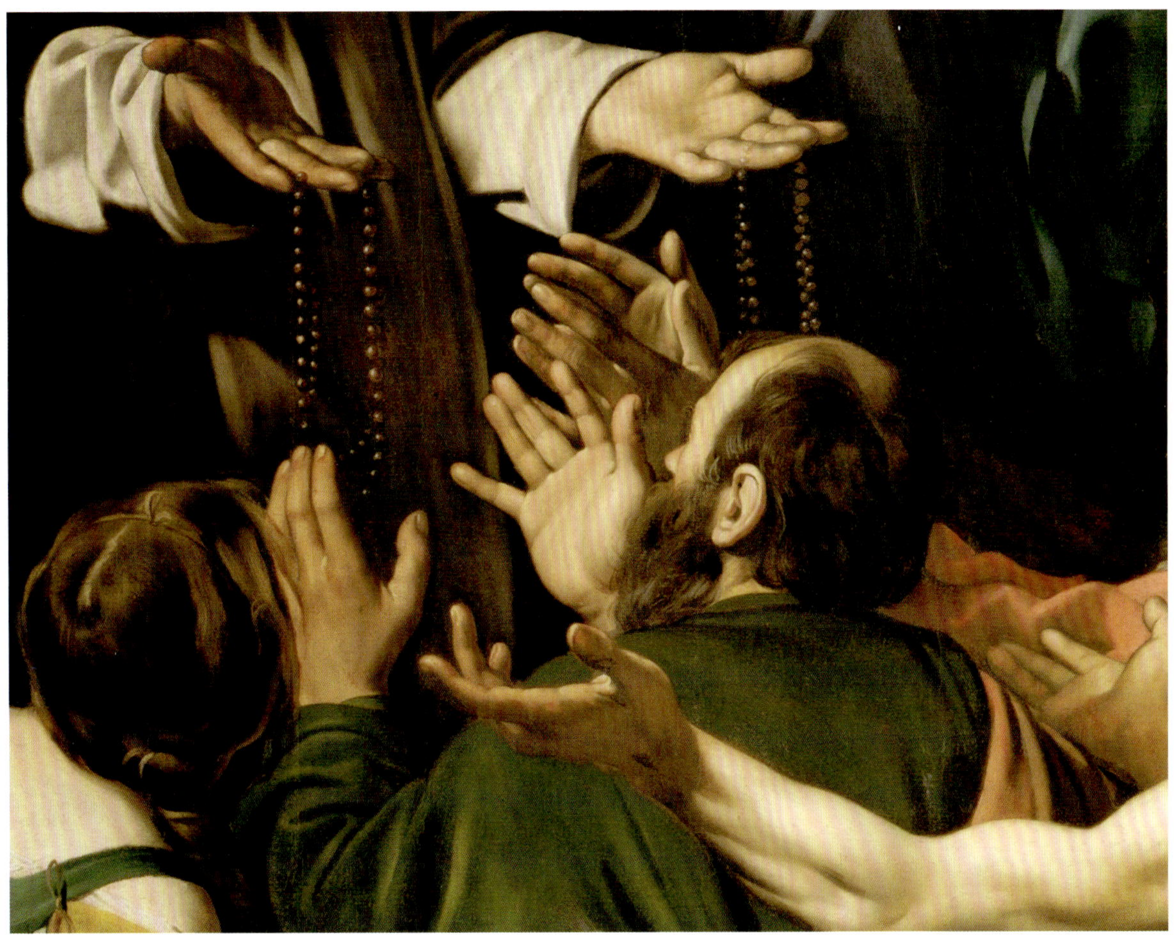

Huida a Nápoles

El 29 de mayo de 1606 Caravaggio mató
a un hombre durante una reyerta,
propiciando que se le buscara por
asesinato. Consiguió escapar de Roma
y esconderse en las propiedades de la
familia Colonna. Aquí pintó una segunda

La fuga a Napoli

Il 29 maggio 1606 Caravaggio uccise un
uomo durante una rissa e fu ricercato
per omicidio. Riuscì a fuggire da Roma
e a nascondersi nei possedimenti
della famiglia Colonna, dove dipinse
una seconda versione della *Cena in*

Vlucht naar Napels

Op 29 mei 1606 doodde Caravaggio
tijdens een ruzie een man en werd
wegens moord aangeklaagd. Het
lukte hem Rome te ontvluchten en op
het landgoed van de familie Colonna
onder te duiken. Daar creëerde hij een

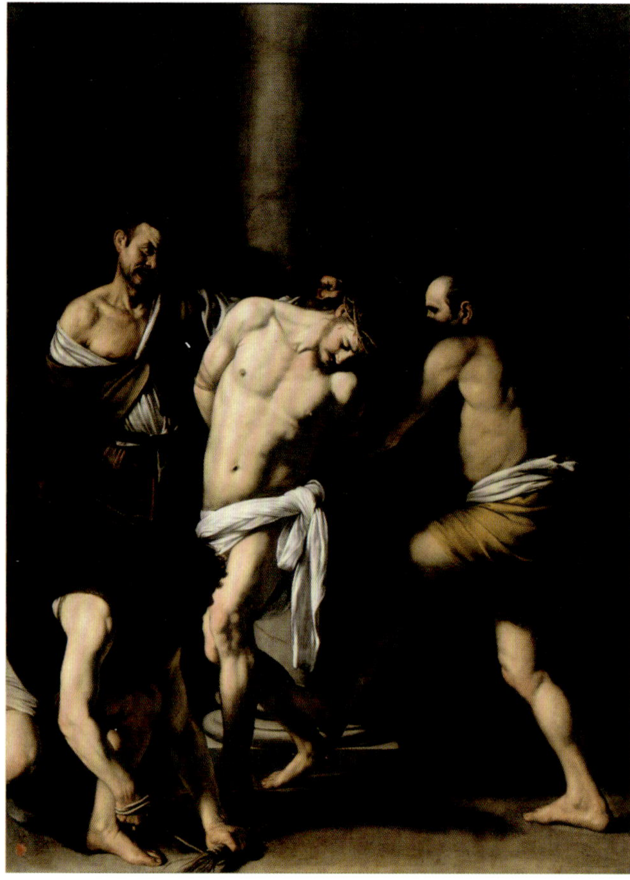

1607, Oil on canvas/Huile sur toile, 286 × 213 cm, Museo di Capodimonte, Napoli

was now an outlaw, had been sentenced to death, and so he fled to Naples.

In Naples, he used his connections to the Colonna family and was given shelter where he continued to paint. During this time, he created masterpieces such as *Our Lady of the Rosary, The Scourging of Christ,* and *The Seven Works of Mercy.*

Mais il est banni et condamné à mort, et doit se réfugier à Naples.

Les relations des Colonna y facilitent son accueil et son séjour, et il peut continuer à peindre. Caravage réalise alors des chefs-d'œuvre tels que *La Madone du rosaire, La Flagellation du Christ* et *Les Sept Œuvres de miséricorde.*

Emmausmahls. Aber Caravaggio stand unter Bann, wurde zum Tode verurteilt und floh nach Neapel.

In Neapel halfen ihm die Verbindungen der Colonna und er wurde freundlich aufgenommen. Er malte weiter. Es entstanden Meisterwerke wie die *Rosenkranzmadonna,* die *Geißelung Christi* und die *Sieben Werke der Barmherzigkeit.*

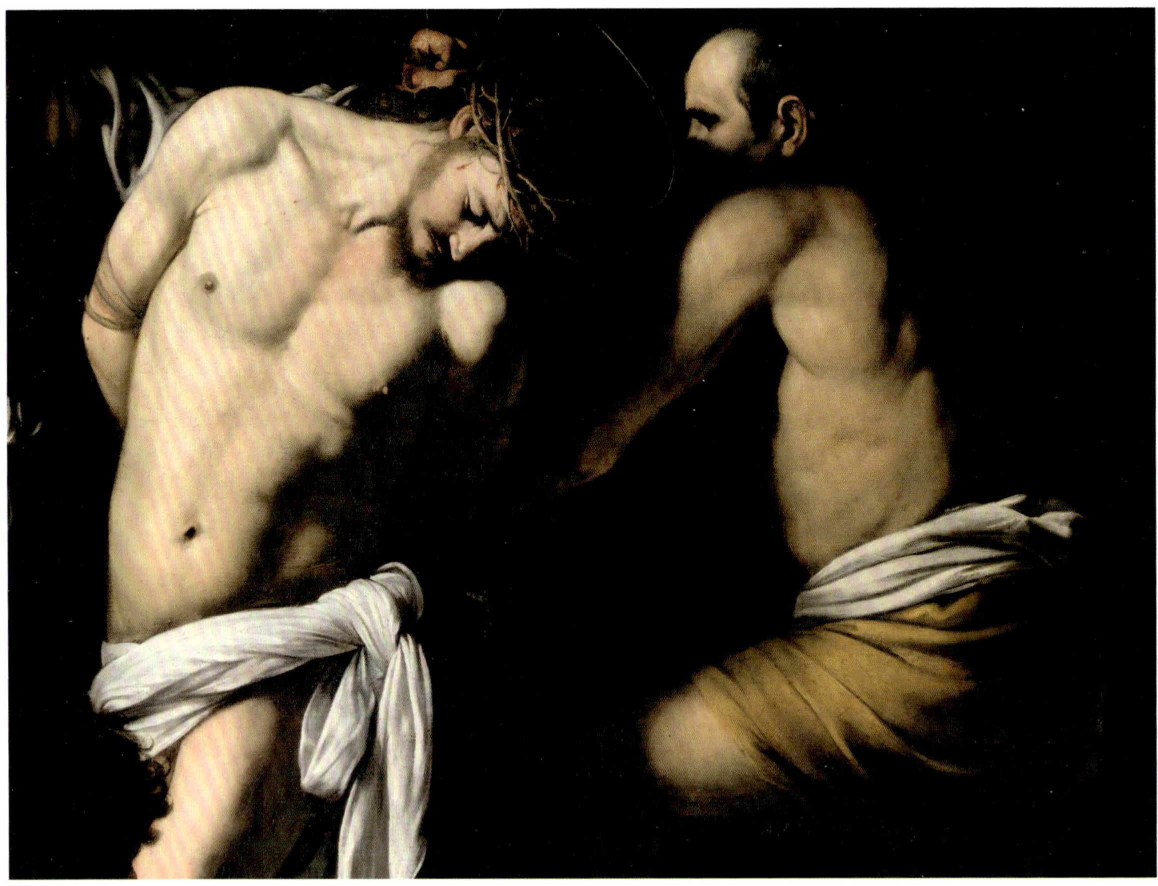

versión de *Los discípulos de Emaús*. Pero Caravaggio fue exiliado, se le condenó a muerte y huyó a Nápoles.

En Nápoles las conexiones de los Colonna le ayudaron, y fue recibido de forma amistosa. Continuó pintando. Creó obras maestras como *La Madonna del Rosario*, *La flagelación de Cristo* y *Siete obras de misericordia*.

Emmaus. Caravaggio era però in esilio; fu infine condannato a morte e fuggì a Napoli, dove fu aiutato da conoscenti dei Colonna e fu ben accolto. Nella città campana continuò a dipingere, dando vita a capolavori come la *Madonna del Rosario*, la *Flagellazione di Cristo* e le *Sette opere di Misericordia*.

tweede versie van *Het avondmaal te Emmaüs*. Maar hij was nu een balling, werd ter dood veroordeeld en vluchtte naar Napels.

Daar werd hij door zijn relatie met de Colonna's verwelkomd. Hij schilderde hier meesterwerken als *De Madonna van de rozenkrans*, *De Geseling van Christus* en *De zeven werken der barmhartigheid*.

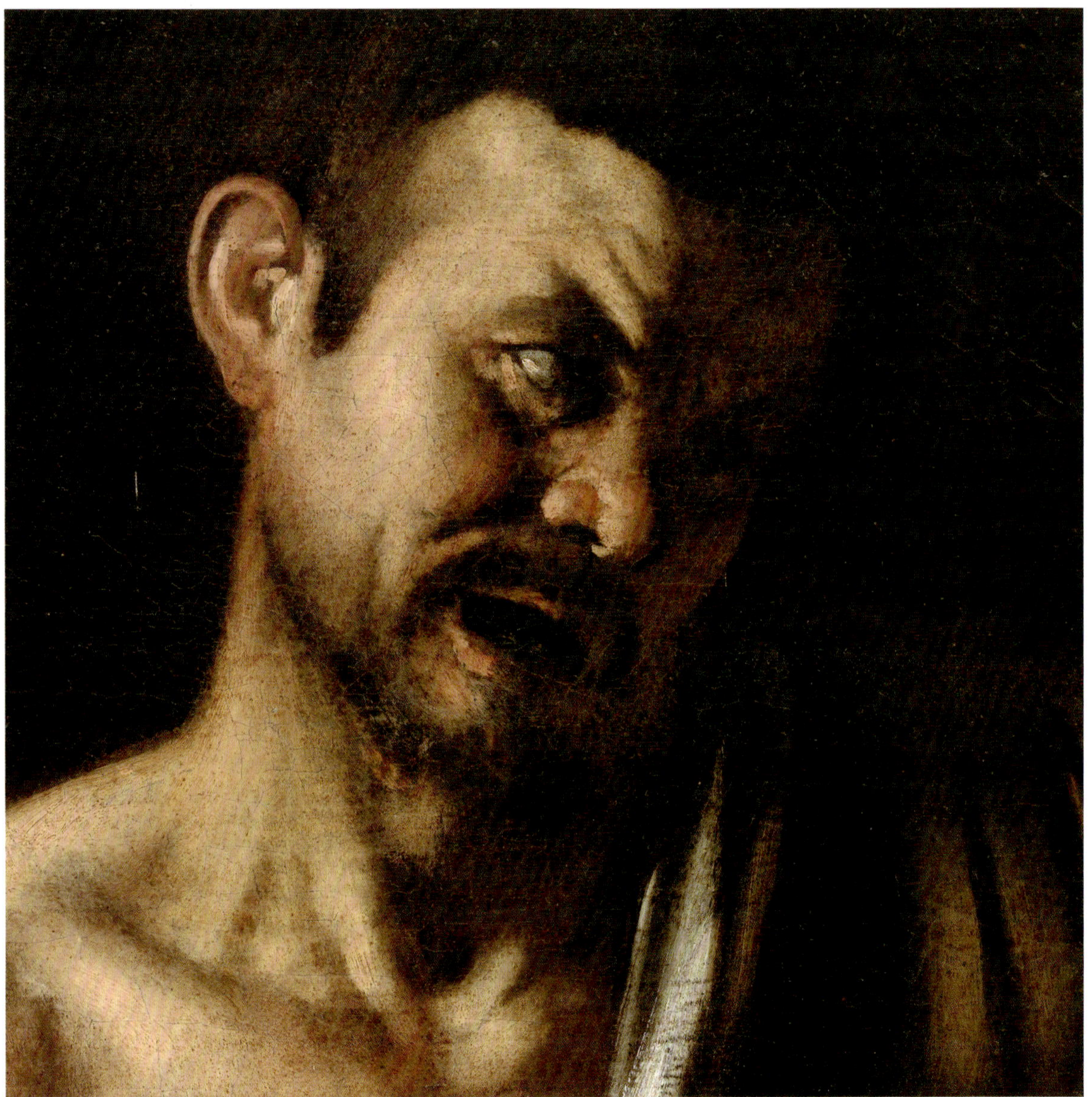

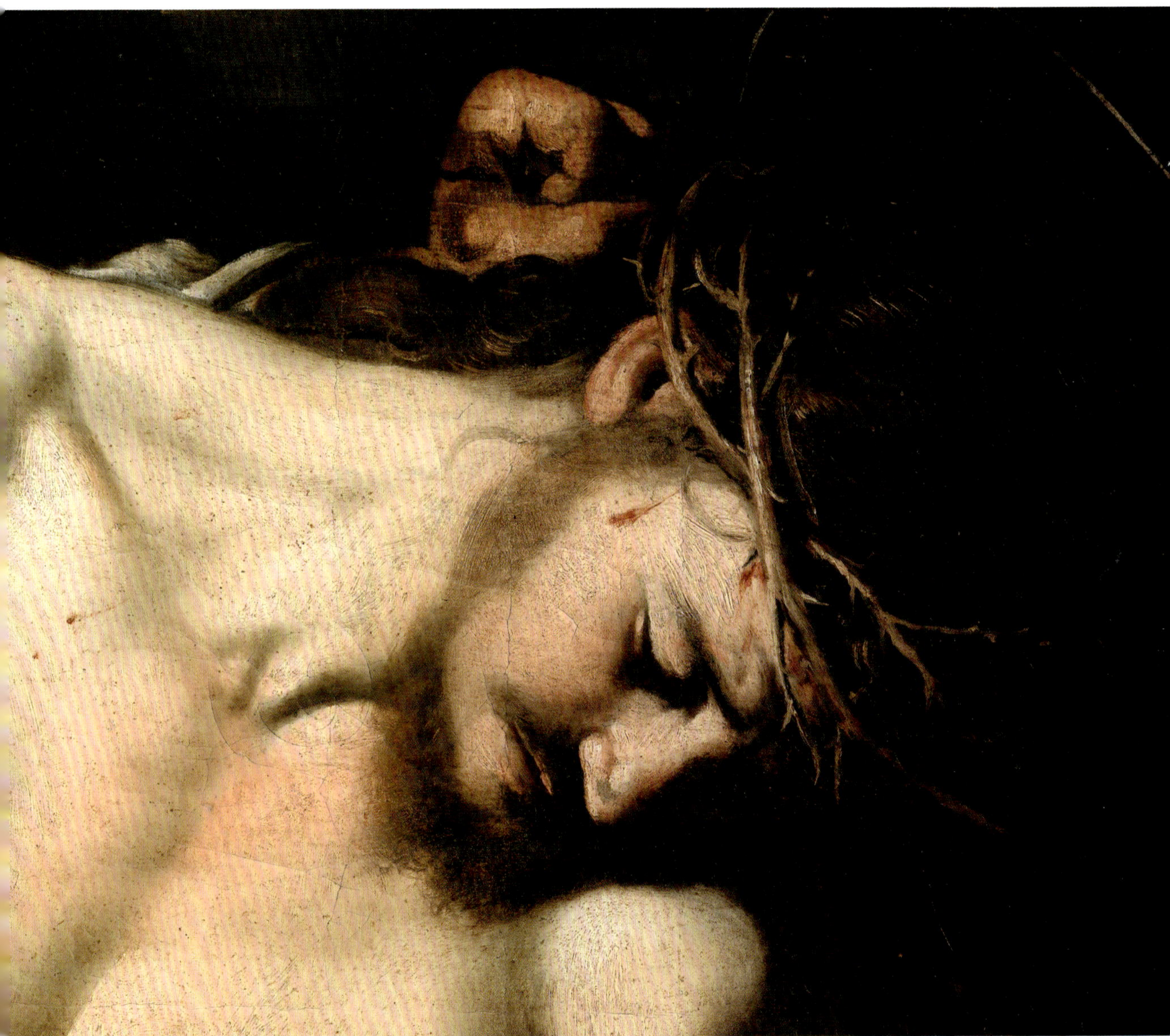

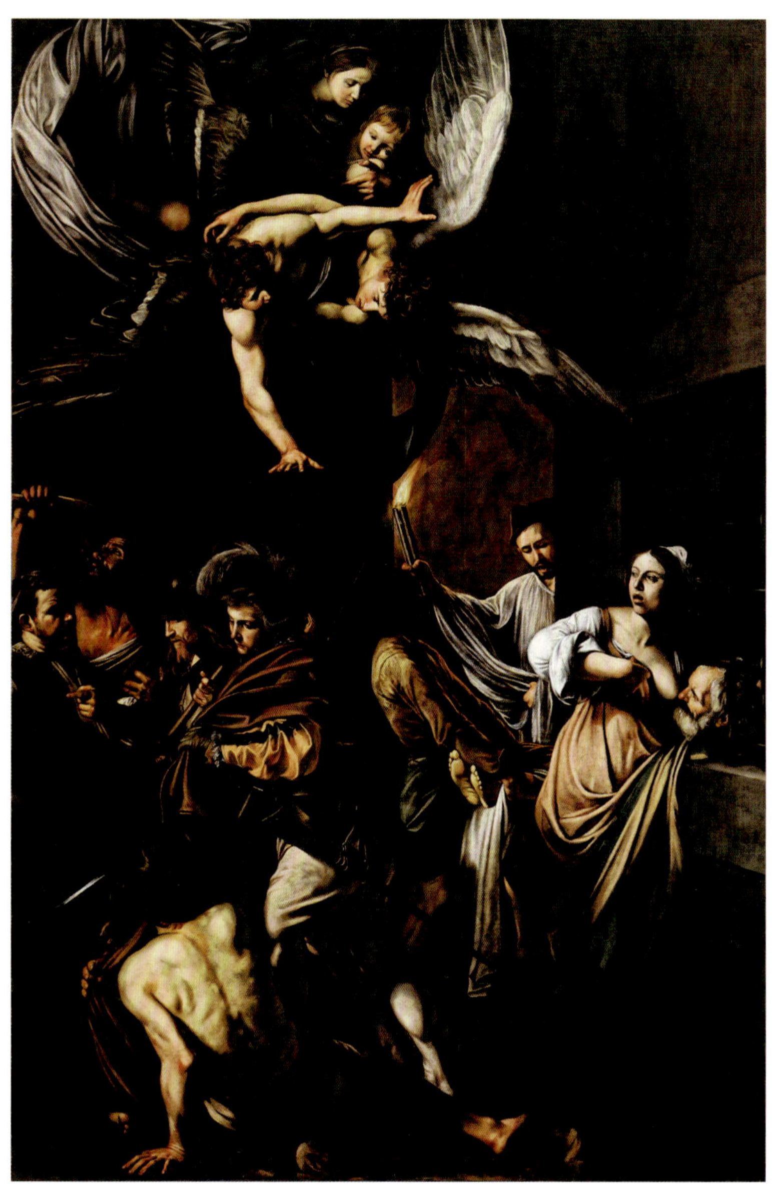

Seven Works of Mercy
Les Sept Œuvres de miséricorde
Sieben Werke der Barmherzigkeit
Las siete obras de misericordia
Sette opere di Misericordia
De zeven werken der barmhartigheid

*1606, Oil on canvas/Huile sur toile, 390 × 260 cm,
Chiesa del Pio Monte della Misericordia, Napoli*

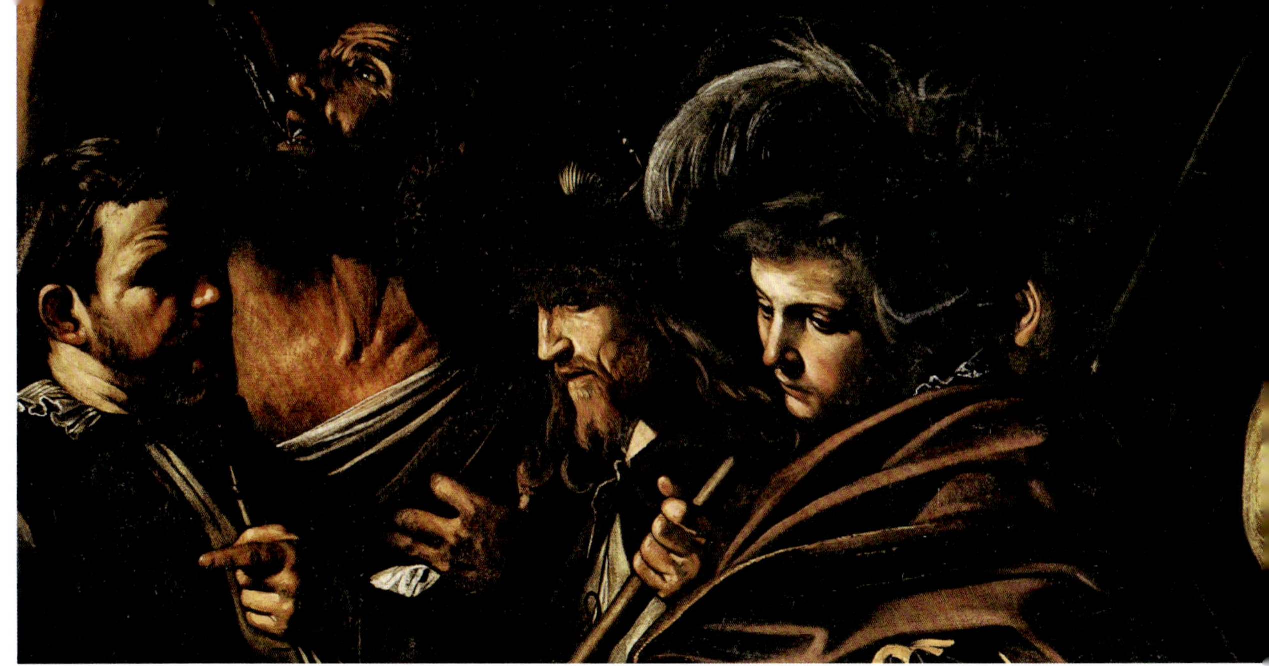

This monumental altarpiece was commissioned by the religious order Pio Monte della Misericordia for their church. Given a generous fee, Caravaggio painted a monumental masterpiece, daring in his inimitable style to be the first painter to represent all seven works of mercy described in Matthew's Gospel in a single image: feeding the hungry, giving drink to the thirsty, sheltering the stranger, clothing the naked, visiting the sick, visiting prisoners, and burying the dead.

Ce retable fut commandé par les directeurs du Pio Monte della Misericordia, pour l'église de la Confrérie. Généreusement payé, Caravage créa un chef-d'œuvre monumental, en osant représenter en un seul et unique tableau – pour la première fois dans la peinture, dans un « défi » très caravagesque – les « sept œuvres de miséricorde » décrites dans l'Évangile de Matthieu : nourrir ceux qui ont faim, abreuver ceux qui ont soif, accueillir les étrangers, vêtir ceux qui sont nus, visiter les malades, visiter les prisonniers et ensevelir les morts.

Das riesige Altargemälde wurde von den Ordensvorstehern des Pio Monte della Misericordia für die Kirche der Bruderschaft in Auftrag gegeben. Mit großzügigem Honorar bedacht, schuf Caravaggio ein monumentales Meisterwerk und wagte es – ganz caravaggesk – als erster Maler, die sieben, im Evangelium nach Matthäus beschriebenen Werke der Barmherzigkeit in einem einzigen Bild darzustellen: Hungrige speisen, Durstige tränken, Fremde beherbergen, Nackte bekleiden, Kranke besuchen, Gefangene besuchen und Tote bestatten.

El monumental cuadro de altar fue encargado por el director de la Orden del Pio Monte della Misericordia para la iglesia de la hermandad. Concebida con un pago generoso, Caravaggio pintó una obra maestra monumental y consiguió –típico de Caravaggio– ser el primer pintor en aunar las siete obras de la misericordia descritas en el Evangelio según San Mateo en una única imagen: Da de comer a los hambrientos, calma la sed de los sedientos, da posada a extraños, viste a los desnudos, visita a los enfermos, visita a los presos y entierra a los difuntos.

Questo monumentale dipinto d'altare fu commissionato dai responsabili della Congregazione del Pio Monte per la Chiesa della Confraternita. Dietro il pagamento di un generoso compenso, Caravaggio dipinse un magnifico capolavoro e fu il primo pittore ad osare, in puro stile caravaggesco, a rappresentare in un unico quadro le sette opere di misericordia corporale descritte nel Vangelo secondo Matteo: dar da mangiare agli affamati, dar da bere agli assetati, vestire gli ignudi, alloggiare i pellegrini, visitare gli infermi, visitare i carcerati e seppellire i morti.

Het monumentale altaarstuk werd besteld door de broederschap Pio Monte della Misericordia en was bestemd voor de kerk ervan. Caravaggio werd goed betaald en schiep een monumentaal meesterwerk: kenmerkend voor hem durfde hij het aan om als eerste schilder de zeven in het evangelie van Matteüs genoemde werken der barmhartigheid in één schilderij samen te brengen. Hij liet de hongerige spijzen, de dorstige drinken en de vreemdeling herbergen; hij kleedde de naakte, bezocht de zieke alsook de gevangene, en hij droeg de dode ten grave.

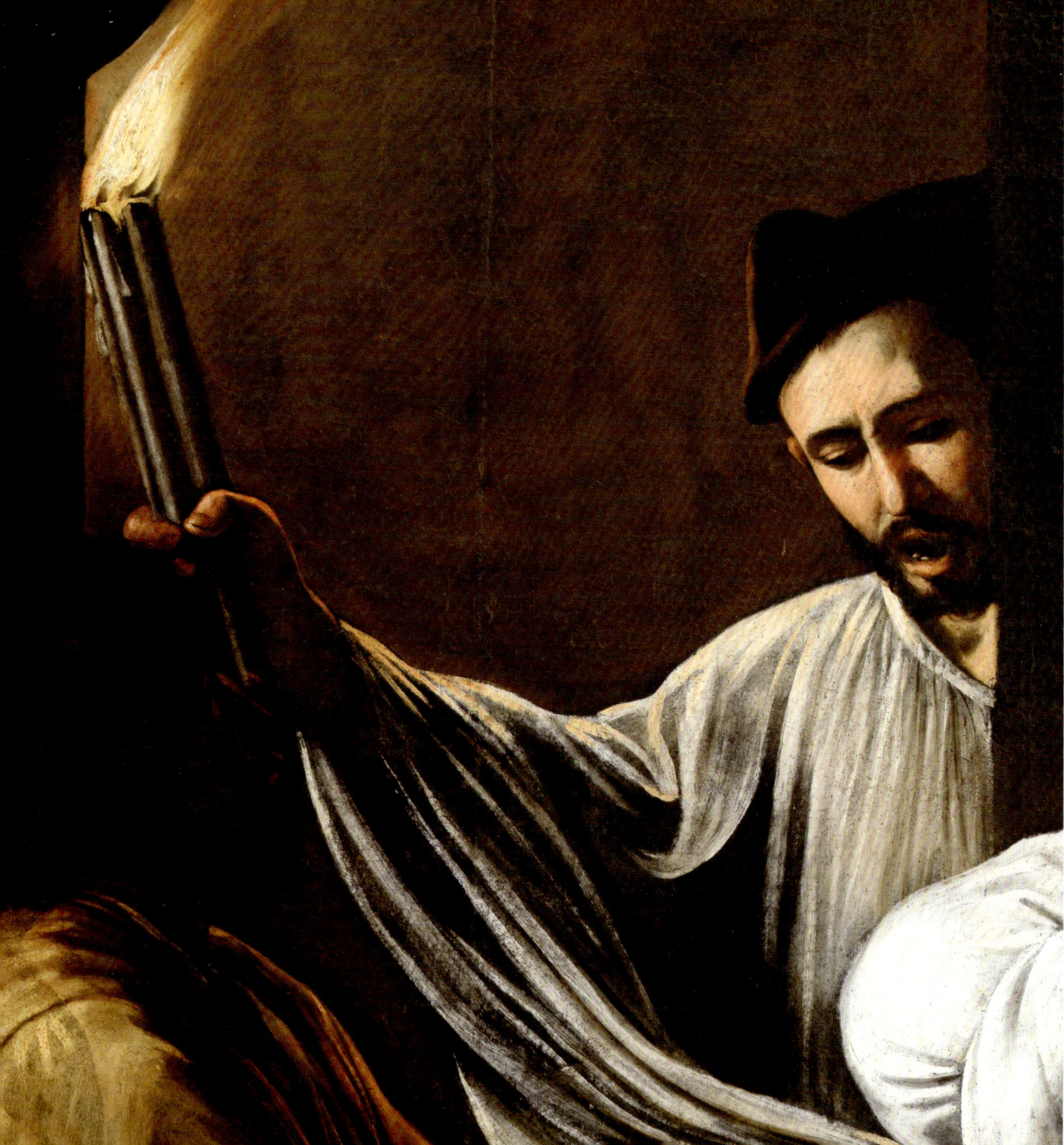

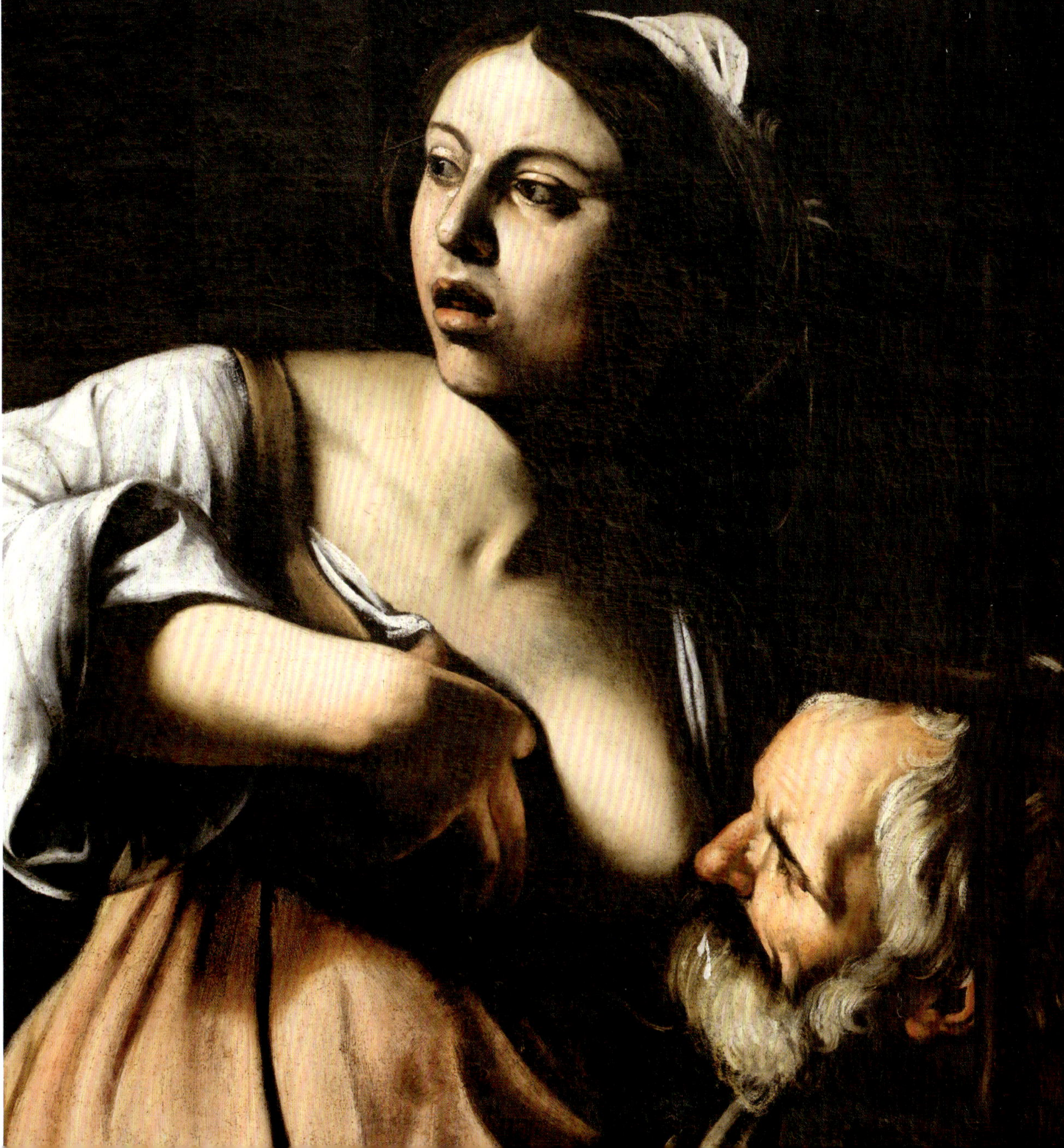

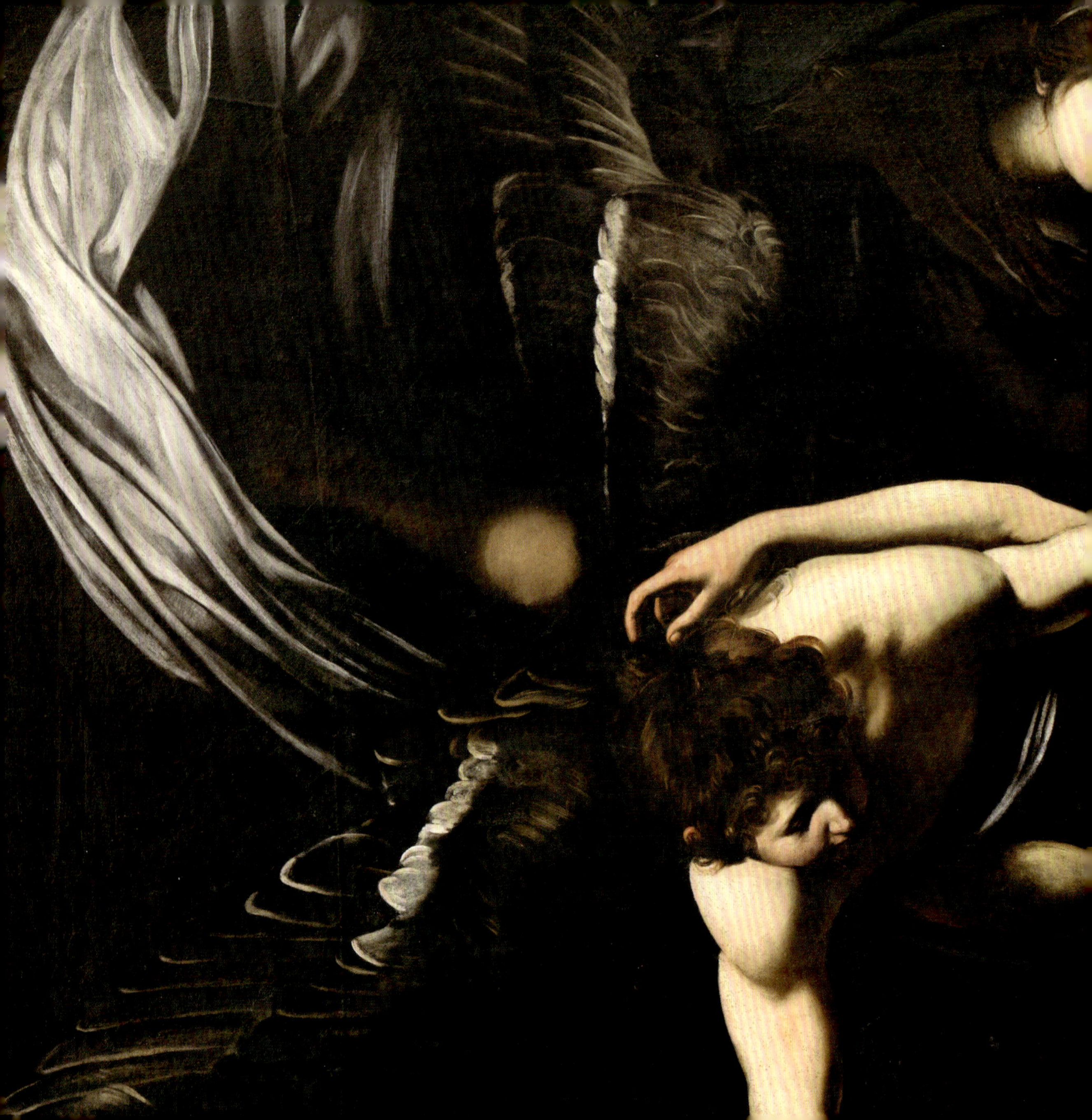

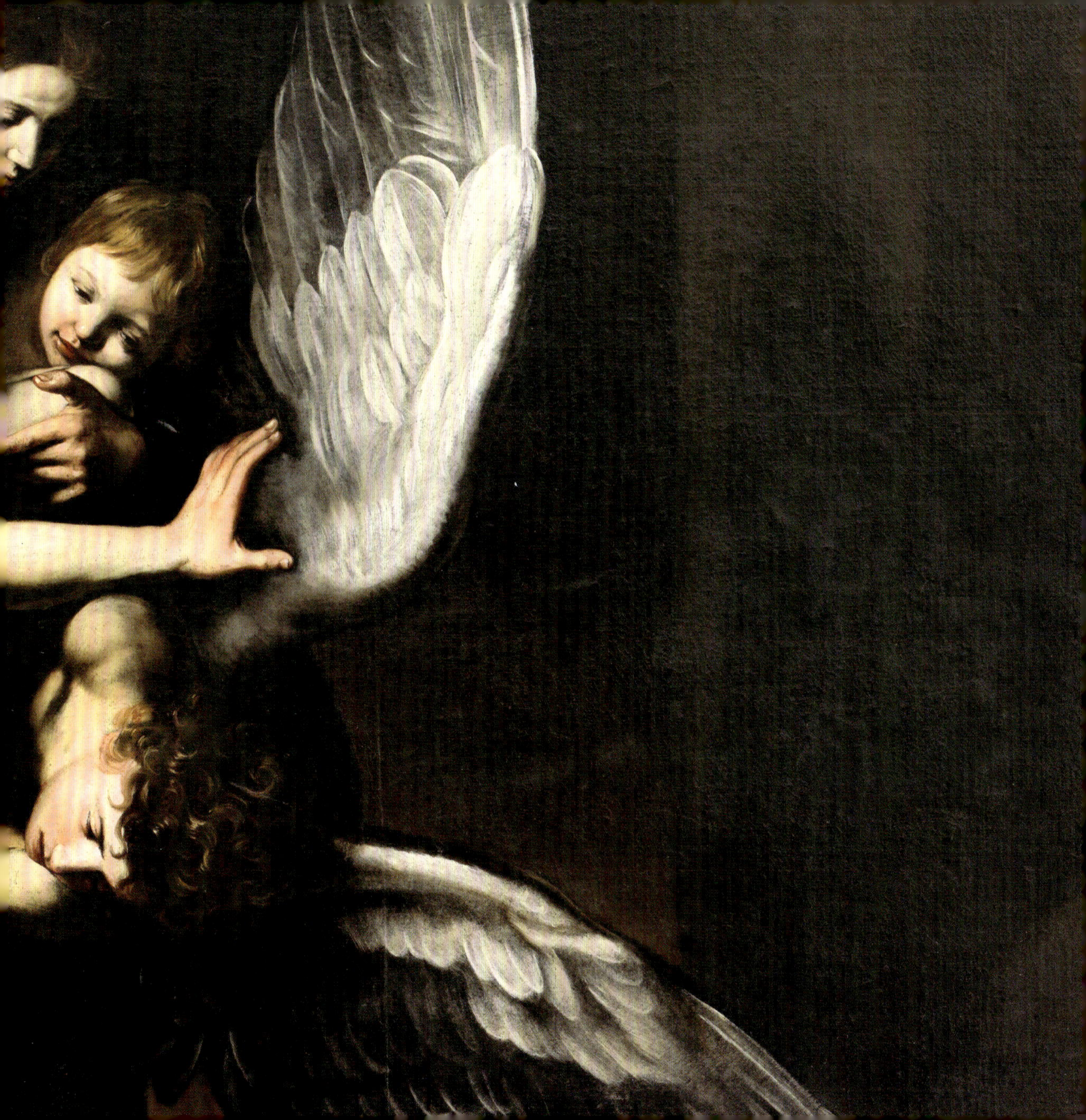

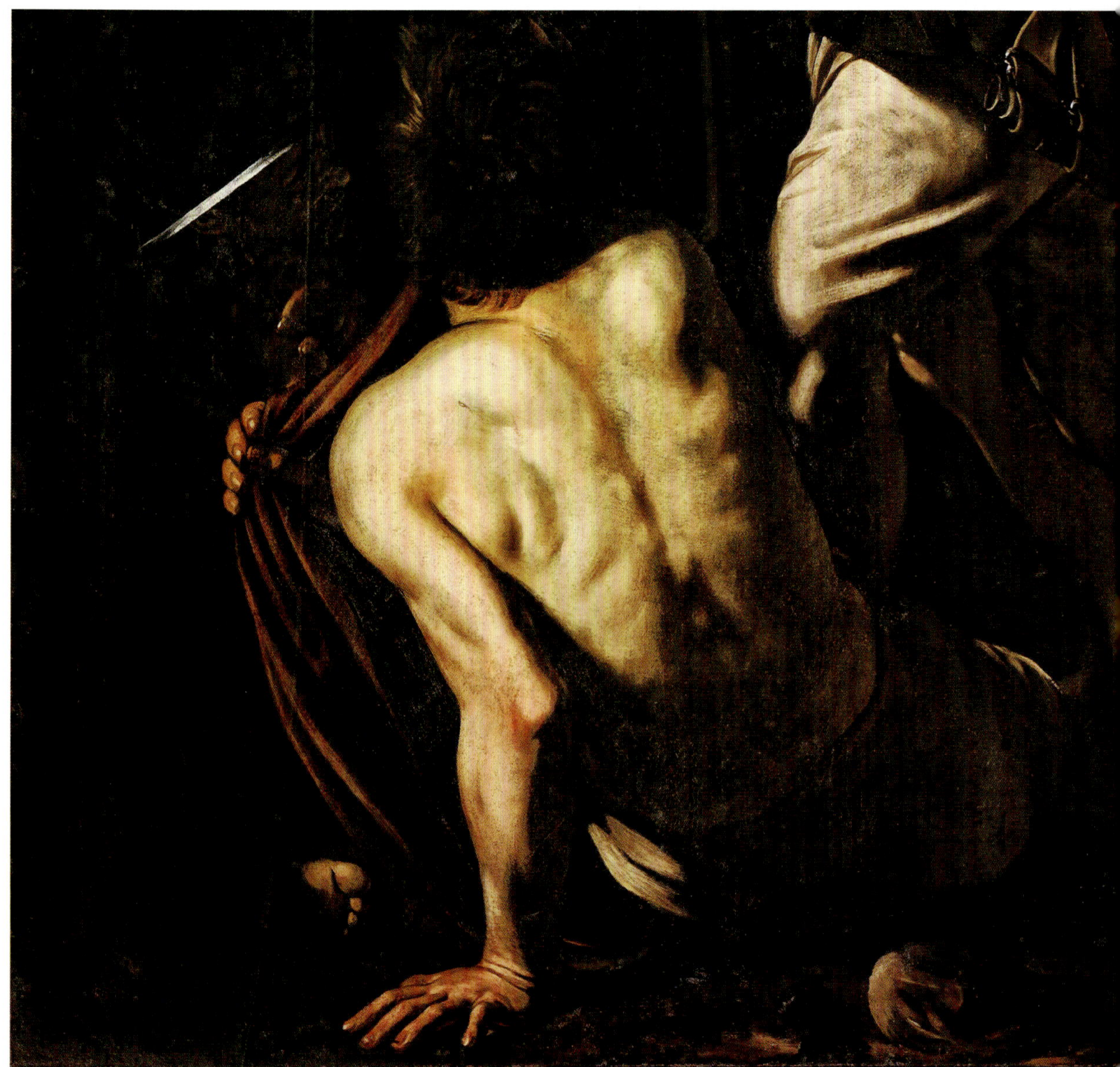

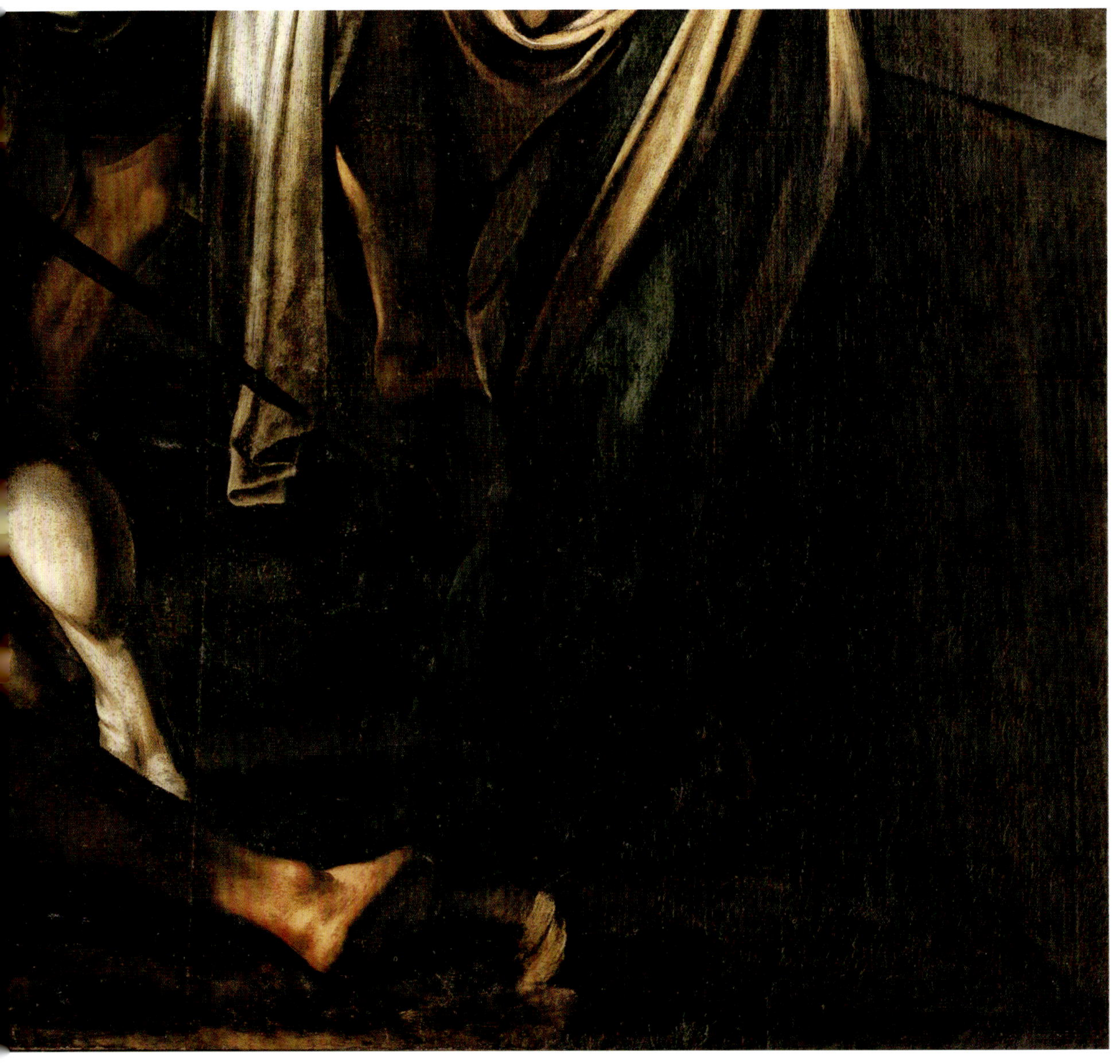

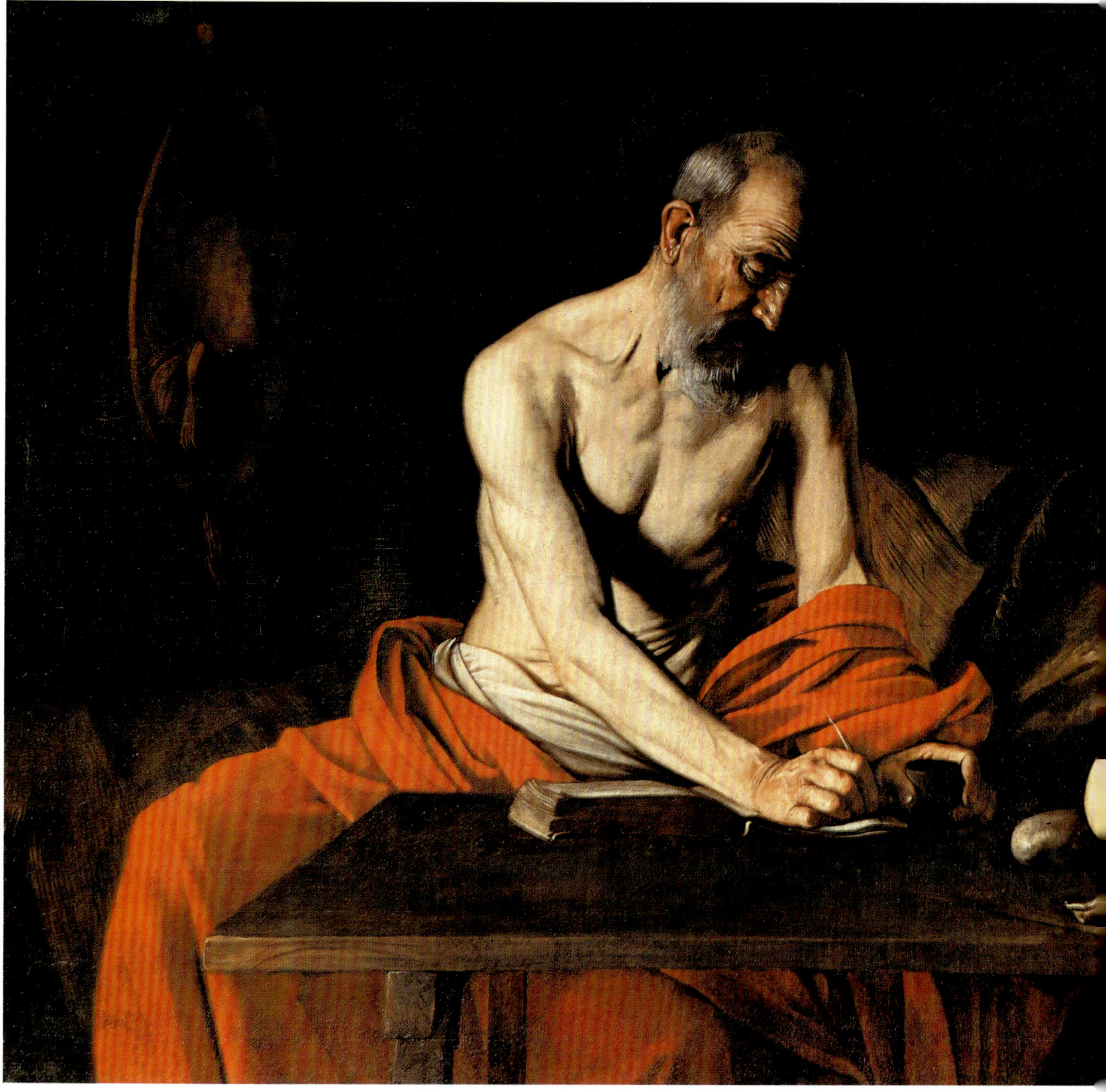

St Jerome Writing

Saint Jérôme écrivant ou *Wignacourt en saint Jérôme*

Der schreibende hl. Hieronymus

San Jerónimo escribiendo

San Gerolamo scrivente

De schrijvende Sint-Hiëronymus

1607, Oil on canvas/Huile sur toile, 117 × 157 cm, Kon-Katidral ta' San Ġwann, Valletta

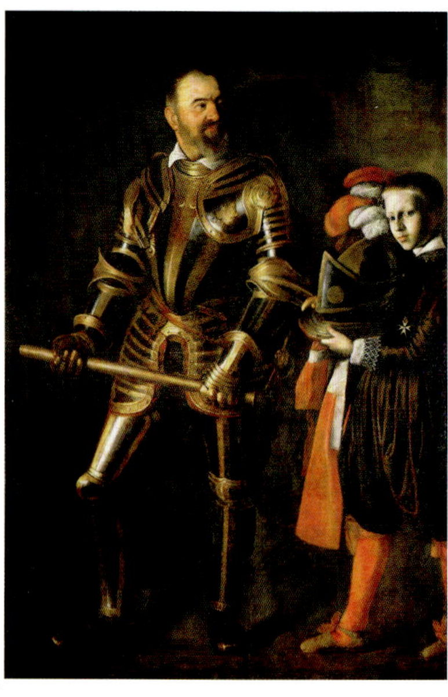

1607, Oil on canvas/Huile sur toile, 194 × 134 cm, Musée du Louvre, Paris

Exile in Malta and Sicily

In 1607, Caravaggio left Naples for Malta. He did everything he could to become a Knight of the Order of Malta, since this was a chance to receive pardon and be allowed to return to Rome. He painted some larger works here such as *The Beheading of John the Baptist* for St John's Co-Cathedral and two portraits of the Grand Master of the Order. He was knighted, but again got into so much trouble that he was expelled from the Order. Caravaggio then fled again, this time to Sicily. Here he created images marked with a harrowing darkness such as *The Burial of St Lucy, The Raising of Lazarus,* and the *Adoration of the Shepherds.* In late 1609, he returned to Naples.

Exil à Malte et en Sicile

En 1607, Caravage quitte Naples pour aller à Malte. Il met tout en œuvre pour devenir chevalier de l'Ordre de Malte, espérant ainsi obtenir une grâce pontificale et pouvoir revenir à Rome. Il peint sur place quelques grandes œuvres comme *La Décollation de saint Jean-Baptiste* (pour la co-cathédrale Saint-Jean de La Valette) et deux portraits du grand-maître de l'Ordre. Mais reçu chevalier, il se compromet dans de telles affaires qu'il est rapidement radié de l'Ordre et doit s'enfuir de nouveau, cette fois en Sicile. Là-bas naissent des œuvres extrêmement sombres comme *L'Ensevelissement de sainte Lucie, La Résurrection de Lazare* et *L'Adoration des bergers.* Il revient à Naples en 1609.

Exil auf Malta und Sizilien

1607 verließ Caravaggio Neapel und ging nach Malta. Hier setzte er alles daran, ein Ritter des Malteserordens zu werden, da er sich damit eine Chance auf Begnadigung und die Rückkehr nach Rom erhoffte. Er malte einige größere Werke wie *Die Enthauptung Johannes des Täufers* für die St.-Johannes-Konkathedrale und zwei Porträts des Großmeisters des Ordens. Er wurde zum Ritter geschlagen, brachte sich aber in solche Schwierigkeiten, dass man ihn aus dem Orden ausschloss und er erneut floh, diesmal nach Sizilien. Hier entstanden Bilder von erschütternder Dunkelheit wie *Begräbnis der hl. Lucia, Die Auferweckung des Lazarus* und *Anbetung der Hirten.* Ende 1609 kehrte er nach Neapel zurück.

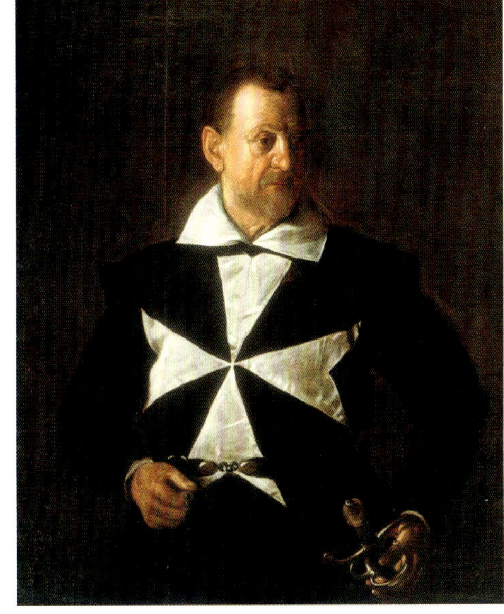

Portrait of Antonio Martelli, Knight of Malta
Portrait d'un chevalier de Malte ou Portrait d'Antonio Martelli
Porträt des Malteserritters Antonio Martelli
Retrato de Fray Antonio Martelli
Ritratto di Fra Antonio Martelli
Portret van de Maltezer ridder Antonio Martelli

1608, Oil on canvas/Huile sur toile, 118,5 × 95,5 cm, Galleria Palatina, Firenze

Exilio en Malta y Sicilia

En 1607 Caravaggio abandona Nápoles y se dirige a Malta. Aquí se concentró en conseguir ser ordenado caballero de la orden de Malta, para poder así tener una posibilidad de conseguir un indulto y volver a Roma. Pintó varios trabajos de gran tamaño como *La decapitación de San Juan Bautista* para la Concatedral de San Juan y dos retratos del gran maestre de la orden. Fue ordenado caballero, pero se metió en tantos problemas que se le acabó expulsando de la orden y tuvo que volver a huir, esta vez a Sicilia. Aquí creó imágenes de una oscuridad demoledora como *El entierro de Santa Lucía, La resurrección de Lázaro* y *La adoración de los pastores.* A finales de 1609 volvió a Nápoles.

L'esilio a Malta e in Sicilia

Nel 1607 Caravaggio lasciò Napoli per recarsi a Malta, dove fece di tutto per diventare un Cavaliere dell'Ordine di Malta in quanto sperava così di poter ricevere il condono e tornare a Roma. A Malta dipinse alcune opere importanti, come la *Decollazione di San Giovanni Battista* per la Concattedrale di San Giovanni Battista e due ritratti del Gran maestro dell'Ordine. Fu nominato cavaliere, ma si mise nuovamente nei guai e fu così escluso dall'Ordine e costretto a fuggire di nuovo, questa volta in Sicilia, dove dipinse quadri con un'oscurità sconvolgente come il *Seppellimento di Santa Lucia, La Resurrezione di Lazzaro* e *L'Adorazione dei pastori.* Alla fine del 1609 tornò poi a Napoli.

Ballingschap op Malta en Sicilië

In 1607 verliet Caravaggio Napels en voer naar Malta. Daar zette hij alles op alles om ridder van de Maltezerorde te worden, omdat hij daarmee hoopte begenadigd te worden en naar Rome te kunnen terugkeren. Hij creëerde enkele grotere doeken, waaronder *De onthoofding van Johannes de Doper* voor de Sint-Janscokathedraal en twee portretten van de grootmeester van de orde. Hij werd tot ridder geslagen, maar raakte dusdanig in de problemen dat hij uit de orde werd gestoten en weer moest vluchten, ditmaal naar Sicilië. Daar ontstonden enkele verontrustend duistere schilderijen, waaronder *De begrafenis van de heilige Lucia, De opwekking van Lazarus* en *De Aanbidding door de Herders.* Eind 1609 keerde hij terug naar Napels.

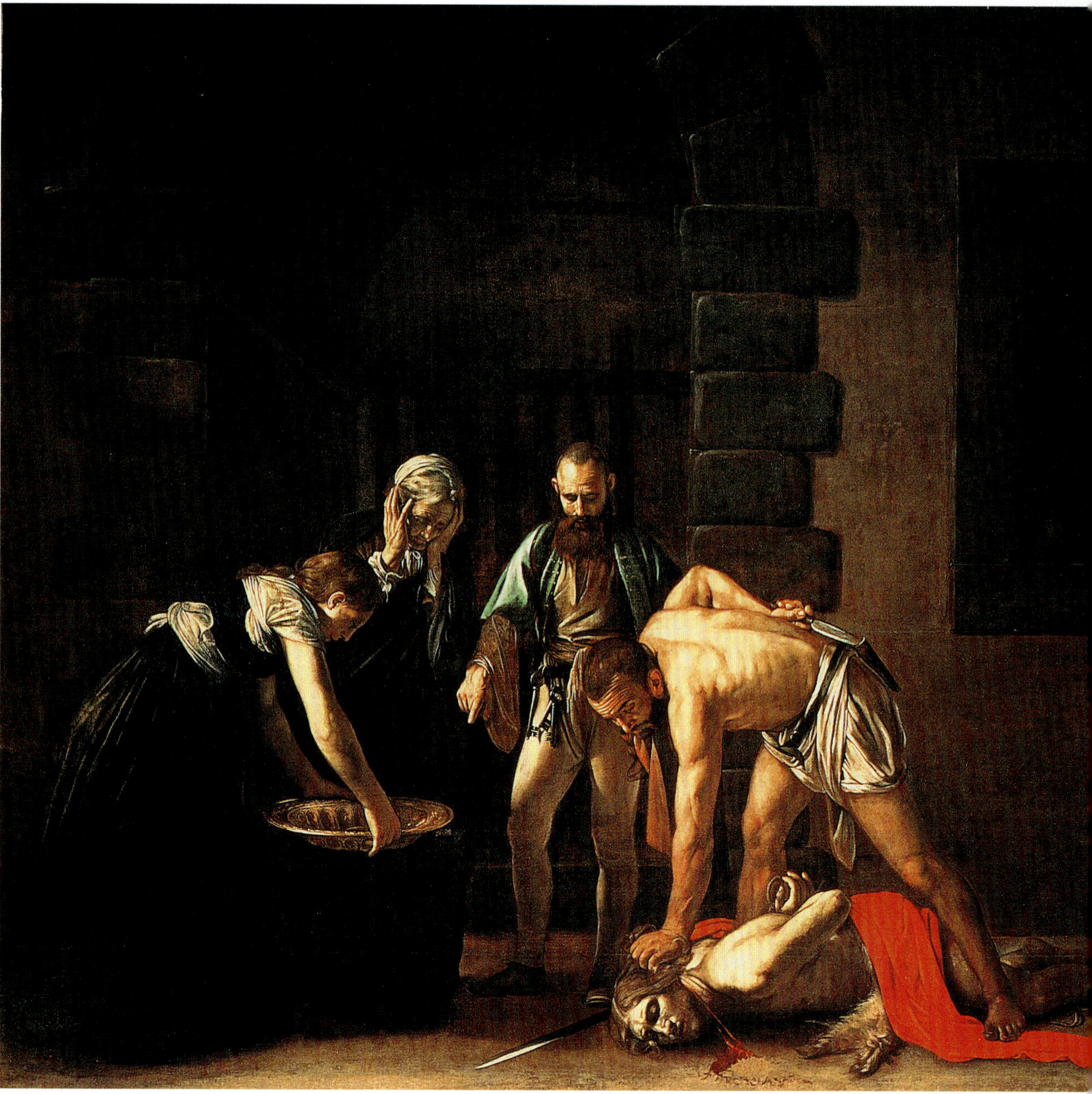

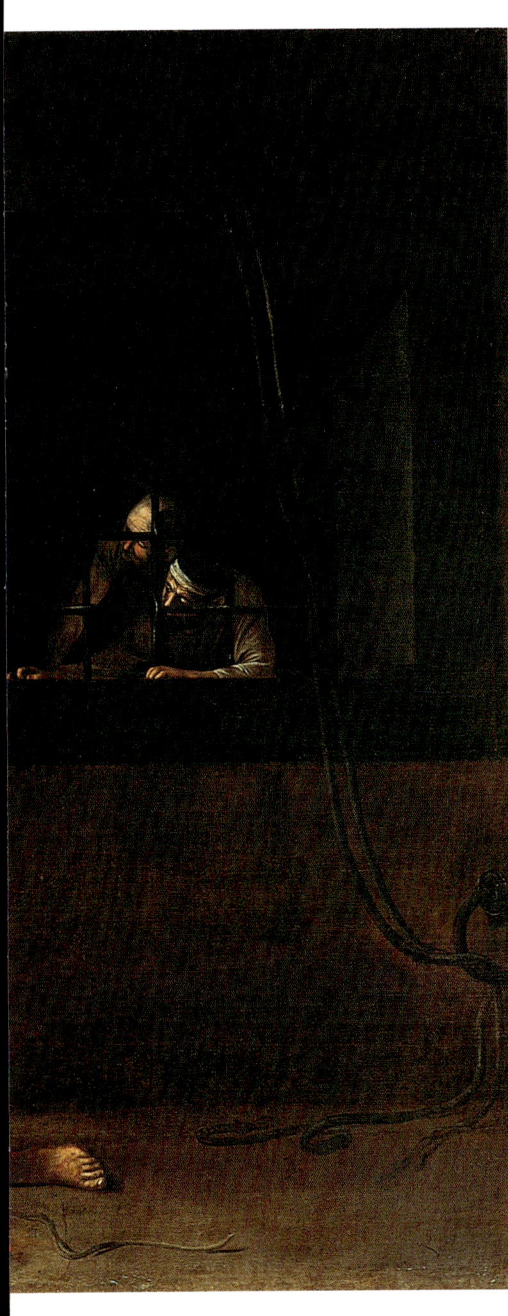

Beheading of John the Baptist
La Décollation de saint Jean-Baptiste
Enthauptung Johannes des Täufers
La decapitación de San Juan Bautista
Decollazione di San Giovanni Battista
De onthoofding van Johannes de Doper

1608, Oil on canvas/Huile sur toile, 360 × 520 cm, Kon-Katidral ta' San Ġwann, Valletta

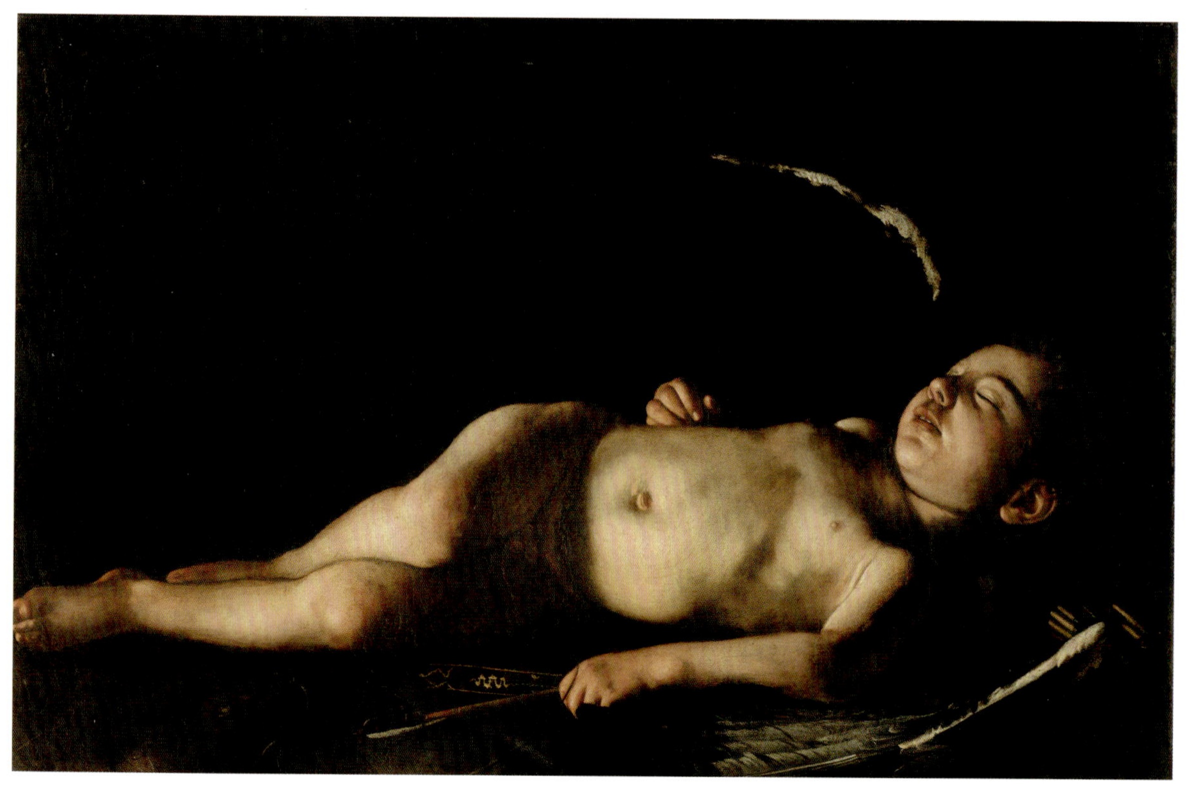

Amor Asleep

Amour endormi

Schlafender Amor

Cupido durmiendo

Amorino dormiente

Slapende Amor

1608, Oil on canvas/Huile sur toile, 72 × 105 cm, Galleria Palatina, Firenze

174

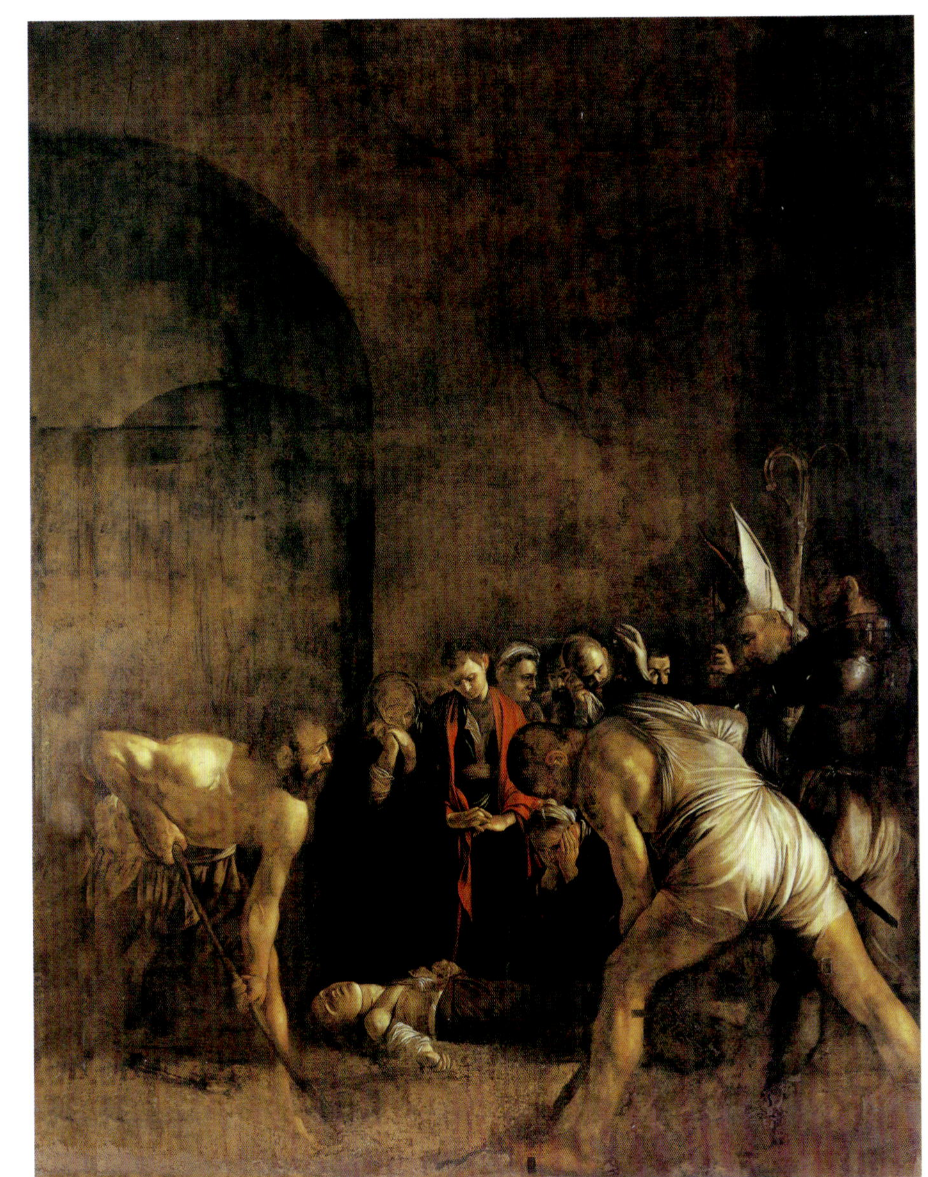

The Burial of St Lucy

***L'Ensevelissement
de sainte Lucie***

Begräbnis der hl. Lucia

El entierro de Santa Lucía

Seppellimento di Santa Lucia

***De graflegging van
de heilige Lucia***

*1608, Oil on canvas/Huile sur
toile, 408 × 300 cm, Chiesa di
Santa Lucia alla Badia, Siracusa*

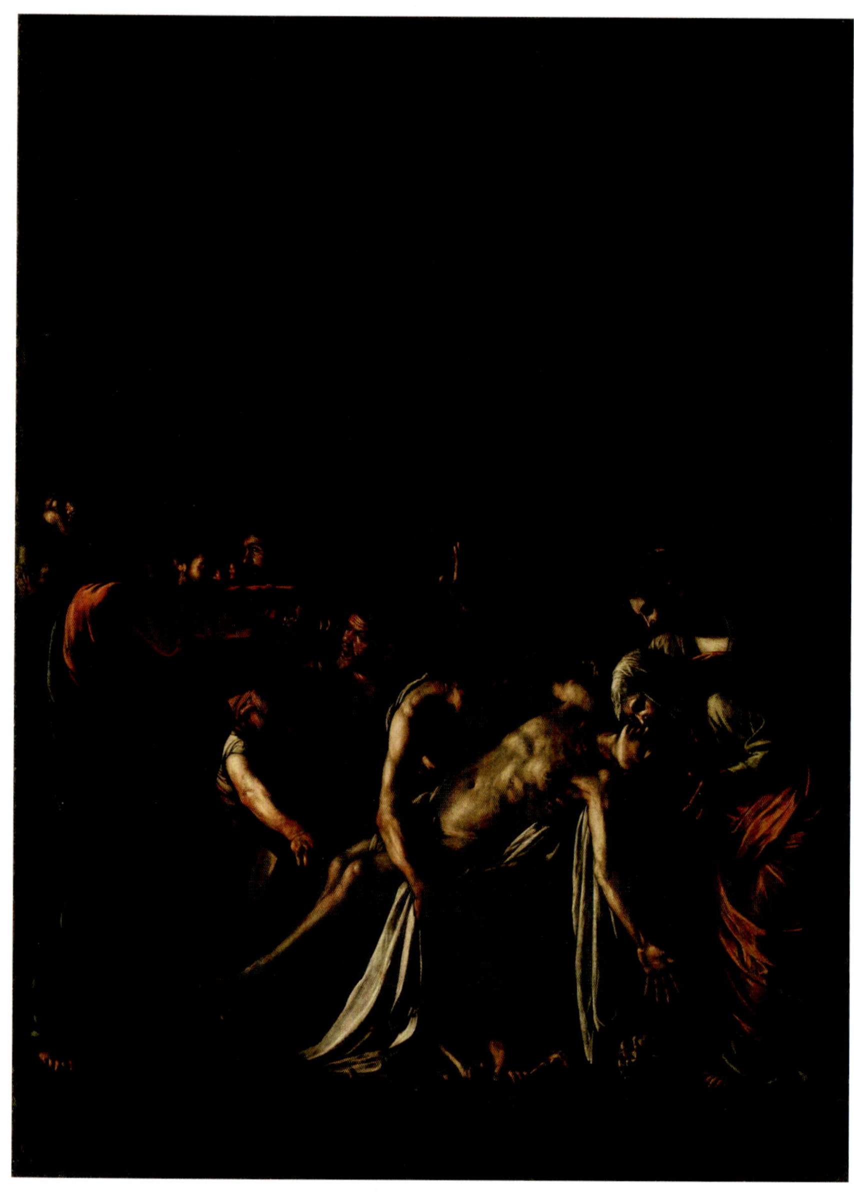

The Raising of Lazarus from the Dead

La Résurrection de Lazare

Die Auferweckung des Lazarus

La resurrección de Lázaro

Resurrezione di Lazzaro

De opwekking van Lazarus

1609, Oil on canvas/Huile sur toile, 380 × 275 cm, Museo regionale interdisciplinare, Messina

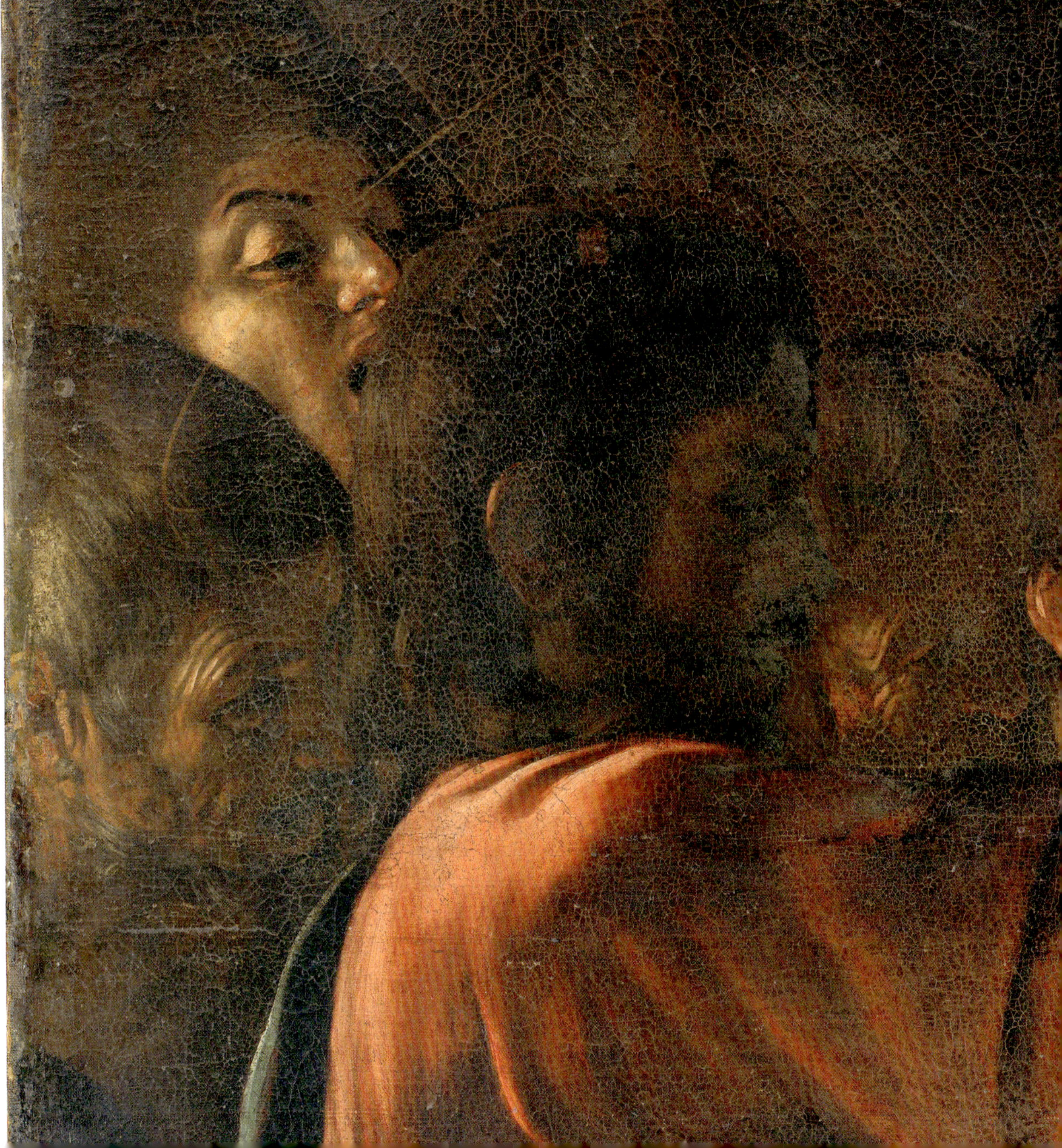

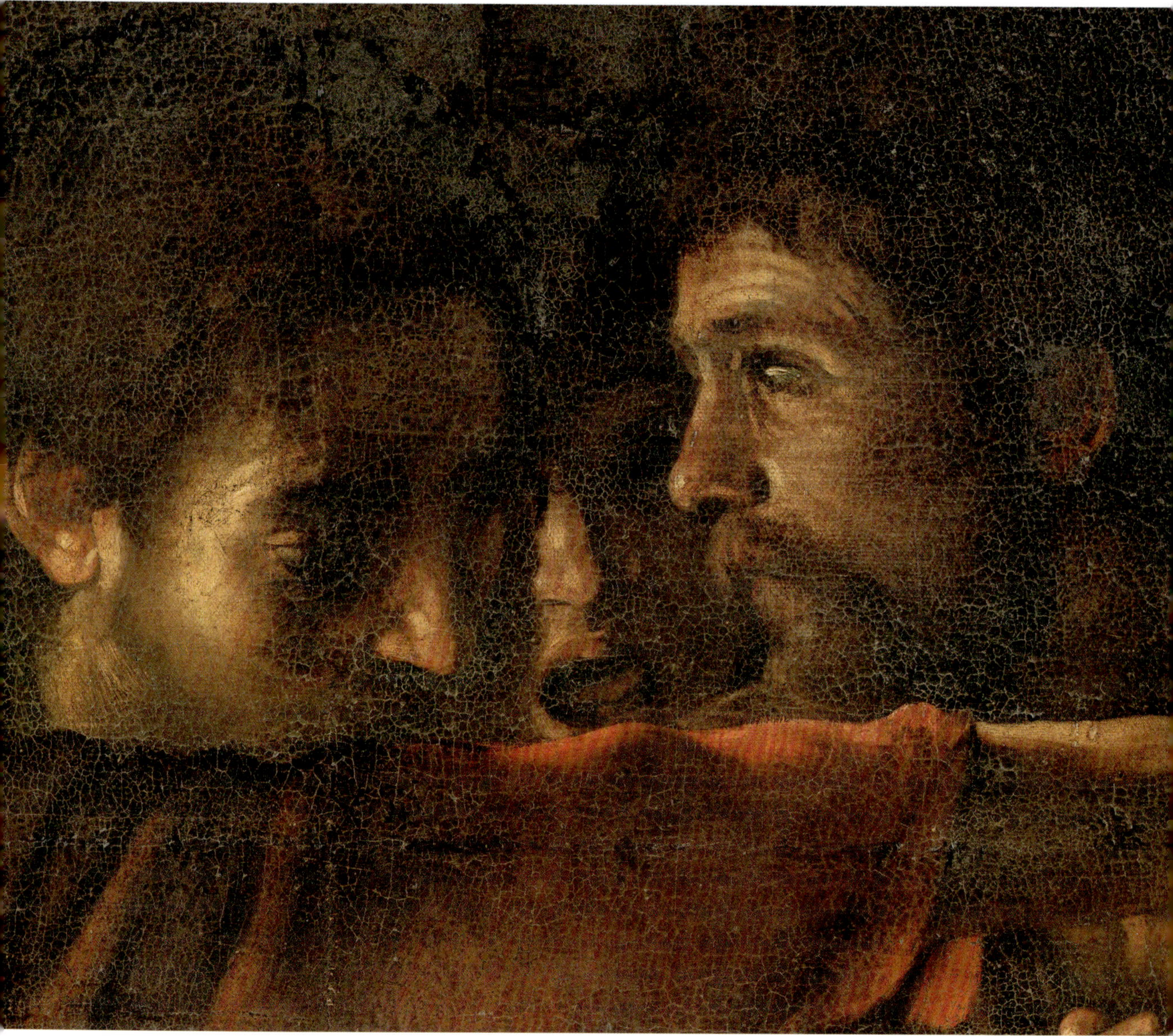

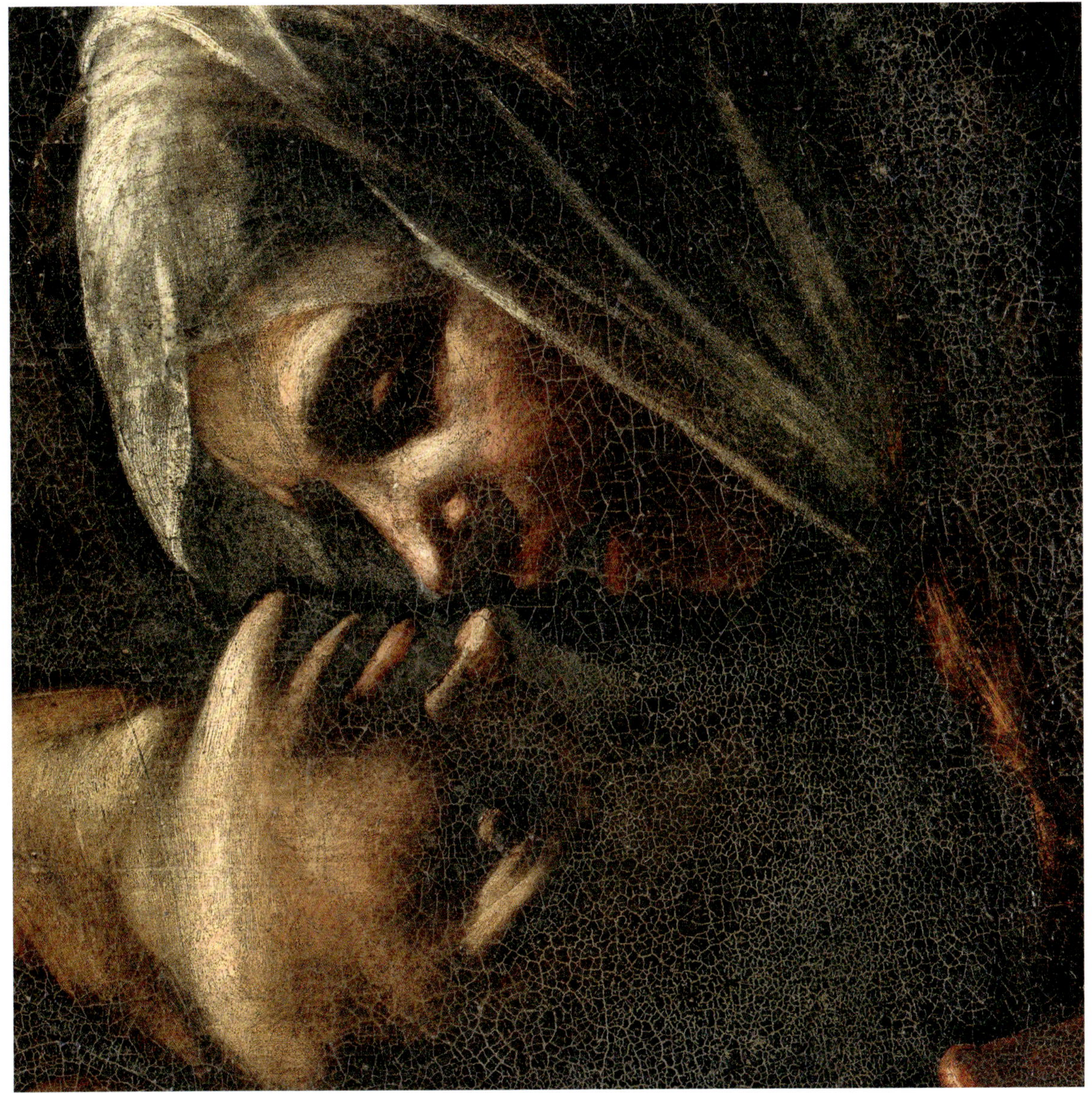

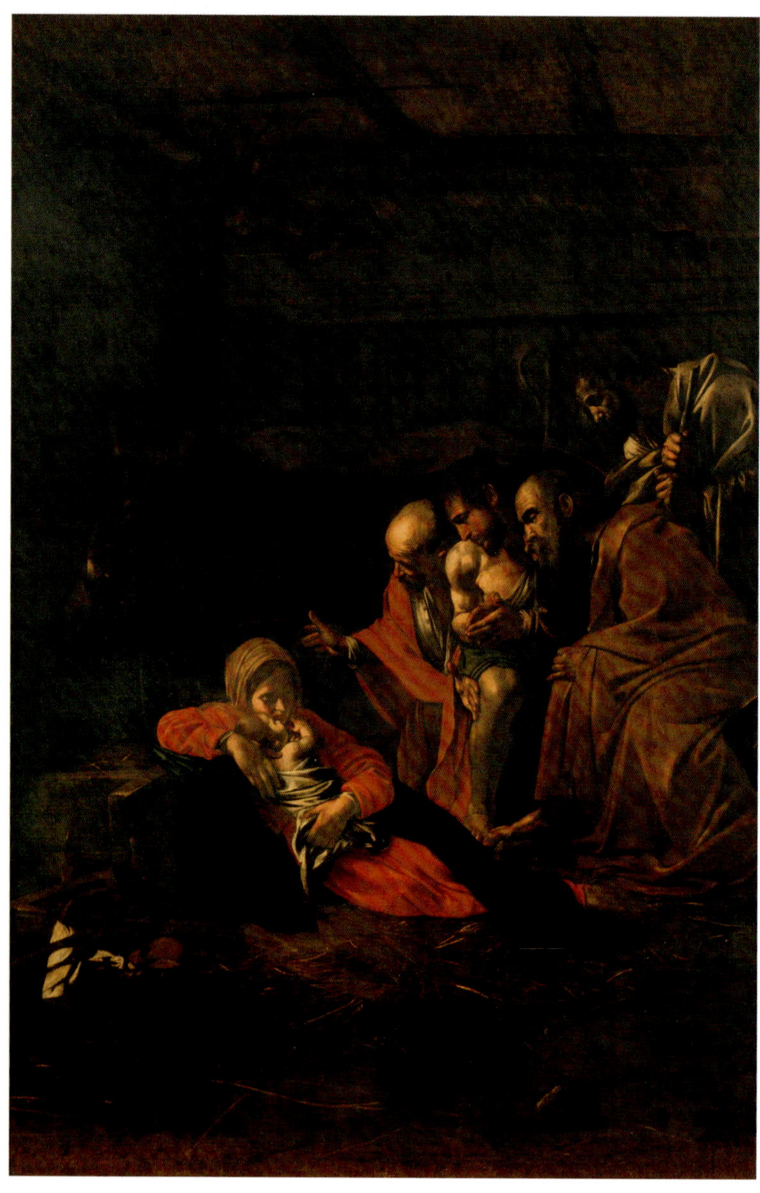

Adoration of the Shepherds

L'Adoration des bergers

Anbetung der Hirten

La adoración de los pastores

Adorazione dei pastori

De Aanbidding door de Herders

*1609, Oil on canvas/Huile sur toile, 314 × 211 cm,
Museo regionale interdisciplinare, Messina*

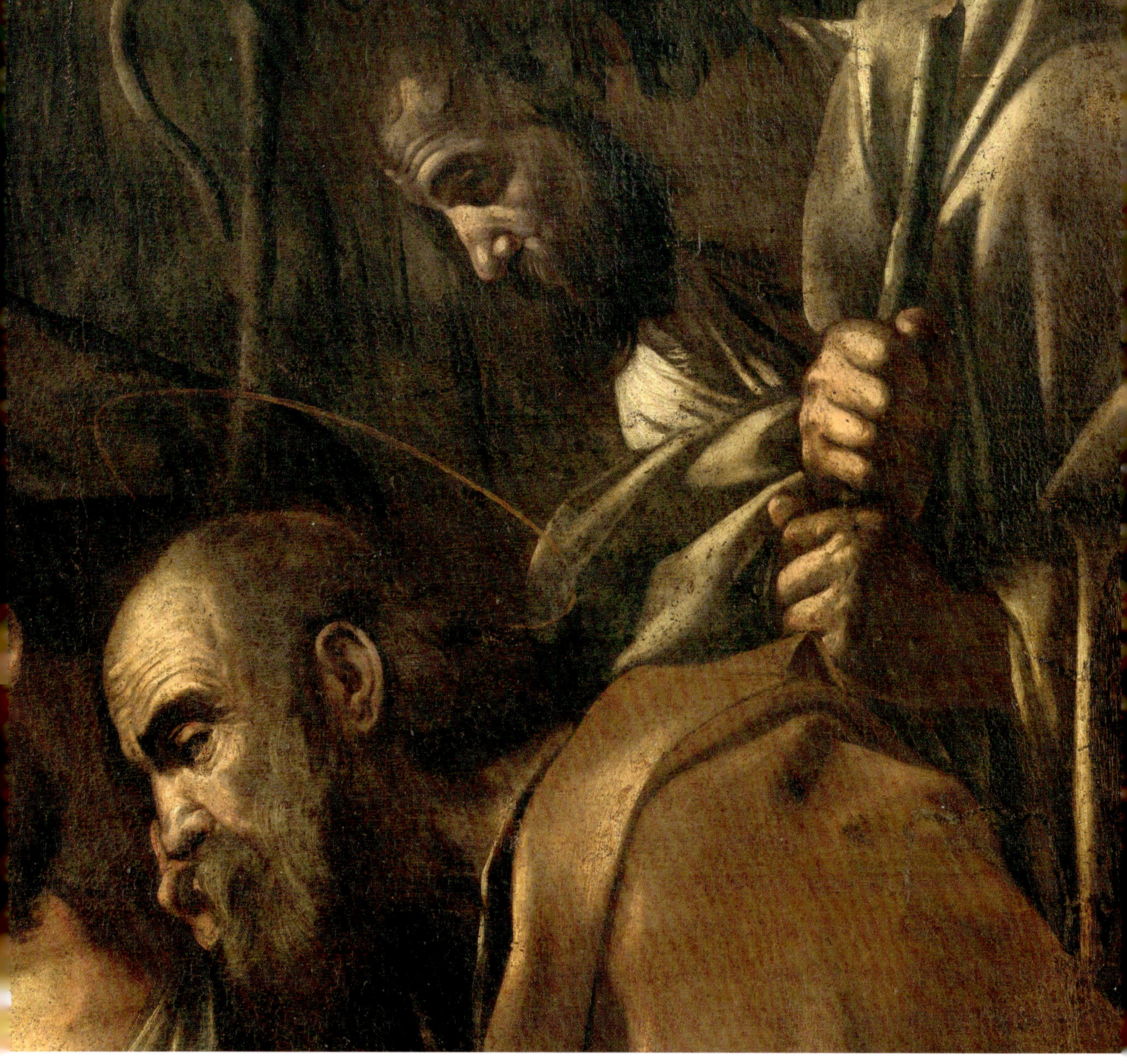

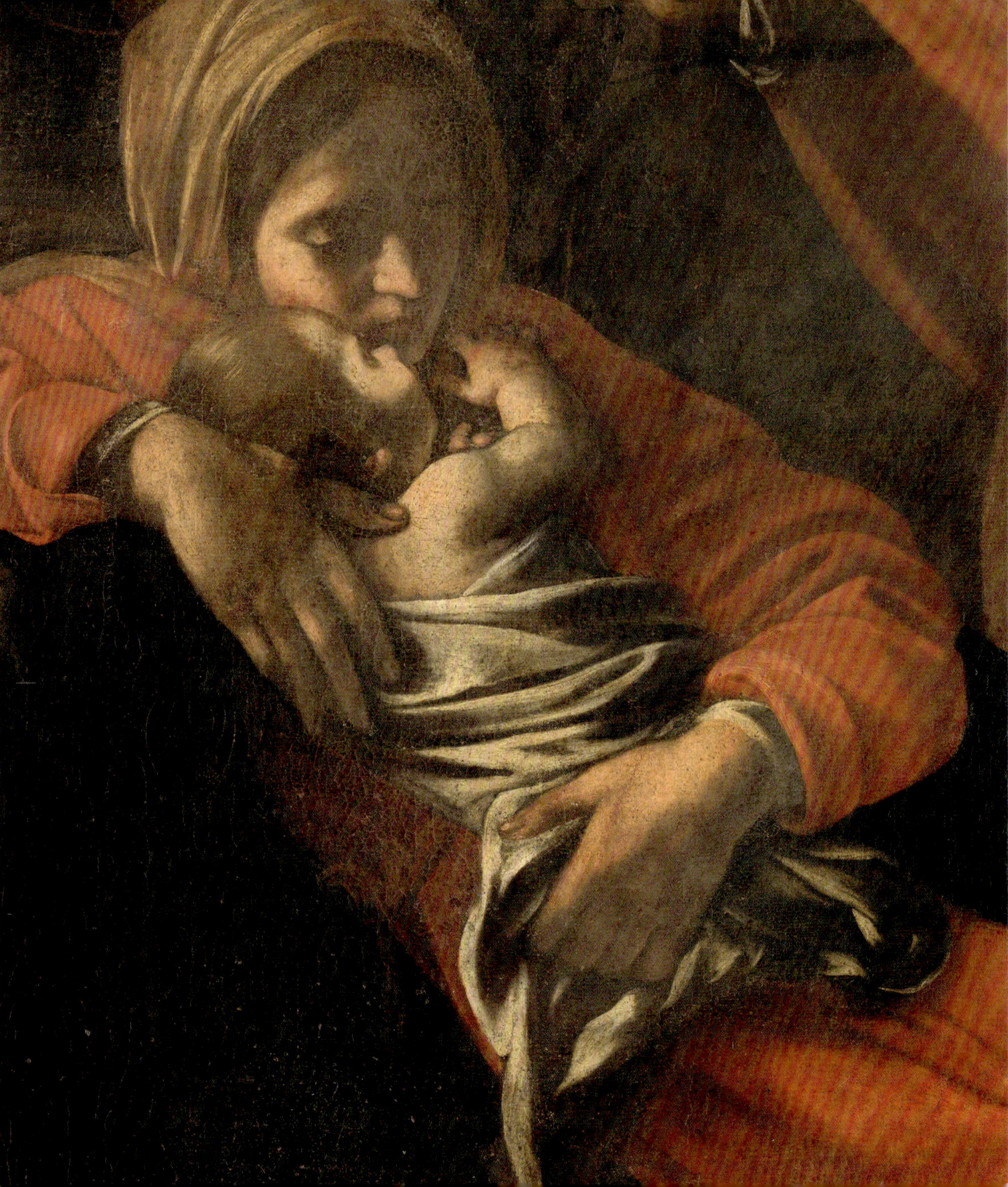

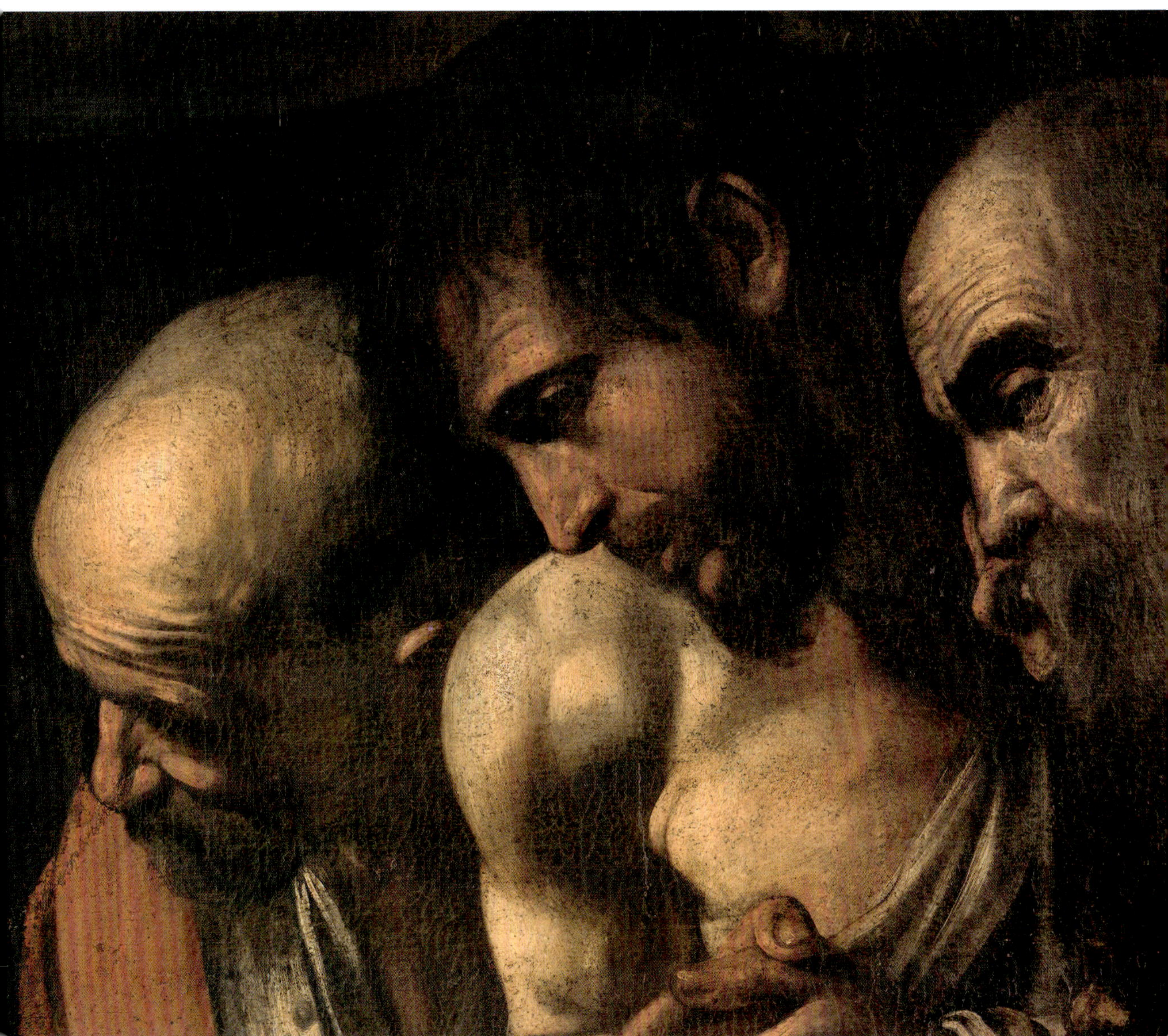

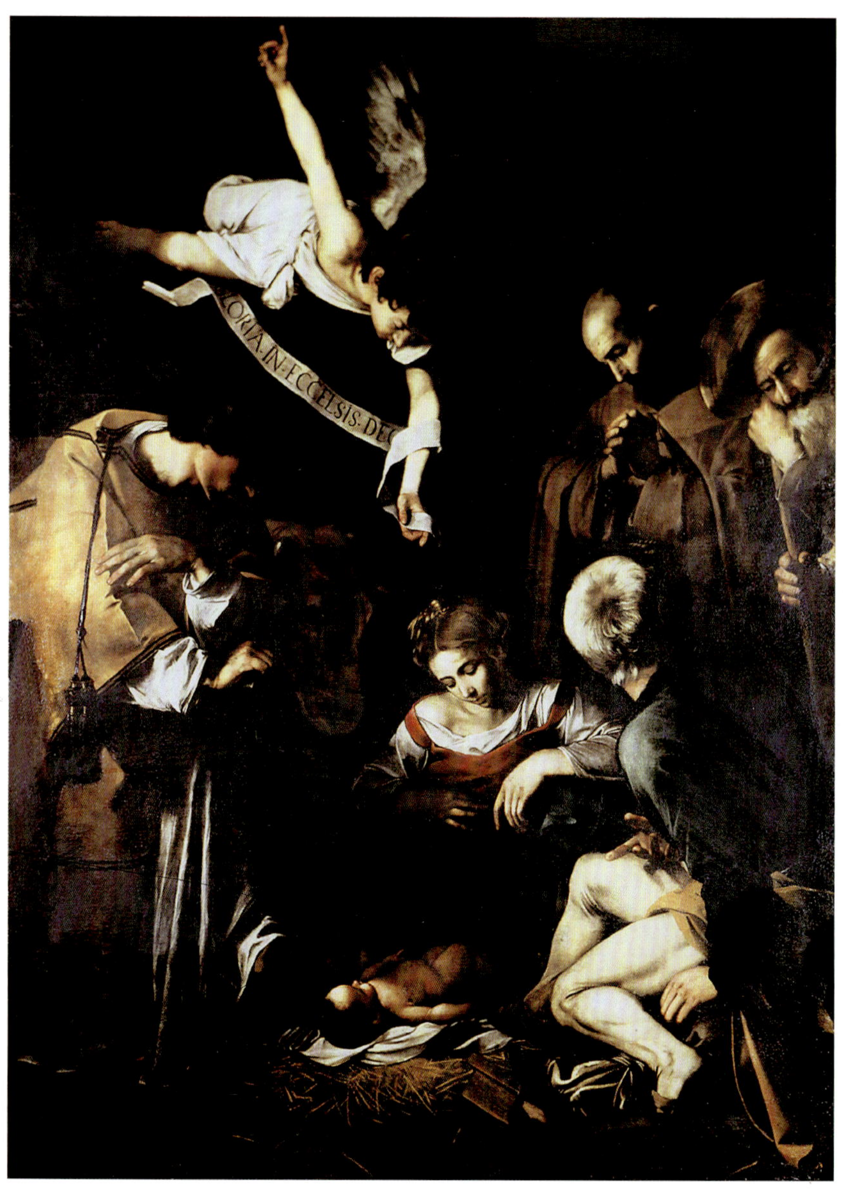

The Nativity of Christ with Saints

*La Nativité avec saint
Laurent et saint François*

Christi Geburt mit Heiligen

Natividad con santos

*Natività con i Santi Lorenzo
e Francesco d'Assisi*

*De Geboorte van Christus
met de heiligen*

*1600?/1609?, Oil on canvas/Huile sur
toile, 268 × 197 cm, stolen in/volé en 1969*

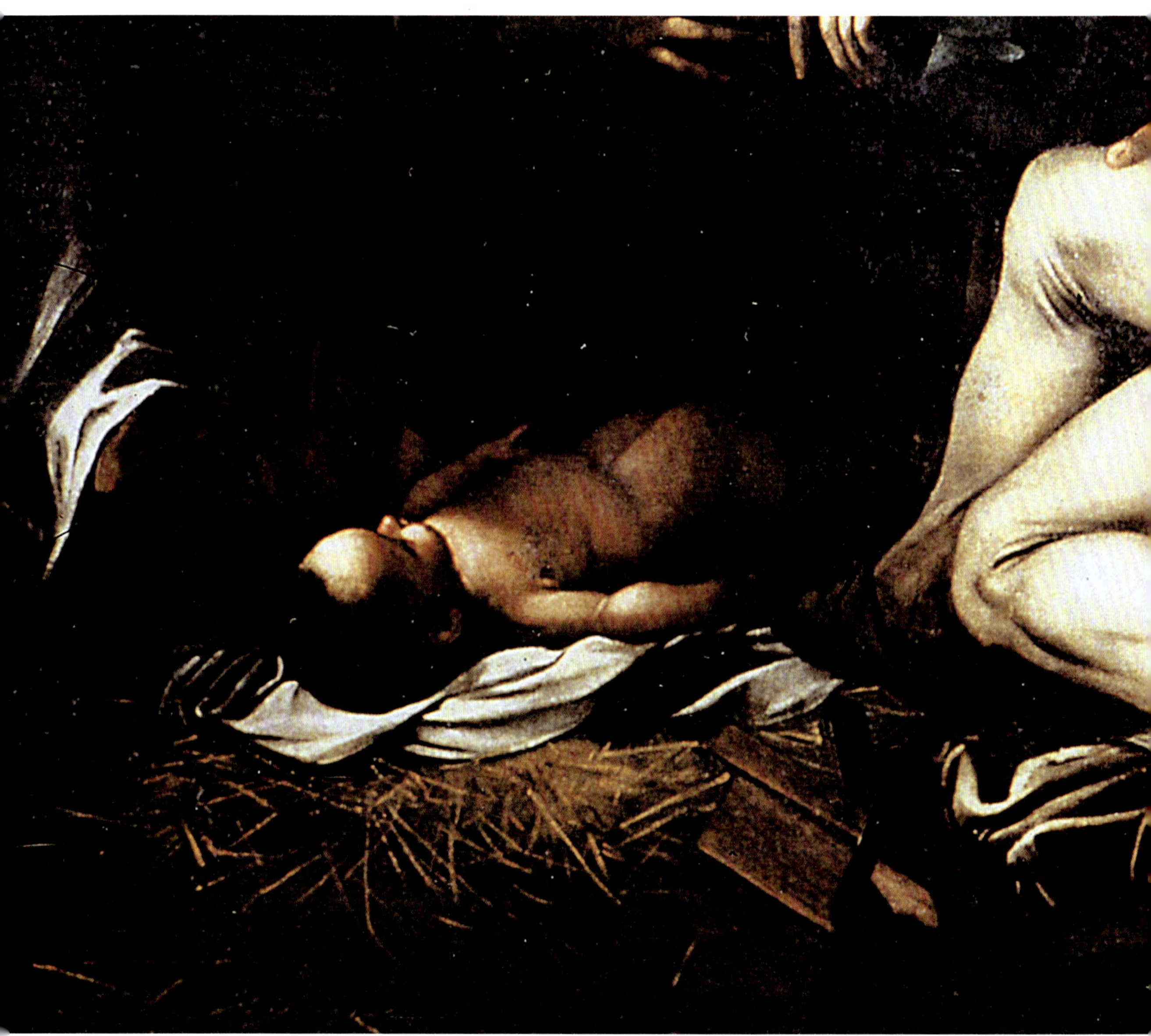

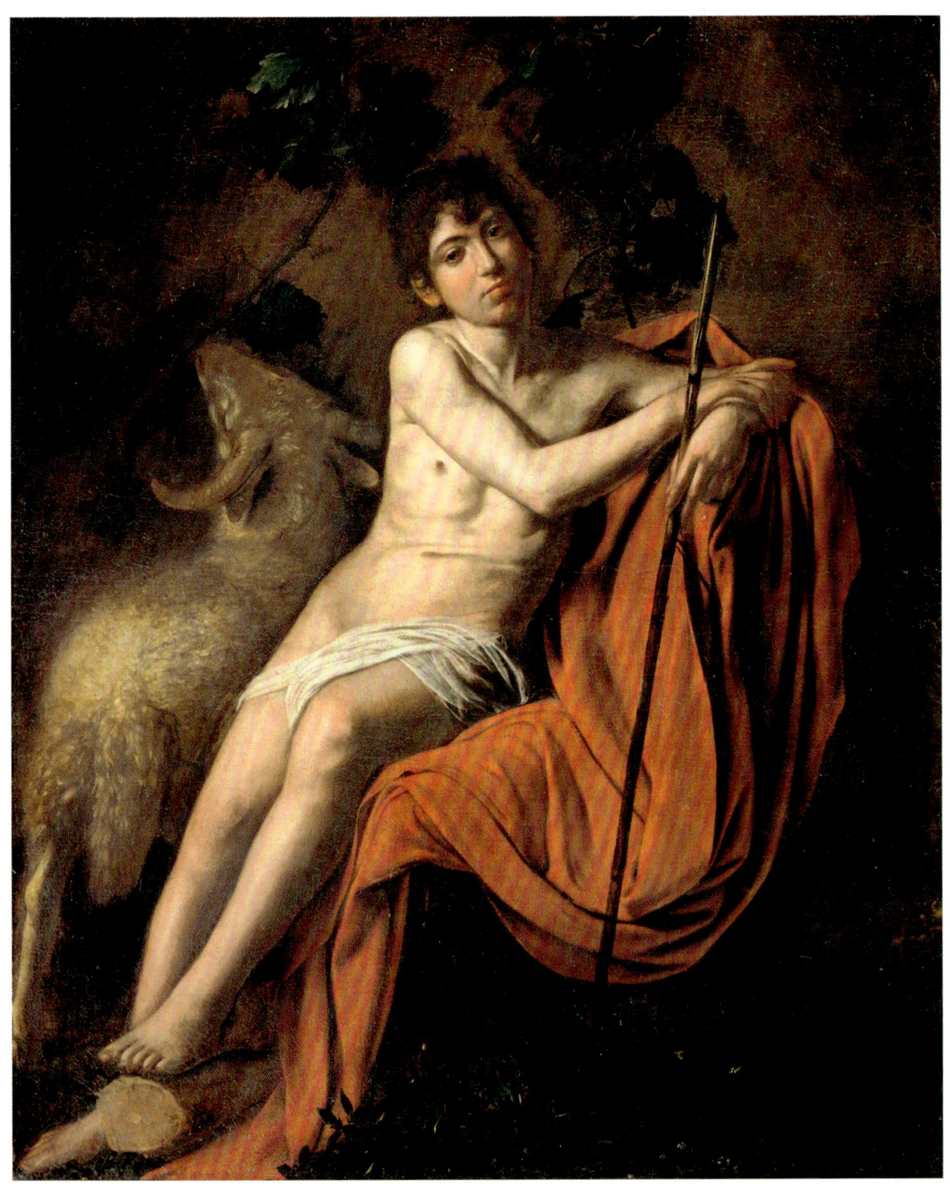

John the Baptist

*Saint Jean-Baptiste
avec un bélier*

Johannes der Täufer

San Juan Bautista

San Giovanni Battista

Johannes de Doper

c. 1610, Oil on canvas/
Huile sur toile,
159 × 124,5 cm, Galleria
Borghese, Roma

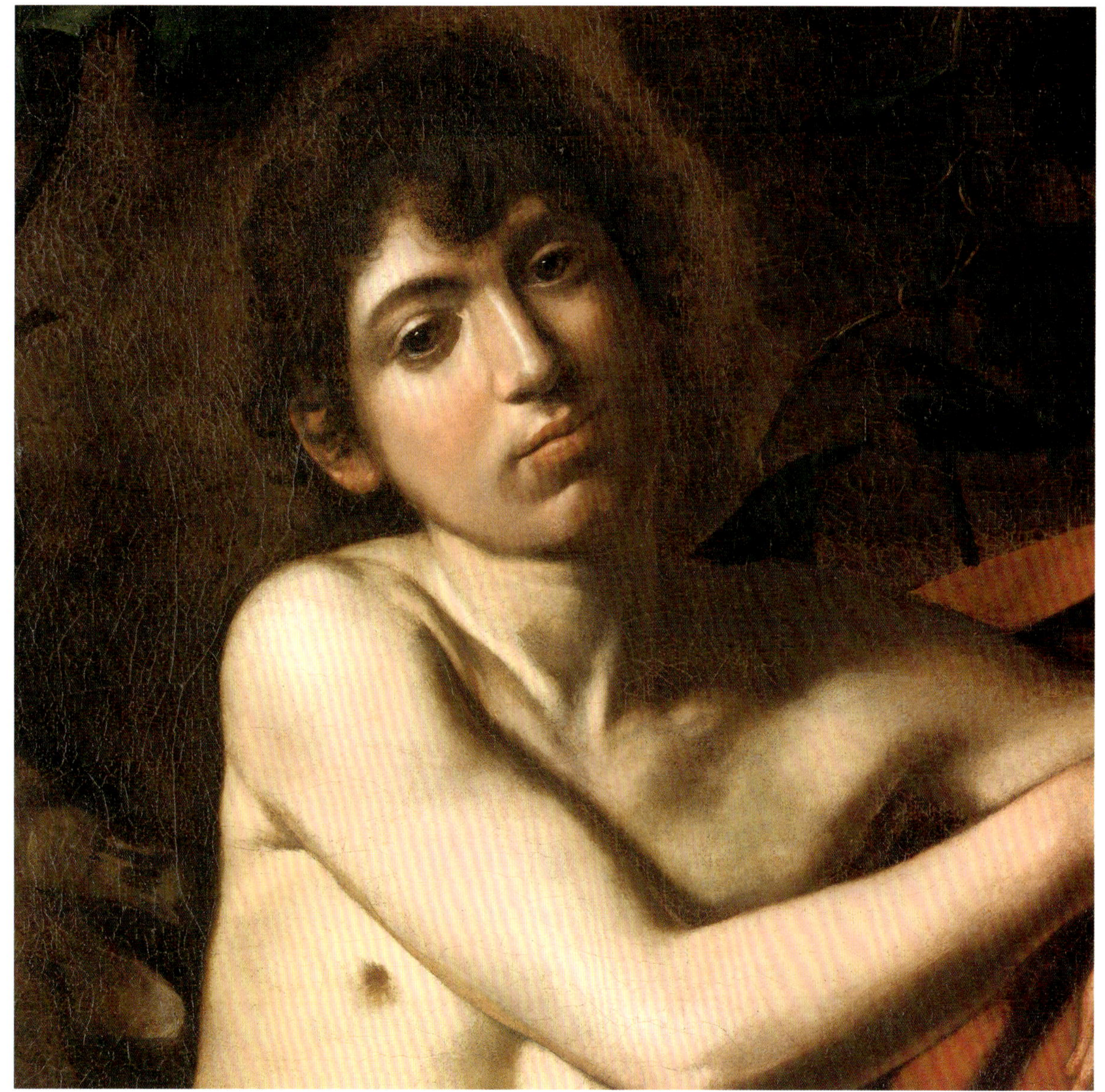

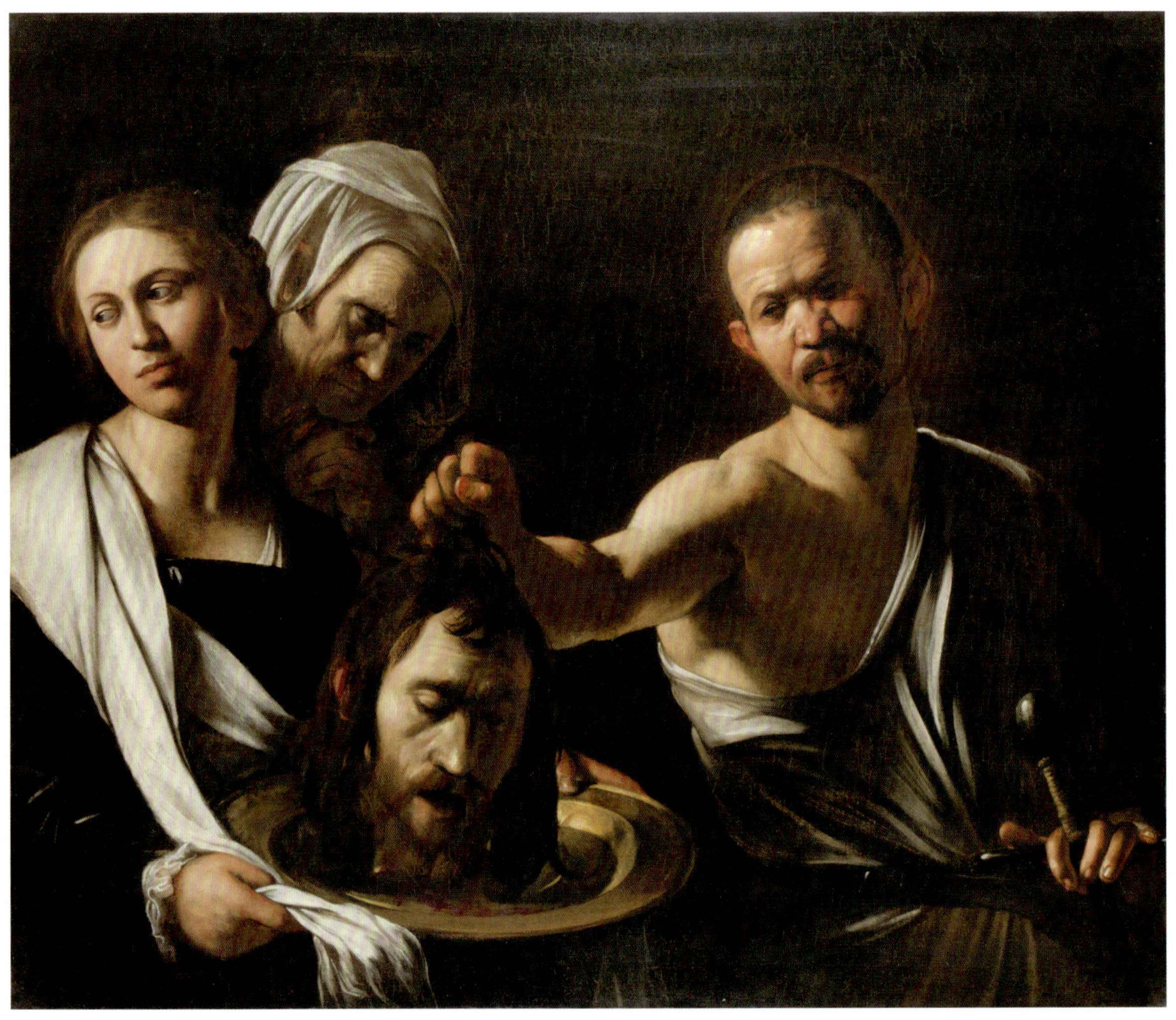

Salome with the Head of John the Baptist
Salomé avec la tête de saint Jean-Baptiste

Salome mit dem Haupt Johannes des Täufers
Salomé con la cabeza de San Juan Bautista

Salomè con la testa del Battista
Salomé met het hoofd van Johannes de Doper

c. 1606/07, Oil on canvas/Huile sur toile, 91,5 × 106,7 cm, National Gallery, London

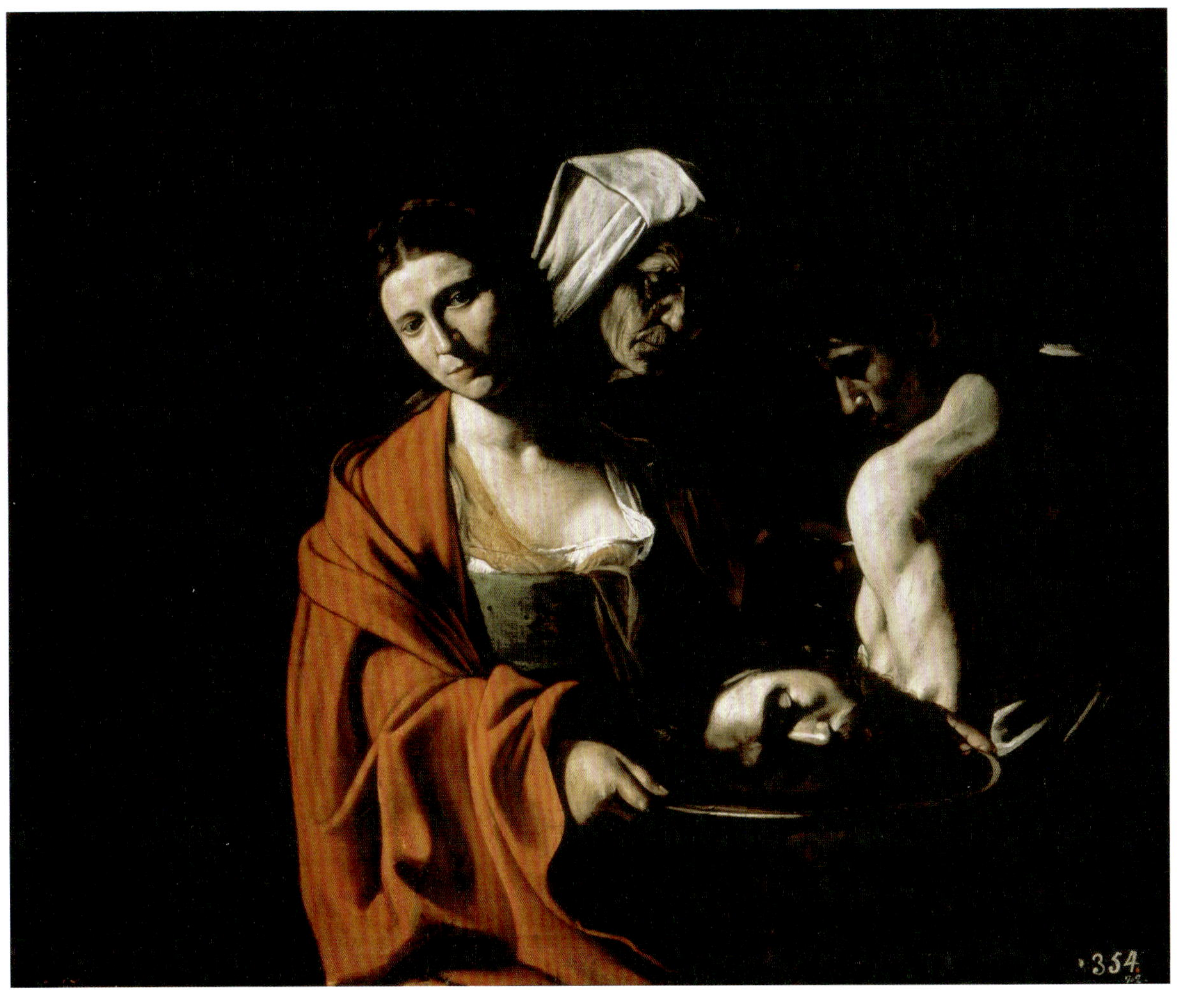

Salome with the Head of John the Baptist
Salomé avec la tête de saint Jean-Baptiste

Salome mit dem Haupt Johannes des Täufers
Salomé con la cabeza de San Juan Bautista

Salomè con la testa del Battista
Salomé met het hoofd van Johannes de Doper

1609/10, Oil on canvas/Huile sur toile, 116 × 140 cm, Palacio Real, Madrid

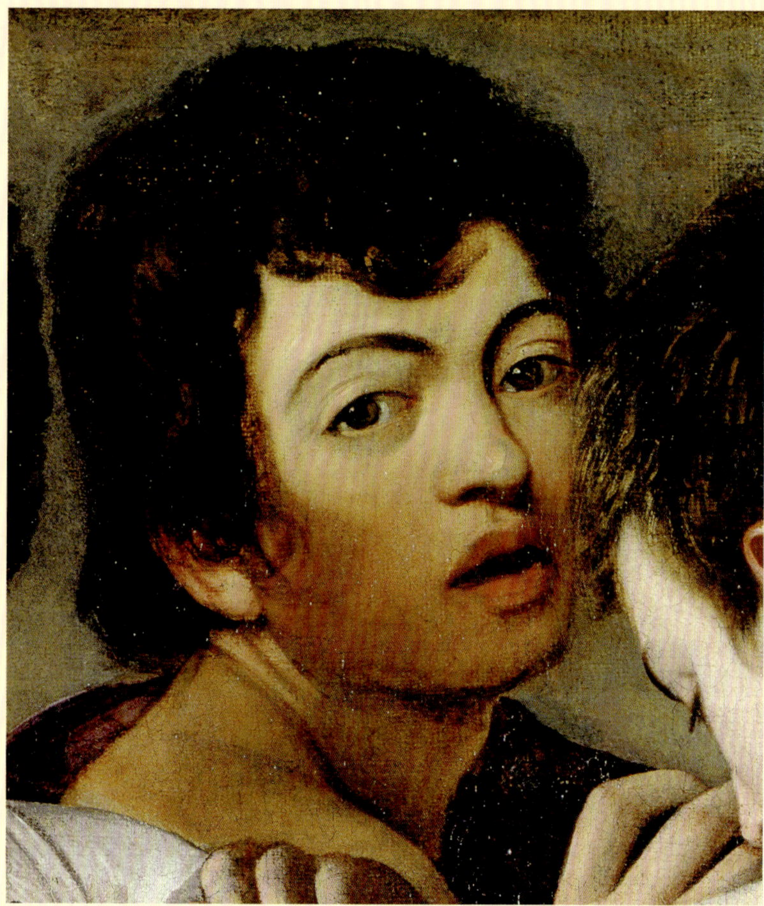

Boys Making Music (detail)
Les Musiciens ou *Le Concert* (détail)
Musizierende Knaben (Detail)
Jóvenes músicos (detalle)
Concerto o *I musici* (particolare)
Musicerende knapen (detail)
see/voir p. 24

Caravaggio's self-portraits

One striking feature in Caravaggio's œuvre is his penchant for the staged self-portrait. He never made a self-portrait as such, although he does appear in a number of his works. He painted himself as a sickly Bacchus and as a boyish musician, he watched

Caravage en scène dans ses tableaux

Une caractéristique surprenante chez Caravage est sa propension à se mettre lui-même en scène dans ses tableaux. Nous n'avons de lui aucun autoportrait autonome, mais on découvre qu'il s'est représenté dans bon nombre de ses œuvres. Il se peint en Bacchus malade

Caravaggios Selbstinszenierung im Bild

Ein auffallendes Merkmal in Caravaggios Œuvre ist dessen Hang zum inszenierten Selbstporträt. Es gibt kein selbstständiges Selbstporträt, wohl aber eine Anzahl von Selbstbildnissen innerhalb seiner Werke. Er malt sich als kranker Bachhus oder knabenhafter Musikant, er zeigt

Sickly Bacchus (detail)

Le Jeune Bacchus malade (détail)

Der kranke Bacchus (Detail)

Baco enfermo (detalle)

Bacchino malato (particolare)

De zieke Bacchus (detail)

see/voir p. 25

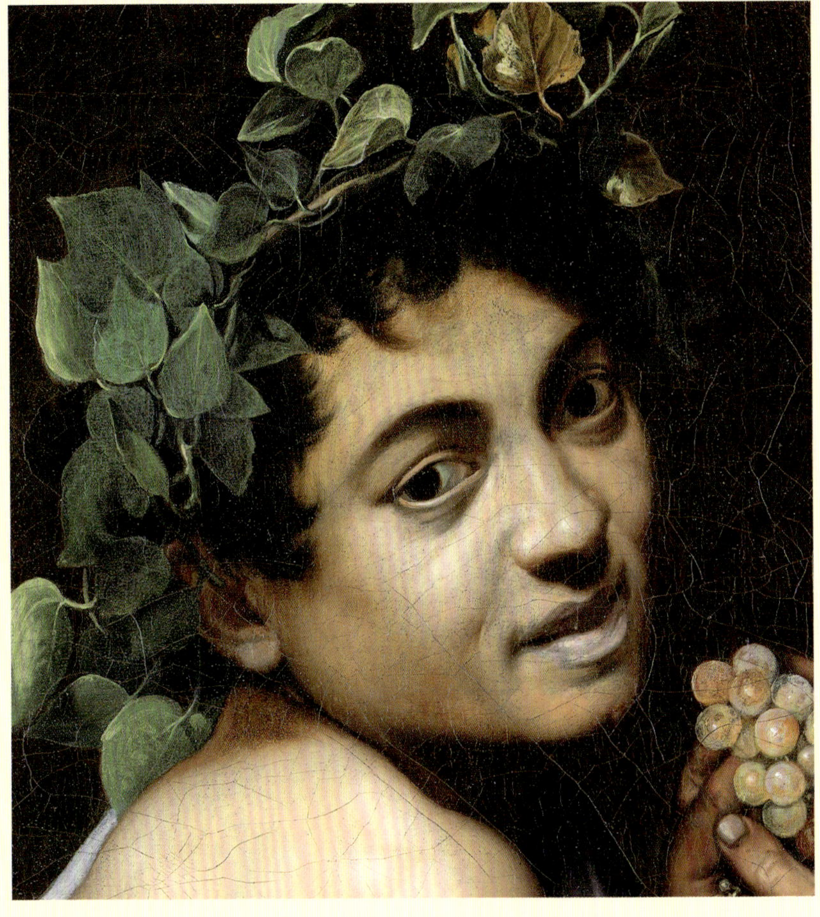

Autorretratos escenificados de Caravaggio

Una característica notable de la obra de Caravaggio es su tendencia a presentar autorretratos escenificados. No existe un autorretrato autónomo, pero sí una serie de autorretratos dentro de sus obras. Se pinta como Baco enfermo o

L'autoraffigurazione di Caravaggio nei suoi quadri

Una caratteristica dell'opera di Caravaggio che colpisce è la sua propensione per l'autoritratto. Non esiste alcun autoritratto indipendente, bensì una serie di autoritratti incorporati nei suoi quadri. Si dipinse infatti come

Caravaggio als figuur in zijn schilderijen

Een opvallend kenmerk van Caravaggio's oeuvre is zijn neiging om zichzelf in zijn werken te portretteren, hoewel er geen zelfstandig zelfportret van de schilder bestaat. Caravaggio schildert zichzelf als zieke Bachhus of jongensachtige

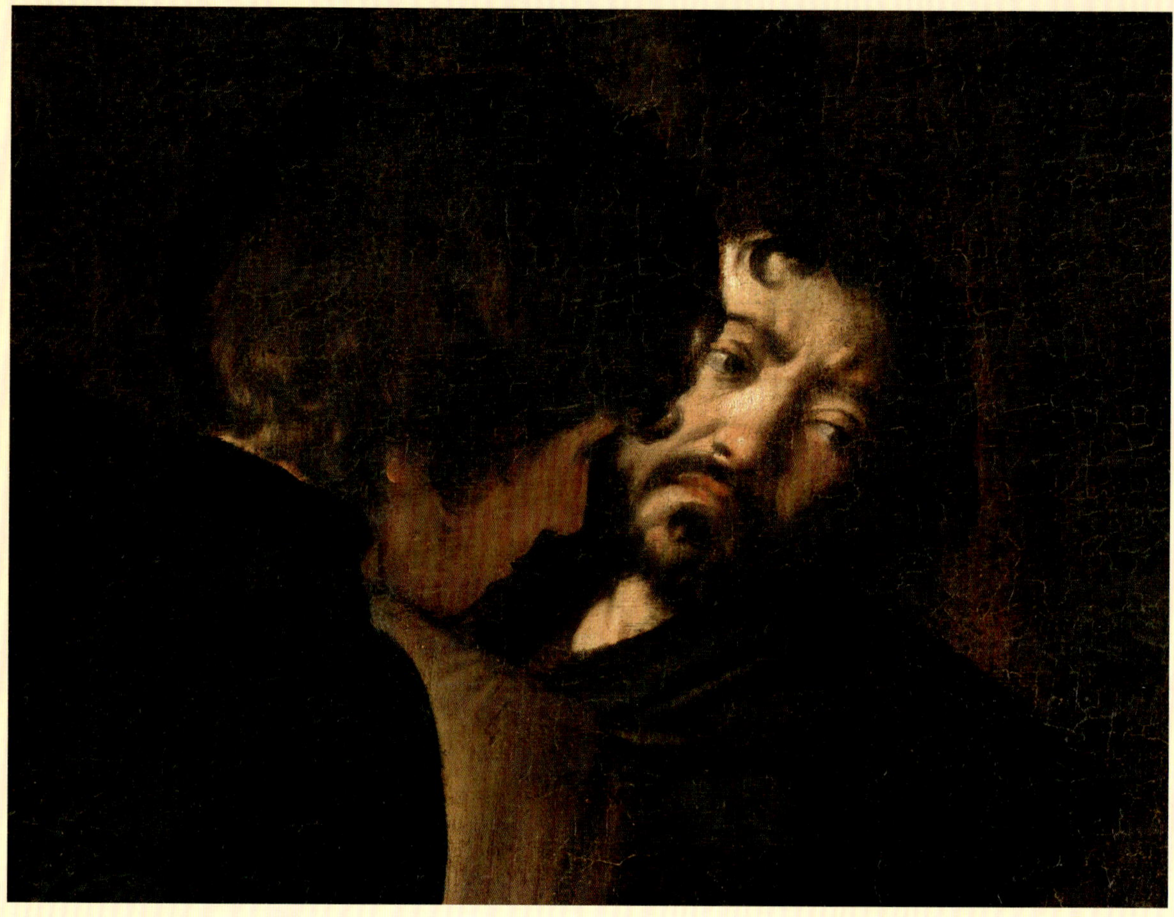

the martyrdom of St Matthew with sympathy, and stands bearing a torch witnessing the arrest of Jesus. In late works such as *David with the Head of Goliath,* the decapitated head has the physiognomy of the artist.

ou en jeune musicien ; il assiste en spectateur affligé au martyre de saint Matthieu et participe – comme témoin et porte-flambeau – à l'arrestation du Christ. Dans la version tardive de *David tenant la tête de Goliath,* la tête coupée du Philistin offre même les traits du peintre.

Anteilnahme am Martyrium des Matthäus und taucht auf als Zeuge und Fackelträger in der Gefangennahme Christi. In späten Werken wie *David mit dem Haupt Goliaths* nimmt sogar der geköpfte Schädel die Physiognomie des Künstlers an.

The Martyrdom of
St Matthew (detail)

Le Martyre de saint
Matthieu (détail)

Martyrium des
hl. Matthäus (Detail)

El martirio de
San Mateo (detalle)

Martirio di San Matteo
(particolare)

Het martyrium van de
heilige Matteüs (detail)

see/voir p. 76

David with Goliath's
Head (detail)

David tenant la tête
de Goliath (détail)

David mit dem Haupt
Goliaths (Detail)

David con la cabeza
de Goliat (detalle)

Davide con la testa di
Golia (particolare)

David met het hoofd
van Goliath (detail)

see/voir p. 195

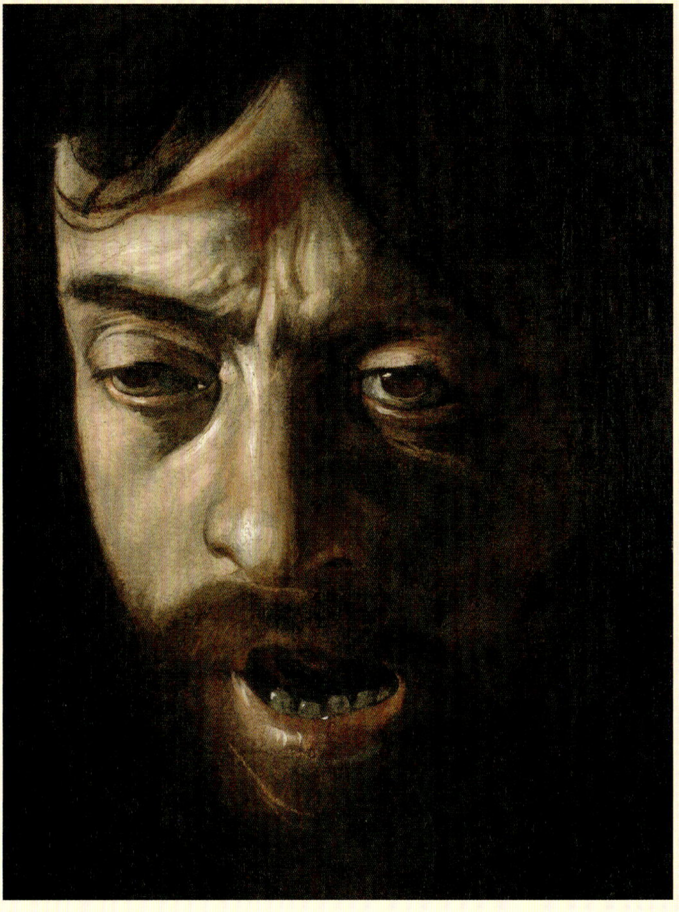

como músico de aspecto juvenil, toma parte en el martirio de Mateo y aparece como testigo y portador de la antorcha durante el prendimiento de Cristo. En obras más tardías como *David con la cabeza de Goliat* incluso la propia cabeza decapitada toma los rasgos del artista.

Bacchino malato, giovane musicista, partecipante al martirio di Matteo, e testimone e tedoforo nella cattura di Cristo. Inoltre, in opere successive come *Davide con la testa di Golia,* raffigura alcuni dei personaggi con la sua fisionomia, in questo caso il volto di Golia decapitato.

muzikant, hij is aanwezig bij het martyrium van de heilige Matteüs en duikt op als ooggetuige en fakkeldrager bij de gevangenneming van Christus. In een laat werk als *David met het hoofd van Goliath* is zijn portret zelfs te herkennen in de onthoofde schedel.

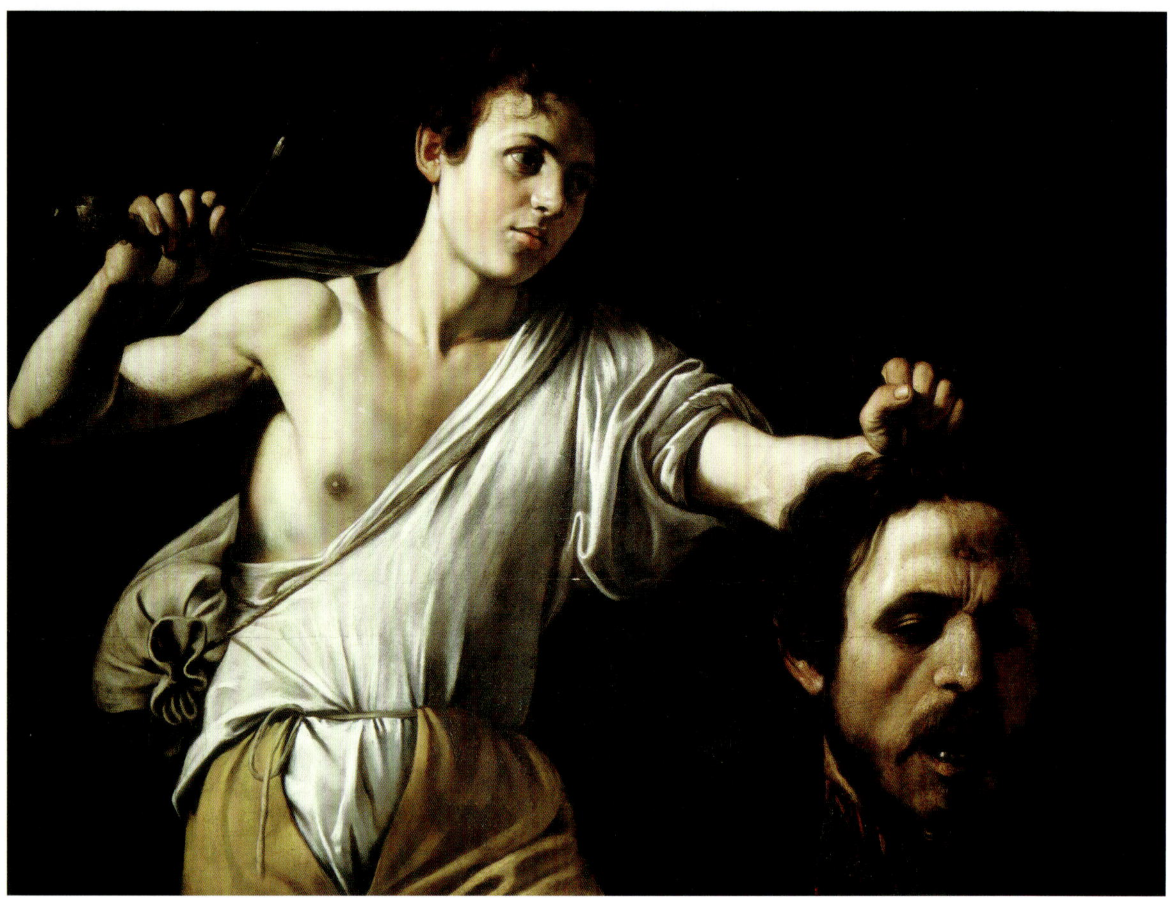

Pardon and early death

When he arrived in Naples, Caravaggio finally heard news that he had been pardoned. With a few paintings in tow, he boarded a ship towards Porto Ercole to travel from there to Rome. He never arrived. He died under tragic and mysterious circumstances alone on the beach of Porto Ercole on 18 July 1610, having not even reached his 40th birthday.

Grâce et mort prématurée

À Naples, Caravage reçut enfin la nouvelle libératrice de sa grâce. Avec quelques tableaux dans ses bagages, il embarqua dans une felouque à destination de Porto Ercole, d'où il espérait pouvoir gagner Rome. Il ne devait jamais y arriver et mourut solitaire sur le rivage, dans des conditions mal élucidées, le 18 juillet 1610. Il avait 38 ans.

Begnadigung und früher Tod

In Neapel erhielt Caravaggio endlich die erlösende Nachricht der Begnadigung. Mit einigen Bildern im Gepäck bestieg er ein Schiff Richtung Porto Ercole, um von dort weiter nach Rom zu reisen. Er sollte nie dort ankommen; unter tragisch-mysteriösen Umständen starb er einsam am Strand von Porto Ercole am 18. Juli 1610, nicht einmal 40-jährig.

David with Goliath's Head

*David avec la tête
de Goliath*

*David mit dem Haupt
des Goliath*

*David con la cabeza
de Goliat*

Davide con la testa di Golia

*David met het hoofd
van Goliath*

*c. 1600/01, Oil on canvas/
Huile sur toile, 91,2 × 116,2 cm,
Kunsthistorisches Museum,
Wien*

David with Goliath's Head

*David tenant la
tête de Goliath*

*David mit dem
Haupt Goliaths*

*David con la cabeza
de Goliat*

Davide con la testa di Golia

*David met het hoofd
van Goliath*

*1610, Oil on canvas/Huile sur
toile, 125 × 101 cm, Galleria
Borghese, Roma*

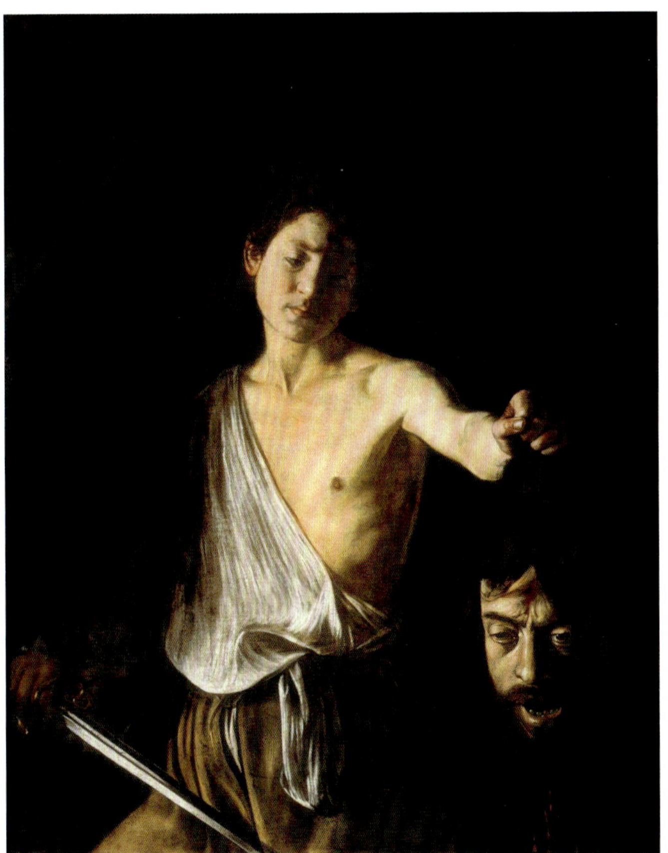

Indulto y muerte prematura

En Nápoles Caravaggio recibió la
liberadora noticia del indulto. Con
algunos cuadros en el equipaje, tomó un
barco en dirección a Porto Ercole, para
desde allí continuar su viaje a Roma.
Nunca llegaría a Roma; murió solo, en
condiciones trágicas y misteriosas en la
playa de Porto Ercole el 18 de julio de 1610,
sin haber alcanzado siquiera los 40.

Il condono e la morte prematura

A Napoli Caravaggio ricevette finalmente
il messaggio salvifico del condono. Con
alcuni quadri nel bagaglio, si imbarcò
in direzione di Porto Ercole, da dove
avrebbe poi raggiunto Roma. A Roma,
però, non vi giunse mai. In circostanze
misteriose e tragiche morì solo sulla
spiaggia di Porto Ercole il 18 luglio 1610,
non ancora quarantenne.

Begenadiging en vroege dood

In Napels ontving Caravaggio eindelijk
het verlossende bericht dat hij was
begenadigd. Met enkele schilderijen in zijn
bagage ging hij scheep naar Porto Ercole
om vandaar naar Rome te reizen. Daar
zou hij nooit aankomen: onder tragische
en onopgehelderde omstandigheden
vond hij op 18 juli 1610 op het strand de
dood; hij was nog geen 40 jaar oud.

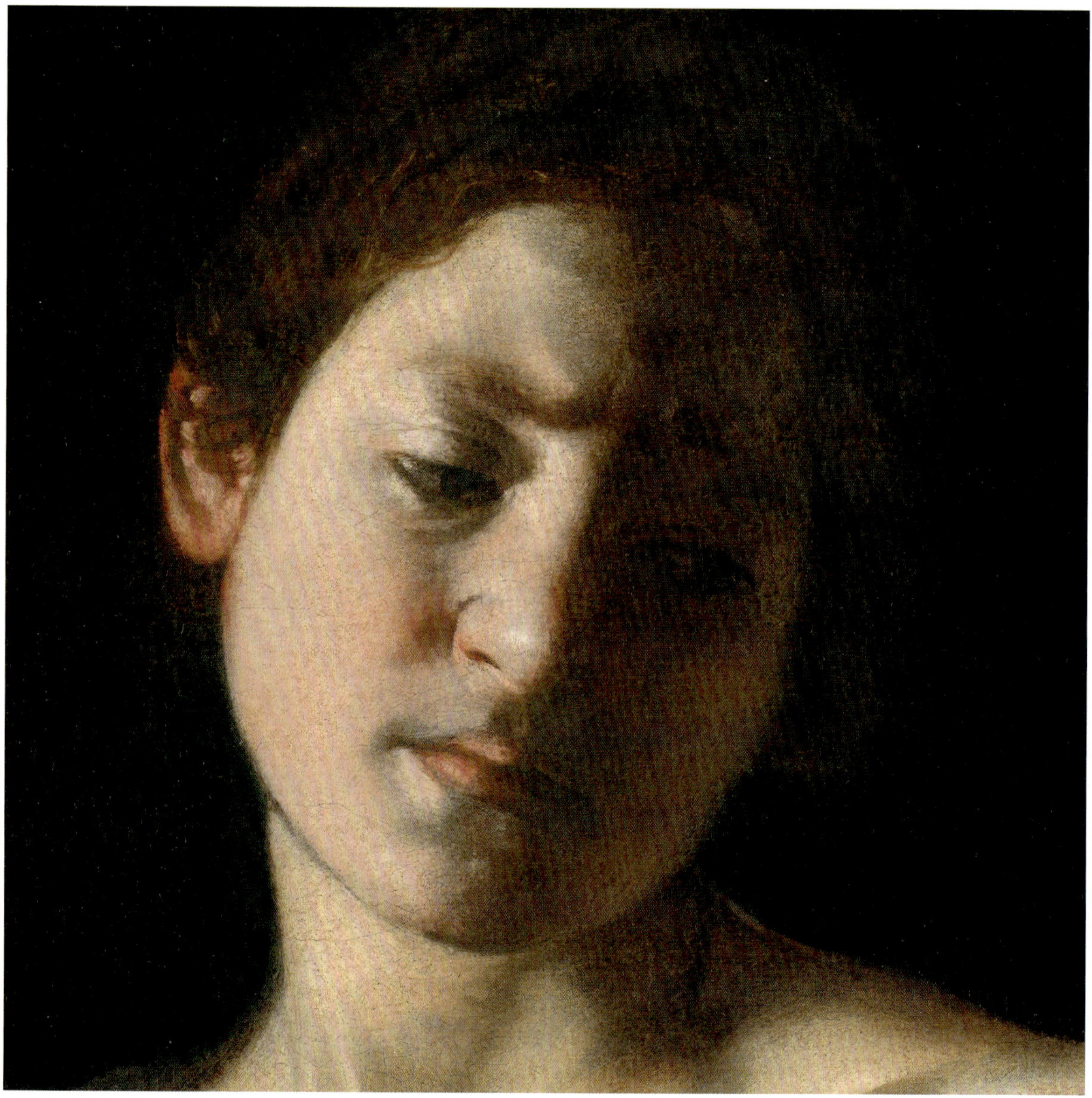

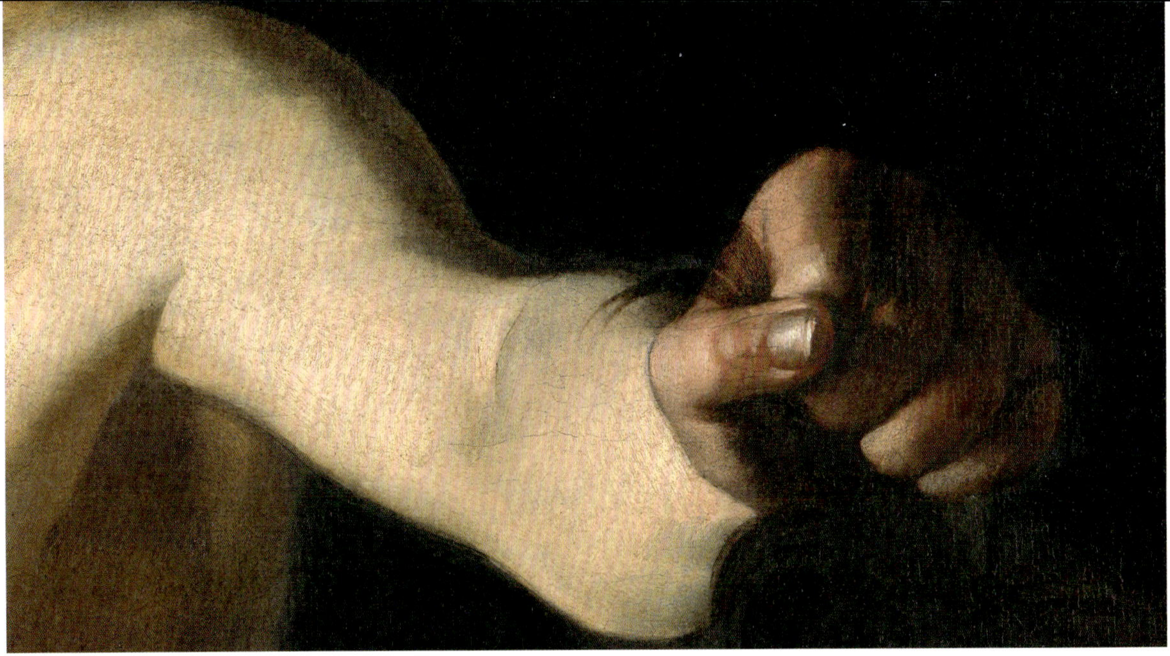

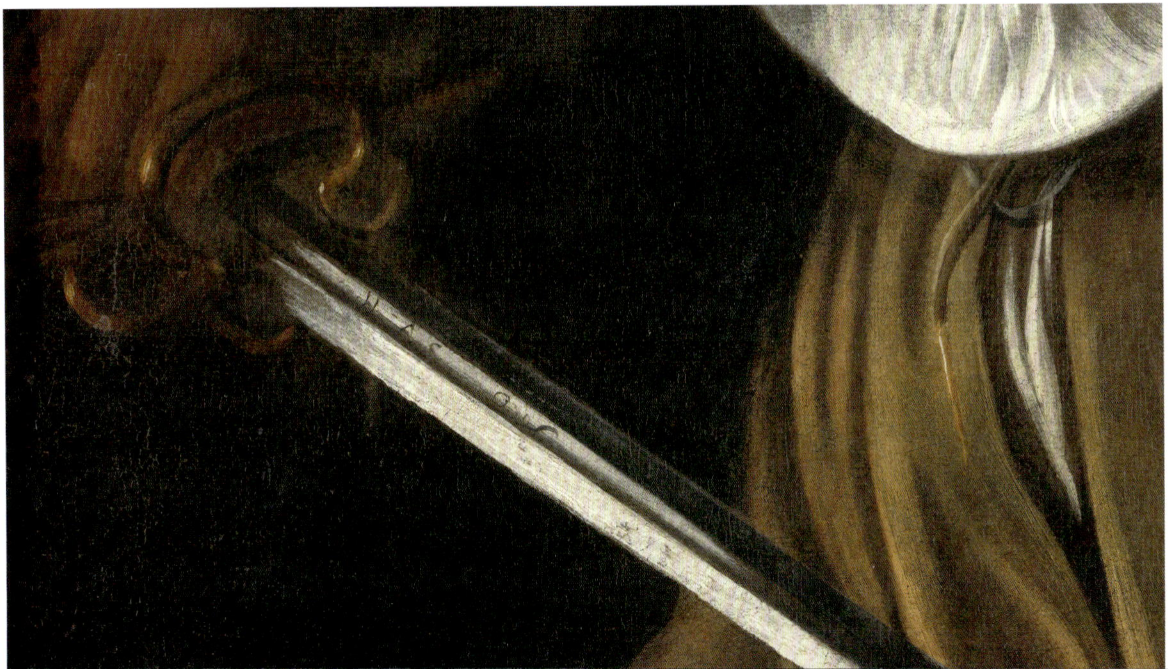

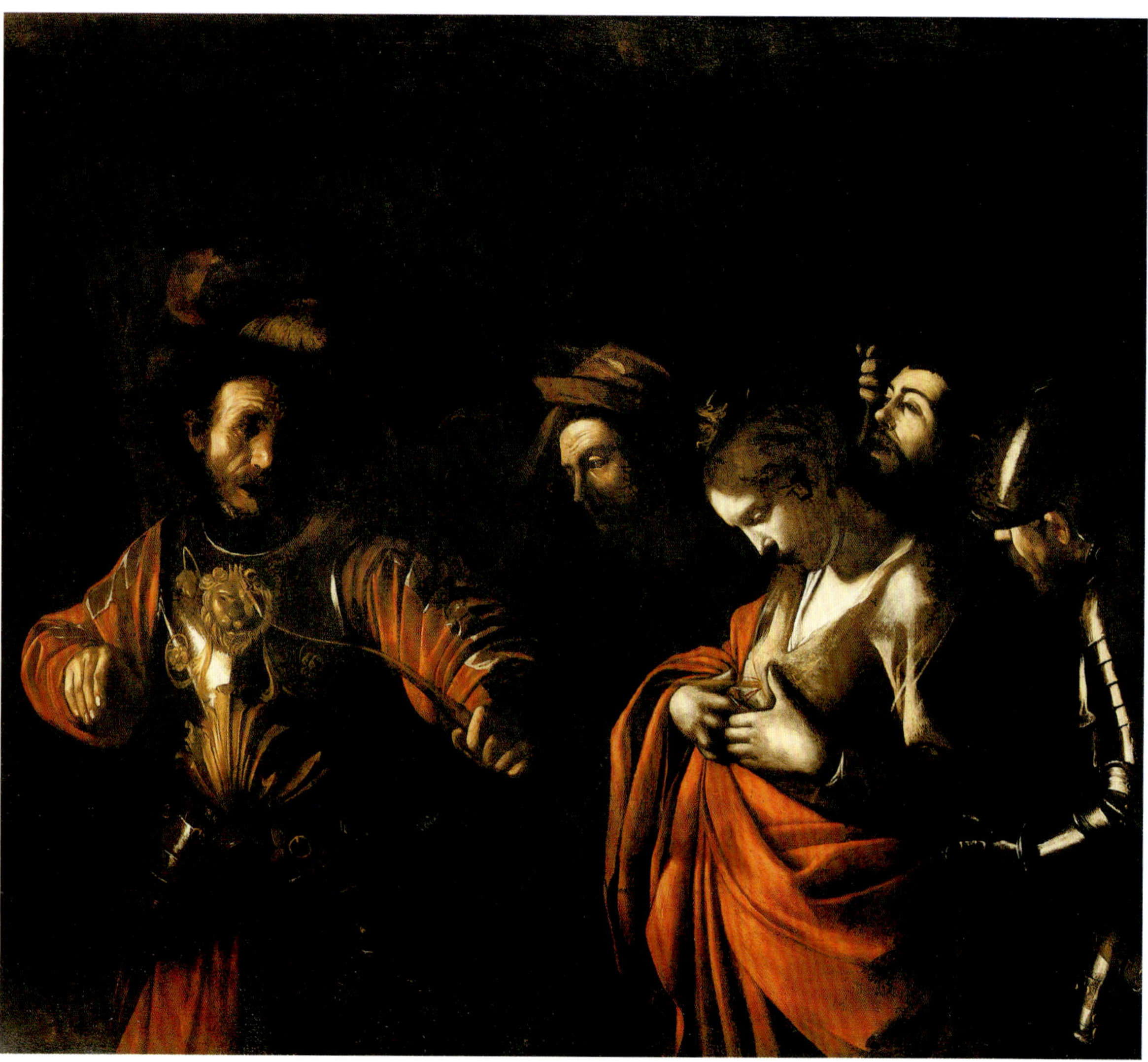

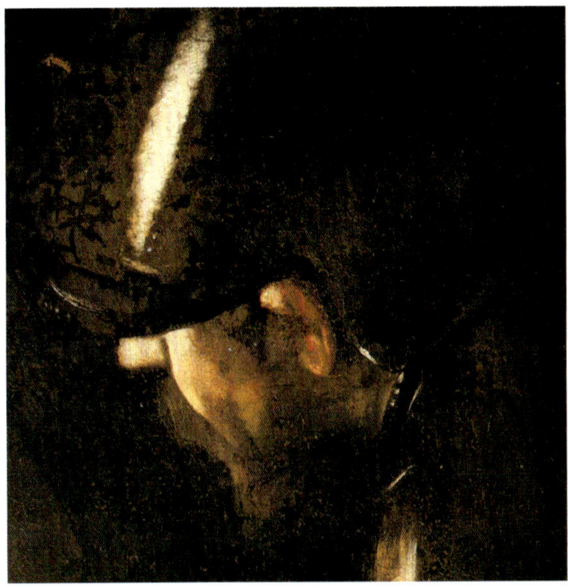 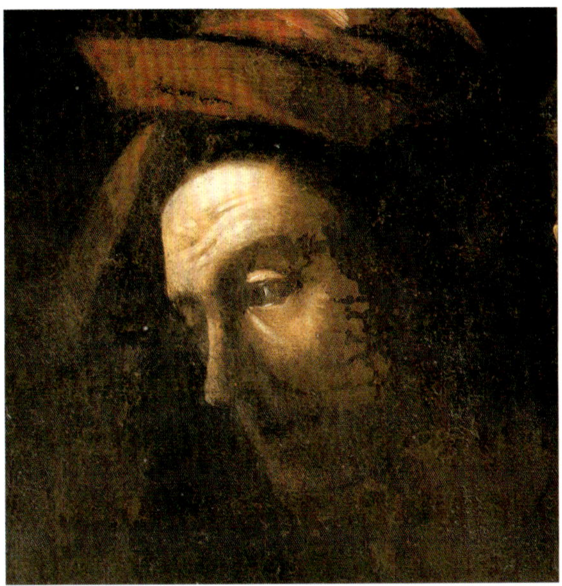

1610, Oil on canvas/Huile sur toile, 140,5 × 170,5 cm, Palazzo Zevallos Stigliano, Napoli

Caravaggio has taken Ursula out of her age-old context with the procession of virgins, heavenly signs, and the presence of God. Instead, Ursula remains for the moment, in silent amazement at the arrow coming her way, and the only one standing by her side at this tragic moment is a simple man of the people.

Caravage débarrasse le thème très ancien de la sainte de ses éléments canoniques : le pèlerinage des vierges, les signes célestes et la présence de Dieu. Sainte Ursule reste immobile, les yeux fixés sur la flèche ; à côté de ses bourreaux, elle n'a auprès d'elle qu'un seul soutien qui est un homme du peuple.

Caravaggio löst das uralte Thema der Heiligen aus den bestimmenden Komponenten wie Pilgerzug der Jungfrauen, himmlische Zeichen und Gottes Gegenwart heraus. Ursula verharrt im Augenblick, im stillen Erstaunen den Pfeil umfassend und der einzige Getreue, der ihr zur Seite steht, ist ein einfacher Mann aus dem Volk.

Caravaggio separa el tema ancestral de la santa de sus componentes más significativos como la peregrinación de las vírgenes, las señas celestiales y la presencia de Dios. Úrsula aparece petrificada en el momento, sosteniendo la flecha en un estupor callado y con un único acompañante leal a su lado, un hombre simple del pueblo llano.

Caravaggio svincolò l'antichissimo motivo dei santi dai suoi elementi caratteristici, quali il pellegrinaggio delle vergini, i segni celesti e la presenza di Dio. Sant'Orsola viene qui raffigurata nel momento stesso in cui, in un silenzioso stupore, viene trafitta dalla freccia. Al suo fianco vi è un unico fedele: un uomo semplice del popolo.

Caravaggio maakte het eeuwenoude motief van deze heilige los van de bijbehorende iconografie, zoals de pelgrimstocht der maagden, het hemelse teken en de aanwezigheid van God. Ursula kijkt verstard en in stille verbazing naar de pijl, en de enige trouwe dienaar aan haar zijde is de eenvoudige man uit het volk.

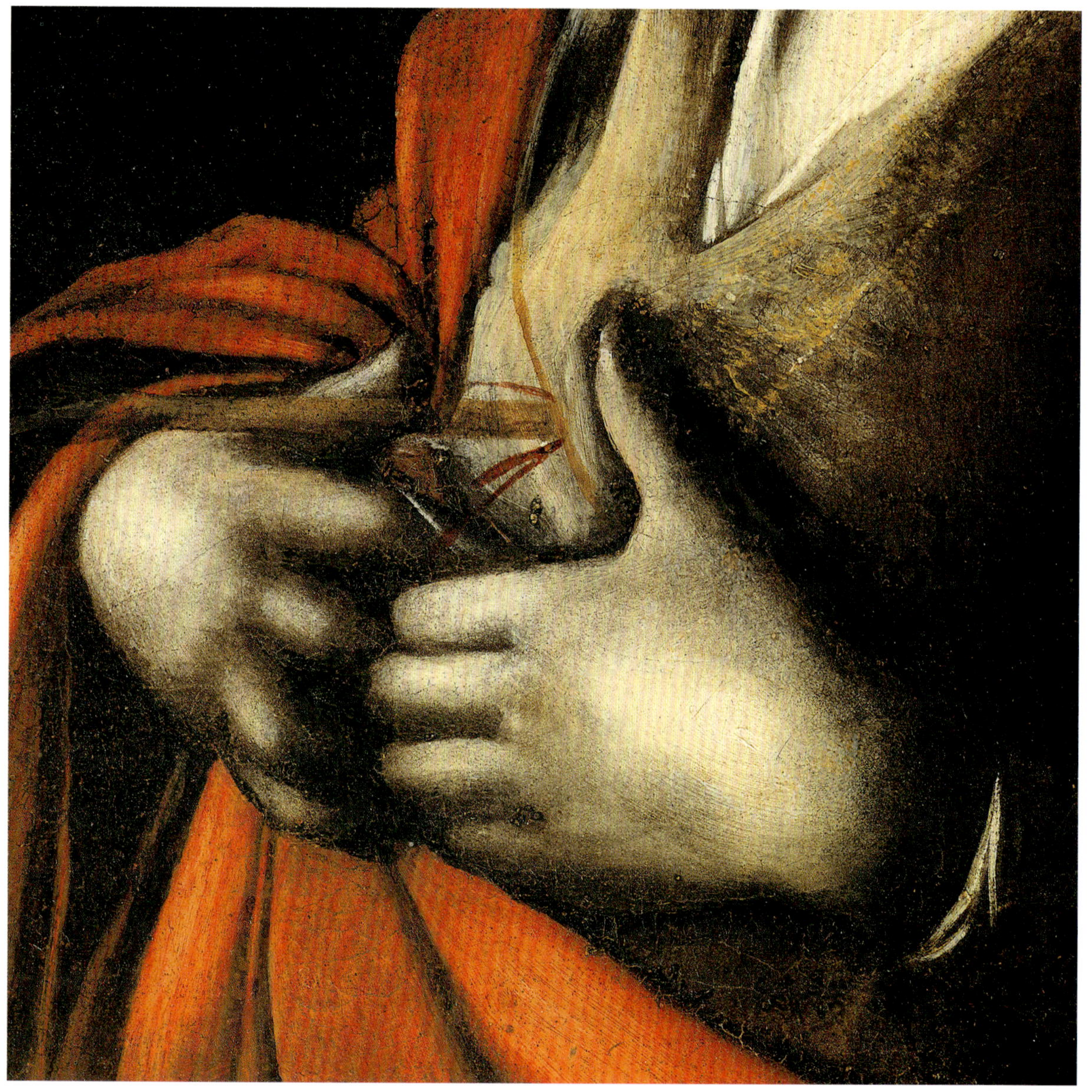

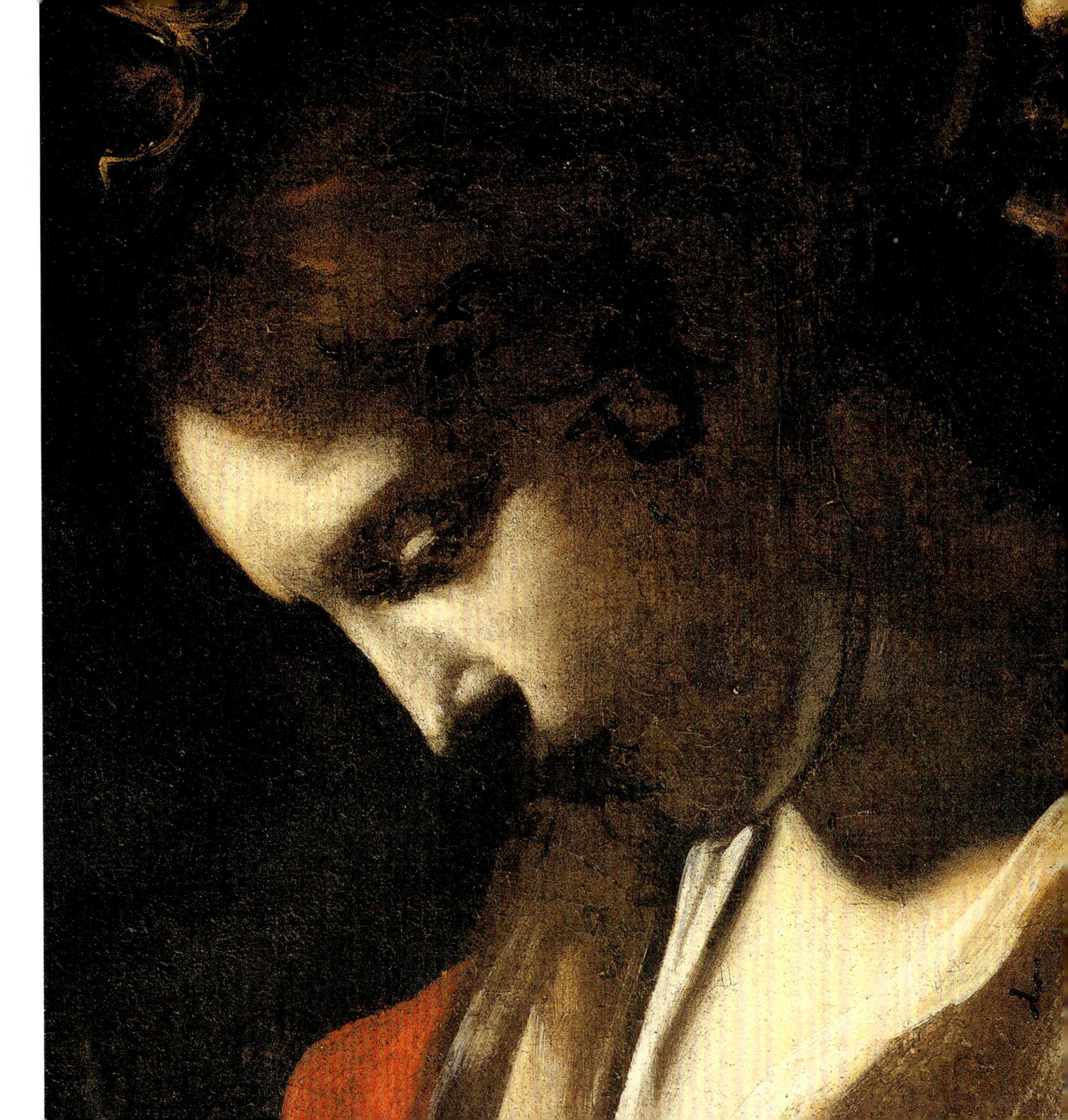

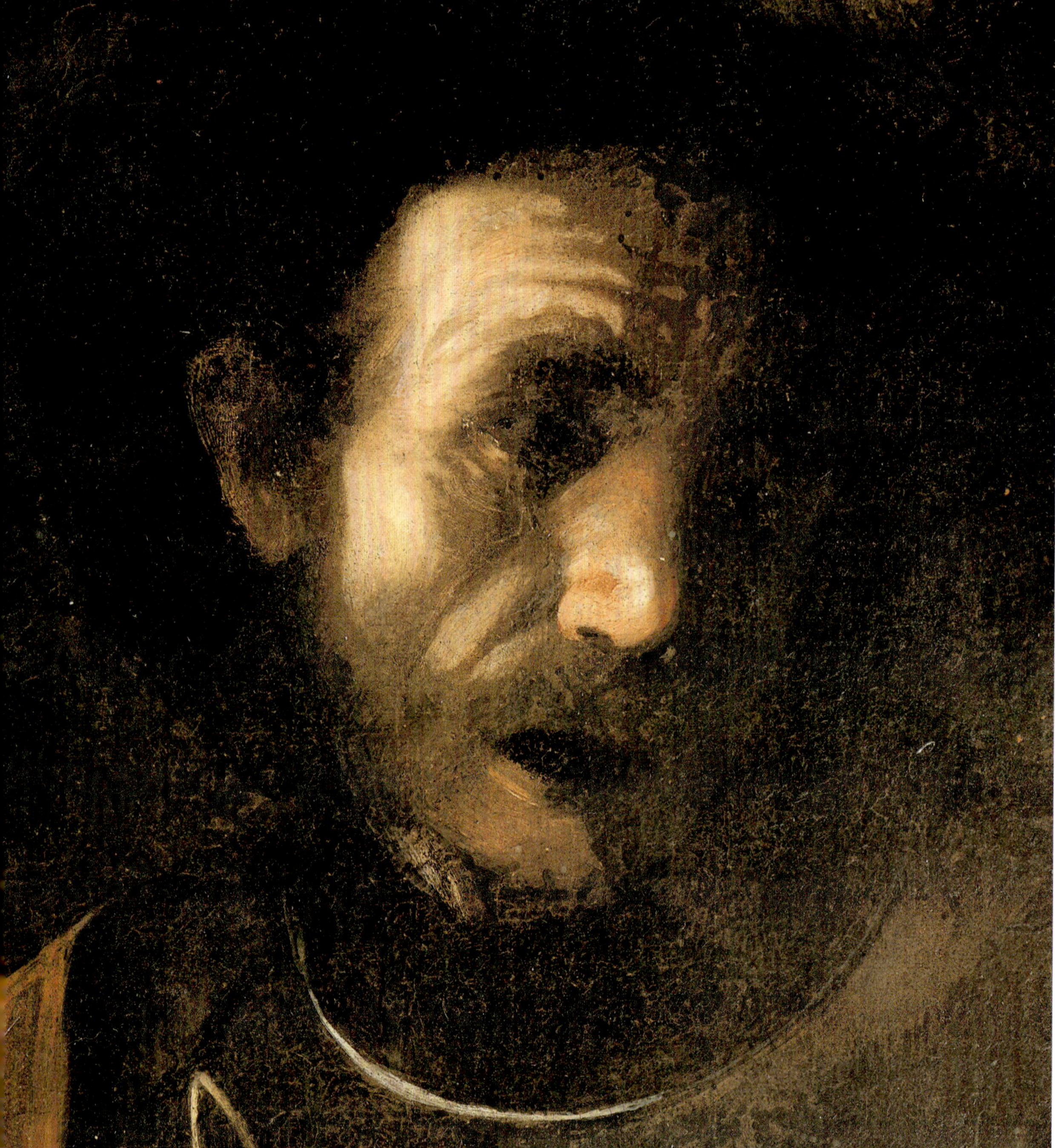

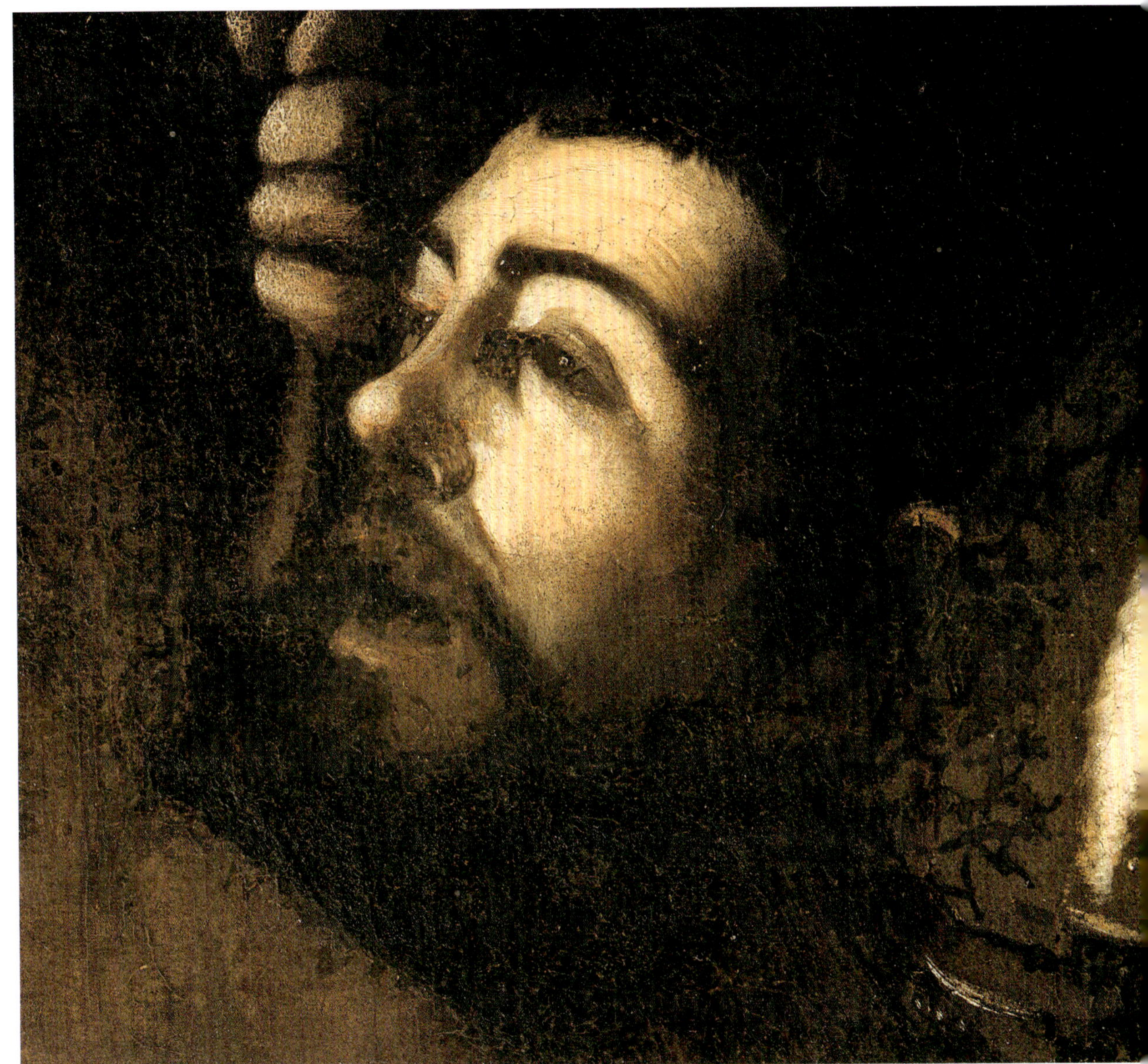

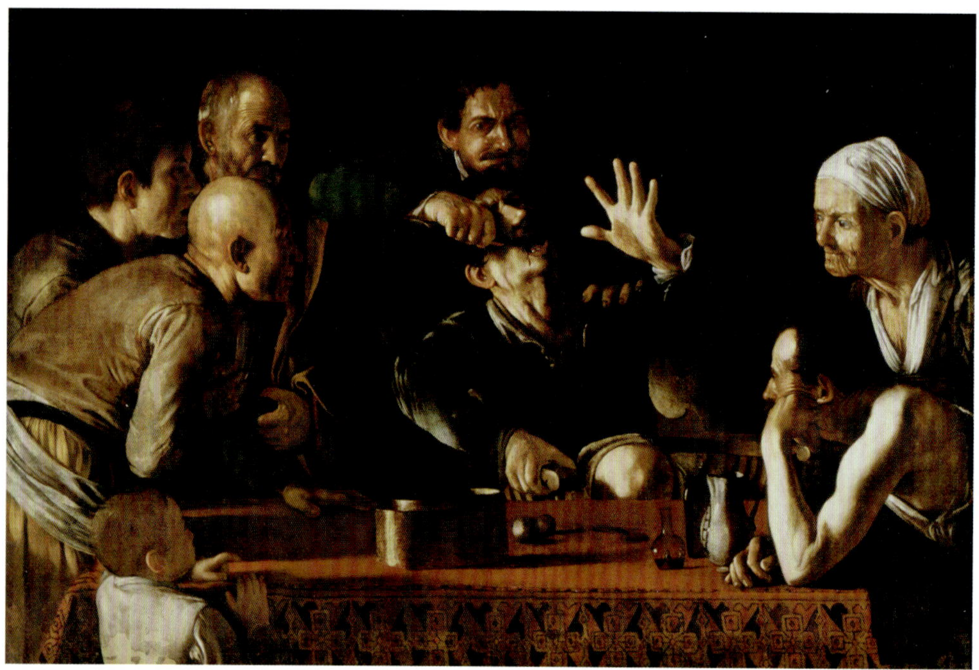

Caravaggio's heirs

In Naples, Caravaggio quickly became
a role model for several generations of
Baroque artists to follow. He inspired the
formation of a local school which trained
artist Artemisia Gentileschi (1593–c. 1653)
among others.

Caravaggio's revolutionary painting had
an impact across the peninsula and his
style became overwhelmingly popular
by the early 17th century. Art history has
called his followers Caravaggists. The
Spanish Baroque painting of Jusepe de
Ribera (1591–1652) or Diego Velázquez
(1599–1660) would be unthinkable
without the influence of Caravaggio. His
influence is also clearly felt in France, for

L'héritage de Caravage

À Naples, Caravage devint en peu de
temps un modèle pour de nombreuses
générations d'artistes baroques. Il inspira
la formation d'une école locale à laquelle
appartint entre autres Artemisia
Gentileschi (1593–c. 1653).

La manière révolutionnaire de
Caravage se diffusa dans toute l'Europe ;
au début du XVIIᵉ siècle, son style
devint brusquement populaire – au
point que l'histoire de l'art nomme
tout simplement ses suiveurs les
« caravagistes » ou « caravagesques ». La
peinture baroque espagnole de José de
Ribera (1591–1652) ou Diego Velázquez
(1599–1660) est inconcevable sans

Caravaggios Erben

In Neapel war Caravaggio innerhalb
kurzer Zeit Vorbild für Generationen
neapolitanischer Barockkünstler
geworden. Er inspirierte die Bildung
einer lokalen Schule, zu der unter
anderem die Künstlerin Artemisia
Gentileschi (1593–ca. 1653) gehörte.

Caravaggios revolutionäre
Malweise wirkte aber auf den halben
Kontinent, sein Stil wurde Anfang
des 17. Jahrhunderts schlagartig
populär. Seine Nachfolger nennt
die Kunstgeschichte schlichtweg
Caravaggisten. Die spanische
Barockmalerei Jusepe de Riberas (1591–
1652) oder Diego Velázquez' (1599–1660)

Anonymous/Anonyme

Cook Cutting Up Fish

Cuisinier découpant du poisson

Koch beim Zerteilen der Fische

Cocinero partiendo el pescado

Cuoco che affetta il pesce

Kok bij het snijden van vis

1610, Oil on canvas/Huile sur toile, 139 × 180 cm, Private collection

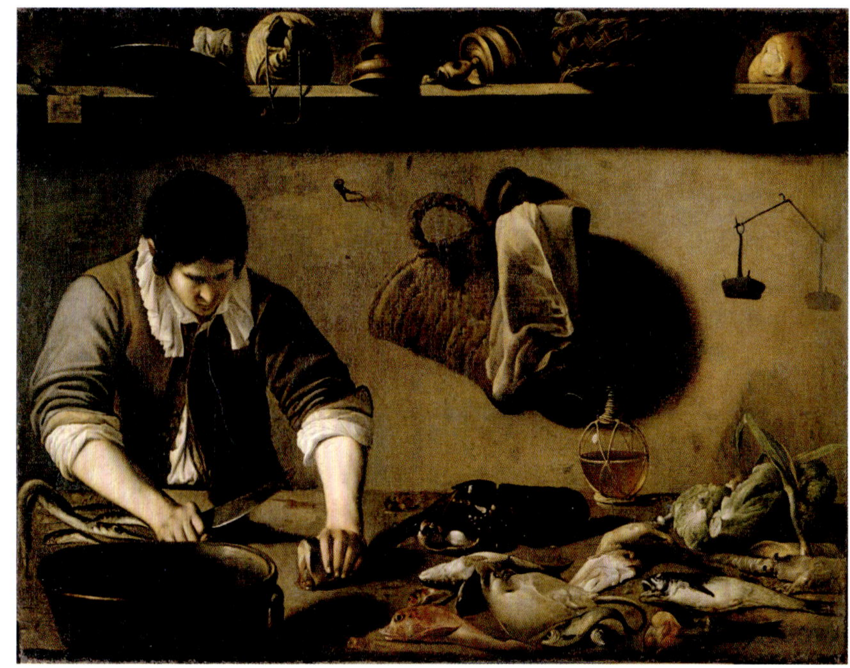

Los herederos de Caravaggio

En el poco tiempo que estuvo en Nápoles Caravaggio se convirtió en ejemplo para varias generaciones de artistas barrocos napolitanos. Inspiró la creación de una escuela local, a la que pertenecía entre otros la pintora Artemisia Gentileschi (1593–c. 1653).

La técnica revolucionaria de Caravaggio mostró su influencia en gran parte del continente, y su estilo alcanzó una tremenda popularidad a principios del XVII. La historia del arte se refiere a sus sucesores como simplemente Caravaggistas. La pintura barroca española de José de Ribera (1591–1652) o Diego Velázquez (1599–1660) no

L'eredità di Caravaggio

A Napoli Caravaggio divenne in breve tempo un modello per diverse generazioni di artisti del barocco napoletano. Ispirò inoltre la creazione di una scuola locale, alla quale appartenne, tra gli altri, la pittrice Artemisia Gentileschi (1593–c. 1653).

La rivoluzionaria tecnica pittorica di Caravaggio fece però sentire la sua influenza in mezza Europa, e il suo stile divenne di colpo popolare all'inizio del XVII secolo. I suoi seguaci vengono chiamati dagli studiosi dell'arte semplicemente caravaggisti. La pittura barocca spagnola di Jusepe de Ribera (1591–1652) e di Diego Velázquez

Caravaggio's invloed

In Napels groeide Caravaggio in korte tijd uit tot voorbeeld voor meerdere generaties kunstenaars en was de inspiratie voor het ontstaan van een Napolitaanse schilderschool, waartoe ook de kunstenares Artemisia Gentileschi (1593–ca. 1653) behoorde.

Caravaggio's revolutionaire composities hadden echter in heel Europa invloed en zijn schilderstijl werd begin zeventiende eeuw razendsnel populair. Zijn navolgers worden in de kunstgeschiedenis "caravaggisten" genoemd. Zonder de invloed van Caravaggio is de Spaanse barokschilderkunst van José de Ribera

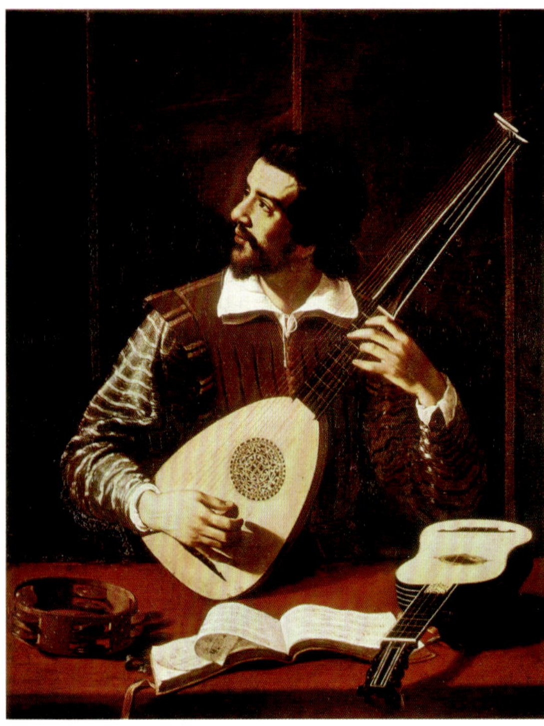

Antiveduto Grammatica (1571–1626)

The Lute Player
Le Joueur de luth
Der Lautenspieler
El tañedor de laúd
Il Suonatore di tiorba
De teorbe-speler

c. 1615, Oil on canvas/Huile sur toile, 119 × 85 cm, Galleria Sabauda, Torino

example in the works of Georges de la Tour (1593–1652).

In the Dutch city of Utrecht, a whole group of young painters devoted themselves to the new style, including Gerrit van Honthorst (1592–1656), Hendrick ter Brugghen (1588–1629), and Dirck van Baburen (1595–1624). Even Rembrandt (1606–1669) and Rubens (1577–1640), both innovators in their own right, could not escape the influence of Caravaggio.

l'influence de Caravage. Cette influence se fait sentir aussi en France, par exemple dans les œuvres de Georges de La Tour (1593–1652).

À Utrecht, dans les Pays-Bas, un groupe de jeunes peintres se consacra au nouveau style : on relève parmi eux Gerrit van Honthorst (1590–1656), Hendrick ter Brugghen (1588–1629) et Dirck van Baburen (1595–1624). Même Rembrandt (1606–1669) et Rubens (1577–1640) – qui développèrent très tôt leur propre écriture – ne purent totalement échapper au rayonnement du Romain si précoce.

ist ohne den Einfluss Caravaggios nicht denkbar. Auch in Frankreich ist sein Einfluss deutlich zu spüren, etwa bei den Arbeiten von Georges de la Tour (1593–1652).

Im niederländischen Utrecht verschrieb sich eine ganze Gruppe junger Maler dem neuen Stil – zu ihnen zählten Gerrit van Honthorst (1592–1656), Hendrick ter Brugghen (1588–1629) und Dirck van Baburen (1595–1624). Selbst Rembrandt (1606–1669) und Rubens (1577–1640), die ihre ureigene Handschrift pflegten, konnten sich der Ausstrahlung des früh verstorbenen Genies nicht entziehen.

Caravaggio (attr.)

St Mary Magdalene in Ecstasy

L'Extase de sainte Madeleine

Die hl. Maria Magdalena in Verzückung

Santa María Magdalena en éxtasis

Maria Maddalena in estasi

De heilige Maria Magdalena in extase

1606, Oil on canvas/Huile sur toile, 106,5 × 91 cm, Private collection

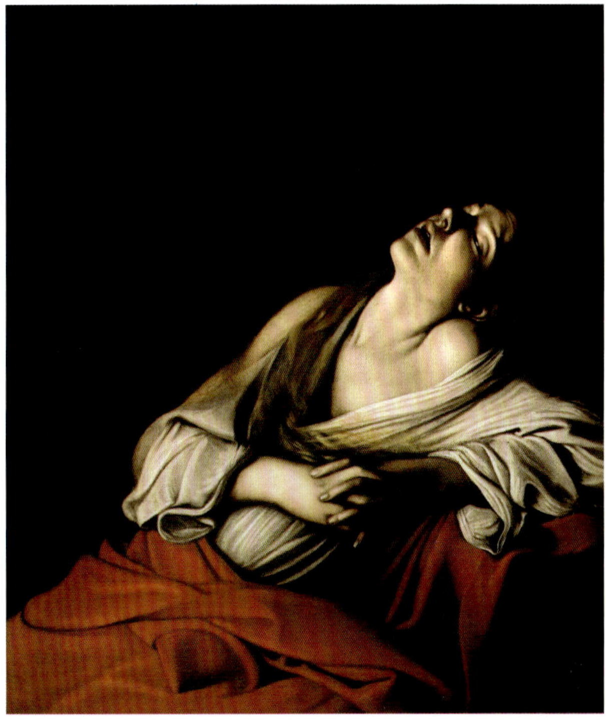

son concebibles sin la influencia de Caravaggio. También en Francia queda patente su influencia, por ejemplo en los trabajos de Georges de la Tour (1593–1652).

En Utrecht (Países Bajos) todo un grupo de jóvenes pintores se dedicaron al nuevo estilo; entre ellos se cuentan Gerrit van Honthorst (1592–1656), Hendrick ter Brugghen (1588–1629) y Dirck van Baburen (1595–1624). Incluso Rembrandt (1606–1669) y Rubens (1577–1640), de los que se conservan sus escritos, no pudieron escapar al cierto atractivo del genio que muere joven.

(1599–1660) è impensabile senza l'influenza di Caravaggio, palesemente osservabile anche in Francia, ad esempio nelle opere di Georges de La Tour (1593–1652).

Ad Utrecht, nei Paesi Bassi, si dedicò al nuovo stile un intero gruppo di giovani pittori, tra cui Gerrit van Honthorst (1592–1656), Hendrick ter Brugghen (1588–1629) e Dirck van Baburen (1595–1624). Anche Rembrandt (1606–1669) e Rubens (1577–1640), pur sviluppando un loro stile personale, non riuscirono a sfuggire al carisma del pittore.

(1591–1652) of Diego Velázquez (1599–1660) ondenkbaar. Ook in Frankrijk was zijn invloed overduidelijk, onder andere in het werk van Georges de la Tour (1593–1652).

In het Nederlandse Utrecht wijdde een hele groep schilders zich aan de nieuwe stijl, onder wie Gerrit van Honthorst (1592–1656), Hendrick ter Brugghen (1588–1629) en Dirck van Baburen (1595–1624). Zelfs Rembrandt (1606–1669) en Rubens (1577–1640) konden zich ondanks hun onmiskenbaar eigen artistieke handschrift niet aan de invloed van de geniale Milanees onttrekken.

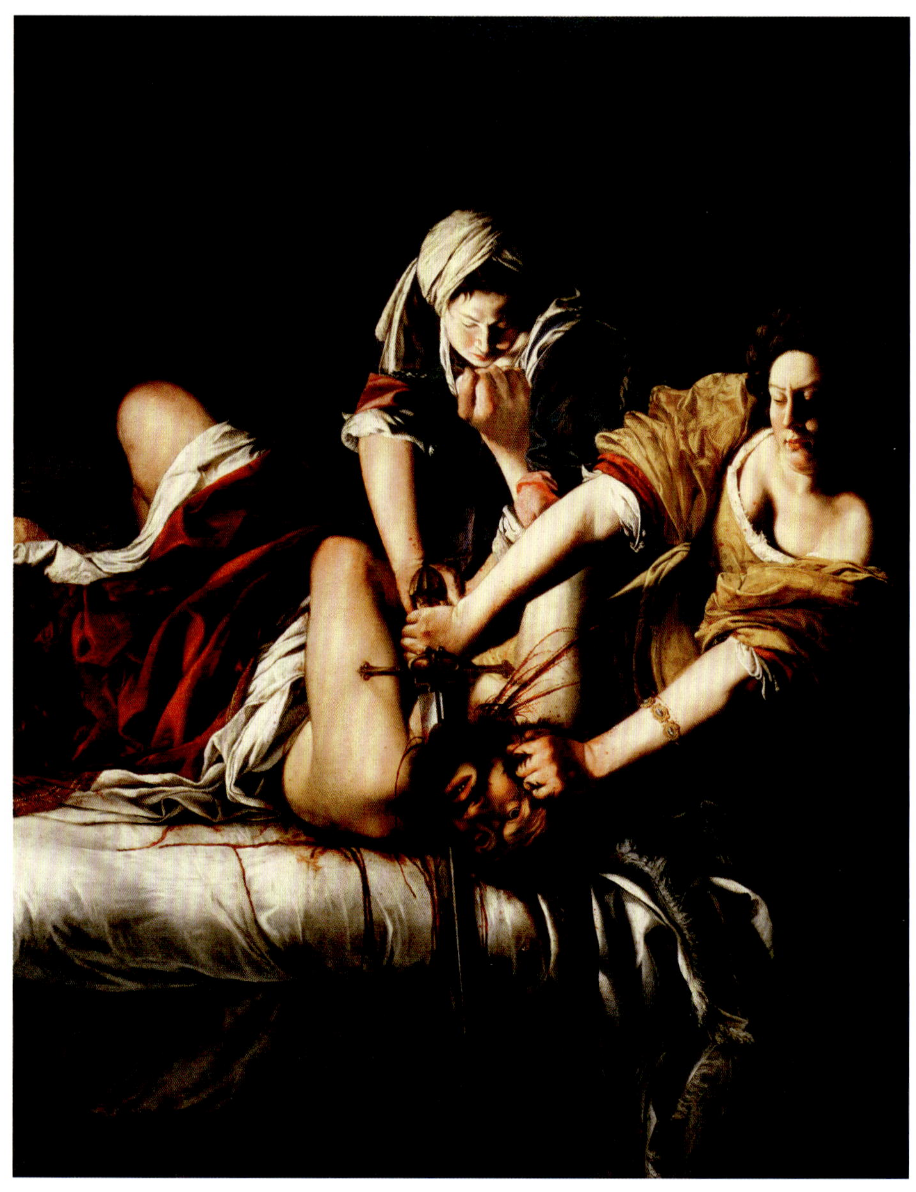

Artemisia Gentileschi
(1593–c. 1653)

Judith and Holofernes

Judith décapitant Holopherne

Judith und Holofernes

Judith y Holofernes

Giuditta che decapita Oloferne

Judith onthoofdt Holofernes

c. 1620, Oil on canvas/Huile sur toile, 199 × 162,5 cm, Galleria degli Uffizi, Firenze

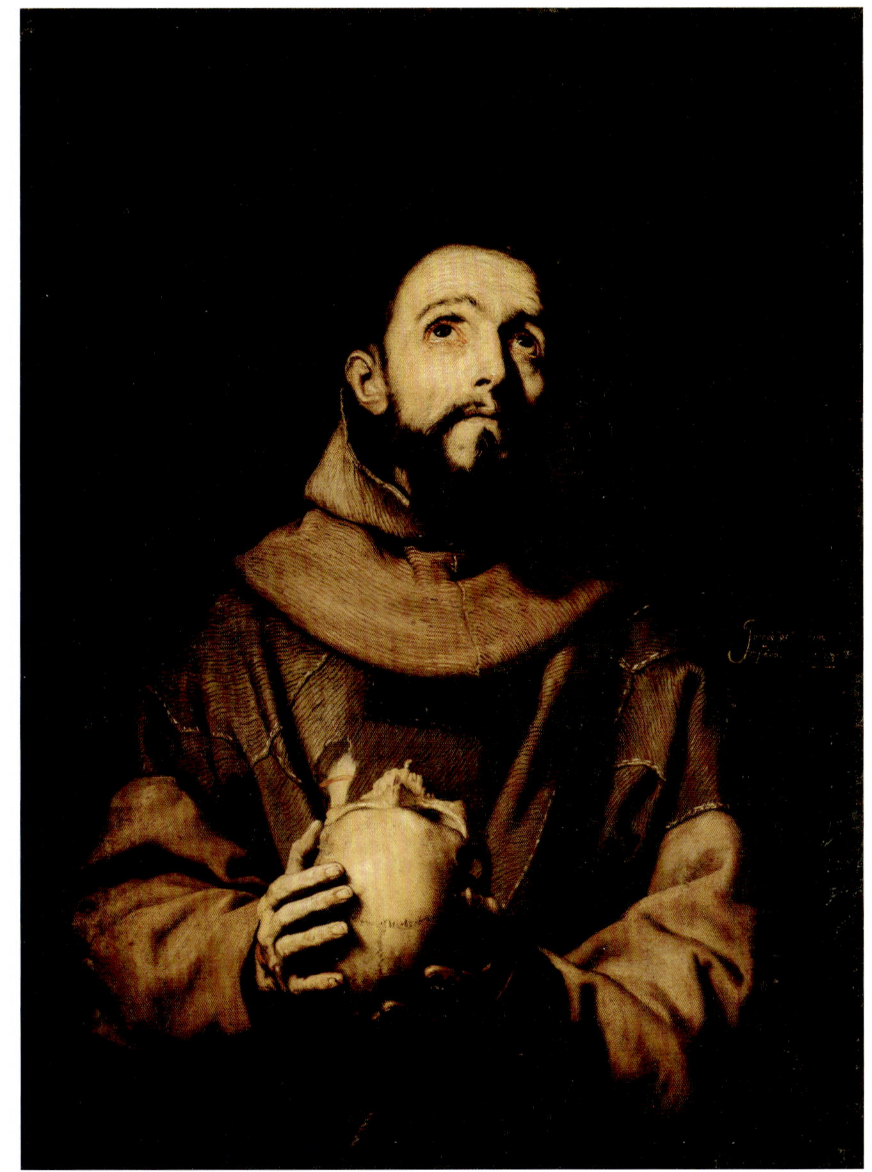

Jusepe de Ribera (1591–1652)
St Francis of Assisi
Saint François d'Assise
Der hl. Franz von Assisi
San Francisco de Asís
San Francesco d'Assisi
De heilige Franciscus van Assisi

1643, Oil on canvas/Huile sur toile,
103 × 77 cm, Galleria Palatina, Firenze

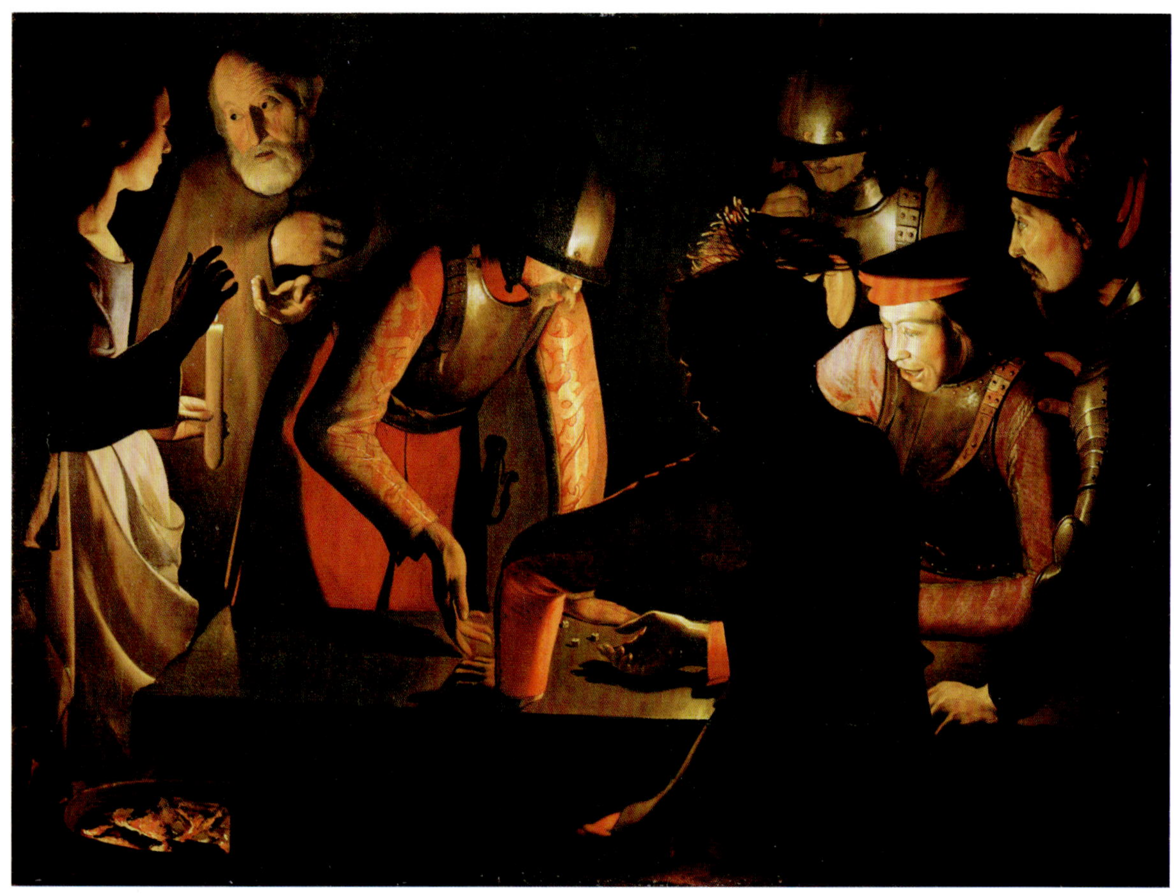

Georges de La Tour (1593–1652)

The Denial of St Peter

Le Reniement de saint Pierre

Verleugnung des hl. Petrus

Negación de San Pedro

Negazione di San Pietro

De verloochening door de heilige Petrus

1650, Oil on canvas/Huile sur toile, 120 × 160 cm, Musée des Beaux-Arts, Nantes

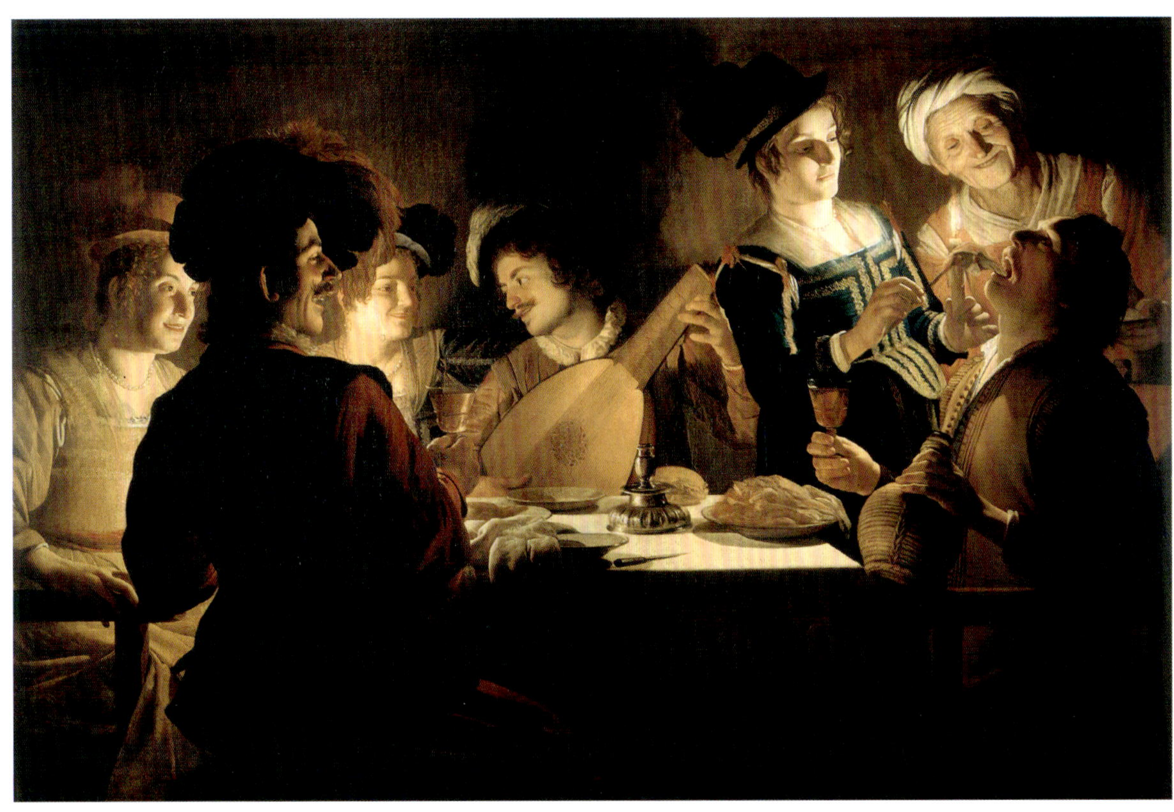

Gerrit van Honthorst (1590–1656)

A Gallant Dinner Party

Le Souper au joueur de luth

Galantes Nachtmahl

Cena de caballeros

Cena con suonatore di liuto

Vrolijk gezelschap met luitspeler

c. 1619, Oil on canvas/Huile sur toile, 144 × 212 cm, Galleria degli Uffizi, Firenze

Curriculum Vitae

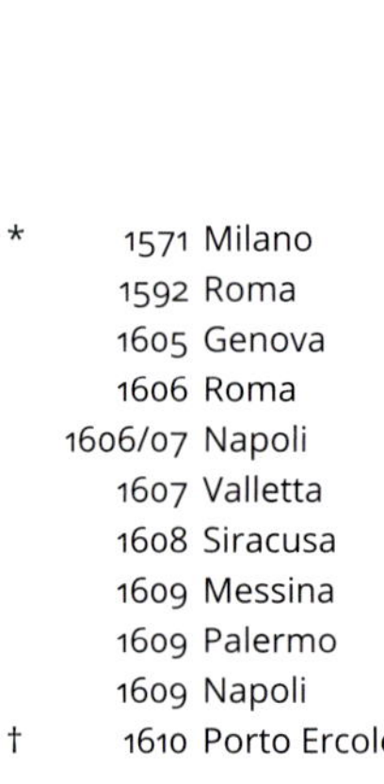

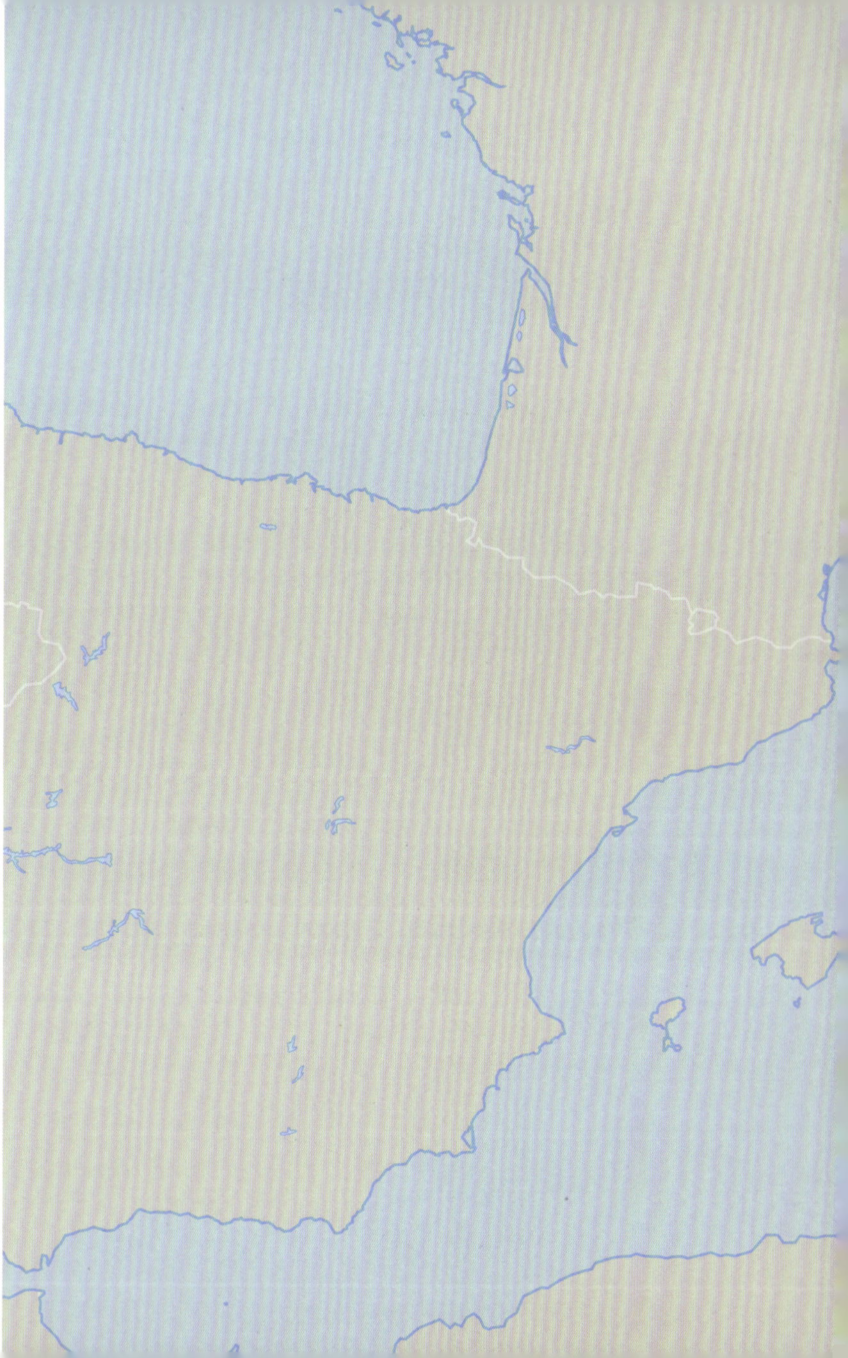

```
*        1571 Milano
         1592 Roma
         1605 Genova
         1606 Roma
    1606/07 Napoli
         1607 Valletta
         1608 Siracusa
         1609 Messina
         1609 Palermo
         1609 Napoli
†        1610 Porto Ercole
```

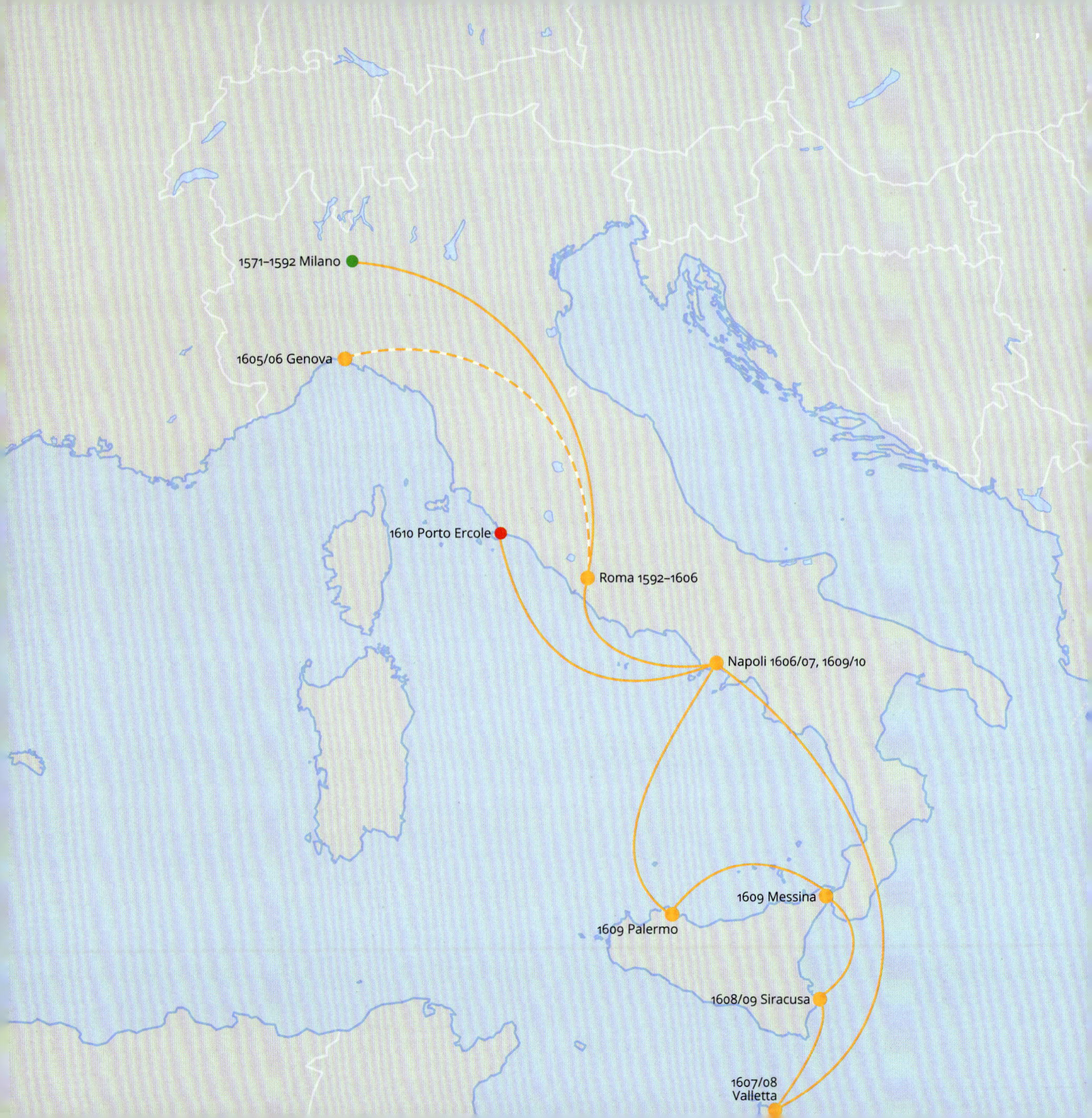

1571–1592 Milano
1605/06 Genova
1610 Porto Ercole
Roma 1592–1606
Napoli 1606/07, 1609/10
1609 Messina
1609 Palermo
1608/09 Siracusa
1607/08 Valletta

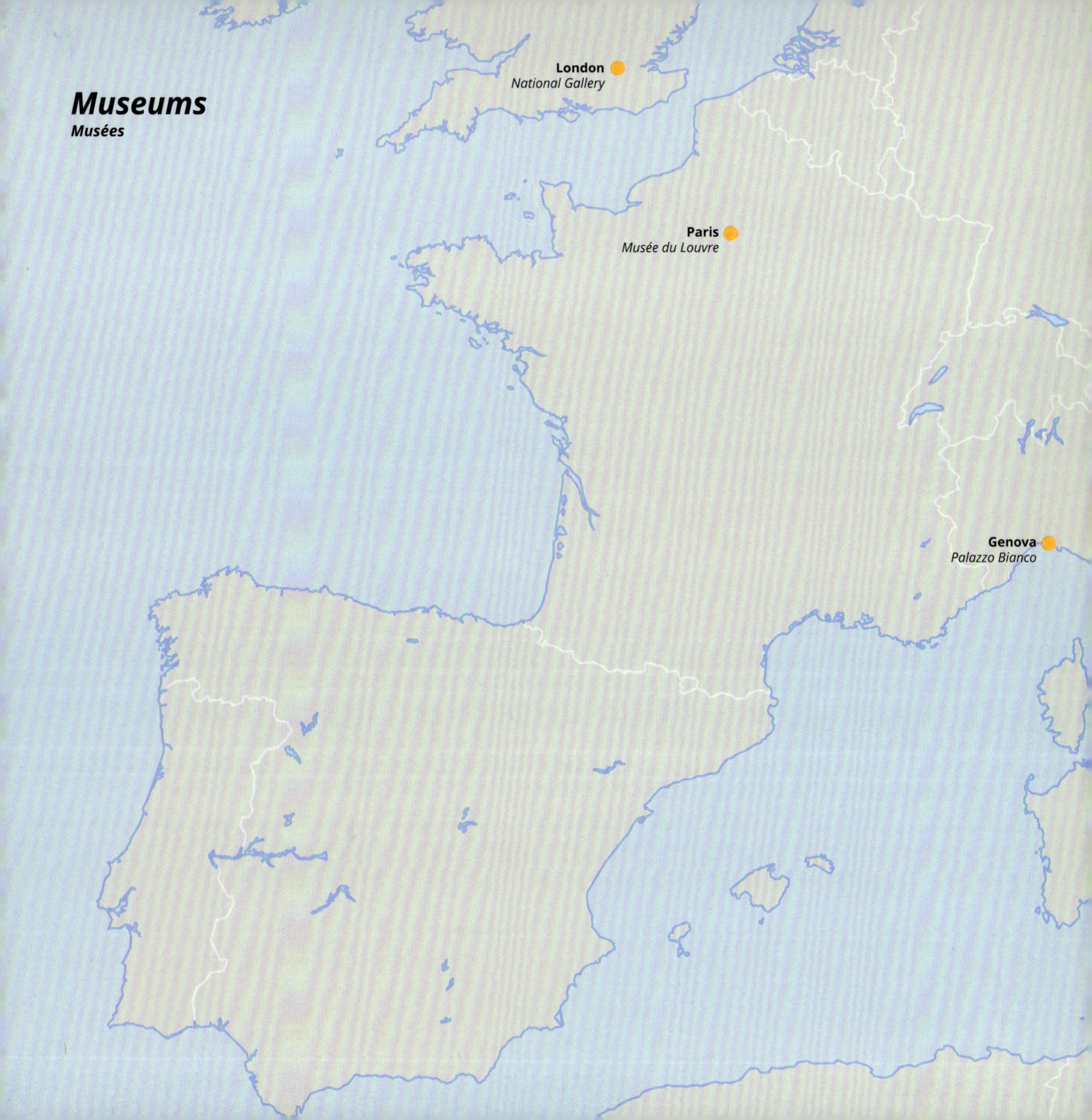

Museums
Musées
London
National Gallery
Paris
Musée du Louvre
Genova
Palazzo Bianco

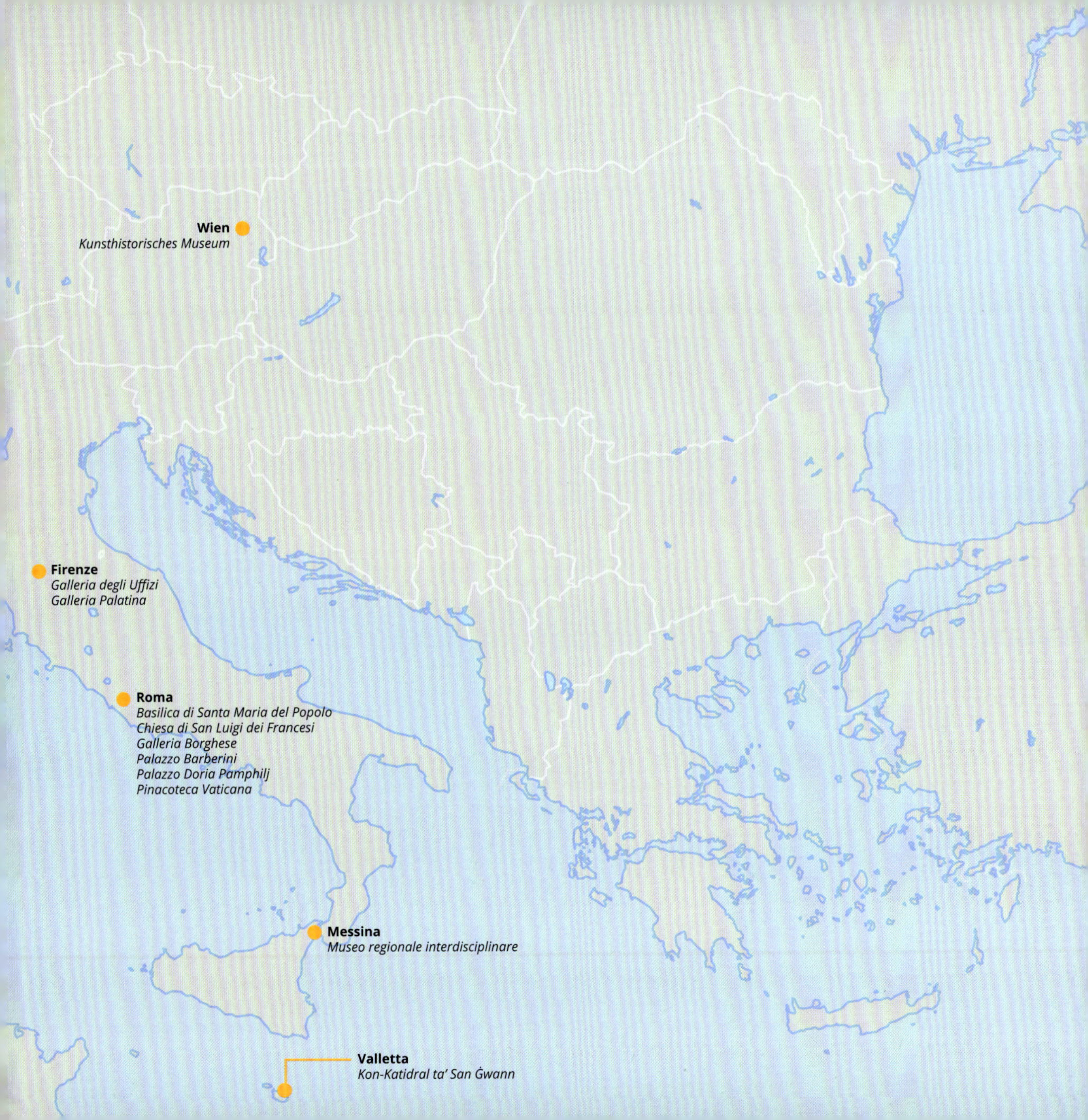

Wien
Kunsthistorisches Museum
Firenze
Galleria degli Uffizi
Galleria Palatina
Roma
Basilica di Santa Maria del Popolo
Chiesa di San Luigi dei Francesi
Galleria Borghese
Palazzo Barberini
Palazzo Doria Pamphilj
Pinacoteca Vaticana
Messina
Museo regionale interdisciplinare
Valletta
Kon-Katidral ta' San Ġwann

Recommended Literature
Cynthia De Giorgio & Keith Scriberras
   (Ed.), *Caravaggio and Paintings of
   Realism in Malta,* Valletta 2007
Michael Fried, *The Moment of Caravaggio,*
   Princeton 2010

Littérature recommandée
Claudio Strinati, *Caravage,* Paris 2015

Literaturempfehlungen
Sybille Ebert-Schifferer, *Caravaggio:
   Sehen – Staunen – Glauben. Der Maler
   und sein Werk,* München 2010
Jutta Held, *Caravaggio: Politik und
   Martyrium der Körper,* Berlin 2007
Klaus Krüger, *Caravaggio. Der Künstler
   und sein Werk,* Köln 2010
Roberto Longhi, *Caravaggio,*
   Dresden 1993
Sebastian Schütze, *Caravaggio.
   Das vollständige Werk,* Köln 2016